Bop Apocalypse

Bop Apocalypse

Jazz, Race, the Beats, and Drugs

Martin Torgoff

Da Capo Press

Designed by Jeff Williams

Set in New Baskerville by Perseus Books

Cataloging-in-Publication data for this book is available from the Library of Congress.

ISBN: 978-0-306-82475-3 (hardcover)
ISBN: 978-0-306-82476-0 (e-book)

Published by Da Capo Press, an imprint of Perseus Books, LLC, a subsidiary of Hachette Book Group, Inc.

www.dacapopress.com

Da Capo Press books are available at special discounts for bulk purchases in the U.S. by corporations, institutions, and other organizations. For more information, please contact the Special Markets Department at Perseus Books, 2300 Chestnut Street, Suite 200, Philadelphia, PA 19103, or call (800) 810-4145, ext. 5000, or e-mail special.markets@perseusbooks.com.

10 9 8 7 6 5 4 3 2 1

To my wife, Laura . . . Confidante, helpmate,
best friend, lover, heart, and soul . . .

Contents

Author's Note

I could hear the election returns and then Nixon's victory speech filtering down to me from the upstairs den where my parents were watching television. It was November 5, 1968, the night Richard Nixon was elected president. As we huddled conspiratorially in the darkened basement of our house, my sister placed a wet towel under the basement door so that my parents wouldn't be able to smell what was about to transpire.

"Here," she said, placing a hookah pipe in my hands.

I was sixteen years old at the time, a high school junior; Carole was four years older, lately a burgeoning hippie around our town on the north shore of Long Island, where I had lived my entire life. We were sitting cross-legged on an old Persian rug down in that black-lighted sanctuary of hers, exactly as I had observed her sitting with her beaded, long-haired, leather-fringed friends over recent months. I was goggle-eyed at the exotic illegality of it all. A sense of fear overwhelmed me as I took the pipe, but mixed with the delectation that comes from being about to do something forbidden. My sister could tell that I was waffling at the last minute, and just to make sure that I would get totally and unequivocally blasted that very first time, she delivered long and highly detailed instructions about how to inhale and exactly how long to hold the smoke in my lungs before I was permitted to exhale. Never one to do things halfway, she then shaved little pieces off a black, gooey little ball she produced from tin foil, and mixed it in with the bowl of leafy green substance.

"This is *hash*," she explained patiently. "*Hashish*. It's just like pot, only a little stronger. You put 'em together, and it's called an Indian mixture." She struck a kitchen match, smiling, and held it to the bowl.

It was obvious that she intended to monitor this operation very closely. "Don't worry, it'll only intensify the effect."

How right she was. Thirty minutes and innumerable bowls passed. My lungs felt like they were on fire. I could feel the beginnings of a warm, tingly feeling spreading up the back of my neck. She peered into my eyes and smiled knowingly. "What do you *feel?* Do you feel *different?* Are you *stoned?*"

"I don't know," I stammered. "I'm not sure."

I wasn't certain of what I was feeling, except that with her flashing dark eyes and high cheekbones and long dark hair parted in the middle, my sister had transformed into a beautiful Native American girl right before my eyes. Lights began whirling across my field of vision in phaser-like traces, like square dancers at some demented psychedelic hoedown. I must have looked like I was seeing a ghost, because all she could do was laugh at me.

"Oh, yeah, you don't know if you're *stoned?* Well, let me tell you, then, you're *wrecked.* Come on over here and I'll prove it to you." She led me over to her little stereo, like a lamb to slaughter. "Here, put your head *right between* those speakers. That's right, *closer . . .*"

I did as I was told, and she put on "Blue Jay Way," from the *Magical Mystery Tour* album. To this day, more than forty years later, I still find it difficult to find the words to describe the feeling that came over me as my head filled with the swelling dirge-like organ as the song faded in, except to say that I felt the music and the lyrics—*There's a fog upon LA . . .*—to the very roots of my soul. And that was how it all began for me, those solitary afternoons of experimentation and self-discovery down in the basement after school, my head between those tiny speakers. When it all came to an end twenty years later, I was thirty-seven, hitting rock bottom on drugs and alcohol and facing the desperate realization that my very survival was in question. How had I gotten there? As I began a new sober life, I realized that recovery had no more produced easy answers about drugs than their use had. Instead, I was forced to wrestle uneasily with the meanings and consequences of the drugs I had taken, no more willing or able to deny the self-expansion of my experiences than I could the state of addiction that had ended my journey. I was aware that some of the substances I'd taken had benefitted me and that others had damaged me; perhaps most of all, I was aware that they had *changed* me. I began thinking about how they had changed my generation, and that led to thinking about how they had changed my country.

When I decided to write about all of this, I realized that the best way to start would be to tell the story of how the marijuana that so altered my life had found its way into a typical middle-class suburban basement on the north shore of Long Island in November of 1968. It was the beginning of a twelve-year odyssey that led to the publication of a book, *Can't Find My Way Home: America in the Great Stoned Age, 1945–2000* (Simon & Schuster, 2004), and a television series based on the book called *The Drug Years*, both of which told the story of how the use of illicit drugs went from the underground to a mass experience that one in four Americans have come to know, and how that has shaped the cultural landscape of this nation. This book tells the story of the underground itself—in essence, how the use of drugs entered the DNA of modern American popular culture in the first place.

In February of 1964, only four years before my virgin marijuana experience, the Beatles smoked pot for the first time when Bob Dylan, thinking that the lyrics to "I Want to Hold Your Hand" were "I get high" instead of "I can't hide," showed up at the Plaza Hotel, where the Beatles were staying, with a pack of rolled joints. This single event would have worldwide repercussions. It didn't take long before the Beatles were "smoking marijuana for breakfast," as John Lennon later described it, which turned them into "glazed eyes giggling all the time. In our own world." As Paul McCartney commented, "This was beginning to get into that period when people were sort of giving up the drink which had been the stimulant of the times, and were getting into herbal jazz cigarettes, and it was changing things."

Herbal jazz cigarettes—a telling turn of phrase. McCartney's description of marijuana says a lot about how it would have entered the life of someone like Bob Dylan in the first place, before it ever came to the Beatles. The roots of drug use by the baby boom counterculture that I was a part of are to be found in jazz and the Beat Generation, two subcultures that commingled beginning in the 1940s and continuing up through the 1950s. Drug-using musicians like Charlie Parker were models for aspiring young writers and poets like Jack Kerouac and Allen Ginsberg, who, in turn, incorporated the use of drugs into a new literary aesthetic. This book is largely the story of the evolution of jazz and its relationship to the Beats: the first time that drug use coalesced with music and literature, becoming a central element in the creation of an avant-garde American voice and underground cultural sensibility. During these decades, the use of marijuana and other substances became a truly interracial and multicultural nexus of American experience. Call it what you will—words like *insurgent, transgressive,* and *oppositional* have been used to describe it—but it was nothing less than revolutionary because it became a vital part of the development of an alternative vision and pursuit of freedom that have shaped our cultural landscape ever since.

The narrative of this book encompasses the birth of jazz in New Orleans, Harry Anslinger and the Federal Bureau of Narcotics, Louis Armstrong, the Chicago of the 1920s, Mezz Mezzrow and the tea pad culture of Harlem in the 1930s, the Marihuana Tax Act of 1937, the Savoy Ballroom, Kansas City and the birth of swing, Billie Holiday, Lester Young, Charlie Parker and the birth of bebop, the initial conjoining of the group of principal Beat Generation characters in New York that included Jack Kerouac, Allen Ginsberg, Neal Cassady, and William Burroughs, the coming of heroin to the streets of Harlem, the addiction and fate of a generation of jazzmen and the impact of heroin on a whole community, the policies and popular attitudes surrounding addiction, the creation of the three jazz-imbued masterworks (*On the Road, Howl,* and *Naked Lunch*) that launched and defined the Beat Generation, and the advent, by 1960, of a new bohemian culture in cities and on college campuses across America.

Although a century has passed since marijuana first appeared in New Orleans and heroin powder became available on our streets, I see this as a living history in the truest sense. Seventy-five years after the Marihuana Tax Act of 1937 was passed and the era of pot prohibition began, Colorado and Washington became the first states in American history to allow the sale of marijuana for recreational use in 2012. Then Alaska, Oregon, and the District of Columbia followed. This year there will be ballots to legalize pot in six more states: Nevada, California, Massachusetts, and Maine. After a Pew poll reported in 2014 that 75 percent of Americans believe the repeal of marijuana prohibition is now inevitable, predictions that up to a dozen states will have legal marijuana by 2017 suddenly do not seem all that far-fetched.

At the same time, a new wave of heroin has arrived. Since the arrival of heroin in the Harlem of the 1940s, any uptick in the population of heroin addicts in America is reflexively labeled an "epidemic" or a "plague," and each one has its own identity. This one is serious and notable for fatal overdoses, which have tripled in three years to more than eight thousand a year. It's a strange version of a heroin wave that has plateaued for years on an epidemic of prescription opiates, largely among white middle- and working-class people, that has taken root in places like Staten Island and in small cities and towns across New England and the Midwest. In 2014, Governor Peter Shumlin of Vermont devoted the entirety of his State of the State address to what he called a "full-blown heroin crisis," and during the 2016 election cycle, it moved center stage. But unlike heroin epidemics of the past, in this one an antidote called naloxone, which can be injected or used as an atomizer, has been distributed to police, emergency medical workers, clinics, and laypeople to reverse overdoses and save lives. In this heroin epidemic, the national attitude toward drug addiction seems entirely different. The police chiefs most affected did not use military metaphors to urge get-tougher policies and longer jail sentences but called for treatment. "These are people and they have a purpose in life and we can't as law enforcement look at them any other way," said one former narcotics officer. Even the Republican presidential candidates in 2016 opened up about struggles with addiction in their own families.

"Paradigm shift," "tipping point," "crossroads"—such are the terms being commonly used to describe momentous changes like marijuana legalization and the unprecedented use of a harm-reduction strategy like naloxone by police, and their implications for drug policy. But as the battlefield fog of the war on drugs begins to lift a little after forty years, forty million arrests, and over a trillion dollars spent, the first thing that one sees is the vast wreckage of disproportionately black mass incarceration. Despite the fact that every study ever done shows that all races in this country use drugs at remarkably similar rates, in some states black men have been incarcerated on drug charges at rates twenty to fifty times greater than whites (as many as 80 percent now have criminal records in our major cities).

"It is heartening to see the eclipse of the generations-long failed war on drugs," writes Ekow N. Yankah of the Benjamin N. Cardozo School of Law in "When Addiction Has a White Face," a *New York Times* op-ed. "But Black Americans are also knowingly weary and embittered by the absence of such enlightened thinking when those in their own families were similarly wounded. When the face of addiction had dark skin, this nation's police did not see sons and daughters, sisters and brothers. They saw 'brothas,' young thugs to be locked up, rather than 'people with a purpose in life.'"

To increasing numbers of people outraged by the injustice of these disparities, it appears that African Americans have been typecast and targeted—as if they were the culprits being pigeonholed and held accountable for the whole American experience with illicit drugs—and even as a movement for prison reform gathered increasing momentum during the Obama administration, the question of how and why it happened this way must be asked. My belief is that any understanding of it at all requires going back to the early part of the twentieth century, when the templates of modern drug law, policy, and culture were first established, along with the concomitant racial stereotypes. Back to the time when the whole culture war over the use of drugs in America first began. It's a fascinating and controversial period that teaches us much about the conflicts and questions that surround drugs today. It is my sincere hope that by looking to the past, we will be able to make more informed decisions as we face the challenges of the future.

"High, I'm telling you, high. What's the law against being high? What's the use of not being high? You gonna be low?"

—Jack Kerouac, *Visions of Cody*

1

Red-Dirt Marijuana

1.

There was something about the way the cow was laying on the ground on that hot summer day that piqued Terry Southern's interest immediately and made him laugh. The animal was just lying out there alone on its stomach in that section of dry scrub brush pastureland, its head stretched out on the ground, a dazed, loopy expression on its face.

Southern had been going out to his cousin's farm in Alvarado, Texas, over the summers to pick cotton as a way of making a few extra dollars and was on his way to go fishing for bullheads in a pond surrounded by cottonwoods and weeping willows with his cousin and C.K., a field hand. The three of them were just meandering through the johnsongrass when they first noticed the milk cow stretched out on the ground.

Funny thing was, the way it was lying there, it looked more like a hound dog than a cow. They walked over and Terry started gently kicking at it to try and get it up. The cow protested his kicks with a soft lowing but refused to budge. Then, examining it more closely, Terry noticed that the animal had very heavy-lidded eyes and seemed awfully contented to be sprawled out there in the middle of a pasture on that scorching Texas afternoon. That was when he saw the half-uprooted green plant in the ground in the midst of the mesquite bushes and a patch of dwarf cactus.

"What's the matter with this cow?"

"Oh, there's nothing wrong with her," C.K. told him, "she's just had some of that loco weed over there."

Southern's cousin thought the weed was toxic and wanted to call a veterinarian immediately. By now C.K. had pulled the big green plant out of the ground and was holding it in his hand, looking at it admiringly. "Yeah, this is mighty good. This is *red dirt*. This is pretty dang strong."

"Well, it must be pretty dang strong," Terry cackled, "look at that cow there!"

"Well, I guess we'd better burn it," said C.K., ever the dutiful field hand, but on the way back to the house, he kept going on about the plant, shaking his head and saying, "This is *mighty fine* gage," and no matter how he tried he couldn't seem to bring himself to accept the idea of burning it. "Oh, well," he finally decided. "I guess we'll dry it out and sell it."

The year was 1936—the year of the Texas Centennial—a year filled with rodeos and parades and barbeques and fireworks displays celebrating the Lone Star State. By no stretch of the imagination was it a common time or place for a twelve-year-old white boy to be smoking marijuana with a black field hand, but Terry Southern was anything but common, even at the age of twelve.

"We went back to the barn and dried the stuff out, and that's when C.K. twisted up a few and turned us on," Southern recounted, tipsily sipping on a glass of cognac in a suite of the Wyndham Hotel in New York. It was the winter of 1993, not long before the writer, who had suffered a stroke and was teaching screenwriting at Columbia at the time, would pass away.

"That first time I was very apprehensive," Southern continued. "Coughing a lot. But intrigued enough to work at it the second time, holding it longer in my lungs. My father was a pharmacist, so I knew a bit about drugs, but marijuana was a totally unknown substance in this part of Texas for white people. My father and uncles were all great drinkers, so I knew a lot about booze already and had been around people who were able to drink a lot and not show it. But I hadn't heard a thing about weed—until that day. It never occurred to me that drink represented any kind of a derangement of any kind; it was just this fortifying thing that people did, almost for their health, it seemed. But this was a totally new and unrelated experience."

By the time Terry Southern smoked his first joint in 1936, marijuana had come to symbolize much more than a cheap high. Public concern over cannabis, or "Indian hemp," in the United States had originated in the Southwest and had been steadily increasing since the end of the First World War, when it had appeared on the Texas border as "Rosa Maria" and black cavalrymen stationed along the border were known to indulge in its use. California and Utah were the first states to criminalize its use in 1915; Texas followed in 1919; and by 1936, pressure was mounting for the federal government to ban it, even though thirty-eight of the forty-eight states had already enacted bans by that time. For fifteen years, authorities throughout the Southwest had been lobbying Washington to do something about it. Headlines like the following, taken from the November 5, 1933, issue of the *Los Angeles Examiner*, had been appearing in newspapers across the country:

> Murder Weed Found Up and Down Coast—Deadly Marijuana Dope Plant Found Ready for Harvest That Means Enslavement for California Children

By 1935, the city of El Paso, then being frequented by Depression-era tourists looking for cheap thrills, had already been identified as a "hot bed of marihuana fiends"—Mexicans, Negroes, prostitutes, pimps, and a criminal class of whites. Add to this hotbed of fiends the twelve-year-old son of the local pharmacist:

"After that incident, I went back to Fort Worth. There was this black guy that delivered big chunks of ice for the refrigerators. He would come every day and I was supposed to pay him and give him his two dollars for the last week, and when I came back with the money I guess he thought he was going to have a little time because there he was smoking his joint. I came out of the back porch screen door and saw him doing it, just the same way that C.K. had taught us—'Gotta suck it in with a lot of air!'—and he would make this, like, *viper* sound as he did it . . .

"I guess I surprised him. He saw the way I was watching him and said, 'Weeel, now, don't guess you'd be innerested in this sort of thing . . .' 'Oh,' I said, 'is that *loco weed?*' He laughed, and said, 'Well, I don't know if you'd call it *that*'—you know, still holding his breath in—'we call it *gage.*' Of course, being a Texas kid, I was still very much in a segregationist mindset, but I asked him if he had any to sell. 'Well, I ain't no pusher,' he said, 'but I'll *give* you some.' And so he gave me a couple of joints, and there I was, holding for the first time. . . . I remember this wonderful mischievous feeling came over me, and I had a friend and invited him over, and we smoked. By that time, you could say I was actually getting a good buzz, and all these strange and funny things were starting to happen."

2.

The marijuana he smoked had no immediate outward effect on Terry Southern's life. He still did the same things he had always done as a boy, still loved odd creatures like tarantulas and armadillos, hunting and fishing, and riding horses under the endless Texas skies. When he went to Sunset High in Dallas he played quarterback on the football team and first base on the baseball team and did his best to get the pretty cheerleaders into the backseats of cars. But as he started smoking with more frequency, he became increasingly more interested in exploring the Central Track area of Dallas.

"It was the part of the city called Nigger Town," Southern pointed out, "and as soon as I was able to make that connection, I realized that smoking was something that I had in common with black people. It brought out that identification, and I would meet more and more of them. I began to see that the effect of this 'gage' was very different indeed from the vodka and grapefruit juice that we drank. Sure, we knew about the Mexicans and the blacks doing it—but it was a part of their culture, not ours. What white people smoked *pot?* My God! I mean, these were just very sporadic occurrences; there was no continuity to them or anything. And yet, I have to say, they completely altered my life. As I became more aware of black people, I found myself really trying to appreciate and understand them in a way I never had before."

In his 1992 novel *Texas Summer*, Southern describes the Central Track area as a dusty place of "lean-to shacks, beside which great black-charred iron wash pots steamed in the Texas sun above raging bramble-fires, and black people sat or squatted in front of these ramshackle front porches, making slow cabalistic marks in the dust with a stick, or gazing trance-like at the road in front of them." The "Nigger Town" he wrote about in the novel was the site of crap games and dingy little bars like the Paradise, which jumped with the "ceaseless swinging wail of the blues guitar"—a place where the barbeque was so dredged in red pepper that it blistered the lips and brought tears to the eyes and sweat to the face.

Along with the life-changing cross-cultural impact of experiencing the black neighborhood of Depression-era Dallas, the effect of marijuana on Terry Southern was most discernible in the long-term development of the way he looked at the world. There is, in fact, one particular scene at the end of the infamous antimarijuana propaganda film *Reefer Madness*, produced right around the very same time Southern smoked pot for the first time, that seems to exemplify the essence of his early marijuana experiences. The scene comes during the climactic trial near the end of the film, when the use of marijuana by several innocent American youths has already led to the multiple tragedies of sexual corruption, madness, addiction, and death. The district attorney is questioning the high school principal for any indication of how a "fine upstanding American boy" could have possibly gone so wrong as to have committed murder under the influence of the weed.

"Well, although you didn't know from your own knowledge that the defendant was using marijuana, did you notice any changes that would lead you to believe as an educator, that he was under some severe mental strain which could have been induced by some drug?"

"I recall something a few weeks ago," the stern principal responds without hesitation. "It was during a class of English literature. There was a serious discussion of Shakespeare's *Romeo and Juliet*, when he suddenly burst into an uncontrollable fit of hysterical laughter!"

Few boys were more prone to an "uncontrollable fit of hysterical laughter" than Terry Southern. An avid reader as a boy, he had already begun to write stories when he was eleven. Right around the time he encountered marijuana, he became interested in rewriting stories by Nathaniel Hawthorne and Edgar Allen Poe because, as he put it, "they never seemed to me to go quite far enough . . . I made them get *really* going."

It was an unusual hobby for a Texas adolescent during the 1930s, to say the least—self-appointed rewrite man for some of the most intense and gothic authors of the literary canon—and the story of Poe's that Southern fixated on the most was, typically, one of his most bizarre, *The Narrative of Arthur Gordon Pym of Nantucket*. "I tried to make it even wilder and showed it to my friend Big Lawrence," said Southern. "'Goddamn, you must be *crazy*,' he said. I think that's when we began to drift apart, Texas and me."

The notion of "getting them really going" and "going too far" became trademarks of a literary sensibility and vision that would eventually make Terry Southern, as both a novelist and a screenwriter, one of the foremost American satirists of his time. By the 1960s he was internationally known for a style of writing characterized by outlandish moments and a skewed but devastating critique of the values, mores, and politics of conventional middle-class American society. At its best, his work exhibits the capacity to provoke, outrage, and subvert while it entertains, displaying a style that shaped the writing of the new breed of humorists who came of age writing for *National Lampoon* and *Saturday Night Live* during the 1970s. To make the connection, one only has to think of the television show "What's My Disease?" in his novel *Flash and Filigree*, where guests strive to identify the gruesome ailments of mystery guests; or the surreal billionaire Guy Grand of *The Magic Christian* inviting the populace of downtown Chicago to go scavenging for hundred-dollar bills in a giant pile of excrement; or the lovely and innocent Candy of that notorious novel coupling with a hunchback—"Give me your hump!"—or Slim Pickens astride the hydrogen bomb at the end of *Dr. Strangelove*, riding it down to earth with the buckaroo whoop of "San Antooooone!" Not for nothing did the Beatles place Southern amidst the assemblage of personalities on the cover of *Sgt. Pepper's Lonely Hearts Club Band* in 1967, right there with his dark ditty-bop shades in the middle of Lenny Bruce, Aldous Huxley, Dylan Thomas, and Dion DiMucci. By the time Southern came to write the celebrated campfire scene for the movie *Easy Rider* and give Jack

Nicholson's character his wiggy digression about UFOs and Venutians, Southern had smoked thousands of joints, sharing them with some of the most interesting cultural figures of the age, not to mention indulging in many other tastes of the pharmacopoeia both ancient and modern, but any tracing of the origins of his satirical sensibility as a writer points right back to the sight of a stoned milk cow lolling comically in a barren and dry Texas pasture in the summer of 1936, and to the first few times he smoked pot.

"How come it's against the law if it's so all fired good?" says Harold the boy to C.K. the field hand in "Red-Dirt Marijuana," the classic short story Southern wrote about his introduction to marijuana.

> "I tell you what it is," C.K. said then, "it's cause a man see too much when he get high, that's what. He see right through ever'thing . . . you unnerstan' what I say?"
>
> "What the heck are you talkin' about, C.K.?"
>
> "Well, maybe you too young to know what I talkin' 'bout—but I tell you they's a lotta trickin' an' lyin' go on in the world . . . they's a lotta ole bull-crap go on in the world . . . well, a man git high, he see right through all them tricks an' lies, an' all that ole bull-crap. He see right through there into the truth of it!"
>
> "Truth of what?"
>
> "Ever'thing."
>
> "Dang you sure talk crazy, C.K."
>
> "Sho', they got to have it against the law. Shoot, ever'body git high, wouldn't be nobody git up an' feed the chickens! Hee-hee . . . ever'body just lay in bed! Jest lay in bed till they ready to git up! Sho', you take a man high on good gage, he got no use for they ole bull-crap, 'cause he done see right through there. Shoot, he lookin' right down to his ver' soul!"

"By the time I wrote that story, twenty years or so after I'd smoked marijuana as a boy, marijuana was already becoming part of a step-by-step breaking away from the mainstream values of the culture," Southern reflected. "For a certain kind of individual smoking it, this one isolated high began to have a growing impact on one's insight. Some people were going to smoke it and get into a light kind of music high, but others were going to see right through to the very heart of the corruption of the system—to how the political parties were both locked in by the same interests and money and lobbyists and how dirty it all was, and how it was all virtually meaningless and quite absurd. So in that respect, marijuana had the potential to be a very seditious thing indeed—the end of everything as we knew it in the good old USA. But it certainly didn't *start out* like that."

Southern took another sip of his cognac and cackled softly at those isolated events of more than half a century ago, and how they were like some crazy distant mirror of everything that was going to happen.

"It's hard to believe what was going on about it, back there in that one year, 1936 to '37, when it all seemed to start—this gigantic rumpus about some little ole weed growing wild . . . right there in a tumbleweed field in Alvarado, Texas."

2

Stompin' at the Savoy

Bernie Brightman was sixteen and had just won the shag contest at the Loew's Oriental on 86th Street in Bensonhurst, Brooklyn, when somebody told him about the Savoy Ballroom in Harlem. The big-band craze was really hitting big, and on those muggy summer nights of 1936, the lindy hoppers would all gather around the ice cream parlor there along 86th Street and Bath Beach like deer at a salt lick.

Dancing meant everything on those nights. Money was very scarce, and dancing in the streets was free. The music of Benny Goodman and Tommy Dorsey and Artie Shaw would come blasting out into the street from some Victrola like glorious hot balm being poured over Depression woes, and the kids would dance with mad desperation until the last possible minute before the cops showed up to clear the area and it was time for them all to go home.

Home was not an especially happy place for Bernie Brightman, who came from a family of poor working-class Jews from Poland. Brightman had been nine when the Great Depression hit, and his father was more than a bit of an Old World tyrant, the sort of unhappy man who had never made much of a living to begin with even before the Depression, but now that Bernie was of working age the pressure was on; the emphasis in his family was on going out and getting a job instead of getting good grades at school and going to college. He needed to bring home every possible extra penny he could earn and was already working as a shipping clerk in the Garment District when he was told that you could get in to the Savoy Ballroom in Harlem on a Saturday night for twenty cents if you got there before eight o'clock, which sounded good to him. He couldn't afford much for an evening's entertainment, so he and his friend Slapsie Sammy Bergman—all of his friends had nicknames like that—found themselves dressed in their only suits that very Saturday night, clutching the straps on the IRT as it rumbled uptown. He had no idea what to expect, other than music and dancing and maybe seeing some pretty colored girls there. Bernie Brightman was a dancer, and they said the Savoy had the very best. He wanted to show them his stuff. They got off at 135th Street, walked north to 596 Lenox Avenue at 140th Street, and saw the marquee—"The Savoy Ball Room Presents the Erskine Hawkins Orchestra, Also Appearing The Savoy Sultans"—and walked right in.

The first thing Brightman noticed after he paid the cover was the huge cut glass chandelier in the lobby, which impressed him, but that was nothing compared to the feeling of walking up the marble steps and seeing the Track—the huge ballroom the size of a whole city block, with its gleaming maple wood dance floor and the bar and the little settees along the sides and the pretty black hostesses. It was like walking into another world. Since its opening ten years earlier on March 12, 1926, the Savoy had become the most famous ballroom in the nation—perhaps the only place in America where white and black kids could dance together in relative peace and harmony.

For the first few minutes Bernie and Slapsie just walked around, completely stupefied by the place. Bernie thought it was the most glamorous thing he'd ever seen in his life. What impressed him the most were the two bandstands set up side by side at the back of the floor, one small and set for a seven-or eight-piece band, the other set for a full orchestra. As much as he loved dancing and music, Brightman hadn't had the money to go to concerts. He hadn't experienced much live music in his life, let alone big-band jazz.

"Hey, what's that stuff those people are drinking?"

"Some stuff called King Kong," Slapsie told him. "You wanna get some?"

Bernie pondered this for a moment and shook his head. King Kong was apparently some kind of cheap hooch moonshine whiskey of indeterminate origin. As neither of them were really drinkers, Bernie figured they would just listen to the music and try to find somebody to dance with.

The place was filling up with mostly black faces, and what faces they were. Everyone was well-dressed, pomaded, and cologned, and what style!—Bernie had never seen such style—and that was when he was approached by this guy they knew from their neighborhood.

Roy had been coming to the Savoy for awhile. He was a tenor sax player, and he had a certain look on his face, an expression that said he was wise to everything that was going on, not just in the Savoy but in the whole universe. He had a kind of gleam in his eye and a wise guy smirk like Leo Gorcey's, who played Muggs McGinnis in the *East Side Kids*.

"You wanna smoke some reefer?"

"Some *what?*"

"You know, reefer."

"What's that?"

"You know. You smoke it, like a cigarette!"

Bernie just looked at him.

"Ain't you ever been *high?*"

He hadn't. Ever in his life. Not on anything.

"You got a quarter?"

Bernie Brightman figured he should try everything in life at least once, and he bought two of these cigarettes for a quarter; Slapsie bought a third. "Where should we smoke it?"

"Just go right over there into the bathroom," Roy said, walking away.

Nobody in the bathroom seemed to mind as they stood there in the brightly lit white tile room and lighted up two slim, white hand-rolled cigarettes. People brushed nonchalantly right past them and went about their business and seemed singularly unfazed about the whole thing.

Bernie smoked half of his stick and really didn't think much of the effect, so he smoked it all the way down and would have kept smoking but there was nothing left except the tiniest burning ember. Then he and Slapsie shared the third stick. He was feeling a little different before they left the bathroom, but as they went out the door it seemed to hit him all at once, the people dancing and the dim, sexy lights and the colors and the music. He felt like he was gliding on air and found himself being drawn to the bandstand, where he positioned himself directly in front of the house band, the Savoy Sultans, who were blowing like crazy.

The Sultans only had about seven or eight guys but they might just as well have been a thousand, ten thousand, Genghis Khan and his entire horde of Mongol warriors. They sounded so full and big and powerful, it sent chills up his spine. They were playing Kansas City style, two trumpets and three saxophones trading solos like a basketball team fast-breaking down a court at breakneck speed, when the alto man, Rudy Williams, took over and started blowing his lead and Razz Mitchell was drumming so fast and hard that Bernie could barely keep track of his sticks. The music just seemed to jump up to another level of intensity, as if suddenly cranked up by some giant invisible hand, and then the whole brass section kicked in together on the chorus. The effect was like a crisp slap hitting him squarely across the face. Bernie Brightman thought his heart was going to leap right out of his chest. At that moment he felt like a weight was being lifted from him, like the Great Depression itself was just blowing away from him like a thin leaf caught in a saxophone hurricane. None of it seemed to matter anymore: the drudgery of his lousy job pushing heavy racks of clothes through the streets for eight dollars a week, the milk lines, relief, the pressure, the stone cold drag of being young and poor in New York and feeling like you had no future.

Brightman had absolutely no interest in dancing at first. He just wanted to stand there alone in front of the bandstand like a solemn worshiper before an altar. He closed his eyes and let the music fill his whole being. But when finally his feet began to move, they moved with a life of their own. It seemed as if he became pure speed and rhythm and style itself as he started to dance.

That was the moment when it really started, with his feet just flying and cutting across the Track as fast as Razz Mitchell's sticks across the high hat. That was the moment when Bernie Brightman understood in his soul exactly why they called it swing, and from that moment on he was a viper.

3

The Paranoid Spokesman

1.

Nobody in America would have more readily agreed with Terry Southern's equation of marijuana and sedition than Harry J. Anslinger, the forty-five-year-old chief of the Federal Bureau of Narcotics. Had Anslinger known about what had happened to the twelve-year-old Southern in Alvarado, Texas, or to the teenaged Bernie Brightman at the Savoy Ballroom in Harlem, he would have wasted no time entering the stories in a file of cases he had been compiling for years about the weed's menace to the youth of America.

Anslinger had been in charge of the Bureau for seven years when he took the chair on the morning of April 27, 1937, to become the first witness in the hearings on H.R. 6385, Representative Robert L. Doughton's House version of the Treasury Department's Marihuana Tax Act, which called for a prohibitive tax upon unauthorized transfers of marijuana.

The purpose of the act, as explained to the House Ways and Means Committee by Clinton Hester, assistant to the chief counsel for the Treasury Department, was to propose a "prohibitive tax upon the production, manufacture, and sale of marihuana, and thus discourage its use in any form in this country." The idea of the bill, as explained by Hester, was "to stop high school children from getting marijuana."

Anslinger was an imposing man with a large, oversized head, big ears, and a solemn, imperious manner. He wore dark funereal suits but had a great flair for the dramatic.

"Mr. Chairman and distinguished members of the Ways and Means Committee," he intoned before the committee,

> this traffic in marihuana is increasing to such an extent that it has come to be the cause for the greatest national concern. This drug is as old as civilization itself. Homer wrote about it, as a drug which made men forget their homes, and that turned them into swine. In Persia, a thousand years before Christ, there was a religious and military order founded which was called the Assassins, and they derived their name from a drug called hashish, which is now known in this country as marihuana. They were noted for their acts of cruelty, and the word "assassin" aptly describes the drug. . . . Here we have a drug that is not like opium. Opium has all the good of Dr. Jekyll and all the evils of Mr. Hyde. This drug is entirely the monster Hyde, the harmful effect of which cannot be measured.

Thus Anslinger evoked the Homer of antiquity and a cult of assassins in Persia to explain the evils of marijuana to the assembled congressmen on the Ways and Means Committee in 1937, many of whom were completely unfamiliar with the weed, despite the mounting onslaught of press about it. That Anslinger's citing of Homer was completely spurious went unnoticed by the congressmen, for they would have had to have been classical scholars to have spotted the inaccuracies. In fact, Homer refers to two different substances in *The Odyssey*. The drug that "made men forget their homes" was actually the "nepenthe" used by Helen of Troy as an assuager of pain and a drug of forgetting; the drug that "turned men into swine" was "moly," and nowhere in the text is there any reference to cannabis, or any image associated with anything remotely resembling cannabis.

Anslinger knew very well what he was doing. He knew that evoking this legend would play upon a fear buried in the Western mind for a thousand years—a fear of what could happen when such a powerful drug as cannabis was administered to the young and unsuspecting minds of the innocent—and that this image would play a central role in building his presentation of marijuana as the assassin of the youth of America.

2.

Thanks to Harry Anslinger, from its very beginning and continuing right up to George Bush's pronouncement in September of 1989 that the drug crisis represented nothing less than "the moral equivalent of war," the movement against the use of drugs in America, whether marijuana or otherwise, would always be cast as a great moral crusade that used the symbols and dire rhetoric of warfare. On the surface it was a conflict as basic as that of a dominant alcohol culture seeking to control and repress a minority culture that would accept and integrate the use of other substances, but it would go far beyond that. It is only when seen in this light that the harshness and distortions and extreme passions surrounding drug use in this country become more comprehensible. The prohibition of drugs in America was always a war to save civilization—and the first casualty of war, as the great Greek dramatist Aeschylus so famously wrote, is truth.

Few men were more suited by natural temperament and ideology to lead America's moral crusade against drugs than Harry Jacob Anslinger, who was a complex blend of cop, crusader, bureaucrat, and propagandist, and few would exert a more singular or longer-lasting impact on the molding of a vital aspect of American national and international policy. An archconservative who fervently believed that people who used drugs were weak and morally corrupt individuals who should be punished to the fullest extent of the law, Anslinger held to the deep Calvinist conviction that people are inherently incapable of controlling their passions and appetites if not strictly held in check by outside authorities. He would always cite an incident that happened in 1904, when he was twelve years old and growing up in Altoona, Pennsylvania, as the essential defining experience for him about the perils of drugs. It happened when young Harry was visiting a neighbor's farmhouse and he heard the piteous scream of the farmer's wife coming from upstairs—the inconsolable shriek of a woman hopelessly addicted to narcotics, caught in the desperate throes of withdrawal. The farmer rushed downstairs and exhorted Harry to take his cart and pick up a package from the local pharmacist and come back as fast as possible, and Harry lashed at the horses, dashing back with the

package. The farmer then hurried upstairs, and the screaming bless-
edly stopped as soon as the drug was administered.

"I never forgot those screams," Anslinger wrote, nor that the narcotics were given to him, "a twelve-year-old, with no questions asked."
The anecdote has become such an oft-repeated part of Anslinger's
biography that Johann Hari uses it as the melodramatic central metaphor for the whole *raison d'être* for the war on drugs in his book *Chasing the Scream: The First and Last Days of the War on Drugs*: "When he
grew into a man, this boy was going to draw together some of the
deepest fears in American culture—of racial minorities, of intoxication, of losing control—and channel them into a global war to prevent those screams. It would cause many screams in turn. They can
be heard in almost every city on earth tonight. This is how Harry Anslinger entered the drug war."

Of course, who knows if it ever really happened in the first place.

By most accounts Anslinger was a diligent, incorruptible civil ser-
vant, but he was also an inveterate liar and a self-promoting blowhard
who would say practically anything if it served his ends. America's first
drug czar and warrior was also a xenophobic racist. From the beginning of his tenure, when he was named to head the newly formed
Federal Bureau of Narcotics in 1930, he preached a gospel that held
that America needed protection not only from drugs but also from the
people who brought them. From his days in the Prohibition Unit of
the Treasury Department, he had come to view the sailors on the ships
that smuggled contraband from "filthy Central American and West Indian ports" as "the lowest scum of the earth" who brought diseases and
contaminated the people of the slums with "contagious and loathsome
diseases."

Many thought that with the election of Franklin Delano Roosevelt
in 1932, Anslinger's days as head of the FBN were numbered, but
by this time he had already consolidated a strong bastion of support
among conservative newspaper editors and congressmen, law enforcement officials, the pharmaceutical industry, patriotic societies, and religious organizations. The most serious challenge to his reign came in
1934 when newly elected Democratic senator Joseph Guffey, of Anslinger's home state of Pennsylvania, called for his head in a letter to

Assistant Secretary of the Treasury Stephen B. Gibbons. It seems that Anslinger had apparently used the phrase "ginger-colored nigger" in a Bureau memorandum to describe an FBN informant.

"It would seem to me that a man in such a responsible position as that held by Mr. Anslinger should have more discretion than to refer to one of such a large part of the population of this country in the manner quoted above," Guffey wrote, "and I doubt very much that one so indiscreet should be allowed to remain in such a responsible position."

Anslinger survived the challenge; above all else, he was a survivor. As a Republican forced to operate in the New Deal administration of FDR, perhaps his greatest talent was his ability to portray the "drug problem" faced by the United States with dramatic flair and in a manner that always justified the existence of the relatively new FBN and presented himself as indispensable to its solution. He became a master at using the tabloid press to manipulate public opinion and bolster his position, getting himself photographed in trench coat and fedora, doing everything possible to burnish his legend as America's number one narc. A rough draft of an author's note he once composed says much about how he viewed himself: "His fame spread throughout the world. His great contributions to rid the world of the worst plague of mankind have won him many awards." Anslinger routinely referred to himself as "the world's greatest expert on the international narcotic traffic." Over time he grew into an increasingly tyrannical and domineering figure, vindictive toward any person or organization that challenged his complete domination of American drug policy. His avowed enemies came to include lawyers such as Rufus King, sociologists such as Alfred E. Lindesmith, any judges he perceived to be too lenient about the enforcement of the drug laws—virtually anyone, in fact, who had the temerity to challenge his policies.

During the early 1930s, Anslinger was initially reluctant to propose federal antimarijuana legislation, and his reasons were well-founded. As much of a born crusader and antidrug zealot as he was, he was also a pragmatist. His experience with alcohol prohibition had graphically demonstrated that enforcing a law without popular support was a very difficult proposition. "Prohibition will never succeed through the promulgation of a mere law observance program if the American people regard it as obnoxious," he wrote. He was reluctant to commit the full resources and prestige of his newly formed Bureau against what his agent in New Orleans had described as a plant that grew "promiscuously. The Police Department here in New Orleans advises this Office that this vegetable is generally grown on vacant city lots and out in the open country. The difficulty of enforcing a restrictive law with regard to production of 'Marihuana' is obvious."

But throughout the early 1930s, pressure from the Southwest was steadily mounting for the Bureau to do something about marijuana. The onset of the Depression had quickly soured the welcome for Mexican workers, who used the weed as a substance of entertainment and relaxation in the states where they provided cheap agricultural labor. Suddenly increasing numbers of unemployed whites had to compete for jobs with Mexicans willing to work at much lower wages, and the association of the "dirty Mexicans" with their dirty evil weed made them a convenient target for a growing backlash. From 1932 to 1936, Anslinger supported the Uniform State Narcotic Act as the best means of combating marijuana and began lobbying state legislatures to pass the act. As developed by the National Conference of Commissioners on Uniform State Laws in 1934 to effectively safeguard and regulate narcotic drugs throughout all of the states, the Uniform State Narcotic Act was designed to give authority to the states to exercise police power regarding either seizure of drugs used in illicit trade or punishment of those responsible. However, as few people had heard of marijuana before 1936, state legislators were initially slow to act. Thus Anslinger began to focus on the "marihuana menace" to raise public consciousness and promote passage of the Uniform State Narcotic Act, setting in motion the very gears that would force him to propose federal legislation, touching off what Yale historian David Musto calls a classic case of "bureaucratic overkill."

Anslinger became convinced that the only way to ensure against any possibility of a recurrence of what had happened with Prohibition—the phenomenon of a significant percentage of the American population wantonly and brazenly breaking an unpopular law they found obnoxious, living as virtual criminals until the law had to be repealed—would be through a national campaign against the weed.

Before 1935, the *Reader's Guide to Periodical Literature* lists not a single article about marijuana in any major national magazine. From July 1935 to June 1937, four appeared; between 1937 and 1939, there were seventeen. Of the seventeen articles during the peak of the campaign, sociologist Howard S. Becker notes that "ten either explicitly acknowledged the help of the Bureau in furnishing facts and figures or gave explicit evidence of having received help by using facts and figures that had appeared earlier, either in Bureau publications or in testimony before the Congress."

To whip up public support, Anslinger was well prepared with horror stories for the congressmen and later the senators considering the antimarijuana legislation—a large file of cases that he had been compiling for a number of years. Many of these cases involved interracial sexual encounters; many others involved murderous rage and carnage and were filed by the Bureau as fact with only the flimsiest documentation or none at all. One particularly grisly piece was a glossy close-up photograph of Thomas Cook, a Pennsylvania man shot point-blank in the face with a shotgun by a man allegedly under the influence of marijuana, whose face looked like it had been shredded by a meat grinder.

But even more horrific was the centerpiece of Anslinger's file, the case of Victor Licata, a Tampa, Florida, man who killed his entire family of five with an ax in 1933. This story, along with Licata's haunting, hollow-eyed photograph, was so widely circulated and recirculated in the media by the Bureau that it became the basis for an insanity defense based on marijuana and was still being cited as evidence of the deranging effects of marijuana as late as 1966. Anslinger's version of the case appeared in his famous *American Magazine* article "Marijuana: Assassin of Youth" in July of 1937:

An entire family was murdered by a youthful addict in Florida. When officers arrived at the home, they found the youth staggering about in a human slaughterhouse. With an ax he had killed his father, mother, two brothers and a sister. He seemed to be in a daze. . . . He had no recollection of committing the multiple crime. The officers knew him as a sane, rather quiet young man; now he was pitifully crazed. They sought the reason. The boy said he had been in the habit of smoking something which youthful friends called "muggles," a childish name for marijuana.

Licata was committed to the Florida State Hospital in 1933 and hanged himself in 1950. In examining the case closely for his book *Marijuana—The New Prohibition* (1970), Stanford University law professor John Kaplan learned that Licata had in fact been diagnosed as suffering from "Dementia Praecox with homicidal tendencies" and uncovered numerous other pathological factors in his case file as well as a long family history of insanity, none of which had anything to do with marijuana (in fact, marijuana was not even mentioned in his case file at the hospital). But Harry Anslinger ascribed Victor Licata's madness to a "marijuana dream." It was a classic example of the Big Lie: Anslinger's version of the story became press fact, and press fact became the public truth. And so it would go with marijuana and other illicit drugs in America: a long tradition of myths fed as a matter of course to an unquestioning and circulation-hungry press shaping laws, policies, and public perceptions, from Anslinger's time into the twenty-first century.

As millions of people who had never heard about marijuana before learned about it from scare stories generated by the Bureau, the political pressure mounted for the very federal legislation that Anslinger sought to avoid by employing the Uniform State Narcotic Act. With no choice but to move ahead for a national law, America's first drug czar picked up the banner in the war against marijuana, waved it even more frenziedly, and prepared to lead the charge toward the next great American Prohibition.

Anslinger was prepared to put forth a number of signature images to isolate what he saw as the greatest threats being posed to American civilization by marijuana. If the first image was that of an ax murderer and the second that of a degenerate schoolyard pusher, the third was equally pernicious and threatening: a Negro jazz musician.

"As you know, some of these musicians acquire followings among juveniles," Anslinger observed in a draft letter to the undersecretary of the treasury. "We are familiar with the type of hero worship in which the juvenile is a slavish imitator of the things, good and bad, which are done by the object of his admiration. In my opinion there is a real juvenile delinquency threat in the marihuana antics of these persons."

3.

Perhaps the historian Richard Hofstadter came closest to putting his finger on the origins and dynamics of the cultural conflict over marijuana and other drugs in America in his classic 1964 essay, "The Paranoid Style in American Politics," even though it isn't about drugs at all. Hofstadter's essay is a study of the traditional right-wing ideologies that manifested so dramatically in the anticommunist hysteria of McCarthyism during the 1950s and the Goldwaterism of 1964. Tracing the roots of these ideologies back to the nativist movements against Catholics, Masons, and the successive waves of immigration that had arrived on America's shores, Hofstadter identifies in them a "paranoid style" that he describes as a "style of mind, not always right-wing in its affiliations, that has a long and varied history." He characterizes this mindset as a "way of seeing the world and of expressing oneself" that tends to be "overheated, oversuspicious, overaggressive, grandiose, and apocalyptic in expression," the impetus for which derived from "the desire of Yankee Americans to maintain an ethnically and religiously homogeneous society." The paranoid style was always expressed as an "all-out crusade. The paranoid spokesman sees the fate of this conspiracy in apocalyptic terms—he traffics in the birth and death of whole worlds, whole political orders, whole systems of human values. He is always manning the barricades of civilization."

Can anyone possibly think of a better example of Hofstadter's "paranoid spokesman" than Harry Jacob Anslinger?

This struggle, according to Hofstadter, is "always a conflict between absolute good and absolute evil, [and] the quality needed is not a willingness to compromise but the will to fight things out to the finish. Nothing but complete victory will do." The enemy in this great cultural war is "clearly delineated: he is a perfect model of malice, a kind of amoral superman: sinister, ubiquitous, powerful, cruel, luxury-loving."

Furthermore, as Hofstadter portrays it, the enemy also represents some deeply repressed part of the paranoid's psyche: "The sexual freedom often attributed to him, his lack of moral inhibition, his possession of especially effective techniques for fulfilling his desires, give exponents of the paranoid style an opportunity to project and freely express unacceptable parts of their own minds."

Whether it sees an "enemy within" or an "enemy without," the paranoid trend as delineated by Hofstader reflects a deep-seated fear of contamination from undesirables.

In 1931, Dr. A. E. Fossier read a paper before the Louisiana State Medical Society called "The Marihuana Menace." One out of every four people arrested in New Orleans was "addicted to marihuana," Fossier claimed in his analysis of the role that the weed had played in that city's rising "crime wave," and seventeen out of thirty-seven murderers in the city that he studied had smoked "muggles," marijuana cigarettes. Although quite characteristic of the "scientific" studies about marijuana and crime of this period, the paper that Dr. Fossier presented on the role of the weed in the New Orleans crime wave and the meaning of the marijuana "menace" is far more telling for what it reveals about the cultural sensibility behind the movement to prohibit the use of marijuana at the time:

> As far as it can be ascertained this addiction has assumed formidable proportions since the advent of that "noble experiment," that fiasco, prohibition. In fact, it is the offspring which bids fair to surpass its dissembling parent in destroying moral inhibition. The lesser of the two evils is alcohol. . . . The debasing and baneful influence of hashish and opium is not restricted to individuals but has manifested itself in nations and races as well. The dominant race and most enlightened countries are alcoholic, whilst the races and nations addicted to hemp and opium, some of which once attained to heights of culture and civilization, have deteriorated both mentally and physically.

Add to this deep-seated fear of contamination by "the races addicted to hemp and opium" the notion that drug use was somehow un-American, and what had been coalescing since the 1920s was a potent conservative ideological context for framing the entire drug issue. Congressmen like Richmond Hobson were quick to blame the "drug problem" on the perfidy and greed of other nations: South America corrupted us with cocaine; degenerate Europe sent its heroin and morphine; inscrutable Asia was the source of opium; backward Africa and the Middle East produced hashish.

"Projection of blame on foreign nations for domestic evils harmonized with the ascription of drug use to ethnic minorities," observes historian David Musto. "Both the external cause and the internal locus could be dismissed as un-American. This kind of analysis avoids the painful and awkward realization that the use of dangerous drugs may be an integral part of American society. Putting the blame on others also permits more punitive measures to be taken against certain of the culprits."

It was a point of view that would naturally incorporate the notion that the practice of using cannabis as an evil euphoriant was a repugnant custom being introduced into the Yankee WASP culture during the twentieth century like some kind of foreign bubonic plague by uncivilized, low-bred Latinos and African Americans. It was a worldview that portrayed drug users and addicts as not only morally tainted but malevolent—as not only "other" but somehow less than human—thereby justifying any and all measures employed against them.

In the end, what was at stake in this great cultural crusade against drugs was always the hearts and minds of America's children, their innocence and future—the lifeblood of the nation, the very destiny of the civilization. Thus for the vast majority of Americans, who had heard relatively little about marijuana before the 1930s, the most incendiary image connected to its use was always that of the degenerate pusher, hanging around schoolyards, handing out reefer to unsuspecting schoolkids, trying to get them hooked. But it didn't end there.

The other most powerful fear had to do with sex and forbidden flesh, for walking hand in hand with the image of marijuana use was an unspeakable fear as old as slavery in the New World. The ethnobotanist and author Terence McKenna has written about how marijuana is a "boundary-dissolving" experience and a "deconditioning" agent that "decouples" users from accepted values. Of course, the single most sacrosanct boundary of American life, particularly in the South, was that of racial segregation. Always implicit in the antimarijuana agenda was the great fear that, as with the sweet smell of burning cannabis rose in the steamy back streets of New Orleans, in dusty towns along the border of Texas and Mexico from Brownsville to El Paso, on the South Side of Chicago, along 12th Street in Kansas City, Central Avenue in South Central Los Angeles, and the Stroll between 131st and 132nd

Streets crossing Seventh Avenue in Harlem, the sexual boundary between the races would vanish as if by some perfidious deed of black
magic, and the great taboo of interracial sex would come tumbling
down forever.

Nothing epitomizes this fear more than the following item in Anslinger's file, which he would trot out over and over again: "Colored
students at the Univ. of Minn. partying with female students (white)
smoking and getting their sympathy with stories of racial persecution.
Result pregnancy."

The notion that marijuana was a powerful aphrodisiac that would
promote sexual promiscuity and interracial sex found voice among not
only fundamentalist Christians but also organizations like the American Psychiatric Association. In 1933, a respected researcher, Dr. Walter
Bromberg, presented a paper on cannabis to the APA that estimated
the number of marijuana smokers throughout the South to be one in
four. His estimation was ludicrously inflated but not surprising considering the panic-stricken press reports of the period, and while Bromberg did not subscribe to the rising hysteria about how the weed caused
crime, he was nonetheless persuaded that it was "a primary stimulus to
the impulsive life with direct expression in the motor field," and that it
"release[d] inhibitions and restraints imposed by society and allow[ed]
individuals to act out their drives openly."

What could possibly be more offensive and threatening to the
moral sensibility of mainstream Protestant American culture, whether
Presbyterian, Methodist, or Southern Baptist, than the use of a weed
that allowed individuals "to act out their drives openly" and promoted
"direct stimulus to the impulsive life"?

After all, the "impulsive life" could easily incorporate behavior
ranging from the ravishing of young white Anglo-Saxon women by
drug-crazed ethnics and blacks, to the most heinous ax murders, to
C.K. the field hand's observation of what would happen if people were
ever allowed to smoke marijuana with impunity in Terry Southern's
"Red-Dirt Marijuana": "Shoot, ever'body git high, wouldn't be nobody
git up an' feed the chickens!"

4

Two Hits of That Stuff, and Jack, You'd Be Mellow

Bernie Brightman wasted little time. He was back in Harlem the very next weekend after his first trip to the Savoy. He was astonished to learn that if you stopped off at a candy store on the corner of 141st and Lenox, and you went in and spoke to Crappy or Mickey, you could buy three marijuana joints for a quarter. When Brightman realized that his friend Roy had bought three and taken one joint for himself before selling them to him, he learned his first lesson about the marijuana trade right there.

"I think I spent every Saturday night there at the Savoy for the next three straight years," Brightman recalled in his office at Stash Records, the jazz label he founded to catalog the music he came to love after that first night at the Savoy in 1936. "It was the absolute height of the big band era. I became part of the first wave of white guys who smoked marijuana in New York. We were all kids from neighborhoods all over the city, kids all looking for something. We all came to Harlem because that was the place to be. We called it different names—*gage, jive, tea, grass*—most of the Jewish guys I knew used to call it 'shit.' I don't know why. After a while, once we got a little more sophisticated, we would try to put together enough money to pick up an ounce, and come up with our own stuff for free."

Brightman was astounded at how very easy it was to get grass at the time. "When I started smoking you could get an ounce for about eight dollars. We were so poor a group of us would chip in, and we all had no privacy at home because we had to share rooms and even beds with people in our families, so we would get a cheap hotel room and clean it and roll it there. We would all then fill up these cigarette packs with our portion. There was hardly any place that sold rolling papers in those days! We'd have to go down to a little Spanish grocery store on 14th Street to get our Bambú papers."

The Harlem on a Saturday night that Brightman began to explore was radiant with life and color. Dress was the first item of business. You always wore a suit, preferably navy. The jacket was long, not the exaggerated zoot jacket of the movies, but just a little long. The pants were wide, narrowing to a very pegged cuff; the tie was knit wool with big knots; the shirt was high-necked with a roll collar; and the hat, if you could afford one, had a three-inch brim, and the place where you got your hats was Big Bill, on Sixth Avenue.

"That's where all the hip guys went. And that was the look, brother. If you saw a guy who looked like that, you knew he was hip, and chances are that he smoked shit, too."

If you didn't have reefer, you could always score before you went to the Savoy. In the early 1930s, before Brightman arrived on the scene, when marijuana was still legal, guys would just light up on the dance floor; later, the bathroom became the place. After a couple of years you couldn't smoke in the bathroom anymore, and sophisticates like Teddy Reig, Count Basie's road manager, who also became a producer for Savoy Records and was later busted for possession, would head into the cloakroom. Brightman and his friends then became habitués of the telephone booth. Once you were good and high the ritual of the evening began in earnest . . .

"Here's how a viper spent the evening at the Savoy after smoking. It was music, dancing, talk, in that order, and each one of those things became like a whole world unto itself. At around eleven thirty, the buses would come up. You'd always get tourists coming in and dancing with the hostesses; they wanted to dance with attractive black women. At around midnight they would put on a big dance exhibition by Whitey's Lindy Hoppers, the famous group that could really throw people around and twirl them, all those incredible steps and moves. We could do a little of that, but not the same level as those people. That really wasn't our thing. Our thing was laying back stoned and being cool, and that was a whole world unto itself too."

The real odyssey began after leaving the Savoy. Brightman fell in with Crappy's sister, who was older and knew all the after-hours tea pads in Harlem.

"There must have been dozens. The three or four that I frequented regularly were places I'll never forget. Mostly they were just very relaxed places where you could go to sit around and be stoned and listen to some music in a nice environment. They were like Harlem's version of an opium den: very simple, not that much dialogue or socializing. You just wanted to lay back on a nice soft couch with mellow red and blue lights and enjoy your head. There was always a Victrola with the latest sides, and sometimes there were women there you could be with in a back room. Some of them were just amazing."

The most famous tea pad was Kaiser's, around 133rd Street. "Kaiser was this big black stud. To get there you had to go through the basements and sub-basements of several different buildings. They wouldn't let you in unless they knew you. They would look at you through a peephole door and if they didn't know you, forget it, the door would slam right in your face. You even had to know the right way to ring the bell, otherwise they wouldn't open the peephole door. Inside was the place to be, man—*everybody* went there, the finest chicks and the best reefer in Harlem. Two hits of that stuff, and Jack, you'd be mellow!"

Then there was Reefer Mae's. "Mae was a black chick from Carolina who used to have a whole group of chicks rolling reefer for her all day long—thin, beautiful, perfect joints, turned out like machines by these girls who could light up and smoke as many as they wanted while they were working. Mae was an illiterate woman, but I'll tell you, she made a lot of money in the marijuana business. She ended up owning real estate all up and down 125th Street."

At first Brightman usually stayed out until about three or four in the morning, but as time went on he began to see the sun rise more and more. After the night was over, ravenous from smoking and with nothing else left to do, he would head over to the Fat Man's, a little greasy spoon that had the most delicious ribs in the world, with potato salad, coleslaw, and bread, all for thirty-five cents. He would eat like a king. And then it would be over, this night of reefer and great music and dancing and adventure and maybe even sex, walking around in this place that had become completely magical to him, and he would be dog tired, and get on the train to go back to his life and job, and he couldn't wait, just couldn't wait for the week to pass so that he could come right back.

Bernard Brightman had found not just a culture but a whole way of life that had been growing around jazz and reefer in Harlem. When he became curious about where it had all come from, he began to ask questions and hear the stories—about the carnival people, and the pimps, and the hookers, and the show biz folks—that had been around since the twenties.

That was when he learned about Pops, and New Orleans golden leaf, and the Mighty Mezz, and the story of how reefer came to Harlem during that first cold, desolate winter of the Great Depression.

5

The White Mayor of Harlem

1.

In the winter of 1930, Mezz Mezzrow's stomping ground was the Stroll, between 131st and 132nd Streets where the streets crossed Seventh Avenue in Harlem. Here, within the course of a few hundred feet of concrete, congregated all the great black entertainers and musicians of the age, all of the dramas and tragedies of life, all of its human colors and variegated emotions simmering in one big bubbling cauldron of a city block.

And what a block it was! Mezzrow had a pick of hangouts that included a barbershop, a drugstore, the Performers and Entertainers Club, Connie's Inn, the Lafayette Theatre, a candy store, and Big John's ginmill. Around the corner of 132nd Street were Tabb's Restaurant and the Rhythm Club; back on 131st Street was the Barbeque, which served the best ribs in Harlem; upstairs were rehearsal halls and a speakeasy and nightclub called the Bandbox; and running around the corner building, a wide alleyway with entrances on Seventh Avenue and 131st Street led to the back of the Lafayette and a little bar that became, along with the Corner, the crossroads of Mezz Mezzrow's universe.

Into this single remarkable alleyway filtered the sounds of the orchestras of Jimmie Lunceford, Cab Calloway, Erskine Hawkins, and Count Basie as they rehearsed the music that would make the thirties swing, but the sounds that gave Mezzrow the most pleasure by far came through a huge exhaust fan built into a shed in the alleyway where, if he didn't choke on the exhaust and funk that pumped into his face, he could hear the sounds of Louis Armstrong's horn and Zutty Single-ton's drums coming through loud and clear from the stage of Connie's Inn, where Pops was performing the number "Ain't Misbehavin'" in Fats Waller's show *Hot Chocolates* and bringing the house down every night.

Chicago-born, Mezz had never been to New Orleans, but a few notes of Pops's horn was all it ever took to bring images of New Orleans rushing to life in his stoned head, its levees and cribs and barrel-houses and honky-tonks. Mezz loved jazz like few Caucasians ever had, and he knew that the real jazz, just like the real marijuana, came from the Crescent City. He would stand there nightly, swaying as he listened, hungrily soaking up every Harlem sight and sound, every nuance, every bit of jive.

Of course, Mezzrow could have easily gone backstage anytime he wanted to enjoy the music. He was a jazz musician himself, a legitimate clarinetist who had once played with the likes of the Austin High Gang—Jimmy McPartland on cornet and alto, Bud Freeman on tenor, Davey Tough on drums, and Frank Teschemacher on alto and clarinet—back in Chicago between '26 and '29. Mezzrow had been part of the first wave of white boys up north outside of Bix Beiderbecke to play jazz seriously. He knew that he was always welcome backstage because he and Pops were very tight, but he preferred to hear the sounds outside in the company of Little Fats and Mark, an orphan boy named Travis, a dancer named George Morton, Oakie, Nappy, Brother Raymond of the dance trio Tip Tap & Toe, two fly girls named Thelma and Myrtle, and his good friend Little Frankie Walker, a skinny teenager with razor legs, snaggleteeth, and dribble lips. It was much more fun for Mezzrow to listen to Louis with his black friends, the first gang of vipers in Harlem.

"When it came to hearing Louis," Mezzrow related in his 1946 autobiography, *Really the Blues*, "you wanted the whole world to dig what he had to say on his horn. Roaches were passed round and round, and even though those vipers were plenty raggedy they loved Louis like nobody else. . . . All the raggedy kids, especially those who became vipers, were so inspired with self-respect after digging how neat and natty Louis was, they started to dress up real good, and took pride in it too, because if Louis did it, it must be right. The slogan in our circle of vipers became, *Light up and be somebody."*

There had been a few pot dealers in the history of Harlem before Mezzrow—early teaheads before his reign had bought their gage from a certain Spanish dealer on Lenox Avenue—but Mezzrow was certainly its most famous, and his marijuana certainly had the most cultural impact. Simply put, Mezz had access to the best Mexican weed ever to hit the streets of New York. It came from a connection he had made in his Detroit days, who brought the stuff directly up from Mexico—quality weed that was heads and shoulders above any reefer ever known along the Stroll. Mezz remembered its arrival on the scene as follows:

> As soon as we got some of that Mexican bush we almost blew our tops. Poppa, you never smacked your chops on anything sweeter in all your days of viping. It had such a wonderful smell and the kick you got was really out of this world. . . . I laid it on the cats in the Barbeque, and pretty soon all of Harlem was after me to light them up. . . . Before I knew it, I was standing on the Corner pushing my gage. Only I did no pushing. I just stood under the Tree of Hope, my pokes full, and the cats came and went, and so did my golden-leaf."

Mezzrow would hang out there day and night at the crossroads of the universe—righteously stoned, just watching the glorious river of life that was Harlem flowing past, his bushy dark eyebrows arching up and his mouth twisting into a friendly smile when he was approached by the never-ending succession of vipers looking to score from him.

"Hey there, Poppa Mezz, is you anywhere?"

"Man, I'm down with it," Mezz tells the cat, "stickin' like a honky."

"Lay a trey on me."

"Got to do it, slot."

The translation of the conversation reads as follows:

FIRST CAT: Hello, Mezz, have you got any marihuana?

MEZZROW: Plenty, old man, my pockets are full as a factory hand's on payday.

FIRST CAT: Let me have three cigarettes (fifty cents' worth).

MEZZROW: I sure will, slotmouth. (A private inner racial joke, suggesting a mouth as big and avaricious as the coin slot in a vending machine, always looking for something to put into it.)

That winter, as he stood on the Corner and the people of Harlem began to feel the bite of the Great Depression, Mezzrow became famous.

> Overnight I was the most popular man in Harlem. New words came into being to meet the situation: *the mezz* and *the mighty mezz*, referring, I blush to say, to me and to the tea both; *mezzroll,* to describe the kind of fat, well-packed and clean cigarette I used to roll (this word later got corrupted to *messerole* and it's still used to mean a certain size and shape of reefer, which is different from the so-called panatella); *the hard-cuttin' mezz* and *the righteous bush.* Some of those phrases really found a permanent place in Harlemese, and even crept out to color American slang in general.

2.

Marijuana was hitting Harlem at a crucial moment in its history. Along with jazz, it became a part of the experience of the first generation of African Americans to come of age in New York after the Great Dispersal had transformed Harlem from a small middle-class neighborhood with housing designed for sixty thousand into a black city-within-a city of three hundred thousand. It arrived right at the time when the promise and cultural fermentation of what had become known as the Harlem Renaissance of the 1920s was fading, dissolving away to the despair of the Great Depression, which would hit African Americans so hard.

If the presence of reefer had been culturally identifiable during the twenties in the experience of a few like Louis Armstrong, during the thirties it came to be reflected in the sensibility and style of many more, in a whole community of "vipers"—in their way of walking, dressing, dancing, and talking. The grassroots of this movement—in effect, the first cultural underground of marijuana users—were young disillusioned African Americans who danced nightly at the Track, the Savoy Ballroom. These were kids who knew that they would never in their lives see the inside of the Cotton Club, Connie's Inn, or Small's Paradise—the fancy black and tan nightclubs only for white patrons from downtown. This was where the socialites and nightlife dilettantes and celebrities who came to party and play in Harlem went.

The hero of the movement may have been Louis Armstrong, but its cynosure and chronicler was Milton "Mezz" Mezzrow, the son of immigrant Jews. What Mezzrow came to discover in the jive-talking hipsters of Harlem was much more profound than merely a new kind of clever slang of razor-sharp witticisms and lightning-quick metaphors; it was a culture of such vitality and originality that he saw it as nothing less than revolutionary. Mezzrow was by no means the first Jewish musician to fall in love with Harlem, with its people and music. George Gershwin's forays into the Harlem of the Renaissance had produced his masterful *Rhapsody in Blue* in 1924, but Mezzrow's identification went much deeper, into the life of the community, into the very soul of its people.

Mezzrow never saw the vipers and hep cats as exotic primitives. His identification with them sprang from the soil of the marijuana he smoked and the music he loved, but what he really fell in love with was precisely what brought this culture to life and gave it such purity and power: the fact that it was "outside." It was the product of a people denied entry into the main track and relegated to becoming musicians, entertainers, maids, butlers, chauffeurs, handymen, gamblers, countermen, porters, numbers racketeers, day laborers, pimps, stevedores. These were the people who became the first vipers, and what Mezz recognized in them was the stirrings of a pariah culture coming to life, seeking to define its destiny on its own terms, not those of the white world.

> You know who they were, all these fast-talking kids with their four-dimensional surrealist patter? I found out they were the cream of the race—the professionals of Harlem who never got within reaching distance of the white collar. They were the razor-witted doctors without M.D.s, lawyers who never had a shingle to hang out, financiers without penny one in their pokes, political leaders without a party, diploma-less professors and scientists minus a laboratory. They held their office hours and made their speeches on The Corner. There

they wrote their prose poems, painted their word pictures. They were the genius of their people, always on their toes, never missing a trick, asking no favors and taking no guff, not looking for trouble but solid ready for it. Spawned in a social vacuum and hung up in mid-air, they were beginning to build their own culture. Their language was a declaration of independence.

Despite the onset of the Depression, it was still a glorious time to be in Harlem. This was the Harlem of Duke Ellington and Cab Calloway, the Harlem of the great dancers and dance teams—Bill "Bojangles" Robinson, the Berry Brothers, Buck and Bubbles, Ada Brown, Nina Mae McKinney—and the new rage in dancing, the snakehips dance, originated by Earl Tucker. This was the Harlem of the great piano players, Fats Waller and Eubie Blake, James P. Johnson and Willie "the Lion" Smith; of breakfast dances and tea pads, conked hair and rent parties. Mezzrow relished his role as a Harlem insider, a kind of cultural transvestite who had crossed over to the "underworld" and could "hip" the white world to what was really going on. He particularly enjoyed bringing the established white musicians he knew from downtown up to Harlem's Lafayette Theatre: "Every Friday night I'd reserve the first three or four rows, and most of the musicians I knew would come up with their friends to gape at the goings-on. Acres of marijuana smoke went up at every show there—and man, many a time even the performers would come on stage and do some comedy routine about vipers, and they'd light up too, right in front of everybody."

It wasn't only the comedians who were performing material about reefer, either. Celebratory songs about marijuana began finding their way onto wax during the twenties and thirties with Fats Waller's "Viper's Drag," "Golden Leaf Strut," and "Chant of the Weed." Stuff Smith's "If You're a Viper," later recorded by Rosetta Howard, even mentioned Mezz himself:

Dreamed about a reefer five foot long
The mighty mezz but not too strong

"If You're a Viper" was followed by a whole succession of tunes throughout the 1930s by some of the greatest artists of the swing era:

Don Redman's "Reefer Man" and Cab Calloway's "The Man from Harlem" in 1932, Benny Goodman's "Texas Tea Party" in 1933, Andy Kirk's "All the Jive Is Gone" in 1936, Georgia White's "The Stuff Is Here" in 1937, Buster Bailey's "Light Up" and Sidney Bechet's "Viper Mad" in 1938. These songs form a vivid portrait of Harlem's reefer culture, and what they convey is the sense that with the deepening Depression, reefer came to be viewed in Harlem as a fun, easy, cheap way to get high and cast off one's cares for an evening—a far cry indeed from the images of the schoolyard pusher or ax murderer being presented by the Federal Bureau of Narcotics throughout the 1930s. In these songs, marijuana was a mild and safe euphoriant that allowed people to be playful and whimsical in the face of worsening economic hardship and social oppression, and the man who brought it to the people was viewed as *righteous, groovy,* a *solid sender,* a *hep cat* who performed a vital social service, a new kind of social hero. And the Mighty Mezz was the first of his kind. On the corner he became known as the Reefer King, the Link Between the Races, the Philosopher, the Mezz, Poppa Mezz, Mother Mezz, Pop's Boy, the White Mayor of Harlem, the Man About Town, the Man That Hipped the World, the Man That Made History, the Man with the Righteous Bush, He Who Diggeth the Digger, Father Neptune . . .

"I don't mean to boast; that's what the cats really called me, at different times," Mezzrow proudly recalled. "I did become a kind of link between the races there. My education was completed on The Stroll, and I became a Negro."

3.

What Mezz found in the Harlem of the 1930s became the most important part of a cultural journey that had begun in Al Capone's Chicago in 1924, when Milton Mezzrow, the man destined to become the first white hipster and write an autobiography that would become a primer for the American counterculture—a book that, when it appeared in 1946, the young Allen Ginsberg studied in the Columbia University bookstore as if it were the Rosetta Stone—encountered marijuana for the first time in the bathroom of a roadhouse in Indiana Harbor.

The son of a middle-class Jewish family on Chicago's Northwest Side, Mezzrow was in trouble on the street from a relatively young age.

He spent his youth around poolrooms and shady street characters and was caught in a stolen car at the age of sixteen, which led to a stretch in the Illinois State Reformatory that changed his life when he encountered a black horn player named Yellow and fell in love with the blues while laying on the dirty corn-husk mattress in his cell. Upon his release, he heard the siren call of jazz, like so many of his time, when he heard the ringing trumpet of Louis Armstrong, and then he fell in love with the sound of Sidney Bechet's soprano saxophone. After purchasing his first horn, he joined the Local Tenth of the Chicago Federation of Musicians, plunging headlong into the scene that became Chicago jazz in the days when Armstrong, Jelly Roll Morton, Joe "King" Oliver, and Nick LaRocca walked the streets of the South Side. By 1920, he had his first band, and he came into contact with marijuana for the first time when the New Orleans clarinet player Leon Roppolo produced a cigarette rolled out of wheat straw paper one night at the Friars Inn and asked, "Ever smoke any muggles?"

Mezzrow was told it was something called "New Orleans golden leaf." He was apprehensive but he watched Roppolo get very high and happy. Then one night between sets out at the Martinique at Indiana Harbor, a "sawed-off runt of a jockey" named Patrick produced some muggles and instructed Mezz how to smoke them ("Say *tff, tff,* only breathe in when you say it"). Mezz did as he was told, and then went sauntering out to the bandstand to play.

> The first thing I noticed was that I began to hear my saxophone as though it were inside my head, but I couldn't hear much of the band in back of me, although I knew they were there. All the other instruments sounded like they were way off in the distance; I got the same sensation you'd get if you stuffed your ears with cotton and talked out loud. Then I began to feel the vibrations of the reed much more pronounced against my lip, and my head buzzed like a loudspeaker. I found I was slurring much better and putting just the right feeling into my phrases—I was really coming on. All the notes came easing out of my horn like they'd already been made up, greased and stuffed into a bell, so all I had to do was blow a little and send them on their way, one right after the other, never missing, never behind me, all without an ounce of effort. The phrases

seemed to have more continuity to them and I was sticking to the theme without ever going tangent. I felt like I could go on playing for years without running out of ideas or energy. . . . I began to feel very happy and sure of myself. With my loaded horn I could take all the fist-swinging, evil things in the world and bring them together in perfect harmony, spreading peace and joy and relaxation to all the keyed-up and punchy people everywhere. I began to preach my millenniums on my horn, leading all the sinners on to glory.

Mezzrow had entered a world that was "stripped of its dirty gray shrouds," that had become "one big bellyful of giggles, a spherical laugh, bathed in brilliant sparkling colors that hit you like a heat wave."

It was a world in which everything seemed funny and light-hearted, everything had meaning, and everything became a feast for the senses. "All your pores open like funnels, your nerve-ends stretch their mouths wide, hungry and thirsty for new sights and sounds and sensations; and every sensation, when it comes, is the most exciting thing you've ever had. You can't get enough of anything—you want to gobble up the whole goddamned universe just for an appetizer."

It was an experience that would not only change Mezzrow's life but also eventually come to resonate in the experience of millions. As Mezz so aptly put it, "Them first kicks are a killer, Jim."

6

Pops

1.

Almost from its beginning, jazz formed the nexus of perhaps the most vital and authentic exchange between the races in American culture—"one of the very few areas in American life where whites and Negroes, otherwise residentially segregated, have been able to form relatively casual friendships," as Nat Hentoff has described it.

Small wonder that jazz incited people against it during the twenties and thirties, since the music represented nothing less than the purest form of cultural miscegenation in America. Moreover, from its very beginnings, jazz and the people who played it and listened to it had seemed to express a sensibility that walked hand in hand with drug use. Marijuana appeared on the streets of New Orleans for the first time around 1910—right around the very same time that jazz began to coalesce—and from its earliest days, both jazz musicians and jazz lovers had been accused of moral turpitude and singled out as carriers of the drug plague. The onus of blame derived from the fact that the roots of the music at the turn of the century were irredeemably attached to those dark denizens of the American night—prostitutes, pimps, gamblers, gangsters, and grifters—populating the humid and languid city of New Orleans, that compellingly permissive Crescent City of sweet and naughty dreams, which had become a port of entry for illicit substances and a hotbed for their use. No city in the history of the republic had ever represented more of a nightmare to the watchdogs of public morality. West Indian and South American sailors brought their *coca* and *ganja* to the city; Mexicans streamed in with their *grefa* and *muta*; and people of all colors used the substances in places like the Storyville district against a rising soundtrack of blues and black and creole jazz music, which drifted through the city streets and reverberated along its misty canals from its street parades, saloon serenades, bawdy houses, barbeques, and picnics.

The cradle that spawned jazz included innumerable dance halls, cabarets, honky-tonks, saloons, barrelhouses, brothels, cribs, houses of assignation, and clip joints. There were roughneck joints like the Red Onion, the Keystone, and Spanola's, where a man could lose his life just by walking in, and fine "sportin'" houses like Countess Willie Piazza's and Lulu White's on Basin Street, which featured the finest cut glass and draperies, deep crimson rugs, sparkling mirrors, gleaming mahogany furniture, and what Louis Armstrong, the poor grandchild of a slave, would remember as "the most beautiful Creole prostitutes in the world." Armstrong, who delivered stone coal in Storyville during his impoverished boyhood in the Third Ward neighborhood around Perdido and Bolivar Streets called "the Battleground," would never forget these beautiful prostitutes "standing in their doorways nightly in their fine and beautiful negligees—faintly calling to the boys as they passed their cribs."

As Jelly Roll Morton remembered his New Orleans youth, music seemed to pour forth from every opened window:

> The streets were crowded with men. Police were always in sight, never less than two together, which guaranteed the safety of all concerned. Lights of all colors were glittering and glaring. Some very happy, some very sad, some with the desire to end it all by poison, some planning a big outing, a dance or some other kind of enjoyment. Some were real ladies in spite of their downfall and some were habitual drunkards and some were dope fiends as follows: opium, heroin, cocaine, laudanum, morphine, etc. I was personally sent to Chinatown many times with a sealed note and a small amount of money and would bring back several cards of hop. There was no slipping or dodging. All you had to do was walk in and be served.

Pate Lala's was the place where all the girls would come after work to meet their men and pimps, and where the musicians would gather after work. The great Joe Oliver would blow cornet there and Jelly Roll Morton and some of the best piano players of the South would play until dawn. Clarence Williams recalled that you could buy "all of the cocaine, morphine, heroin, and hop you wanted in the section, almost right out in the open. . . . But I never knew hardly any musicians who took dope. It was mostly the girls who were out to destroy themselves if their man left them or something like that. And in those days there were no teenagers or anything like that takin' dope."

Who knows when a piano player first blew some New Orleans golden leaf and put his fingers to the ivories of an upright and liked the roll of his left hand better, or a trumpet player picked up some and blew his horn and his mind at the same time? It might have been at one of the "cutting contests" on the streets, where musicians like Freddie Keppard would square off against all comers and it was a battle to the death, when a blast or a blow of something might have fortified some musician's chops and made him feel more loose and ready to reach for that perfect high C. Suffice to say that from the earliest days of jazz, the use of marijuana and other substances had slowly but surely ingrained itself into the lifestyle of the city's musicians.

When the US Navy decided it was of paramount importance to protect the innocence of its young servicemen from the twin vices of dope and prostitution in the district and closed down Storyville in 1917, it was only natural that all the Negro jazzmen of the dance halls would turn out to play "Nearer My God to Thee" as the weeping prostitutes were all forced to pile their belongings into carts and wheelbarrows and the green shutters of the red-light district of New Orleans were closed forever.

The closing of Storyville coincided with the Great Migration of African Americans in the South to the industrial centers of Chicago, Detroit, and New York, which was greatly accelerating right at the time the district was shut down, throwing a great many musicians out of work and sending them north, where their hot and bluesy intonations and improvisational styles and embellishments would revolutionize jazz and American popular music.

Marijuana made its way upriver right along with the roustabouts and the sound of Fate Marable's steam calliope on the colorful riverboats, like the *JS* and the *Bald Eagle* and the *Capitol,* as they tied up to ports from Natchez to Chicago, calling out to the people along the riverfronts with melodies of heart-stopping gaiety, beckoning them to the great party that would become the Roaring Twenties.

As jazz spread, so did a backlash that not only associated the music with drugs but also often made it a metaphor for the evils of the substances themselves. The popular song composer Harry Von Tilzer called jazz "the opiate that inflames the mind and incites to riotous orgies of delirious syncopation"—perhaps not a surprising statement at all from a man who wrote songs with titles like "Mammy's Kinky-Headed Coon."

"I can say from my own knowledge that about fifty percent of our young boys and girls from the age of sixteen to twenty-five that land in the insane asylum these days are jazz-crazy dope fiends and public dance hall patrons," declared the head of a state hospital in Napa, California, in 1921. "Jazz combinations—dope fiends and public dance halls are the same . . . where you find one, you will find the other."

In August of that same year, the twenty-one-year-old Louis Armstrong arrived in Chicago at the Royal Gardens, where he had been invited to play with King Oliver and his Creole Jazz Band. Armstrong showed up wearing a brown box-back coat, straw hat, and tan shoes, looking like a rube in an undertaker's coat and with his corny country boy's haircut. Everyone remembered him as a real bumpkin when he arrived, fumbling and insecure in just about everything but his music. In the simple words of Preston Jackson, Louis Armstrong played a horn "like nobody had ever heard."

2.

Nobody really knows exactly when Louis Armstrong first started smoking his muggles. The reason for this lack of precise information may have to do with the fact that Armstrong's lifelong manager, Joe Glaser, literally confiscated the part of his memoirs (published in 1954 as *Satchmo: My Years in New Orleans*) that dealt with his early years in

Chicago, in which Armstrong had been characteristically candid about his marijuana smoking. Armstrong was busted for marijuana in Los Angeles in 1930, and Glaser, who had always strongly disapproved of marijuana, no doubt wanted to protect Armstrong's public image and suppressed the material about his being a viper. However, it was also well known that Armstrong didn't give a damn what his manager thought about this particular aspect of his life—perhaps the only serious disagreement in a very fruitful and harmonious partnership between the two men. Suffice to say that sometime soon after his arrival in Chicago, the man who would become jazz's first and most influential soloist, singer, personality, folk hero, and one of the most beloved entertainers in the history of America started smoking marijuana. Call him what you will—Dippermouth, Old Gatemouth, Satchmo, Pops— but call him a pothead, because Louis Armstrong smoked it practically every day for the rest of his life.

"We did call ourselves vipers," Armstrong told John Chilton shortly before his death in 1971, "which could have been anybody from all walks of life that smoked and respected gage. That was our cute little name for marijuana, and it was a misdemeanor in those days. Much different from the pressures and changes the law lays on a guy who smokes pot. . . . We always looked on pot as a sort of medicine, a cheap drunk and with much better thoughts than one that's full of liquor. . . . The respect for gage will stay with me forever. I have every reason to say these words and am proud to say them."

Armstrong seemed disposed to look positively on the weed from his youth, as a kind of medicine, when his mother, Mayann, advised him to take a daily laxative and gave him a potion concocted out of "Pepper Grass, Dandelions, and lots of weeds similar to gage" that grew wild in New Orleans, which she boiled into a "physic." The other telling comment about the role his particular background played in how he may have viewed the prospect of trying it also involved his mother: "I was never born to be a Square about anything, no matter what. . . . My mother always told me to try anything at least once."

From the beginning of his days in Chicago, Louis Armstrong displayed a musicianship that was as remarkable for its pure feeling and expression as for its technical virtuosity and execution. It was a sound and tone that Armstrong himself would characterize as "gutbucket," so named after the contents of a chitterlings bucket filled with the entrails of a slaughtered hog. Armstrong is credited with coining, in addition to this word, many other phrases that became staples of the hip cultural vernacular, such as *you cats, mellow, solid, chops, jive, scat, Pops, Face,* and *Daddy.* He played a style of jazz as old as the blues itself, one that had evolved from his days as a teenager with the Colored Waif's Home Brass Band in New Orleans, through his time in the Tuxedo Brass Band and later in Fate Marable's band on the S.S. *Capitol* on the Mississippi River. However you analyzed it, the result was the same: Louis Armstrong played music that could make people stand on their chairs and shout.

Coming to Chicago was like going off to college for Armstrong, and when he found marijuana he was like a little kid with a sweet tooth suddenly loose in a candy store. He took to marijuana with an exuberant joy that must have seemed a sharp and enormously pleasurable contrast to the hard conditions of his New Orleans youth, timed as it also was to his ascent as an artist. It's not hard to picture him playing stoned with his colleagues in the Creole Jazz Band (Baby Dodds, Honoré Dutrey, Bill Johnson, Johnny Dodds, and Lil Hardin, soon to the be first of his four wives) at the storied Lincoln Gardens Café on Chicago's South Side. The Lincoln Gardens was a large ballroom with a balcony that had suspended over the center of the dance floor a big mirror ball, which threw swirling bright nuggets of light all over the dance floor and dancers as it turned and was hit by a couple of spotlights. It was an effect that would become popularized and forever associated with the party atmosphere of the twenties, from bathtub gin speakeasies to gala ballrooms, but to Louis Armstrong and the other vipers on the bandstand and in the audience at the Lincoln Gardens, this light show must have been a particularly astonishing sight.

The fact that Armstrong became such an avid user of marijuana is momentous for many reasons. For one thing, he was so unabashedly devoted to it. At least within the community of jazz musicians, his marijuana smoking would always be identified with his genial, generous, live-and-let-live nature, with the side of him that caused Duke Ellington to characterize him as a man who was "born poor, died rich, and never hurt anyone on the way."

Pops became the first in a line of powerful musical innovators and improvisers who are renowned for the use of a particular substance, and who also changed the face of the music after them. In Armstrong's case, his impact on the jazz community is hard to overestimate, which raises the perennial and thorny question of the relationship between the effect of the substance (or substances) and the artist's musical development and creativity. It's an intriguing question that arises over and over again in the evolution of the music, but it's one that can never be answered with any absolute certainty.

"Anytime you make generalizations about an artist of such extraordinary magnitude, you're bound to get into trouble, whether they're based on sociological assumptions or on what an artist might have used in his private or public life," remarked the author and critic Stanley Crouch, who spent many years researching and writing a magisterial biography of Charlie Parker. "There's always a lot of erroneous information about these things. But what I think is important is whether or not, for certain people, these drugs functioned as a kind of courage; how they might have turned a person who might have been timid into a different personality musically, who might play in a different way."

Others are nothing less than unequivocal about the central role that they think marijuana played in the evolution of jazz. "For the early jazz artists, marijuana was a revelation," writes Martin Lee in *Smoke Signals*, his history of marijuana. "While high on gage, they experimented with melodic phrases, slurs and offbeat syncopation that became the cutting-edge sound."

Armstrong played his horn with majesty, with a stunning emotional sweep and depth, inventing and rephrasing jazz and blues at will, playing his notes in audacious doubles and triples—repeated eights—in essence, turning them into "rhythm notes"—playing in stop time, double time, sustaining his notes for unheard-of amounts of time and with unprecedented vibrancy and power.

In 1928, he made a series of recordings for Okeh Records with Earl "Fatha" Hines on piano that are considered to be among his most innovative. "West End Blues" displays a blazing opening cadenza that by itself seems to signal the change in jazz from what had been primarily an ensemble form into a soloist's art form. As the trumpeter and bandleader Max Kaminsky described the impact of first hearing it, "I felt as if I had stared into the sun's eye. All I could think of doing was run away and hide until the blindness left me."

Armstrong also recorded a dramatic blues that year called "Muggles," a song named for the marijuana that he was by then no doubt smoking regularly, which contains another climactic solo, a series of soaring and growling blues notes that sound dredged from the deepest depths of his soul, notes that seem to tell not only the story of his life but also the whole story of his people—all of their passion and pain— within the course of four electrifying bars.

The degree to which marijuana may have influenced or in any way enabled these musical breakthroughs need not be the subject of debate here. The simple fact of the matter is that the marijuana that Pops smoked on a daily basis had to have had a significant impact on the way he experienced and played music. Its possible effects were many, from limiting inhibition and increasing his ability to improvise and experiment to stretching time and changing metrical structure. Pops had an uncanny ability to visualize, to bring his musical ideas to life—"You see, he tried to make a picture out of every number he was playing to show just what it meant," was how Mutt Carey once explained it. As the poet Charles Baudelaire once accurately characterized the effect of hashish as "a mirror which magnifies, yet no more than a mirror," it's certainly not unreasonable to assume that the marijuana was enhancing an already prodigious talent.

The other effect of the substance was external. The impact of Pops's artistry and personality was felt everywhere in the world musical community. For perhaps for the first time, the association was made—however accurately or erroneously—between an artist being high and his "chops"—indeed, his very musical personality. As Stanley Crouch related, "Budd Johnson once told me that back there in the twenties, a lot of musicians never even got high, they just drank some whiskey here and there, but when they found out that Louis Armstrong smoked reefers, they began to think, 'Oh, maybe *that's* the key to him being able to play all that stuff.'"

Pops liked to blow reefer as much as his beautiful gleaming Selmer trumpet, rolling giant panatela-sized muggles on his tour bus, sitting in the front seat and blasting so much that the other musicians would get a contact high in the back of the bus. In St. Louis a group of vipers presented him with a joint the size of a baseball bat and a card that dubbed him "the King of the Vipers." He was practically always high onstage. "You could really tell when Pops was high," the trumpeter and arranger Zilner Randolph remarked with a kind of awe. "Man, he would blow! When he'd come back off intermission, Pops would be, like, 'I'm ready! I'm ready! So help me, I'm ready!' When he said that, the folks just rolled, and the band laughed too. And he was really ready!"

Two of its main attractions for Armstrong and other musicians was how well they could function under the effects of marijuana, given the rigors of their schedules, and the fact that there was no hangover, as there is with alcohol. For one thing, the New Orleans golden leaf that Armstrong smoked was relatively mild compared to the dense, resinous, powerfully psychoactive bud that is consumed today. Moreover, Armstrong always maintained a disdain for hard drugs and excessive alcohol. He had already observed the destructive effects of the lush life on another great New Orleans horn player, King Buddy Bolden, who is often credited with becoming the first recognizable jazz star and who ended his days in an insane asylum in Jackson, Mississippi—one of the first casualties of life in the fast lane.

"Buddy got to drinking too much," Armstrong remembered, "staying up two or three nights a week without sleep and going right on to work like so many hot musicians. They get low in their minds and then drink some more." As a result, from the beginning Armstrong set strong boundaries between smoking his gage and doing other things—and he never crossed them into immoderate drinking or any kind of hard drug use whatsoever.

"Now, when it comes to summing it up, the difference between the vipers and those using dope and all other kinds of drastic stuff, one could easily see who were actually dope addicts," Pops observed. "First place—they were never clean, and they stays dirty-grimey all the time. Show most addicts a bucket of water and they'll run like hell to keep it from touching them. But a viper would gladly welcome a good bath, clean underwear and top clothes—stay fresh and on the ball."

On November 14, 1930, Louis Armstrong became the first celebrity marijuana bust in American history. The incident occurred when Pops was playing Frank Sebastian's Cotton Club in Culver City. He was enjoying his first trip to California as well as a muggle outside the club, as was his habit during intermission, with Vic Berton. Berton was white, a well-known drummer who performed with symphony orchestras. By that time the first wave of his records for Okeh had become a sensation, and the place was "packed and jammed with all sorts of my fans including movie stars," as Pops recalled it. "Anyway, Vic and I were blasting this joint—having lots of laughs and feeling good, enjoying each other's company. We were standing in front of some cars. Just then, two big healthy Dicks came from behind a car and nonchalantly said, 'We'll take that roach boys.'"

Armstrong was told that a rival bandleader who was jealous of the good business he was doing in town had "dropped a dime" on him by making a phone call to the narcotics police. He spent nine days in the Los Angeles city jail, an experience that instilled in him a lifelong sense of compassion and solidarity with the people he would call "the poor cats in jail" for marijuana.

Armstrong's manager from Chicago at the time, Tommy Rockwell, sent an underworld character named Johnny Collins out to California to fix the case. Palms were greased; deals were struck; whatever need the powers that be had to make an example of Louis Armstrong was apparently satisfied by his public apology and renunciation of his beloved muggles.

"His protestations were considered hilarious in jazz circles," noted critic and Armstrong biographer Gary Giddins in his book *Satchmo*. "I interviewed more than a dozen musicians who said that Armstrong introduced them to it. Most of them shook their heads with laughter at how much he loved rolling cigar-sized joints after leaving the bandstand. It wasn't just a recreational substance to him but a nostrum on the order of his favorite physic, Swiss Kriss. He swore by it and proselytized for it—even wrote a letter to Eisenhower asking him to make it legal."

Whatever fear Pops may have had about the bust having a negative impact on his career quickly vanished; in fact, quite the opposite happened and he returned to Chicago more popular than ever. On his first tour after his marijuana bust, he supplied coal for the entire neighborhood when he appeared at the Royal Theater and realized his fans were freezing and too poor to afford it during that cold and bleak Depression winter. If Harry Anslinger was looking for stories of how the use of marijuana lowered the morals of those who smoked it, he could not have found a more obstinately disobliging example than Louis Armstrong, a man who would walk happily through life with a muggle in his hand and have no compunction about honestly acknowledging it. "As we always used to say, gage is more of a medicine than a dope. . . . But if we all get as old as Methuselah, our memories will always be of lots of beauty and warmth from gage. Well, that was my life and I don't feel ashamed at all. Mary Warner, honey, you sure was good and I enjoyed you 'heep much.'"

But at the same time, Pops recognized how Harry Anslinger and his Marihuana Tax Act had changed the game by outlawing his revered New Orleans golden leaf in 1937. "But the price got a little too high to pay (law-wise). At first you was a misdemeanor. But as the years rolled on, you lost your misdo and got meanor and meanor (jailhousely speaking). Sooo, bye-bye-Dearest, I'll have to put you down."

Of course, Louis Armstrong would never really put marijuana down, but for the rest of his life it would always puzzle and pain him to see it connected to narcotics in any way.

7

The Misdo Gets Meanor and Meanor
(Jailhousely Speaking)

1.

Harry Anslinger may have been a master at inflaming public fears, pitching scripts for low-budget exploitation movies that demonized cannabis, such as *Marihuana* in 1935 ("Weird orgies! Wild parties! Unleashed passions!") and the classic *Tell Your Children* in 1936, later titled *Reefer Madness*. But in preparing for the congressional hearings on the Marihuana Tax Act, he knew that in addition to depicting marijuana as the devil's weed, the government would have to be prepared to rebut any suggested use of cannabis, whether medical or commercial, or to allow it through some exemption should such use be deemed valid.

Although marijuana as a medicine had mostly been supplanted by drugs such as aspirin and barbiturates, there were still twenty-eight pharmaceutical products containing cannabis extracts on the market in 1937, and there was absolutely no conclusive scientific or medical evidence indicating that the substance did not have legitimate use for any of the ailments for which it was being prescribed. Anslinger also knew that any legislation would have to satisfy companies like the Sherwin-Williams Paint Company, which used hempseed oil for drying purposes, and distributors of canary birdseed, who were actually complaining that canaries would not sing as well or might stop singing altogether if marijuana seeds were eliminated from their diet, and

Anslinger knew that Congress would have to recognize the legitimacy of their argument and amend any bill to include sterilized marijuana seed.

The congressional and Senate hearings have been much described and reviewed and are notable for several highlights because they contained the origins of furious controversies that persist to the present day.

As chief witness, Anslinger set the tone and trotted out the horror stories: "Marijuana is the most violence-causing drug in the history of mankind," he proclaimed, reading aloud into the congressional record half a dozen of the Narcotics Bureau–generated articles that he had collected into his file, claiming that 50 percent of all violent crimes in the United States were committed by Mexican Americans, Latin Americans, Filipinos, Greeks, and Negroes and could be directly traced to marijuana, without any statistical evidence whatsoever. (FBI statistics for that year actually showed that 65 to 75 percent of all murders in the US were in fact—as they are today—alcohol-related.) The district attorney from New Orleans then testified about the city's great crime wave, which had hardly existed in the first place, and how criminals used marijuana in that city, graphically corroborating Anslinger's testimony.

Other witnesses stressed that marijuana "addicts" went crazy. Dr. James C. Munch, a ten-year veteran of the Food and Drug Administration who had a background in pharmacology and toxicology, testified that "continuous use will tend to cause the degeneration of one part of the brain, that part that is useful for higher or psychic reasoning, or the memory."

Even though Munch was making claims about human behavior on the basis of experiments with dogs, his assertion about the deleterious effects of marijuana on the brain became the basis of the "memory loss" theory that would frame future marijuana studies.

In a particularly telling exchange, Anslinger was asked by Representative John Dingell of Michigan, "I was just wondering whether the marihuana addict graduates into a heroin, an opium, or a cocaine user."

"No, sir," Anslinger replied, "I have not heard of a case of that kind. The marihuana addict does not go in that direction." Fifteen years down the road, Anslinger would reverse his opinion on this matter. By the 1950s, marijuana as a "gateway" or "stepping-stone" to harder drugs would become the cornerstone of the Bureau's marijuana policy and would frame the mindset of institutional policy for the next fifty years.

Then came testimony from the various companies that used parts of marijuana for industrial purposes, which generally supported the bill but wanted exceptions for legitimate uses, such as pigeon feed.

"Does the seed have the same effect on pigeons as the drug has on individuals?" Chairman Robert L. Doughton asked William G. Scarlett of the birdseed industry.

"I have never noticed it," Scarlett responded. "It has a tendency to bring back the feathers and improve the birds. We are not interested in spreading marijuana or anything like that. We do not want to be drug peddlers."

After Scarlett explained the process of how the marijuana seeds would be sterilized, the committee, apparently satisfied that the pigeons would not be turned into some species of avian drug addicts, agreed that the birdseed industry would indeed be allowed to use the cannabis plant in its product.

The only witness hostile to the views of the Bureau to appear before the committee was Dr. William C. Woodward of the American Medical Association, who appeared on the final day of the hearings and was assailed with hostile questions. Woodward was a specialist in legal medicine as well as a lawyer and a doctor, and his very presence at the hearing was a source of ire in the wake of the AMA's recently successful opposition to FDR's plan to include health insurance as part of the Social Security Act. (It should be noted that New Deal "liberals" on the committee were every bit as eager to pass the Marihuana Tax Act and protect the public by banning marijuana as conservatives.) There was no need to burden the medical profession with such a bill, Woodward argued. The states could readily handle any marijuana problems without the federal government. These were views consistent with the AMA's opposition to the intrusion of big government into medical affairs. At the time there was no love lost between the Narcotics Bureau and the American Medical Association. In the wake of the 1914 Harrison Narcotics Tax Act and under Anslinger's hard-nosed directives, twenty thousand doctors in America had been successfully prosecuted for prescribing narcotics to addicts in what many doctors had always felt should have been a medical affair.

What rankled Anslinger and the committee the most were the doctor's pointed assertions that the evidence against marijuana was woefully incomplete. If it was indeed true that the drug had such degenerative effects on the brain as claimed, and if it represented a national scourge for the schoolchildren of America, then where were the experts from the Public Health Service and the Children's Bureau with conclusive proof?

Woodward suggested in no uncertain terms that any increase in marijuana use was probably the result of "newspaper exploitation of the habit." He pointed out that marijuana was a recognized medicine in good standing, distributed by leading pharmaceutical firms, on sale at many pharmacies. Even worse to Anslinger, Woodward offered a view that addicts were sick people who needed treatment rather than fiendish criminals, and that the solution to any conceivable drug problem in the United States was to be found in the real education of its citizens, implying that such education was a very different matter than media hysteria and propaganda. His testimony alone pointed toward future debates about medical marijuana, the nature of addiction, drug education, and the fundamental question of treatment versus punishment as the most effective policy for dealing with the drug problem in the United States.

In the end, of course, none of Woodward's testimony mattered. He was accused of attempting to misrepresent the AMA's position and obstruct the protection of the public from the marijuana menace, and was dismissed without even being granted the professional courtesy of a thank-you. It is a striking example of how very easy it was to portray individuals with views about drugs that challenged official policy and laws—no matter how reasoned—as weak and misguided on the issue and as promoting policies that would send civilization down the slippery slope of increased drug use, endangering the health and well-being of the public.

A week after the hearings, Chairman Doughton reported the bill to the full House. A month later it was presented for debate on the House floor, where the House members displayed almost complete ignorance of the subject.

"What is this bill about?" Congressman Bertrand Snell asked Sam Rayburn, the House majority leader.

"It has something to do with marijuana," explained Rayburn. "I think it is a narcotic of some kind."

After brief Senate hearings that required just one session to examine six witnesses—Anslinger was again the chief witness and asserted with complete conviction that marijuana produced homicidal tendencies in the user—the bill was reported favorably out of committee and sent back to the House, where it was considered again. Passed by voice vote without a recorded tally at the end of a Friday afternoon session when many members were absent, the law was signed into law by President Roosevelt on August 2, 1937, with no fanfare whatsoever, and took effect sixty days later, on the first of October.

2.

Only four years after the repeal of alcohol prohibition, Harry Anslinger had the second great American prohibition firmly in place. At a time when the federal government was passing the groundbreaking legislation of the New Deal, the Marihuana Tax Act represented the American legislative process at its shoddiest, a shameful display of how the most egregious kind of demagoguery, yellow journalism, and racism could be used to shape and implement our drug laws.

"This nation's drug laws were born in imperialism, nurtured in racism, and sealed in deliberate deceit," asserted the drug historian and marijuana rights activist Michael Aldridge, the first person in American history ever to receive a doctorate in "Marijuana Studies." "Anti-marijuana laws in America rose in the twentieth century as a direct part of racist imperialism, the prejudice that says white Westerners are the only good people on earth."

Aldrich's observation typifies the critique of the drug laws mounted by the counterculture during the 1960s, when millions of white, middle-class, left-wing college students were coming to smoke pot, but his statements are nonetheless rooted in historical fact. The taking of drugs had always been equated with the menace of race, going back to the period between 1898 and 1914, when fears of uniquely murderous "Negro cocaine fiends" with superhuman strength throughout the South were commonly cited by prominent newspapers, doctors, and politicians, becoming part of the testimony at the congressional hearings that produced the Harrison Narcotics Tax Act. Not only were they sexual predators ("most of the attacks upon white women of the South are the direct result of the cocaine-crazed Negro brain," testified one "expert") but the drug also produced a "resistance to the knock down effects of fatal wounds. Bullets fired into vital parts that would drop a sane man in his tracks, fail to check the 'fiend.'" These "cocaine niggers" were the reason that police throughout the South began carrying more powerful handguns.

Harry Anslinger had succeeded in his primary goal: creating a menace that made the Federal Bureau of Narcotics seem invaluable in countering it. Not only had he established the Bureau as a mainstay of the federal government, he had also ensured that it would have an adequately escalating budget for its continual growth. And finally, by successfully exploiting racial apprehensions to secure passage of the Marihuana Tax Act (exactly as the authors of Harrison Narcotics Tax Act had made use of alarm about "cocaine niggers"), he had established fear and racism as essential ingredients in the template of American drug legislation, policy, and enforcement.

The first arrest of the new era of marijuana prohibition occurred only a day after the law went into effect, when a fifty-five-year-old peddler and farmhand named Samuel R. Caldwell was caught selling a couple of joints to eighteen-year-old Moses Baca in Colorado before police found three pounds of cannabis in his apartment. Unlike the penalties for alcohol during Prohibition, possession of even the most minute quantity of marijuana was now punishable by five years' imprisonment and a $2,000 fine.

Anslinger was seated in the Denver courtroom and must have felt that he had done his work very well indeed when US district judge J. Foster Symes, declaring that "under its influence men become beasts . . . Marijuana destroys life. I have no sympathy for those who sell this weed," fined Caldwell $1,000 and sentenced him to four years of hard labor at the federal penitentiary in Leavenworth, Kansas.

Anslinger had urged judges to "jail offenders, then throw away the key." Caldwell had been arrested by narcotics agents on a Wednesday night, indicted by a grand jury on Thursday, and sentenced on Friday—processed through the judicial system in a mere forty-eight hours. "Marijuana has become our greatest problem," Anslinger told the *Denver Post* after the verdict. "It is on the increase. But we will enforce the law to the very letter."

It was the first marijuana arrest of twenty-three million that followed.

With the new law in place, the Bureau began planning a concerted attack on the jazz community, waging a vigorous public relations campaign that linked swing music directly to the marijuana menace.

Since the early 1930s, Anslinger had directed the Narcotics Bureau to keep a file on jazz musicians that would come to be known as the "Marijuana and Musicians" file. As a young man Anslinger had played piano and had dreamed of being a classical concert pianist. He seems to have been as fascinated by jazz musicians as he was revolted by them, and his obsession with them only grew over the years. From the beginning of his tenure, he directly equated the music itself with the effects of the weed and was especially outraged by the songs, like "Reefer Man," that were written directly about the substance: "Music hath charms, but not this music. It hails the drug. The well-informed would just as soon hear a song about sitting in the pleasant shade of the hood of a cobra." Anslinger considered it his personal mission to go after musicians, dreaming of a large-scale national roundup of "teahound" jazz musicians that would result in stiff prison sentences and a windfall of publicity. In addition to Louis Armstrong, the file came to include the likes of Les Brown, Thelonious Monk, Count Basie, Duke Ellington, Dizzy Gillespie, Jimmy Dorsey, Lionel Hampton, Billie Holiday, and many others.

Employing a policy that foreshadowed the dirty tricks and smear tactics of the FBI in later years, the FBN established a fund for paid informants to infiltrate the jazz world and help set up musicians for arrest. In the long run, however, with the exception of a few notable celebrity busts like Gene Krupa's in 1943, the strategy would fail as the tight-knit world of jazz bands closed ranks and turned out to be very difficult for narcotics agents and their informers to penetrate.

With the outbreak of the Second World War, the US government faced a scarcity of industrial fibers and was forced to promote the growing of *Cannabis indica*—the nonpsychoactive industrial strain of the plant. In 1942, a government film called *Hemp for Victory* was produced about how to cultivate the plant and was shown widely to farmers, telling them it was their patriotic duty to grow the stuff. An estimated three hundred thousand acres were planted. (The program would be dropped as soon as the war ended, and the government would later disavow the very existence of the film.) But as cannabis was helping the US war effort by providing everything from rope to lubricants to parachutes, Harry Anslinger was turning up the heat on jazz musicians. Plants, setups, shakedowns, smear tactics, attempts to have cabaret licenses revoked and passports canceled, would all result in an atmosphere of paranoia among the vipers that in 1945 would lead Cee Pee Johnson to write a song about Anslinger and his narcs called "The G Man Got the T Man," in which the fun in a jumpin' joint crashes to a halt when a knock comes on the door and in steps a man "with a shiny badge" and a "brand new forty-four."

No single piece of legislation more effectively guaranteed the growth of an underground alternative culture in this country than the Marihuana Tax Act of 1937, and no single piece of legislation more decisively declared war on that culture. It was a war declared by middle America and waged by its puritan bureaucrats, patriotic societies, and conservative religious and law enforcement organizations, aimed initially at Mexican and African American laborers, and jazz musicians and their followers, but also bringing under fire a growing population of cultural outlaws, rebels, outsiders, eccentrics, bohemians, individualists, romantics, artists, writers, dreamers, adventurers, sexual experimenters, self-explorers, hedonists, spiritual seekers, thrill merchants, and black marketeers. It was a war against a part of America that would find itself commingling and percolating in an ever-growing underground, dwelling in what the writer John Rechy would call that "one vast City of Night stretching from Times Square to Hollywood Boulevard."

8

The Great Tenor Solo
in the Shoeshine Jukebox

1.

When Billie Holiday finally made her way to the stage of Café Society at the age of twenty-four, it was abundantly clear that she had traveled the length of an entire world to get there from Harlem, and it was just as clear that even though she was now performing for a crowd of well-heeled New Dealers and society people, there were certain things about her that would never change.

Holiday had arrived in the chic demimonde of the small downtown nightclub on Sheridan Square and was no longer in the familiar atmosphere of Clark Monroe's Uptown House in Harlem, but she wasn't about to stop smoking reefer. She liked to smoke between shows in a taxicab riding through Central Park, alone with a stick of tea burning in her hand, dressed in a beautiful white off-the-shoulder gown with a single string of pearls around her neck, wearing a white gardenia in her smartly lacquered hair above her left ear. She would always return from these forays soaringly high and liked to have a glass of sweet wine to relieve the parched dryness in her throat before taking the stage again. Each night she was performing three sets of six songs, and her audiences at Café Society were usually raptly attentive, but for some reason not on this particular night in the winter of 1939. The crowd seemed stiff, a bunch of squares, and some of them were even talking loudly. Billie stopped after the first song, her eyes flashing with anger.

She stood for a moment in silence, alone in the pink light against the darkness. She then whirled around, her back to the audience, bent way over, and flipped her gown up over her derriere.

What the audience saw for a brief and shocking instant was that Billie Holiday wore no underwear underneath her gown—in short, what the audience saw was everything—before she strutted boldly past the tables, back to her dressing room. Members of the audience gasped at the display, but the underlying message of the gesture was clear enough. If those fancy white folks weren't hip enough to appreciate what she was singing, they could just kiss her big beautiful black ass.

Club owner Barney Josephson, the Jewish ex–shoe manufacturer from New Jersey who had opened the place, was stunned. Billie Holiday was the singer he'd hired to perform at the club when it opened in December of 1938. Josephson was attempting to attract a progressive audience to the club. It was Clare Boothe Luce who would call it "the right place for the wrong people," meaning that it was the antithesis of the Stork Club with its right-wing politics, snootiness, and racial discrimination. Café Society was decorated with murals done by left-wing WPA types. The doormen wore rags and ragged white gloves and stood by as people opened the doors for themselves; the bartenders were veterans of the Abraham Lincoln Brigade from the Spanish Civil War. Blacks and whites fraternized freely onstage and off—that was the whole *raison d'être* of the club. On any given night the audience might include Dorothy Parker, Charlie Chaplin, Errol Flynn, even Eleanor Roosevelt. But as much as Josephson wanted Café Society to become known as "a nightclub to take the stuffing out of stuffed shirts," this was something else. Josephson signaled Teddy Wilson at the piano to begin a dance song as soon as Billie left the stage, and hurried back to her dressing room.

"Billie, why did you do that? Please, don't *ever* do anything like that again."

"Fuck 'em," said Billie. It was as simple as that.

As Josephson would later say about the incident, "That was one time a black person said, 'Kiss my ass' to a white audience and showed it."

Billie Holiday was and would always be defiant. What Josephson and the audience of Café Society did not understand was that she had once worked in an establishment where she was expected not only to lift up her dress but to pick up her tips off the tabletops with the labia of her vagina. She had refused to do so at the time, and if she hadn't played by the rules then, when she was starving and desperate, it wasn't likely that she would play by the rules now. She was a natural-born rule breaker—the first African American performer to integrate an all-white orchestra when she joined Artie Shaw. Billie had come to Café Society only after quitting Shaw's band when they were playing the Blue Room of the Hotel Lincoln in New York, outraged that owner Maria de Ramirez Kramer had demanded that she use the freight elevator so that hotel customers would not think that colored people were welcome there as guests. Right before that, Billie and the Shaw orchestra had gone so far as to tour the Deep South— a recklessly daring undertaking that had involved hair-raising late-night escapes from southern police across state lines. It was this very attitude that would draw her toward Abel Meeropol's searing anti-lynching ballad "Strange Fruit" when it was brought to her the following year by Robert Gordon, the floor show director at Café Society.

According to the Tuskegee Institute, between 1889 and 1940, 3,833 African Americans were lynched in America—and this was a conservative estimate—90 percent of them murdered in the South for "uppitiness," which might include anything from an imagined glance at a white woman to the use of any language deemed offensive. In 1937, Congress rejected an antilynching law that even President Roosevelt did not support after a bitter debate and filibuster by southern Democrats in the Senate. To perform and record this song was an act of brazen courage and defiance of the highest magnitude, and it would become the signature closing song of Billie Holiday's sets. The room would go completely dark when she performed it. All service in the club would stop. Billie would sing the song, eyes closed, with her face starkly delineated in a pin spotlight.

Southern trees bear a strange fruit,
Blood on the leaves and blood on the root

Some in the audience simply did not understand the song; others were discomfited and angered and got up to leave; but as the heartbreaking lyrics sank in, depicting a black body "swinging in the southern breeze," the audience would grow ever more still, until they were completely immobilized, stunned by the simple understated elegance and emotional honesty with which Billie Holiday could render such a raw subject, and by the time she left the stage she had succeeded in turning Café Society into a cathedral of tears and mourning. Sometimes after finishing the song she would have to head straight for the bathroom—"When I sing it, it affects me so much I get sick. It takes all the strength out of me." Josephson recalled a hysterical woman following Billie into the powder room after one performance of the song.

> "*Don't you sing that song again!—Don't you dare!*" she screamed—and ripped Billie's dress. I asked her to leave. She started to cry again. She explained she came to Café Society to have fun and here she heard Billie sing about "burning flesh" and it brought back a lynching she had seen when she was seven or eight years old down South. She saw a black man tied by the throat to a back fender of a car, dragged through the streets, hung up and burned. She thought she forgot it and Billie brought it back.

Leonard Feather would call the song "the first significant protest in words and music, the first unmuted cry against racism," and Ahmet Ertegun would later insist that it marked the true beginning of the civil rights movement in America, but Billie Holiday would pay a price for it. As David Margolick aptly notes in his book *Strange Fruit*, "Surely a song that forced a nation to confront its darkest impulses, a song that maligned an entire portion of the country, did not win her any friends in high places who might have cut her some slack as she degenerated into substance abuse and assorted scrapes with the law." As Billie herself later told *DownBeat*, "I've made a lot of enemies. That song hasn't helped any."

In fact, it was this song that first brought Billie Holiday to the attention of the FBI, Harry Anslinger, and the Federal Bureau of Narcotics.

2.

Lady Day had always found her philosophy of life in the streets. According to her famous autobiography, *Lady Sings the Blues*, it hadn't taken long after arriving in New York before she encountered reefer on the streets of Harlem. Her mother, Sadie, learned that she smoked it one day when they were crossing Seventh Avenue on their way to see Louis Armstrong at the Lafayette Theatre. Billie was fourteen years old at the time. A guy called them over and told her, "Jim's got the best panatela you ever smoked in your life." With her mother there at her side, Billie tried to shut the fellow up, but he persisted: "Who's she? Your sister? Bring her along too. They'll be blue lights and red lights and we'll pitch a ball!"

> Mom knew about reefers but she didn't know I'd been smoking them for a year. She flipped. "You get out of here," she told our friend. "If you don't, I'm gonna put her away until she's twenty-one, and you in jail." We never got to see a movie, or Louis Armstrong, or nothing that day. When we got home I told her I'd been smoking reefers for a year. . . . I tried to tell her they hadn't done me any harm. It was just the shock she got from finding it out this way that made her angry. But she had been taken in by the stuff she'd read and heard about what marijuana does to you. She'd believe that before she'd believe her own eyes. She thought I was headed for trouble and that it was my own fault because I was weak.

Billie Holiday's entire life is shrouded in myth, but perhaps no part more so than her early years. Biographers disagree about even the most basic facts, and Billie herself recrafted her life story as she saw fit in interviews and later in her autobiography, ghostwritten by William Dufty—a book that over time would come to be regarded as both an American classic and one of the most confounding and controversial autobiographies of a major twentieth-century musical figure ever published. But the book is so interesting for so many reasons that one is hard-pressed not to quote from it even as one questions its veracity, particularly on the role of drugs in her life—a subject in which the myths actually *become* the story. Assuming the above story is true, what Billie didn't tell her mother was that she had been smoking reefer for several years, probably from the age of ten or eleven. Reefer was just a natural part of where she came from. It all came into her life at the same time: reefer, jazz, the fast life, balling, satin slips and panties, glamorous and dangerous hustling men who wore double-breasted

pin-striped suits with monkey backs, and handsome musicians who re-
minded her of her father and grandfather.

The discrepancies begin with the very date of her birth. It was long
assumed that Billie Holiday was born Eleanora Fagan (her mother's
last name) on April 7, 1915, in Baltimore, until biographer Stuart
Nicholson established that she was born three years earlier in Philadelphia. Eleanora was the child of unmarried teenagers, the great-
granddaughter of the slave mistress of an Irish plantation owner.

Clarence Holiday was a guitar and banjo player of some stature who
played with Fletcher Henderson. "She was just something I stole at
fifteen," he once reportedly said of his daughter, never acknowledging
her until she was famous. It was later, after moving to New York, that
Eleanora would rename herself by combining the names of her father
and the silent-screen star Billie Dove.

Billie's mother, Sarah Julia Harris, nicknamed Sadie, moved to New
York soon after Billie's birth, leaving her with relatives. Sadie later returned to Baltimore, to an unsuccessful marriage and a series of affairs. Billie was living with her mother in 1925 when she was brought
before the juvenile court for playing hooky and "being without proper
care and guardianship," after which she spent a year at the House of
Good Shepherd for Colored Girls.

According to Nicholson, on the morning of December 24, 1926,
Sadie discovered her daughter being raped by a neighbor named Wilbur Rich. Billie later called him Mr. Dick in her autobiography, which
stated that she was once again remanded to the House of Good Shepherd for Colored Girls after the rape trial because the judge felt that
she might have somehow "provoked" the man, where she suffered the
indescribably horrible trauma of being locked overnight in a closet
with a dead girl as a form of punishment—"I screamed and banged on
the door so, I kept the whole joint from sleeping. I hammered on the
door until my hands were bloody."

Another biographer, Donald Clarke, claims that none of this ever
happened. "The documentary evidence is that she went to Good Shepherd when she was nine, for playing hooky. She wrote that while she
was there she was locked up with a dead girl, but nobody remembers
that either. Billie's stories were a poetry of their own, a paradigm of a
hard, fast life."

Whether truth or legend, the rape is cited as fact in most of the reputable Holiday biographies and histories of jazz. Given what we now know about the central role that sexual abuse and trauma can play in the psychosexual makeup of an addict or alcoholic, it must certainly be considered a watershed episode in her story if it is true. Billie herself once told Nat Hentoff that her childhood left her feeling "like a damn cripple," but we'll never know for sure what really happened.

What we do know with absolute certainty is that Billie grew up very fast. Her education never progressed beyond the fifth grade. Her youth in the Fell's Point district consisted mostly of a scrub brush and running errands for Alice Dean, the madam of the whorehouse in her North Baltimore neighborhood, which she did in return for being able to listen to her first jazz and blues records: Louis Armstrong's "Irish Black Bottom" and Bessie Smith's "Stormy Weather."

Billie learned a lot of things at Alice Dean's, like how to clip the white men of their money when they came up from the waterfront to Pratt and Dallas to get laid. According to a pimp named Skinny "Rim" Davenport, she started smoking reefers at a place called Ethel Moore, where there was a bar upstairs with a gramophone, where the women could turn a trick and smoke and drink and play records. "Eleanora sings if we ask . . . until six in the morning," Davenport remembered. Then there was Miss Ella's and Pop Major's, where Eleanora "sung and boozed and smoked them real skinny reefers that seamen used to roll for the foreigners. . . . Sell 'em three for a quarter," recalled a girl-friend, Mary "Pony" Kane. "Eleanora used to love them . . . and bootleg whiskey, corn liquor, white lightning . . . and she coming down the street cursing and hollering, 'You *motherfucker, cocksucker,* kiss my ass.'"

Eleanora was the sort of girl who liked to carry on in the streets, and men and boys were always buzzing around her. There was already a pattern with men that would shape her destiny. As Pony Kane put it, "The fellas that was crazy for her, she didn't have no time for, and the ones that have somebody else was the ones she wanted. She wanted who she wanted."

In 1928, Billie left Baltimore in a white voile dress and a shiny red belt and moved to New York. "When I was thirteen I got real evil one time and set in my ways. I just plain decided one day that I wasn't going to do anything or say anything unless I meant it. Not 'Please, sir.' Not

'Thank you, ma'am.' Nothing. Unless I meant it." One of the other "things she decided was that no matter what, she was never going to be somebody's damn maid."

Billie lived with her mother in a brothel on 141st Street run by Florence Williams, the biggest madam in Harlem. She was turning tricks there herself when police raided the establishment and arrested her, along with her mother. Billie was sent to Welfare Island, first to the hospital and then to the workhouse. By the spring of 1930 she was living in a tiny room in Harlem with her mother, waitressing at a club called Mexico's, singing at tables "like a gypsy fiddler in a Budapest café," as composer and bassist Spike Hughes recalled. She and her mother were starving by the time she auditioned as a shake dancer at Pod's and Jerry's on 133rd Street. She was a terrible dancer but desperate for a job; she asked if she could sing and performed a version of "Trav'lin' All Alone" that left the audience "crying in their beer," as Billie described it. She was hired as a singer.

Prohibition was on its last legs, and for a brief period Billie sang in Harlem after-hours joints like Basement Brownies, the Shim Sham, and the Log Cabin. One night when she was singing at Monette Moore's club, in walked John Hammond with his crew cut and bow tie—the producer who would become one of the most important figures in the development of American music. The blue-blooded descendant of Civil War general John Henry Hammond and a long line of Vanderbilts, Hammond devoted his life to bringing African American music and musicians before the public. As much as he loved the music, recording seminal blues artists like Bessie Smith, he was also a board member of the NAACP and was deeply committed to the idea that music was the one thing that could bridge the great racial divide in America.

What Hammond saw was a beautiful young woman with smooth mocha skin, a sensuous mouth with rose-petal lips, lazy bedroom eyes, and the figure of a ripe voluptuary. Despite the battering that life had already dealt her, she was full of stubborn pride, sass, and independent spirit. What Hammond heard was a singer with a unique sensibility. Somewhere back there in those red-light rooms of Fell's Point, on a young girl's reefer ride deep inside the music coming from a scratchy record on a gramophone, Billie Holiday had grasped something wondrous about music and her voice. She had come to understand in the deepest musical sense that however she decided to sing it—slurring, singing off the beat, groaning low from the back of her throat—she could sound like a horn—no, she could actually *be* a horn—and she had been doing it ever since. This was no scat singer but rather a vocalist who instinctively understood how to use her voice instrumentally. Hammond couldn't believe his ears: "She was the first girl singer I'd come across who actually sang like an improvising jazz genius—an extension, almost, of Louis Armstrong."

Hammond began raving about her in his influential column in *Melody Maker*, dragging lots of musicians and music-business people around to hear her—Benny Goodman, vibraphonist Red Norvo, songwriter/A&R man Bernie Hanighen, pianist Teddy Wilson, agent Joe Glaser—and began arranging for her first recording sessions. Her first two sides, "Your Mother's Son-in-Law" and "Riffin' the Scotch" were backed by Benny Goodman's studio band. The songs displayed a distinctive and original sense of phrasing and timing but went nowhere. Billie Holiday was still unformed, unknown, uncertain, searching for an artistic home of her own. As Hammond arranged for her first session with members of the Count Basie band, the pressure was mounting on her to sing in a more commercial style.

On February 25, 1937, when Billie found herself in the American Record Corporation studio at 1776 Broadway, the only experienced studio musicians she knew there were clarinetist Benny Goodman, who'd had an affair with her in 1933, and pianist Teddy Wilson, by now an old friend. The other Basie musicians who had been assembled by John Hammond to back her were bassist Walter Page, drummer Jo Jones, tenor saxophonist Lester Young, and the two most recent additions to the band, guitarist Freddie Green and Wilbur "Buck" Clayton, the trumpet player. Clayton's nickname was well-deserved. He looked like a dusky, pomaded Adonis, and Billie, who had always liked handsome men, had eyes for him at first glance (she would later refer to him as one of the most beautiful men she had ever seen). She also liked the looks of guitarist Freddie Green. All of them were complete strangers to her, with the exception of Lester Young; they'd met once before, briefly, on Young's first trip to New York to join the Fletcher Henderson Orchestra as Coleman Hawkins's replacement in 1934.

Billie remembered being struck by his heavy-lidded light green eyes and thinking they were some of the deepest and saddest eyes she'd ever seen.

Lester Young's first sojourn in New York had been a brief and unhappy one when he'd realized that he was expected to sound exactly like the Hawk. Coleman Hawkins played in a style that was as heavily ornamented as it was rhythmically and harmonically complex, in a rich tone that was laden with vibrato—the antithesis of the style Lester was developing. Instead of demoralizing him, however, the experience had only strengthened Lester's resolve to be original. He had promptly handed in his notice, but upon his return to the Midwest, he'd raved to the drummer Jo Jones about the most amazing girl singer he had heard. Neither Lester Young nor Billie Holiday knew very much about the other personally, and certainly neither knew what to expect.

When some reefer started going around, nobody hesitated.

A vanguard of jazz musicians was already incorporating marijuana into the making of wax, and the reason had as much to do with the music business and the way the sessions were run as the euphoric effects of the weed. With the proliferation of the jukebox and the growing popularity of dance music, men like John Hammond had come to realize that the market for jazz was growing, but the records that were made at these sessions were still for a limited urban black audience and therefore low-budget affairs. The artist was asked to show up at the studio with the best group of studio musicians they could gather to cut the usual quota of four sides in a single day. There were no preparations or rehearsals; the artist was given lead sheets to some of the latest songs being pitched, very often encountering the song for the first time. Under these conditions and limitations, the jazzmen were expected to transmute the material into their own idiom—in effect, to conjure the magic of jazz out of thin air.

Each session had its own challenges, emotional and creative mysteries, and subtexts. At least in the case of this particular recording session, they were obvious. The men from the Basie band had never played with Benny Goodman, but they were particularly unsettled by Teddy Wilson. They were swing musicians and were worried that his easy style might not fit in with them. And how would Lester Young fit in?

3.

Kansas City, where Lester Young had been, on and off, since 1933, was the next center of attraction in the progression of cities that demarcate the history of jazz in America. The musical sensation that was ignited in New Orleans and traveled upriver to Chicago and then came east to Harlem was burning brightly all through the 1930s in the bars and clubs between 12th and 18th Streets in the business areas south of the Kansas River, where most of the city's African American inhabitants lived. It was here in this red-hot crucible that swing was being forged and fired. Kaycee was a musical hothouse, Saxophone City.

Under Mayor Thomas Joseph Pendergast, the city had scarcely felt the Great Depression at all, not to mention the effects of the Volsted Act and Prohibition. Pendergast was a brawling demagogue who controlled the unions and the Democratic Party machine, while his friend, the gangster Johnny Lazia, controlled the production, distribution, and sale of beer and spirits. It produced a happy marriage of convenience between politics and the Sicilian Mafia. Kansas City, or "Tom's Town," as it was called, was wide open territory, the closest thing the 1930s would ever get to the concept of a Wild West Las Vegas–style town where vice could openly flourish. Along with gambling and prostitution, loan-sharking, extortion, and narcotics also thrived. The party never seemed to end, and it produced a musician's paradise. Pendergast would rule over the city until 1938, when he was convicted of tax evasion and tied to several gangland killings.

Music was a twenty-four-hours-a-day affair in Kaycee, played in a rich, blues-soaked idiom that was drawn from an ever-growing reservoir of what was then coming to be called *riffs*: short, rhythmically marked, boogie-woogie-inspired phrases of two or four bars, consisting of melodies that became the basis for the very arrangements and songs that would identify the swing sound of the mid to late 1930s. The arrangements were called "head" arrangements because they spontaneously emerged from the head and required no sheet music, preparation, or discussion. It would not be flippant to suggest that they might just as accurately have been called "pothead" arrangements, because some of the greatest improvisers ever to play jazz were by now indulging in the practice of smoking marijuana as a way of life.

The Kaycee clubs were small, cramped, jumping wild, overflowing onto the streets; each place had its signature, and even the smallest bar had a piano and drums. At the Sunset, which was about twelve feet wide and sixty feet long and looked like a dingy hallway, Pete Johnson banged out boogie-woogie on an old upright piano and the bartender was Big Joe Turner, who would pick up a cue for a song and break out into a spellbinding blues while mixing a drink, and Lester Young and Ben Webster played tenor saxophone until ten or eleven in the morning.

The musical life of the city revolved around marathon jam sessions, and the traveling bands passing through included those of Duke Ellington, Fletcher Henderson, Jimmie Lunceford, and Cab Calloway, featuring a host of great musicians—Chu Berry, Coleman Hawkins, Johnny Hodges—always looking for cutting sessions like visiting gunslingers. Some of these encounters became mythic, like the night at the Cherry Blossom when Lester Young, Herschel Evans, and Ben Webster squared off against the great Coleman Hawkins, who had no idea that the Kansas City tenor men were so formidable. Until the mid-1930s, the dominant instrument in jazz had been the trumpet, as personified by Louis Armstrong. Perhaps it was at this very moment, when the cool, unflappable Lester Young blew down the shirtless Coleman Hawkins in a saxophone whirlwind at the Cherry Blossom, that the saxophone came into true prominence, and the legend of Lester Young was born.

4.

Lester Willis Young was born on August 27, 1909, in Woodville, Mississippi, the son of Willis Handy Young, a traveling carnival musician and bandleader known as Billy, and Lizetta Johnson. He grew up in New Orleans, where he was nurtured on music and the love of a mother who adored him and whose light skin and expressive green eyes he inherited. He was a sweet-natured, pensive, extremely sensitive boy who could be shy and withdrawn at times, but until the age of ten his childhood was stable and happy. The sadness in his eyes that Billie Holiday would perceive began with the dissolution of his parents' marriage in 1919. When he remarried, Billy Young was granted legal custody of the children and sent his sister Irma to fetch Lester and his siblings from Lizetta, who was at work and had no idea that her children were about to be taken from her. The children were told it was only going to be a visit. Lester, who wouldn't see his mother for ten years, was inconsolable.

Billy Young had joined the Hagenbeck-Wallace Circus as the band-leader of its sideshow, which was set up in the form of a minstrel show in its own tent. He moved the family to Minneapolis and set about forming his entire extended family into a band, the New Orleans Strut-ters, that would barnstorm throughout the South and Midwest. It was Billy Young who gave Lester his musical education and his first saxo-phone, and it was Billy Young who induced more sadness into his eyes. He was a dignified Baptist who always kept his composure but was a stern taskmaster, strict and authoritarian, who freely used his strap to punish the children, and Lester's languid nature drove him crazy. As a result, Lester ran away from home several times during his teenaged years, sometimes for months at a time.

But perhaps it was the many harrowing incidents of racism encoun-tered during the family's musical travels through Jim Crow America that produced in Lester Young the most overwhelming sadness of all. He was particularly haunted by a church service he had attended with his brother and sister in a small southern town at the age of twelve, at which a white preacher had inveighed against "black sin" and said that the only path to salvation was to receive the forgiveness of sins, but only the whites were allowed to approach the altar for redemption. The experience traumatized him, as did the time he helped his cousin Isaiah "Sports" Young escape a lynch mob in their early teens, running for their lives. Racism was so abhorrent to his extremely sensitive and gentle nature that he quit the family band at the age of eighteen rather than continue to endure it. "I feel a draft" became the code phrase he would use for racism in whatever form he encountered it for the rest of his life. The other phrase he used for it was far more chilling: "Von Hangman is here."

From his earliest days, Young began developing an original ap-proach to the tenor saxophone he played, having been attracted to the C-melody sax of Frankie Trumbauer, which was pitched between an alto and a tenor. It was a light, sweet sound that he approximated on his lower-pitched tenor—a clean tone without vibrato, with a phrasing and economy of notes that represented a distinctively cool and relaxed departure of style for swing. By the time he joined the Basie band at the age of twenty-four, he was already an incomparable instrumentalist, a preternaturally inventive musician who could pull ideas from a seemingly inexhaustible creative wellspring. Crossing lines and altering harmonies at will, floating high above Basie's sound, he put his indelible stamp on many of Basie's classics: "Every Tub," "Taxi War Dance," "One O'Clock Jump," "Shoe Shine Boy," "Oh, Lady Be Good."

When it came to blowing reefer, Lester Young was every bit the viper that Louis Armstrong was. He had been introduced to the practice by the Texas-born composer and tenorman Budd Johnson in 1933, and by the time the nine-member Basie band began their year-and-a-half stay at the Reno Club in 1934, during which time John Hammond would hear them broadcast from the club over an experimental radio wire that he heard on a car radio in Chicago and make plans to bring the band to New York, he was a confirmed daily user of marijuana. He called his reefers "New Orleans cigarettes," and before it became illegal in 1937, he carried his marijuana around in an elegant leather bag that was always with him.

It was at the Reno, seated on the crowded little bandstand, that Lester Young began holding his tenor, which was held together with india rubber and ribbon tape, with his arms extended and thrust out at a forty-five-degree angle—almost like he was playing a flute—to avoid poking his fellow musicians in the back and to be able to play without interference in such a cramped space. It would become one of his trademarks, like the way he could play with a cigarette burning between his fingers as he played his notes. He would stand up and blow, the riffs shooting out of his upthrust tenor like rich, coruscating sparks of cool fire.

Located at 12th and Cherry, the Reno served beer for a nickel, whiskey for a dime, hamburgers for fifteen cents; there were girls available to dance with and a cathouse conveniently located upstairs. The air outside was usually acrid with marijuana smoke, people drank cheap hooch whiskey and wine while crouching in the neighboring alleyways, and by this time musicians had also become aware of how the tops could be pried off of white metal Benzedrex inhalers and the amphetamine-soaked strip of yellow gauze inside that said "Poison" could be soaked in coffee or soda or cocktails and drunk, or just plain rolled up into a nasty bitter little ball and swallowed. The effect was immediate, like a mule kicking inside the nervous system and the top of one's scalp lifting off. All it took was one of them to send a person flying for a couple of days, and just a couple of them could crank up the level of any jam session and keep it going long after your body was telling you to quit. Manufactured by Smith, Kline and French Laboratories and readily available at the local grocery or corner pharmacy, Bennie inhalers—along with reefer, of course—had become the new fad during that historic season of 1936–37.

Lester Young may have smoked marijuana with the same frequency as Louis Armstrong, but the effect on him was markedly different. Whereas Pops turned outward to give of himself to the world, getting high only pulled Lester deeper into himself. It detached him, allowing him to withdraw into his own private world. As self-contained as the world of jazz was, marijuana enabled him to retreat even further. It spun a cocoon around him, creating a pleasant bubble in which he could move through space and time and play music and invent himself as one of the most memorable, eccentric, and influential personalities in the history of jazz.

As Lester liked to move unhurriedly through life, so he seemed to approach music. Again using Baudelaire's maxim that hashish was "a mirror which magnifies, yet no more than a mirror," one is tempted to draw parallels among his personality, the effects of the marijuana he smoked, and the musical innovations he became known for: the way he used space; the way he would relax on his horn, for example, and lay out three beats before coming in with another phrase, just like a born laggard, always giving you the feeling that he was just revving up. And especially for the sweet splendor of his tone and playing.

"He didn't like nothing harsh," trombonist Trummy Young recalled of him. "Harsh talk or harsh playing or nothing. He just liked nice, pretty things all the time. You see, this is the secret. . . . When he swung, it was always . . . I don't care how harsh you were playing. He swung pretty."

He was about to blow the prettiest music of his life.

5.

Sometimes the mere act of smoking reefer together could be a facilitator of musical intimacy. But while it was becoming increasingly more commonplace for musicians to smoke marijuana in 1937, lighting up at an actual recording session was a very different matter. It was one thing to blow reefer in a club in Harlem, but in a Midtown recording studio it was quite a rash thing to do. There were executives, like John Scott Trotter of Decca, who were known to be dead set against it in any form. When one of the top ARC executives walked in that day when Billie Holiday and the Basie musicians were meeting for the first time and sniffed the air, he exploded with anger and demanded that the session be canceled.

Certainly his reaction should have come as no surprise. The marijuana scare was at its height; front-page headlines and feature articles in some of the most popular magazines were screaming about a killer drug that triggered crimes of violence and sexual excess.

John Hammond was no lover of marijuana—his moral and societal objections aside, he felt that smoking the weed played hell with a musician's sense of time—but he sensed the possibility of magic in the studio that day. It was only after Hammond personally interceded and talked the executive out of pulling the plug that one of the great recording sessions in the history of American popular music was allowed to proceed.

The sequence of songs recorded that day was "He Ain't Got Rhythm," "This Year's Kisses," "Why Was I Born?," and "I Must Have That Man." That the songs steadily improved as the session progressed should not surprise anyone, because as musicians feel each other out and get more comfortable, they tend to make better music. What was so utterly phenomenal was how much better they kept getting, how the level jumped with each song, from good to great, from great to sublime.

The first two songs were Irving Berlin tunes from a Dick Powell–Madeline Carroll–Alice Faye musical, *On the Avenue*. "He Ain't Got Rhythm" was passable enough, but no sooner did Lester Young put his mouth on the reed of his tenor to blow the introductory solo to "This Year's Kisses" than electricity seemed to fill the air of the studio.

The mood he set for Billie, how she picked it up and made it her own like nothing and nobody else, was beyond mere rapport, beyond the kind of mutuality of musicians playing well together. It was as if the very tone of his instrument elevated her to a place she had never been before as a singer. A kind of telepathy began to evolve between them, as if they were always meant to play with each other and had lived their whole lives for the moment. Billie would describe it as an intuitive understanding that what Lester was doing was singing with his horn—"you listen to him and can almost hear the words." For Lester, they sounded "like two of the same voices . . . or the same mind or something like that."

Lester Young's solo was a masterpiece, a breakthrough that kicked up the session to a height where anything was possible, and Billie Holiday picked up the torch. On the next song, "Why Was I Born?," Buck Clayton contributed a muted solo that was equally magnificent, joining the interplay at the same level as Lester Young, and the stage was set for the jewel in the crown of the recording session, "I Must Have That Man," a song by Jimmy McHugh and Dorothy Fields.

There would be men in Billie Holiday's life in the years to come, like Jimmy Monroe and John Levy and Louis McKay, who would use her and beat her and manipulate her through sex and dope and even set her up for arrest—hard and nasty but fetching men who would steal her money and her heart. Billie sang the song like a soul confession, with a feeling that seemed to augur the heartbreak of every man she would ever make the mistake of loving who would betray her, even as she remained seemingly helpless to stop herself.

I ain't much carin'
Just where I will end
I must have that man.

Then Lester Young came in again and blew a sixteen-bar solo of such tender feeling and fecundity that subsequent generations of horn men seeking to learn the basic vocabulary of jazz would study its phrases like holy scripture.

What began by sharing a stick of "tea" turned out to be one of those rare instances when the music that went onto the wax was the equivalent of lightning in a bottle—and to a significant degree, it was a day that sealed their musical destinies.

As many have noted, the truth is that Billie's voice was an instrument that would never project strongly, with a limited range of only one and a half octaves. She would never possess the chops of an Ella Fitzgerald or the velvet clarity of a Sarah Vaughan, but as wonderfully gifted as Ella and Sassy were, neither would ever become mythopoeic like Billie Holiday. This was the session that signaled her arrival as a singer capable of transforming popular ballads into intensely personal and poignant works of art. Henceforth she would become the most spontaneous, emotional vocalist of the swing era. Billie Holiday would literally pioneer the use of the microphone and the art of jazz singing.

As for Lester Young, he would often talk about how playing a solo was like telling a story—a conception he took from one of his heroes, Frankie Trumbauer. Billie would become lovers with two of the men who had backed her on that session, Buck Clayton and Freddie Green. As for Billie and Lester, it was never meant to be. Billie was attracted to men who were dangerous and Lester was anything but that; Lester liked women who were small and delicate and Billie was anything but that. But the truth is that he had already made love to her with his horn in a way he never would have been able to with his body had he even wanted to. That was the story he had told, and it was a message that Billie Holiday fully understood. Theirs would be a great musical romance, a deep meeting of sympathetic souls. Lester had always been the soloist featured in Basie's quicker numbers while Herschel Evans was featured on the romantic ballads. It was this session that consolidated what seemed to be his innate musical identity, that signaled his arrival as a musician who, like Louis Armstrong before him and Charlie Parker after him, would create a new aesthetic in jazz. That aesthetic would become known as *cool jazz*.

"I Must Have That Man" seemed to be playing everywhere on the Victrolas in the blue- and red-light tea pads and buffet flats and rent parties and clubs of Harlem during that season when Lester Young dubbed Billie Holiday "Lady Day" and she called him "Prez," for "President of the Tenors."

The name Lester gave Billie was immediately resonant with meaning. At a time when, as Farah Jasmine Griffin points out, "the dominant cultural stereotypes of black women were Mammy and the Tragic Mulatto," when black women were rarely seen as "ladies" at all by white America, here was a name that bestowed the dignity and grace of just such a social status. From this time on, Billie Holiday would forever be known as Lady Day, and Lester Young as Prez.

One day when Prez was in his room at the Hotel Theresa, a rat poked its head out of a drawer. It was most definitely the kind of unpleasant thing he was always seeking to avoid, and he decided to move in with Lady and her mother, whom he dubbed "the Duchess." That was when Lady really began showing him her Harlem—cabarets and after-hours joints like Basement Brownie's, the Nest, the Clam House, Mexico's, and Pod's and Jerry's—"welcoming gathering places for women, gays, those at different economic levels, as well as people who lived close to the color line on either side, or crossed it," as John Szwed describes them. "These nightspots and the way of life they represented have been described as the other side of the Harlem Renaissance, another kind of racial uplift." Because of the people attracted to these small venues—novelists, poets, musicians, and journalists all mixing together with the night people—they would have an impact far beyond their neighborhoods that presented a "new kind of social and cultural reality."

Along with the tea pads, these places represented a new kind of underground freedom where the kind of moral judgments so common to the daylight were simply left at the door. At the Daisy Chain on 141st Street, operated by ex–chorus girl Hazel Valentine, "everybody would get buck naked," as vaudeville comic Clarence "Pop" Foster remembered. "Women going with women, men going with men. They had a girl named Sewing Machine Bertha and she went down on all the girls. . . . Entertainers went up there and it was half-colored and half-white. Hell yeah! *Real* integrated!"

Lady and Prez became a kind of royal couple in this world. Their arrival at any establishment became cause for great excitement—"Lady's in the house! Prez is in the house!" They smoked prodigious amounts of reefer and shared a love of alcohol, enjoying a drink they called "top and bottom" that was port or sherry mixed with gin. Each had a penchant for profanity that bordered on the lyrical, particularly their use of the word *motherfucker*—"Lester's flow of obscenity was magnificent," as Reverend John Gensel recalled. "Nor was it really obscene, because it was not aggressive and was said as his personal poetry. No one, surely, could say 'mother-fucker' like it was music, bending the notes until it was a blues."

It was, for Lady and Prez, the happiest time of their lives. Both were at the top of their game, they were doing some of their finest work, and their reputations grew along with their relationship. And as Lady's star ascended, so Prez became a rage.

"To me, he epitomized everything that I could aspire to in terms of music and style, the way he carried himself," Bernard Brightman related. "We were just so completely captivated by Basie and Lester Young at the Savoy."

Brightman would never forget when the Basie band played the Savoy on New Year's Eve of 1940. "Lester Young was blowing, and bodies were flying everywhere—legs, arms, skirts whipping around above the girls' heads—just this sea of wild motion and energy—it felt like the roof was going to lift right off the place. . . . I swear, there was a moment I saw that floor *jump*—move up and down! People have told me that there was something in that floor that made it give like that, which might have created that effect. I don't know, but from where I stood, it sure seemed like Lester Young was doing it with his saxophone!"

6.

To John Hammond, Prez was the greatest musician of the swing era, but for the life of him Hammond could never understand what the hell Prez was talking about. Beyond "Lady Day," Prez invented nicknames and jive with the same fluent creativity with which he improvised melody, altering the English language to create his very own brand of hip eloquence. There were many other "ladies," of course, but they were all men, like Lady Stitt (aka Sonny). The rotund Basie vocalist Jimmy Rushing was "Mr. Five-By-Five," and the candy-loving trumpeter Harry Edison became "Sweets." Prez coined the expressions "I got it made," "I got eyes for that," and "copycat," "the Big Apple" as the nickname for New York, "crib" for one's home, and "bread" for money, and would end sentences in conversations by saying, "y' *dig*?" These usages survive to the present day as a common part of our vernacular. As people in the jazz world began picking up on virtually everything about him, many of Prez's trademark characteristics became the quintessence of what became known as "cool." In fact, scores of musicians of the era would confirm that Lester Young was indeed the first person ever to use the expression "cool"—as in, "That's *cool*, man"—becoming the very personification of the usage he created.

Cool was the word used to describe Prez's light, relaxed tone, a riff or a lilting melody he played—in short, cool jazz. It wasn't only Charlie Parker who would study his records but a whole generation of saxophonists—Stan Getz, Gerry Mulligan, Al Cohn, Zoot Sims, Paul Quinichette—all of them blowing on Prez's aesthetic and spreading it beyond the world of jazz to pop music, bossa nova, commercials, film scores. As musician and author Ted Gioia points out, "The vision of jazz that entered the mainstream of American life was not the New Orleans stylings of Satchmo or the modal explorations of Coltrane or the so-called jungle sound of Ellington. It was Lester Young's cool jazz."

Along with his musical impact, there was the way Prez dressed: sharp pin-striped suits of impeccable elegance with double-breasted silk vests, tab collars, knit ties, collar pins. He liked pointy shoes with Cuban heels, but he also had a predilection for suede crepe-soled shoes that made a certain squishy sound as he walked. He wore an ankle-length black coat with a fur collar over his shoulders like a cape, and with his long wavy hair and wisp of a moustache, it gave him the air of some new dandified species of ultra-hip jazz grandee. When he saw a picture of Victorian ladies in their riding habits with broad-brimmed low-cut hats, he paid a milliner twenty dollars to make the prototype of what became famously known as the porkpie hat—another of his trademarks that have stood the test of time.

And finally there was just the way Prez was, his droll and extraordinarily singular being. The way he would pull out a little brush and disdainfully sweep his shoulder off with it if he heard something he didn't like. The way he would pull out a little bell during rehearsal and ding it ever so delicately if someone was sharp or flat or off the beat. The way he always spoke quietly in his soft, whispery voice. Gil Evans once observed that he moved "like a parakeet on a perch." Many have remarked that his manner was so fey and effeminate that they thought he may have been a homosexual, but this was only his extreme shyness.

Ted Gioia, who wrote a whole book about cool, observes that many of Prez's personal traits were self-defense mechanisms that served to insulate him from the slings and arrows of the world. There was also an important cultural backstory to Prez's cool that went much deeper than his personal speech, mannerisms, or wardrobe. It was an attitude, a philosophy, a way of looking at life that can be traced all the way to Africa, where *itutu*, or "mystic coolness," was one of three pillars of a religious philosophy created in the fifteenth century by the Yoruba and Igbo civilizations of western Africa. Within these cultures, the sensibility of cool contained meanings of conciliation and gentleness of character, of generosity and grace and the willingness and ability to defuse fights and disputes, as well as physical beauty. As noted by Yale art historian Robert Farris Thompson in his study of the Gola people of Liberia, there was in their version of cool a connotation of the kind of spiritual imperturbability that one associates with Eastern philosophies and wisdom traditions like Zen—an ability to be mentally calm or detached, in an otherworldly fashion, from one's circumstances; to be nonchalant in situations where emotionalism or eagerness would be natural and expected. Over the four centuries of slavery and the African diaspora, it steadily evolved as a way of dealing with the chain and the lash and the terrible need to navigate between your inner truth and every nuance of what it meant to exist and survive in a world where you were owned and exploited and brutalized. It was a way for male slaves to harness rage at the sight of wives and mothers and daughters being raped. The poet and journalist Lewis MacAdams, author of another book about cool, calls it "the ultimate revenge of the powerless. Cool was the one thing that the white slaveowners couldn't own. Cool was the one thing money couldn't buy. At its core, cool is about defiance."

All through the era of Jim Crow, cool was developing among African Americans as a cultural stance, a critical tool for self-esteem and survival—"I play it cool," wrote Langston Hughes in his poem "Motto," "And dig all jive / That's the reason / I stay alive"—until it melded and found singular expression in the being of this shy, hypersensitive, unfailingly polite boy who was snatched from his mother, once escaped a lynch mob, and grew up to become one the most gifted musicians of his generation, believing in his soul that a musician was also a philosopher and that nothing expressed the principles of democracy and equality more than jazz. Cool would take on many shades of meaning in years to come, but to a significant degree, the modern version of it began as a way of looking at the world through the dark glasses that Prez wore onstage at the Savoy—he was one of the first ever to do it— hiding his stoned, heavy-lidded green eyes as he came to define the very essence of cool. After Prez started doing it, there were people all over Harlem wearing their shades at night. Today it's done all over the world as a statement of cool.

For all of these reasons, one could easily make the case that Prez was possibly the most influential jazz musician of them all.

7.

The writer who would do more to romanticize jazz and marijuana than perhaps any other was a twenty-one-year-old student at Columbia when he first encountered Lester Young. Jack Kerouac was a working-class kid from the mill town of Lowell, Massachusetts, who came to New York to attend the elite Horace Mann School before entering Columbia. A fellow classmate at Horace Mann named Seymour Wyse introduced Kerouac to jazz and black life, and he was enthralled. He was just starting to write about jazz when he met Lester Young in 1943, during one of the nocturnal forays that would change the course of his life. They shared a cab from the Village up to Minton's Playhouse, the nightclub in the Hotel Cecil on 118th Street between St. Nicholas and Seventh Avenues in Harlem, where the bebop revolution was percolating and where, according to Edie Kerouac-Parker, Kerouac's girlfriend at the time, who later became his first wife, young Jack encountered something else as well. "Lester Young turned Jack on to marijuana," Edie Kerouac Parker related. "I believe it was the first time Jack was ever really high on it. And I mean *high.*"

Kerouac was fortunate to have encountered Prez before he was drafted into the army, because it was there that his fragile paradise was burst. Prez was taken into the military just after he filmed *Jammin' the Blues,* Gjon Mili's 1944 short for Warner Brothers, which fades in with a shot of his porkpie, pulling back to a smoky close-up of him that would so perfectly exemplify Prez and the jazz of the era. He was playing the Plantation Club in September of 1944 when "this young guy came out one night—zoot suit on, big chain down to his knees like Cab Calloway," as Buddy Tate recalled. "He introduced himself, and we thought he was a fan." It was a disaster from the moment the guy pulled a badge after buying them rounds of drinks and revealed himself to be an FBI agent, telling Lester and Jo Jones to report at nine in the morning or else go to jail for five years.

To his superior officers and fellow soldiers at Fort McClellan, Alabama, the thirty-five-year-old Lester Young might just as well have come from outer space. Everything about him—the way he talked, the way he moved—set him apart and drew attention to him. The sudden rigors and discipline of military life were harsh enough for a man who had lived his kind of free life. One of his many unusual personal traits was always telling the truth, and when asked questions about drugs and alcohol, he admitted to having smoked marijuana for eleven years, along with consuming large quantities of whiskey. His medical examination revealed both epilepsy and syphilis, and when the examiners decided to give him a spinal (lumbar puncture), he became so upset that they put him in a padded cell. He was in deplorable physical condition and after being injured trying to run an obstacle course, he was examined in the hospital by a neuropsychologist and declared to be in a "Constitutional Psychopathic State, manifested by drug addiction (marijuana, barbiturates) chronic alcoholism and nomadism." From that time on he was watched closely, and when he was acting strangely one day in his barracks and admitted that he was high, they searched his foot locker and found one and one half joints and eleven barbiturate pills. The photo found by Captain William Stevenson—a white officer from Louisiana—of the white woman that Prez had recently married, Mary Dale, could not have helped his cause.

Busted and charged according to the 96th Article of War, Prez was given a mental examination and once again declared to be "a constitutional psychopath." After a trial that lasted only an hour and thirty-five minutes, Private 39729502 Lester Young was given the maximum sentence, without any mitigating circumstances being taken into account. He was condemned to be dishonorably discharged and "to be confined at hard labor, at such place as the reviewing authority may direct, for one (1) year." That place turned out to be the stockade of Fort Gordon, Georgia, and it was there that the greatest musician of the swing era found himself in the very kind of situation he most feared in his life—incarcerated by Von Hangman himself. Prez could never even talk about it after his release except to call it "a nightmare, man. One mad nightmare." All that is known is that it got so bad he actually tried to escape, but one can readily imagine the humiliation, the beatings. He did get to play a little music there—it may very well have saved his life. Many have said that Prez was never the same after he came out— "The army just took all his spirit," as Sweets Edison commented—and that the alcoholism that would consume him began to accelerate in the years after the war.

But on that glowing night in Harlem in 1943, Prez was still at the top of his form, and young Jack Kerouac was mightily high. Kerouac was thrilled to be hanging out with the man everyone called Uncle Bubba, the apotheosis of cool, who had this funny pigeon-toed walk; who called the police "Bob Crosby," white people "grays," and black people "oxford grays"; and who, after encountering a pretty woman, would turn to say, "Man, what a *fine* hat. How'd you like to *wear* that hat?" Of course, there was a different hat for every type of woman: "Skullcap?" "Homburg?" "Mexican hat dance?"

Kerouac never wrote about the experience specifically, but Prez certainly made a deep impression that night. When Kerouac sat down in April of 1951 and spewed forth the 125,000 words that would become *On the Road* in a cathartic twenty-day marathon, the manuscript contained a dithyrambic evocation of the history of jazz in America, later published as "Jazz of the Beat Generation"—a long jazz-enrhythmed passage that used Lester Young as its central driving force and inspiration and that epitomized the essence of Kerouac's developing spontaneous prose style.

The point of departure for the passage was the Chicago jazz club where Sal Paradise and Dean Moriarty stop on their cross-country spree. As they watch a bop group play, Kerouac invokes Prez as

that gloomy saintly goof in whom the history of jazz is wrapped: Lester. Here were the children of the modern jazz night blowing their horns and instruments with belief; it was Lester started it all—his fame and his smoothness as lost as Maurice Chevalier in a stage-door poster—his drape, his drooping melancholy disposition in the

sidewalk, in the door, his porkpie hat. . . . What outstanding influence has Dean gained from the cultural master of his generation?
What mysteries as well as masteries? What styles, sorrows, collars,
the removal of collars, the removal of lapels, the crepe-sole shoes,
the beauty goof—that sneer of Lester's, that compassion for the
dead which Billie has too, Lady Day—those poor little musicians in
Chicago, their love of Lester, early heroisms in a room, records of
Lester, early Count, suits hanging in the closet, tanned evenings in
the rosy ballroom, the great tenor solo in the shoeshine jukebox,
you can hear Lester blow and he is the greatness of America in a
single Negro musician—he is just like the river.

For Kerouac, jazz would become exactly like the great Mississippi
itself, "a roar of subterranean excitement that is like the vibration of
the entire land sucked of its gut in mad midnight, fevered, hot," and
right there in the middle of it all was Prez,

> hands up, arms up, horn horizontal, shining dull, in wood-brown
> whiskeyhouse with ammoniac urine from broken gut bottles around
> fecal pukey bowl and a gal sprawled in it legs spread in brown cot-
> ton stockings, bleeding at belted mouth, moaning "yes" as Lester,
> horn placed, has started blowing, "glow for me mother blow for
> me," 1938, later, earlier, Miles is still on his Daddy's checkered
> knee, Louis' only got twenty years before him, and Lester blows all
> Kansas City to ecstasy and now Americans from coast to coast go
> mad, and fall by, and everybody's picking up.

"Picking up" was one of the underground catch phrases for getting
high, and as jazz continued to spread across America, drawing greater
numbers of people to the dance halls, more people experimented with
the weed called marijuana, despite the possibility of stiff jail sentences
and even the most fiendish prospects of madness and mayhem. In the
years after the Second World War, as the use of illicit mind-altering
substances began to find a literary as well as a musical voice, the weed
came to play a central role in what transpired, reverberating over
the landscape of a newly emergent alternative culture like a tocsin of
rebellion.

But as Prez, "the cultural master of his generation," taught this underground culture how to be cool, the man who would personify how to be hip wasn't even mentioned in Kerouac's passage. In 1937, as Prez was blowing "the great tenor solo in the shoeshine jukebox," Charlie Parker was still a teenager back in Kansas City.

9

You Mean There's Something Like This in This World?

1.

As Lester Young played at the Reno Club with Count Basie in 1936, he was being carefully studied by a sixteen-year-old who lived only blocks away, at 1516 Olive Street.

Charlie Parker would thread through the rowdy crowd spilling out onto 12th and Cherry Streets. He would make his way upstairs to the small balcony, where he would sit, high on tea and Benzedrine and liquor or anything else he could get his hands on, his eyes growing large and lambent with the passing hours, until the coming of the morning and the "spook breakfasts," and still he wouldn't leave.

That he was a truant from Lincoln High, or that his mother may have been worried sick about him, didn't seem to matter to the boy, dogged and hell-bent as he was on becoming a great musician. What mattered was the music, the thrill, the pure sensation of being there and doing what he wanted to do. Even at the age of sixteen, Charlie Parker was a seriously advanced gourmet of the moment—"a devout musician," as he would later call himself—grasping at life with a reckless, insatiable hunger.

Sometime that year, an event occurred that galvanized Charlie Parker's musical ambition into high gear and has become a part of his legend. It happened one night after Basie's set at the Reno, during a jam session with drummer Jo Jones. Most of the young up-and-coming musicians adhered to a strict pecking order of sorts when it came to participating in a jam, like playing in the bush leagues before you were allowed to play in the majors; they didn't just jump from the farm club to the big stage with a guy like Jo Jones unless they were acknowledged to be ready. These jams were serious tests of musical manhood; sometimes there were a hundred musicians waiting to get on the stand. The instrument that Charlie carried up on the stage was a pathetic-looking alto saxophone tarnished with age and patched with tinfoil, cellophane, and rubber bands. As Gary Giddins tells the story, "Charlie decided to jump during Jones's jam session, and after he played a couple of faltering choruses at a racing tempo, Jones hit his bell in imitation of Major Bowes. Charlie didn't take the hint. After a couple of additional unheeded gongs, Jones lifted his cymbal off its stand and sent it crashing at Parker's feet. The altoist left amid cruel laughter."

"I'll fix those cats," Parker was heard to say after the incident. "Everybody's laughing at me now, but just wait and see."

The incident precipitated a critical period in Parker's life commonly referred to as *woodshedding,* that period of endless and intense practicing so crucial to the development of a jazz musician's craft, so vital to the evolution of his musical voice. Parker's woodshedding set him on the path to becoming a great artist, a musical revolutionary, and the apotheosis of an entire subculture that would coalesce around him. At the same time it set him on the path to becoming one of the most romanticized drug addicts of the twentieth century—a central but unwitting figure in the proliferation of drugs in the avant-garde jazz underground of postwar America and beyond.

2.

There was nothing in the early years of Charles Parker Jr. that seemed to indicate such a predisposition, with the possible exception of his hard-drinking father. He was born on August 29, 1920, in Kansas City. His father, Charles Parker Sr., a Mississippi-born and Memphis-bred singer and dancer who eventually went to work as a chef on the Pullman line, was hardly around during Charlie's youth and died when Charlie was seventeen, stabbed to death by a woman in a drunken quarrel. The central character in Charlie's life was undoubtedly his mother, Addie Parker, a hard-working and upright woman of part-Choctaw ancestry who hailed from Muskogee, Oklahoma. Charlie spent the first several years of life at 852 Freeman Street, in a Kansas City suburb, before his mother moved them to the two-story frame house on Olive Street, in the heart of the black district. His parents separated when he was nine. He was a quiet and unprepossessing boy, the object of his mother's complete attention and adoration. Addie Parker always said, "Bird was the cutest and prettiest child I ever saw," and she treated him accordingly. Although her wages from Western Union were modest, she still managed to dress the boy in fine custom-tailored suits and give him virtually anything he wanted. His years at Charles Sumner Elementary School and then Crispus Attucks Public School were largely uneventful, normal enough. He loved movies and ice cream sodas and shooting marbles. As he got older he turned into a bright, well-mannered boy with a fondness for reading who slept in the largest room in the house, which had its own pot-bellied stove. His mother claimed that he professed interest in becoming a doctor as a young boy, a dream he apparently abandoned after hearing Rudy Vallée at the age of thirteen and becoming interested in music.

From the very beginning, there seemed to be a strange and powerful sense of symbiosis in Charlie Parker's life between altered states of mind and music that would define the course of his life. Parker himself said that he was already a serious drug user by the age of fourteen, and there is no reason to disbelieve him. The problem began his freshman year at Lincoln High, when Charlie was asked to repeat the grade. By that time, he was playing baritone in the school band, which was led by his friend Alonzo Lewis. Apparently, as his interest in music began to surge, so did his curiosity about other things. That year, despite being forbidden to go there by his mother, his interest gravitated to the buckets of blood along 12th Street. Soon enough he was staying out late, sometimes overnight. A strapping, handsome boy with a bright smile who had always been well groomed and well behaved, Charlie began to look quite dissipated and frayed for a fifteen-year-old. Certainly, at the time that others were just beginning to encounter reefer, he was already a ravenous polydrug user, well on his way to addiction, as highly adept at mixing and crossing states of mind as he would later become at crossing boundaries in his art. Perhaps this is one of the reasons why his use of drugs seems so inextricable from the development and display of his talent in the minds of so many people. The speed with which he became infatuated with music was matched only by his passion for getting high.

His first discovery was wine ("Sweet Lucy," as his friends called it), but he went on quickly from there. The stories and impressions of his use of drugs during this crucial period of adolescence abound as he went from wine and reefer to nutmeg and Benzedrine, and then to narcotics. He loved drugs from his first high, and every time he tasted something new he displayed an addict's natural proclivity for doing it in ever-growing quantities. He also possessed a very fertile mind and seems to have channeled this quality directly into his drug use almost immediately. As his manager Teddy Blume later put it, "Bird's mind was of such a keenness that anything he did he did creatively. He was inventive about drugs. . . . He was too bright for his own good."

As soon as Benzedrine entered his life, sleep seems to have made a hasty departure, and what little sleep he did get came upon him like a sledgehammer, overtaking him in strange places, at inopportune moments, for brief snatches or long drawn-out periods when he was completely dead to the world. He would use amphetamines in one form or another for the rest of his life, and no single drug is more physically and psychologically ravaging to a user over a long period of time, with the exception of alcohol. As club manager Tutty Clarkin remarked, "When Bird was sixteen he looked thirty-eight. He had the oldest-looking face I ever saw."

Amphetamines would push Charlie Parker to his physical limits, but it was narcotics that would define him more than any other substance. Precisely when and how he acquired his first narcotic is not known, except that it happened and was disturbingly conspicuous to all around him. According to Clarkin, his first dope connection was a local drummer named Little Phil; according to his second wife, Doris Syndor Parker, "some character in Kansas City" had put him onto drugs at fifteen. Nor is it certain that heroin was the first narcotic he tried, or became addicted to, for that matter—it may very well have been morphine. Biographer Stanley Crouch cites a "Negro hustler" who ran an after-hours place called Happy Hollow and maintained that heroin did not come to Kaycee until 1940, "when he went north and got permission from the Chicago mob to bring it in himself." In that case, it had to have been morphine, and Crouch mentions a "darkskinned, nicely proportioned and vivacious" woman named Little Mama, who may have worked as a nurse and had access to a supply. On the other hand, in his study of opiate addiction in America before 1940, David Courtwright indicates that heroin was already very likely in Kansas City by the summer of 1937, when Charlie became addicted for the first time at the age of seventeen.

It was heroin that became the new wave in narcotics due to its potency, compactness, and profitability—the illicit opiate par excellence. After Congress effectively outlawed all domestic use of heroin in 1924, the drug became more plentiful; it was cheaper, stronger, and faster-acting than morphine, and easier to smuggle; it could also be snorted, which appealed to the needle-shy. In 1932, the Bureau of Narcotics declared that heroin had supplanted morphine as the drug of addiction "in every part of the United States except the Pacific Coast" and claimed that the ratio of heroin use to morphine use was 7.7 to 1. Dealers quickly discovered that they could effectively adulterate it with milk sugar and it would still pack a wallop. By 1938 heroin sold in the United States was 27.5 percent pure, very potent by the standards of later decades but weak to the generation of addicts that had become hooked on pure morphine during the 1920s.

Under Tom Pendergast, Kansas City became the Midwestern metropolis for narcotics, and Charlie Parker was never the self-denying type. Wherever he first encountered heroin, it had the irresistible cachet of the new thing. In actual fact, narcotics were entering his life during the first surge of underground heroin use in America, right at the time that hypodermic needles and intravenous technique, which greatly accelerate addiction, were also spreading. And whether it was morphine or heroin, the overall impact was quite the same.

Stanley Crouch surmises that Parker's curiosity about narcotics may have been stimulated by reading Sir Arthur Conan Doyle's Sherlock Holmes mysteries, especially *The Sign of Four*, in which Holmes takes a hypodermic needle from a "neat morocco case" and shoots up. Gary Giddins mentions the death of his close friend, a trombonist named Robert Simpson, who died on the operating table from a heart ailment, as a factor that "may have contributed to his sudden appetite" for drugs and liquor. The most telling and oft-cited anecdote that seems to exemplify his basic attitude about drugs is told by Buddy Jones: "Getting high the first time at fifteen, Bird told me what he felt. He pulled out $1.30, which was all he had and which was worth more in those days, and he said: 'Do you mean there's something like this in this world? How much of it will this buy?'"

There's something heartbreakingly guileless and honest in this anecdote that certainly helps explain the precipitousness of Charlie Parker's addiction. As it took hold, strangers began showing up at his house, and various items of value that belonged to his mother—her jewelry, her iron—began to disappear. He was already married to his childhood sweetheart, Rebecca Ruffin, a beautiful girl who resembled the young Lena Horne. The Ruffins had shared the Parkers' home for a number of years before the romance blossomed, much to the dismay of Rebecca's mother, who viewed Charlie as a no-good bounder. Rebecca was soon pregnant, but the relationship turned increasingly volatile. Marriage between adolescents is difficult enough, but it was made worse by Charlie's increasingly unpredictable moods. That July, according to what she told Gary Giddins, Rebecca "got her first look at a needle."

> She was three months pregnant when Charlie called her upstairs and told her to sit on the bed. He was wearing a dark suit and a long tie. It was night and the shade was down. She looked toward the window and saw in its reflection the tie pulled tight around his arm, the needle plunging in and the blood coming up. She screamed, "What are you doing?" He just looked and smiled. He wiped the blood, and slipped the tie off his arm and put it around his neck, and said, "Well, I'll be seeing you, Rebec." He kissed her on the forehead and left.

Rebecca promptly told Addie Parker what was going on, and Addie confronted him immediately: "Charlie, I'd rather see you dead than use that stuff." Charlie's response was typical of how he would handle many such predicaments in the years to come: he simply disappeared for a couple of weeks. Addiction forced him to cultivate that lying, conning part of himself that becomes a part of every junkie's character makeup as the search for drugs becomes an overriding compulsion. It made him unreliable as a band member and friend; it made him an easy mark for pushers everywhere seeking to fleece him of whatever amount of cash he had in his pockets; it made him completely helpless against any narco bulls trying to roust him, checking his arms with magnifying glasses for tracks and even demanding to put some instrument up his rectum to search for hidden contraband.

But as much as drugs may have been molding Parker's experience and outlook, they never seemed to impede the development and expression of his music. In fact, the truly astounding aspect of this period in his life is how the onset of addiction coincided with such a quantum leap in his musical abilities. As Charlie plunged more deeply into drugs, his search for musical knowledge and growth became even more relentless and all-consuming. He later said that he practiced "from eleven to fifteen hours a day." He was known to kiss his sax and call it "baby." Anybody who passed the Parker home heard his saxophone continuously. He just played. Played all the time. Played in his house, and played out back walking around in circles. Played so much that he would get frustrated and smash his saxophone in a rage against the street curb. He was on fire, burning, haunted by music; he was seen standing alone in the dim alleyways outside clubs with his horn at all hours, eyes closed, listening against walls and doors as he silently fingered his instrument. He would go out alone into Paseo Park, and shoot dope, and blow his horn into the empyrean of the night sky.

As Gene Ramey remembered, "In the summer of 1937, Bird underwent a radical change musically. He got a job with a little band led by a singer, George Lee. They played at country resorts in the mountains. Charlie took with him all the Count Basie records with Lester Young solos on them and learned Lester cold, note for note. When he came home, he was the most popular musician in Kansas City. He had gone up in the mountains; and when he came back, only three months later, the difference was unbelievable."

The wonder of Charlie Parker's musical gifts was only starting to emerge. He became a melting pot of other influences in addition to Lester Young, notably Coleman Hawkins, Roy Eldridge, and Leon "Chu"

Berry. He wisely apprenticed himself to older musicians who could teach him the ropes of the business, like Buster Smith and Tommy Douglas. He experimented with flatted fifths and augmented thirteenths and was constantly rearranging Ray Noble's "Cherokee." Whatever he was feeling, he learned to express it through the silver Conn alto saxophone he'd acquired. "He got into his music all the sounds around him—the swish of a car speeding down the highway, the hum of wind as it goes through leaves," Ramey observed. "When we used to take carriage rides on our free hours, we would sometimes roll along the country roads and look at the trees and leaves falling from the branches; he had notes to express all these phenomena presented by nature."

From now on, the bandleaders that hired him had to do so knowing that he might be late, or fall asleep on the bandstand, or not show at all. But as Stanley Crouch points out, "Charlie might bring disorder to your border, but then he could turn around with disheveled grace and pull a mother lode of what everybody was looking for right out of thin air."

The event that precipitated Parker's departure from Kansas City involved a scrap with a cab driver over a ten-dollar fare. Charlie couldn't pay it, and when the cabbie tried to grab his horn as payment, Charlie cut him with a knife. The knife wound was not serious, but it was enough to get him arrested for assault; he spent a brief time at a prison farm and was released. Had the incident never occurred, Parker would have left anyway because he knew that his destiny lay elsewhere. The bands he'd played with were gone—Jay McShann was off touring in Chicago and Buster Smith was arranging for Basie in New York. One morning early in 1939, he called his wife downstairs.

"Rebecca, you are a good person, and I want you to take good care of our son. I love you. But I believe I could become a great musician if I were free. Rebecca, please free me. Please free me, Rebecca. I have to have my freedom."

Then he called his mother over and made her promise that for as long as Rebecca and his newborn son Leon would live, "they would have a roof over their heads and food in their mouths."

And with that, he was gone. Addie Parker would outlive her son by thirteen years.

3.

He carried very little with him as he made his way to the Kansas City freight yard. Having pawned his alto to get some money for his great adventure, he wore a pair of pants so big they were held up by a cloth belt, a pair of worn workmen's brogans, a threadbare suit jacket, and a scruffy topcoat. But despite this shabby appearance, and even without the horn, Charlie Parker could command attention. He was an autodidact with a lightning-quick mind that allowed him to discourse learnedly on many different subjects. He was also a brilliant mimic. And although he looked older than his eighteen years, he was handsome, with an easy smile and the natural-born charm of a con man.

What he also took along with him was blind ambition and a lust for music and life that was bottomless. Charlie Parker would cram more into the short span of his lifetime than most human beings could ever dream. Since early adolescence, he'd been the exact polar opposite of Louis Armstrong when it came to setting boundaries about drug use. Not only did Parker indulge his appetites, he made an ethos out of it. His passions would burn up his life like a raging brushfire—and yet, as he jumped a train heading north to Chicago, he was clean. Recognizing that he would need all the clarity and discipline he could possibly muster to establish himself when he got to New York, he had somehow managed to kick his habit, and he would stay clean until he accomplished that goal. Above all else, the overriding force that drove him was to find what was his and his alone musically—"to unlock the genie that was hidden somewhere in his soul," as Crouch describes it. And he was always willing to work for it, no matter how hard.

The nickname he would shortly acquire—"Bird," for "Yardbird"—would follow him for the rest of his days. The mundane origin of the name concerned a couple of chickens in the road hit by the car that he was traveling in with the Jay McShann Orchestra on the way to a date at the University of Nebraska. Charlie insisted they stop and go back; he scooped up one of the dead birds and took it along and asked the lady at the boarding house if she would be so kind as to cook it for them.

As Charlie Parker's music became a miraculous presence, as he spearheaded the reworking of the aesthetic of jazz that became known as bebop, the name would come to mean so much more: the Bird who took magnificent flight as his fingers flew over the keys of his instrument; the Bird of unpredictable migratory patterns, who could turn up anywhere at any time; the Bird of wild beauty; the Bird who was free. For what Bird would come to represent to so many, the power of his image, was about freedom, musical and otherwise. But the great contradiction of Bird's life was also well in place by the time he hopped that train, for his habit would return with ill-fated consequences, and as the metaphor of Bird was about freedom and release, his path would also be marked by self-destruction: the Bird who skyrocketed, enveloped by the drugs that would immolate him during flight.

As soon as he arrived in Chicago, he showed up at a breakfast dance at the 65 Club, where the singer Billy Eckstine was performing in a group with King Kolax on trumpet and Goon Gardner on alto.

"We were standing around when a guy comes up that looks like he just got off a freight train," Eckstine later recollected, "the raggedest guy you'd want to see at this moment. . . . And he asked Goon, 'Say, man, can I come up and blow your horn?' . . . And this cat gets up there, and I'm telling you he blew the hell out of that thing! It was Charlie Parker, just come in from Kansas City on a freight train . . . no more than eighteen then, but playing like you never heard."

One cannot help but think of Icarus, who flew too high and close to the burning radiance of the sun. But before Charlie Parker went plummeting, a whole generation of jazzmen, along with painters, poets, novelists, dancers, and composers, came to cite him as inspiration and catalyst for their own breakthroughs.

10

Once Known, Never Forgotten

1.

"I've always wanted to be an opium addict," declared Herbert Huncke. "I just want to go to Thailand and smoke opium until the end. That would be a marvelous way to take off, wouldn't it?"

As I was walking down St. Mark's Place on my way to Huncke's subterranean apartment on the Lower East Side of Manhattan, the fragment of a poem called "A Remembrance of Walking Past the Hotel Wilson," which Jack Kerouac had written about William Burroughs almost half a century earlier, kept sounding in my head—"Here once the kindly dope fiend lived."

Just then I passed a kid seated on the sidewalk at the corner of Second Avenue, dressed in a ratty leather jacket and ripped jeans, who stared up at me with sullen junkie eyes and reached out his hand. "Hey man," he rasped hoarsely, "can you spare me some change? I just need some more money for some *beer*, man."

I wondered, had this kid ever heard of Herbert Huncke?

"Oh, yeah," said the kid. "He's the guy that gave William Burroughs his first shot of dope. . . . He lives right around here."

When I told Huncke of the kid and what he said, he appeared uncomfortable at first. Seated on his bed, he reached for the joint in the ashtray and leaned his frail frame against the wall.

"I'm sort of legend here down on the Lower East Side. A *strange* legend, to be sure. People meet me and are in awe of my survival—as am I. . . . Nobody could have convinced me at your age that I would live for this long—never in my wildest imaginings! When I was twenty-one, I was perfectly satisfied with the idea of packing it in at thirty; forty was out of the question. I wanted to live fast, see and do as much as I could, cram it all into a speedy exit. And now here I am, hanging on, and I'm rather beginning to enjoy it. I neither regret nor anticipate. Once in awhile, when things go wrong, I say, Jesus, I wish I were *dead.* But I've been saying that all my life."

The man who first put the word *beat* in what became known as the Beat Generation was then seventy-eight years old. Huncke would never get to go to Thailand and smoke opium until the end but would live out his days in the Chelsea Hotel, in a room paid for by the Grateful Dead through the Rex Foundation—an acknowledgment of the role he had played in the lives and literature of Allen Ginsberg, Jack Kerouac, William Burroughs, Neal Cassady, and others. It was Huncke who became Elmo Hassel in Jack Kerouac's *On the Road*, Herman in William Burroughs's *Junky*; he was the original "angel-headed hipster" who walked all night with shoes "full of blood on the snowbank docks waiting for a door in the East River to open to a room full of steam-heat and opium" in Allen Ginsberg's *Howl*. To Ginsberg, the whole journey of illicit drugs through the culture and consciousness of mid-century America seemed to begin with this man: "As far as I know the ethos of what's charmingly Hip, & the first pronunciation of the word itself to my fellow ears, first came consciously from Huncke's lips; and the first information and ritual of the emergent hip subculture passed through Huncke's person."

Of course, Huncke himself became a writer of some renown in underground circles. In the title story of a collection called *The Evening Sun Turned Crimson*, he describes a particular sunset as follows:

On the evening of this story as I walked from the interior of the house out to the porch I became aware of the sky which had turned a wild furious crimson from the huge and glowing red disk of the sun radiating shafts of gold light and at rushing speed plunged below the horizon. I stood—nearly riveted to the spot bathed in pinkish tint and surrounded by an almost red world—everything reflecting the sunset—and filled with awe and an inward fright I felt the intenseness of my being alone, and although I've suffered acute awareness of my loneliness many many times throughout my life, I've never seen it quite so thoroughly or traumatically as on that evening when all the world turned into burning flame and it was as though I was already in the process of being consumed.

And so he talked on that day, like a man being consumed by the burning flames of his loneliness and memories, his voice deep and sonorous, the stories flowing one right into another—his boyhood and adolescence in Chicago, his early years in New York—but mostly he talked about drugs, bringing it all to life in a way that made one understand and appreciate why Burroughs and Ginsberg and Kerouac had been so captivated by him as he told his stories hunched over coffee in the Times Square cafeterias of 1945, when Huncke was procuring subjects for Dr. Albert Kinsey's groundbreaking sexual research at the same time that he was scoring junk, tea, and benny inhalers . . .

"I was a little late for the hard-core old junkies of New York that just prior to my hitting the streets had already become established. In *Naked Lunch*, the material about 'Sailor'—that was Phil White, and he was a part of that scene. Burroughs constantly refers to 103rd Street. Those were the old-time schmeckers who hung around there. A lot of Irish, people like that who hung around in cafeterias. The Jewish guys were all hooked up to the mobs and they lived on the Lower East Side; that's how it got started, really, the Jewish guys hanging around the bars on East Broadway, Henry Street, Madison Street, all that below Canal and east of Chinatown. You would hear about some of the old guys way back there in the twenties, guys like Louie the Lip and Crazy Ozzie, guys who remembered what it was like when you could buy heroin right across the counter in a cold cream jar. Imagine that! The Italians got into it later; they took it over from the old schmeckers, and when they did the scene got bigger, heavier, and they started cutting the dope more and more, which changed everything. Eventually, it moved up to Harlem and 110th Street."

Thus Huncke sketched the historical origins of the narcotics scene in New York, and there was nobody better to do it. He took a hit and brooded silently for a few moments before chuckling in his sad, world-weary way.

"Oh, it's quite a story, dope in America. Oh, yes, indeed! One thing it did was teach one a certain contempt for the stupidity of all the hard-core rules that were just fouling up the human race. But, man, at the same time it's kind of *sad*, you know?"

In his first novel, *The Town and the City*, Kerouac described him as "a small, dark, Arabic-looking man with an oval face and huge blue eyes that were lidded wearily always, with the huge lids of a mask. He moved about with the noiseless glide of an Arab, his expression always weary, indifferent, yet somehow astonished too, aware of everything. He had the look of a man who is sincerely miserable in the world."

Huncke was now an old schmecker himself, one of a dying breed, the last living connection to a part of our past that we had always sought to disavow and deny and bury in jails: the time of Louie the Lip and Crazy Ozzie, Harry Anslinger and *Reefer Madness*. He may very well have ended as just another nameless junkie and petty thief had his orbit not intersected with a group whose lives and literature would all change as a result of meeting this lifelong drug addict. It was Kerouac who called him "the greatest storyteller I know, an actual genius at it, in my mind."

2.

Born in Greenfield, Massachusetts, in 1914, Herbert Huncke was the son of a German Jew who hated Jews and later actually joined the German American Bund, an American Nazi organization of the 1930s; his mother was the daughter of a Wyoming cattleman. His parents separated after they moved to Chicago. "Everything I did was wrong," was how he remembered his youth, "and what was supposed to be a substantial American middle class home was really a household of screaming hysterical women and an angry, confused and frustrated man."

Huncke was one of those perennial problem kids who always hated the very idea of being confined in any way. From the very beginning of his life, he felt trapped by family, gender, and school. He was twelve when his mother sent him to live with his father, giving him a dime to ride the trolley. Young Herbert never got off. He rode the trolley all the way to the end of the line in Gary, Indiana—and then, for good measure, he decided to see how far he could get with his thumb. He got all the way to Geneva, New York, before the police picked him up. It was a harbinger of things to come. Huncke would always like to go all the way to the end of the line. Growing up in Prohibition-era Chicago, he liked to hang around Rush Street and Chicago Avenue—the "Village" area of town.

"Man, I started to use drugs back in the thirties, that's when I started. There were very few kids at the time that messed with them—it was quite unheard-of, especially for white kids." It was the taxi drivers around town and "guys in the sporting life, so to speak, boxing joints, pool halls" who were the first drug users he became aware of, and it was a cabbie who one day said, "You look like a pretty wise kid. Did you ever smoke marijuana?"

"No, but I've heard of it."

"Be my guest," the cabbie said, handing him a joint.

Huncke smoked it the next day, but nothing much happened. He was also the kind of kid who wanted to get the full effect of everything, and he was determined to try it again. It took him several months to find some more, but this time when he smoked it he was "unable to move. It was up to then the most unusual and conscious experience of my life. I heard music for the first time—that is, really heard it—and saw people I had known in a whole new perspective. . . . I couldn't stop laughing. I felt like a damn fool—like somebody had pasted a smile on my face and I couldn't take it off."

There are a number of watershed moments in the story of how Huncke became a teenage heroin addict adrift in Depression-era America—Huncke the Junkie, as many would call him. The first was encountering a book called *The Little White Hag* by Francis Beeding (actually a pseudonym for a pair of collaborative British authors) about "smugglers and Chinese junks and opium dens in Shanghai, posh layouts with cushions on the floor and naked or half-naked men and women laying about," as he recalled it. Huncke was fascinated: "Of course, it ended up that everybody went to hell, but so be it. It sounded like a pretty interesting way to go to hell to me."

The next linchpin experience was meeting Elsie John, a six-foot-five man who called himself a hermaphrodite and worked on West Madison in a freak show, "with hennaed hair a fire engine red, and gigantic deep blue eyes, the most expressive eyes I've ever seen." Huncke would regale the young Allen Ginsberg with the exploits of Elsie John until Ginsberg's eyes would go wide-eyed with astonishment behind his glasses. "At that time in my life I could scarcely have imagined that such a person could really exist," Ginsberg related. Elsie John was a precursor of melodramatic drug-using drag queens like Miss Destiny in John Rechy's *City of Night* or the Holly Woodlawn of Lou Reed's "Walk on the Wild Side." Huncke was only fourteen when he met her. It was Elsie John who gave Huncke his first taste of heroin when he visited her in her room in an old vaudeville hotel on North State Street, where she would hold court in the center of her huge brass bed, surrounded by her five Pekingese dogs. It was a taste he would never forget. But it wasn't until his friend Johnny was shot dead by a Treasury agent while making a delivery of heroin that Huncke packed everything he owned into a little cigar-box toilet kit and took to the rails and highways. By the time Huncke hit the road in 1934, he was a full-blown heroin addict, faced with the prospect of having to score dope in every place he landed. As William Burroughs expressed his dilemma, "At an early age Huncke was cut off from family support, leaving him with a life-long drug habit to support as best as he could. The protagonist is thrown into the water to sink or swim. So he learns something about the water."

Huncke would learn many things about the "water" during his journeys. Mostly what he learned were the bare-bone basics of survival through petty crime. He became a thief of suitcases and overcoats, a pickpocket, a grifter, a parasite, a hustler never afraid to use his body to get what he needed—he belonged to the world of "petty cheats, phony braggarts, double clockers, elbow sneaks, small-time chiselers, touts and stooges and gladhand-shakers," as Nelson Algren described such petty criminals in *The Man with the Golden Arm*—but that was as far as Huncke ever went. Heavy crime like armed robbery was out of his league—for one thing, he abhorred violence. All he ever really wanted to do was just to get high and hang out in a cafeteria, or take a walk down the street. "It's still my favorite thing to do. You never know what you're going to find. I just liked to look at people—the stranger, the better."

Wherever Huncke went in America, he was hounded, rousted, and reviled. "If you were a drug addict, you were truly among the damned"—without rights, beneath all dignity. The word that Huncke first began using for this woeful and degraded state of being was *beat*. He also had an expression he often used to express his profoundly weary disdain for the ways of the world and how he couldn't possibly be expected deal with any of it: "Oh, mother, I can't dance!"

3.

Stone-broke as usual when he arrived in New York, Huncke headed right to 42nd Street with a red carnation in his lapel, right into the life of the hustler and the world of cafeterias like Bickford's, Chase's, Hector's, and the Automat. "I was a natural for it. It was exciting. I didn't see all the tinsel and tawdriness about it then, it took me quite a while to finally detect the horror of the surroundings. But the Pokerino with its neon flashing, the little passageways from one street to another that were off the record, guys sitting around the table talking about the clip they'd made—all of this was completely new to me, and I was captivated by it."

When the war broke out, Huncke found himself in a pad on 47th Street. While millions of American men were donning uniforms, he was absolutely thrilled with his 4-F status, delighted that the government would take men, women, and boys into the service before him. He happily withdrew into a world of marijuana, Benzedrine, Seconal, Nembutal, eyedroppers, no. 26 half-inch spikes, hypodermic needles and wires for cleaning them. Times Square, the very crossroads of the world, had become his living room.

At the time the streets of New York teemed with soldiers and sailors—lonely and bewildered—and many found their way to the pad where for a little while at least life took on some meaning. It surprised me how many servicemen got strung out during the war. Often they gave love and always found it. Some found God and hardly knew of their discovery. There many heard the great Bird and felt sad as Lady Day cried out her anguished heart. . . . Others came also—42nd Street hustlers—poets—simple dreamers, thieves, prostitutes (both male and female) and pimps and wise guys and junkies and pot heads and just people—seeking sanctuary in a Blue Glade away from the merciless neon glare.

Huncke was breaking into cars and stealing topcoats and other items when he first got picked up. By that time he had come to be known as "the creep" by the cops on the Times Square beat, and he was treated accordingly. He was thrown into the Tombs, then remanded to Hart Island.

"In those days all the so-called drug addicts were sent up there because they had this theory about the fresh air. Also, they needed people to bury the dead, the poor and the nameless derelicts who had dropped dead on the streets and in the flophouses and were buried out in [the] potter's field, so that's what they made us do. If they knew you were a junkie, you automatically went right out on the grave detail, no matter what condition you were in. They were very righteous about it, absolutely convinced it was the appropriate way to treat a drug addict. The job would have been bad enough for anybody, but if you were withdrawing from heroin it really felt like you were on some chain gang in hell." Because of this experience and so many others like it, Huncke would always revile Harry Anslinger as somebody who'd been bred "in some stool pot in hell, who caused more misery in the name of saving so-called civilization than anyone since Hitler."

Now with a police record in New York, Huncke knew that he could be picked up for questioning at any time. If he continued to use drugs when he got out and got strung out and got arrested again, he knew that he would be thrown right back, and what that meant was that every time he got arrested, he would just have to kick in a jail cell, cold turkey. In the summer of 1943, he was nabbed once again, this time for prescription fraud, and was thrown back in jail, which presented its own challenges for survival and lessons to be learned beyond withdrawal from drugs. Huncke was physically small, and the last thing he wanted was to become a "punk" in the joint. One had to be careful of the dreaded "blanket job"—"Six big black guys would throw a blanket over your head and have a crack at you. This one guy Joe it had happened to had gone completely out of his mind." By now the sounds and feelings of prison had become forever lodged in his consciousness—"the guard passing with the flashlight and the jingling keys, farts, snoring, groaning, sleep talk, flushing toilets, phone ringings, muffled conversations, closing doors, church chimes, traffic, shouts on the streets below and the constant noise of people sick and unable to sleep, moving and adjusting, seeking the more comfortable position"—and if you were kicking cold turkey, the misery could go on for as long as four weeks without sleeping as you suffered from the shakes, the shivers, and the chucks.

"Later on I went to the US Public Hospital at Lexington, Kentucky, twice for a six-month cure. One stretch I did and the other I left— signed out. You could volunteer or be sentenced. Because of the research they did there it was set up very nicely in a sense. You got a bit of orientation, during which they'd try to judge how sick you were. You might get some sleeping medication but generally you were just cut off. They would try to make you as comfortable as possible under those conditions. A little work assignment; chow time; Sunday movies in the auditorium; if there were enough people in who could blow there'd be a concert. Therapy and shrinks weren't mandatory. You wouldn't have to do anything. It was the only place you could go at the time."

Huncke copped dope on his first day back in New York.

"After all that pain and discomfort, you'd think a man wouldn't want to subject himself to it all over again. . . . But man, I never *stopped* using drugs. I even use a little horse from time to time if I want."

The Band-Aid on the back of his hand where he had taken his last pop was graphic evidence that heroin was still a part of Huncke's life even at his advanced age, and there were no judgments or apologies about it. "Yes, man, one does what one does," was all he had to say about it. "That's what a lot of people really don't understand about drugs . . . Here, let me read you something . . . "

Huncke began reading an elegy he was writing about his lifelong love affair with the needle, which had begun in Elsie John's hotel room sixty years earlier.

"There are innumerable ways to woo," he intoned. "On one's knees, while gazing fondly into the eyes of the one being wooed; and then words are, so I'm told, effective; not to mention the ever-handy kiss, the stroking, the touching, those tenderly whispered endearments. But nothing surpasses that titillating first tiny prick—slightly painful, although not quite, as the eye watches and then looks away, only to once again become aware of the tiny point against the outer casing of the waiting vein. One instant of rejection, and then the moment of penetration, recognizing the sensation felt as the little point has entered the flowing blood already seen through the glass of the thirsty syringe, beginning the pressured force, sending it back to rejoin the original stream diluted now with a wondrous new sensation, once known, never forgotten—"

Huncke stopped himself. "'Once known, never forgotten'—it's a little romantic, perhaps, but how true, how very *true*, man," he said with his melancholy laugh. "Isn't that the truth about all drugs? Of course, if it *wasn't* a little romantic, none of us would ever start fucking with it in the first place."

I pulled out my own notebook. "Let me read you my favorite passage about you," I said, and began reading from *Desolation Angels*:

and everything is going to the beat—It's the beat generation, it's *béat*, it's the beat to keep, it's the beat of the heart, it's being beat and down in the world and like oldtime lowdown and like in ancient civilizations the slave boatman rowing galleys to a beat and servants spinning pottery to a beat—The faces! . . . —A face like Huck's in New York (Huck whom you'll see on Times Square, somnolent and alert, sad-sweet, dark, beat, just out of jail, martyred, tortured by sidewalks, starved for sex and companionship, open to anything, ready to introduce new worlds with a shrug).

"Yes, it's good," Huncke said as I finished, with a deep sigh. "Kerouac had a marvelous way with words, there's no question about his language, but there's a hedging that comes through that just saves it from being really, really great, because he was beautiful, you know. He copped some of what he felt might have been some of the strange poetry in me. It's artistic license in some instances, but that's the cop-out."

Huncke took another hit, closed his eyes again, and gently rocked back and forth on his bed, continuing his strange communication of lonely afternoons and dope-dimmed sunsets, hearing the sound of distant music, seeing the faces of long-gone and faraway people, and remembering the needle and the one shot of dope he gave, once known, never forgotten . . .

"It's funny now, because Burroughs has turned into such a dignified old gent. Who could have ever imagined that he'd turn out to be such an outstanding historical figure, this man who became such a junkie. . . . Who could have imagined that any of them would. When I first met them they were just kids, really. Kids looking to get high."

11

The Shot Heard 'Round the World

1.

The way Huncke remembered it, William Burroughs was standing stiffly at the door in his Chesterfield coat, gloves in hand, when Bob Brandenburg first introduced them.

"This is Bill, the guy I've been telling you about."

Huncke had just come out of the back room. He took one look—the horn-rimmed glasses, the snap-brimmed fedora, the gray three-piece suit—and warnings began sounding off in his nervous system like alarm bells after a bank heist. This man was much too straight-looking even for the narcotics squad. This man was *FBI*.

"Jesus Christ, get him out of here, man," Huncke told Bob under his breath, grabbing him aside. "This guy is *heat*!"

Brandenburg, who was working as a soda jerk up around Columbia at the time, vouched for Burroughs, but Huncke still wasn't persuaded. "Waves of hostility and suspicion flowed out from his large brown eyes like some sort of television broadcast," Burroughs would later write. "The effect was almost like a physical impact."

What calmed Huncke was one simple unvarnished fact. The man had arrived with a pocketful of one-half grain syrettes of morphine tartrate, the kind commonly distributed to medics for easy use on the battlefields of the Second World War. As usual, Huncke's desire for a shot superseded any other impulse. Desperate for a fix, he was caught in the basic equation of what Burroughs would come to call "the Algebra of Need."

"Huncke, let's you and I shoot up," Phil White said. "You don't mind, do you, Bill?"

"No, not at all," Burroughs said, taking off his coat. "I've been thinking about this. You know, I'd like to try that myself. I've always had an interest in that sort of thing."

Huncke found the man's interest in drugs surprising enough, but there was something about his voice that struck him even more. It was formal, educated, delivered with a kind of nasal *hrumpf hrumpf,* as if he had some kind of sinus trouble, his accent as dry and flat as the Midwestern plains.

Burroughs took the place in. The apartment looked like someone's version of an opium den. The living room was painted black with garish yellow panels, the ceiling done in Chinese red with a huge Oriental medallion in the middle of plum, yellow, orange, and green. When they went into the bedroom, Burroughs followed them and watched the three of them prepare to shoot up, studying them carefully. He liked these characters. They were obviously a disreputable crew. There was Phil White, the tall, rawboned Tennessean; Brandenburg, the dashing and slim soda jerk from Cleveland who was always talking about capers and drugs; and the little one, Huncke, "small and very thin, his neck loose in the collar of his shirt. His complexion faded from brown to a mottled yellow, and pancake make-up had been heavily applied in an attempt to conceal a skin eruption. His mouth was drawn down at the corners in a grimace of petulant annoyance."

When the three had finished fixing, Huncke said to him, "Now look, there's enough in the cooker for you to shoot up."

"Well," Burroughs said, "what do you think? How do you go about this?"

Huncke began to explain to Burroughs about the morphine, what it would feel like. He was concerned that it would be too much for the newcomer and tried to prepare him for the terrific pins-and-needles sensation he would feel as the drug traveled through the system and whacked him in the back of the neck like a karate chop.

Burroughs wanted to rub a little alcohol on his arm first. He also thought it would be a good idea to clean off the spike before the shot. There was something careful, methodical about his manner, Huncke noticed. He may have looked and sounded like a bank president, but there was something of the doctor in him as well. But when the moment came and they tied him off, Burroughs turned his head the other way. It would always strike Huncke as ironic that the man who would one day write that he had "an open sore where I can slip a needle right into my vein, it stays open like a red, festering mouth, swollen and obscene" couldn't bear to watch the needle penetrate his virgin veins.

By that time Huncke had more than ten years of experience with a needle—the shot was expertly administered.

"Loosen the tourniquet," Huncke told him.

Burroughs stared down at the tiny pinprick in the crook of his arm. The feeling hit him in the back of the legs first, rushing, then the back of the neck. He felt like he was moving off the ground at great speed. He was floating, a wave of pleasure spreading through his tissues, "without outlines, like lying in salt water."

"Well, that's *quite* a sensation," Bill Burroughs said, glancing around. "Well, that's very *interesting*."

Burroughs was exactly like a scientist, Huncke later observed. He became an addict principally as a result of doing "research."

2.

In *Call Me Burroughs*, his exhaustive and authorized biography published in 2013, Barry Miles avows that none of this ever happened. Miles states in his notes that "Huncke's various accounts of watching Burroughs take his first shot are, like many of Huncke's stories, fabricated. Burroughs was alone and did not have the syrettes with him at the first visit to Henry Street. He undoubtedly watched Burroughs shoot up later."

Huncke's version, if indeed false, would obviously fit the very definition of a myth as a widely held but false belief or idea. It was commonly assumed to be true for half a century and was therefore replicated in numerous biographies and memoirs. Why Huncke may have fabricated it is anybody's guess. Memory plays tricks. He may have believed it in the way that lies can become real in one's mind over time. But the far more likely reason is that Huncke was a storyteller and this was a far better story to hustle than Burroughs returning to his own apartment to experiment with the syrettes alone—which is probably why

Burroughs himself would also proffer this version of what happened to William Lee in *Junky*. The story also perfectly fits the definition of a myth as a traditional story, especially one concerning the early history of a people or explaining some natural or social phenomenon, for in the literature and lore of the Beat Generation and the drug culture engendered by it, this tale of Huncke's injection would resonate powerfully. Real or imagined, it would become a proverbial shot of narcotics heard around the world.

One thing is certain. Over the following weeks Burroughs kept returning to the flat yellow box of syrettes, and when the syrettes ran out, he figured out a way to get more, and Herbert Huncke was a part of that way. Burroughs would soon come to understand exactly what Phil "the Sailor" White meant when he said, "If God made anything better he kept it to himself."

Seven years later, after an untold number of injections, Burroughs would write: "The question is frequently asked: Why does a man become a drug addict? The answer is that he usually does not intend to become an addict. You don't wake up one morning and decide to become a drug addict. It takes at least three months' shooting twice a day to get any habit at all. . . . You become an addict because you do not have strong motivations in any other directions. Junk wins by default."

The notion of drugs entering the life of William S. Burroughs "by default" is all the more remarkable considering his background, because unlike Huncke and the Sailor, here was a man who was Harvard-educated, who could quote Shakespeare at will, and who had ingested the whole of Western literature before knowing the needle. And yet Burroughs would also become a junkie—"a disgrace to his blood"—quite by conscious design.

The facts of his life pointed the way to those morphine syrettes like a series of obviously placed stepping-stones. As surely as the bloodlines of his family had combined the American types of the Yankee inventor and the southern preacher, so would Burroughs blend in a single person the two most loathed types of outsider in postwar American society: the drug addict and the homosexual.

William Seward Burroughs II, born February 5, 1914, in St. Louis, Missouri, to an affluent family—he was the grandson of the inventor of the Burroughs adding machine—always viewed himself as "another species." Some of his earliest childhood memories were colored by nightmares. Although it cannot be confirmed with absolute certainty, it may have been the result of some gross and improper sexual activity of some kind introduced by Mary Evans, a beloved family nursemaid. It was Mary Evans who took the four-year-old Billy on a picnic with her girlfriend, who had a veterinarian boyfriend. Ten years of analysis would not recover the memory of what really happened. According to Barry Miles, "The general consensus among his analysts was that Mary had encouraged Billy to fellate the vet, and that, scared, Billy had bitten the man's penis, causing him to smack Billy on the head."

As a young boy Billy Burroughs was a complete loner, an oddball at the John Burroughs School (no relation) who would stand on the banks of the Riviere des Peres, the open sewer that meandered through his affluent St. Louis neighborhood and emptied into the Mississippi, and watch the turds shooting out into the water ("Hey, looky, someone just did it"). One St. Louis matron likened him during his youth to "a walking corpse." His first literary effort was a ten-page essay written at the age of eight called "The Autobiography of a Wolf," inspired by Ernest Thompson Seton's children's book *Biography of a Grizzly Bear*. "People laughed and said: 'You mean the biography of a wolf,'" Burroughs would recall. "No, I meant the autobiography of a wolf and still do."

At thirteen, William found a book called *You Can't Win*, a turn-of-the-century memoir of a thief and drug addict. In the book was a family of thieves and outlaws called the Johnsons who, despite their criminality, helped those in trouble and lived by their own code of outlaw ethics. William made the Johnsons a part of his own personal mythology—a stark contrast to what he saw as the exclusionary, elitist, hypocritical double-dealing of the right-thinking, blue-eyed aristocrats of the St. Louis establishment—and from that time on, Burroughs would use the paradigm of the book to divide the world between those he saw as "Johnsons" and those he viewed as "Shits."

At the age of sixteen, while at the Los Alamos School in New Mexico, he managed to get his hands on some chloral hydrate and had to be sent to the infirmary. "He claimed he just wanted to see how it worked," the headmaster wrote to his father—a prescient bit of observation. At Harvard, where he kept a ferret in his closet while he took

George Kittredge's celebrated Shakespeare class, Burroughs smoked marijuana and laughed so hard that he had "rolled around on the floor and pissed all over himself."

While the other members of his class formed the officer corps that was leading the United States in the Second World War, William Burroughs became an expert in the extermination of bedbugs. Tenacious little devils they were, too. Amazing survivors. He would knock on the doors of apartments and inquire, "Got any bugs, lady?"

By the time Burroughs began his odyssey into narcotics at the age of thirty-one, he had exhausted every possibility in a search for any kind of viable identity in midcentury America. He accepted the arrival of drugs in his life as the fulfillment of a destiny, becoming an exile in his own country, deliberately seeking out a criminal life as far away from the stately homes of Pershing Avenue in St. Louis and the smug fraternity houses of Harvard as he could possibly get.

The rest of America would have viewed Herbert Huncke as the scum of the earth, but to William S. Burroughs, Huncke and his cronies in drugs and crime appeared as guides to a new underworld. Eventually Burroughs took Huncke to the big, rambling six-room apartment at 419 West 115th Street, where the whole group seemed to live and congregate. The apartment was the home of two women, Joan Vollmer and Edie Kerouac-Parker, who had married Kerouac the year before and was working as a cigarette girl at the Zanzibar. The women were like the den mothers of the place. Edie, who had fled the stultification of her wealthy family in Grosse Pointe, Michigan, was fun-loving and adorable, but it was Joan Vollmer who really intrigued Huncke. She was an attractive young woman with dark, penetrating eyes and a cynical, questioning mind, sexually and intellectually voracious, who read everything she could get her hands on—the sort of girl who liked to sip kümmel while discussing Plato and Kant and who would receive visitors in her bubble bath while reading Proust. "I had never met a girl quite like Joan, and to this day I remember her as one of the most interesting people I have ever known."

Joan had a little girl named Julie from a previous bad marriage and was having a romance of some sort with Bill Burroughs, who was then just about to move into the apartment, into the large room past the bathroom, which puzzled Huncke quite a bit because Bill Burroughs was most definitely a homosexual. Once, in fact, Burroughs had developed an obsessive infatuation with a hustler named Jack Anderson and, smarting from rejection, had taken poultry shears and lopped off the end of the pinkie finger of his left hand in an act of Van Gogh–esque self-mutilation and presented it to his psychiatrist.

Huncke had never known people like this, who constantly rushed about declaiming lines from poems and books and seemed to compulsively reveal their most intimate secrets, fears, and neuroses. They could be dazzling with their wit, merciless in their sarcasm. Huncke was amazed by their interest in him. "My storytelling ability has always stood me in good stead, and even then my experience had been varied and considerably out of the ordinary as far as Bill's friends were concerned. Frankly, I derived a certain pleasure in being candid and open about myself."

So Huncke told them the story of his life, and they started to follow him down to Times Square, to the Angler Bar, where a small underground of drug users mingled with criminals and people of every imaginable sexual persuasion, and they all became the same.

That year, 1945–46, Bill Burroughs's habit would bloom in red florets at the bottom of his droppers like the mushroom clouds over Hiroshima and Nagasaki.

12

You're Buzzing, Baby

Not long after Burroughs's first visit to the apartment on Henry Street, Benzedrine entered the life of Jack Kerouac.

Burroughs and Kerouac were sitting on a bench in Washington Square Park at the time, talking about death. "Well, what do *you* think happens when we die, Bill?" Kerouac wanted to know. "What do I think happens when we die? When you die, well, then, you're *dead*, my boy," Burroughs was saying, "that's what happens when you die," when they saw Huncke passing by.

Burroughs made the introduction. Huncke thought Kerouac looked like "a typical clean-cut American . . . like the Arrow Collar Man, his eyes were flashing all around as he took everything in." Huncke recalled that Burroughs then tried to talk Kerouac into shooting up, but Kerouac was wary. "At that time Jack would smoke a little pot, but he was leery of the needle."

Kerouac may not have been interested in shooting up, but he was very interested in visiting the apartment on Henry Street. Several days later, he found himself walking up the five flights of rickety steps with Burroughs and knocking on the door. A statuesque redhead dressed only in a robe opened it. Kerouac peered in and was intrigued to see her stockings and undergarments all drying on a line across the apartment. Burroughs informed the girl that they had been hanging out with Huncke up on 103rd Street. "We were talking, you see," he sniffed, "and we thought we might pick up a little *junk*."

Vicky Russell found the thin man with the glasses looking for junk quite amusing. She could appreciate a character like Burroughs. The daughter of a Detroit judge, she had run away to New York and was staying at the apartment and using drugs with Huncke and Sailor and Brandenburg. She also happened to be a prostitute, though she kept that particular detail to herself for the time being. At first glance she knew that Burroughs was naive about drugs, despite his request for "junk." Few people in town knew more about drugs than Vicky Russell, in fact, or where and how to get them. She invited them in, but it wasn't drugs that Jack Kerouac seemed interested in. He was trying to pick her up in his own shy, stammering way.

"I have a boyfriend in the navy," she told him.

Kerouac banged his head comically against the wall to demonstrate his profound disappointment regarding this tragic fact. "Aw, it makes no difference," he said.

She looked him over, the dark hair, the football player's build, the sad blue eyes that always looked about to cry. "Well, all right, man," she said, "we'll *pick up*," using the jazz code phrase for getting high on the kind of stuff you could go to jail for.

Kerouac was overjoyed. "Do you pick up, jazz baby?"

"I pick up with Charlie Ventura."

So they all got in a cab and went racing uptown. They were sitting in Benny Goodman's Pick-a-Rib when Vicky Russell produced these Benzedrine tubes. Kerouac had known about Benzedrine but had never tried it. He knew that Charlie Parker and many of the other musicians he admired who were playing at Minton's Playhouse took it, prying the tops off of the little white Benzedrine inhalers and taking out the amphetamine-soaked strip of yellow gauze marked "Poison." Vicky cracked one open, extracted the folded paper, and handed each of them three strips.

"Roll it up into a pill and wash it down with coffee."

The stuff reeked of menthol and made you gag as you swallowed it but they did as they were told.

As the drug began to hit, Kerouac began looking quickly around. Almost immediately he found himself dissociating from his environment. Times Square had completely transmogrified into a place he no longer recognized. It was funny, wild, he had gotten so high, so fast, he began to think he was in another country.

"Are we in St. Petersburg? Are we in St. Petersburg, *Russia?*"

Kerouac knew he was talking nonsense but couldn't stop himself. Talking up a storm was one thing, but this was a kind of hyperloquaciousness he had never known. He couldn't seem to control his mouth.

"Are we in *Chicago? Are we in Kathmandu?*"

Then they got in a cab, all of them riotously high, and Burroughs paid the fare as Vicky took them all around Times Square looking to pick up on some tea. It was a tour unlike any that either of them had ever experienced. She made them cruise up and down each and every block, repeatedly, and at every street corner she would scream, "Stop!"—and go jumping out of the cab, running up to every zoot-suited character on the street—

"Hey, Ray!"

"Hey, Mac!"

"Hey, *ba*-by!"

"*Any*thing, man?"

—before hearing, "Nothing, *ba*-by!"—then clamber back into the car on her high heels, pouting, and order, "Drive on!"

It went on like that until it was obvious there was no tea to be had in all of Manhattan, but now Kerouac was even higher and more entranced by her. Before he knew it he found himself clutching a strap on the F train as it went barreling downtown, pressed tightly up against Burroughs and Vicky Russell, his heart pounding and his mouth dry as cotton balls, the words rushing out of his mouth unable to catch up with the thoughts firing off in his racing brain, digging Burroughs as if he had never really appreciated him before, the two of them looking into each other's eyes, feeling like they were really connecting for the first time as people and friends, digging everything and everyone not only on the train but in the whole world, especially this crazy gone redhead named Vicky—

"My ears are *ringing*," he kept exclaiming, "I don't know where I *am*!"

"You're *buzzing*," she kept laughing. "You're *buzzing*, baby!"

For the next forty-eight hours straight Kerouac had sex with her— "fucked her solid," as he later described it—and when it was over he felt like he had lost ten pounds. He had never been so high in his life and had never felt so spent after it was over, so jangled and lost after the great towering exhilaration of the high. He had been so high, in fact, that he had completely forgotten about his father, Leo, who was sick out in Ozone Park, and thinking about his father after coming down was like the sudden reacquisition of some shattering knowledge.

But during the escapade, Kerouac had noticed something about Times Square. He had felt something about all the people passing by. It was an observation that would resonate more and more during subsequent Benzedrine adventures in and around Times Square. As he later described it in his first novel, *The Town and the City*, the people he had observed were

> the same people he had seen in so many other American cities on similar streets: soldiers, sailors, the panhandlers and drifters, the zoot-suiters, the hoodlums, the young men who washed dishes in cafeterias from coast to coast, the hitchhikers, the hustlers, the drunks, the battered lonely young Negroes, the twinkling little Chinese, the dark Puerto Ricans, and the varieties of dungareed young Americans in leather jackets who were seamen and mechanics and garagemen everywhere. . . . All the cats and characters, all the spicks and spades, Harlem-drowned, street-drunk and slain, crowded together, streaming back and forth, looking for something, waiting for something, forever moving around.

There was a quality of furtiveness about them, Kerouac realized, something lost and rootless. He had perceived a quality in the people that he had long felt deep inside himself, and the experience of the drug he had taken had only seemed to heighten the perception. As depleted as he felt after these Benzedrine adventures, he couldn't get his impressions down in the little five-cent notebook he always carried in his shirt pocket fast enough.

13

And the Hippos
Were Boiled in Their Tanks

1.

As a bespectacled nineteen-year-old Columbia student caught in the throes of hard questions about his sexuality and purpose in life, Allen Ginsberg pursued experience with the same unbridled curiosity that had sent him chasing after the strains of Brahms Piano Trio no. 1 filtering down the hall of the Union Theological Seminary, when he followed the music to its source and knocked on a door and found himself face to face with a young man named Lucien Carr.

Lucien Carr was a very different kind of person than anyone Ginsberg had ever known. He was a born rebel and iconoclast, a strikingly handsome, green-eyed golden boy from a blue-blooded St. Louis family—wild, well-read, dashing, and quite drunken. Allen was immediately smitten by him, and they began engaging in lengthy discussions about literature. Carr was obsessed with something he referred to as the "New Vision," which he derived from his reading of moral revolutionary poets like Rimbaud and Baudelaire. The New Vision put forth the notion that self-expression was the highest goal of art, and that the writer experiences a supreme reality through what Rimbaud called *le dérèglement de tous les sens*—"a derangement of all the senses"—rather than be limited by strictures of language or morality or any styles of established literature. Lucien told Allen that he was also discussing the New Vision with another Columbia student named

Jack Kerouac, an ex–football player and seaman who wanted to be a great writer, and Allen went looking for "this romantic seaman who wrote poem books."

The two most dynamic forces that had shaped Allen Ginsberg's emotional life before getting a scholarship to Columbia were his mother's mental illness and his increasing awareness of his own homosexuality. Naomi Ginsberg's illness had begun when he was young but had steadily worsened through his teenage years in Paterson, New Jersey. The experience of taking her to Greystone had been the most harrowing of his life and had left his family emotionally exhausted. As homosexuality was widely considered to be a form of mental illness at the time, it isn't hard to understand Ginsberg's thorny, tormented, and conflicted feelings about it, which would reach critical mass during his years at Columbia. As Huncke observed, "Ginsberg was going through a stage where he didn't know whether he was heterosexual, homosexual, autoerotic or what."

As for Jack Kerouac, who claimed to remember everything he'd ever heard, he was only four and living over an ancient cemetery in a house on Beaulieu Street in Lowell, Massachusetts, when his older brother, Gerard, died of rheumatic fever after a two-year illness. During his illness Gerard had experienced visions of the next world and had grown increasingly tranquil before his death, progressing into martyred Catholic sainthood in the eyes of the family. Jack had experienced swarms of white dots in his vision when Gerard passed, which unleashed the profound gloominess and guilt over his brother's death that he would carry inside for the rest of his life. Thus began his life-long habit of looking up into the night sky for solace and wondering where the universe ended.

In their very first conversation, Ginsberg shared with Kerouac that as a boy, he, too, would feel a ghostly presence and wonder where the universe ended, and it was then that Allen realized that "my soul and his were akin, and that if I actually confessed the secret tenderness of my soul he would understand nakedly who I was."

Although they did not yet have the language to express it, Allen and Jack were talking about what they would later come to understand as cosmic consciousness, and it was this spiritual connection that formed the underpinning of their relationship from the beginning.

Few were more disposed to talk about ghostly presences or the infinitude of the universe or "New Visions" than Jack Kerouac, a man for whom, in the words of biographer Gerald Nicosia, "nothing was secure, not even his own name." A curious blend of deeply sensitive poet and football-playing all-American boy, Kerouac had watched his father's printing business fail during the Depression. It was the beginning of a long period of poverty during which he witnessed the complete breakdown of his father and the disintegration of his family. At Horace Mann, where he went on a scholarship, Kerouac was as much of an outsider as Burroughs was at Harvard, reading Whitman off by himself during his graduation because he was too poor to afford a suit. After breaking his leg playing football at Columbia, he joined the merchant marine and set off on a deadly ice-ridden run to Murmansk on the S.S. *Dorchester.* By the time he returned he was deeply immersed in Thomas Wolfe and the stories of Jack London; he wanted to write "noble words" and never returned to the gridiron. From his first day at navy boot camp at Newport, Kerouac was bored, irascible, and insubordinate. When an officer caught him smoking and slapped the cigarette out of his mouth, Kerouac hauled off and slugged him. "I'm not a warrior, I'm a scholar," he explained to the naval psychologists after his arrest. When asked if he would like to join the elite submarine corps, he responded, "I'm not a frogman, just a frog"—a droll reference to his Canuck ancestry. The navy classified him as a Section Eight and released him to pursue a very different calling.

Lucien Carr's impact on Kerouac was immediate. He began reading Rimbaud, Baudelaire, de Lautréamont. One day in February of 1944, an acquaintance of Carr's from St. Louis showed up at the apartment on 115th Street looking for Kerouac. William Burroughs had been working as a bartender and for a detective agency serving papers, and had come seeking information about shipping out to sea. Kerouac found Burroughs "inscrutable because ordinary-looking . . . like a shy bank clerk with a patrician thin-lipped cold blue-lipped face, his eyes saying nothing behind steel rims and glass," and they soon began developing a friendship. The whole group of them—Carr, Ginsberg, Kerouac, Burroughs, Edie Parker, Carr's beautiful girlfriend, Celine Young, and Joan Vollmer—were soon to be found drinking in the heavy oak booths of the West End, arguing passionately about literature, debating the fate of the earth, listening to jazz, and watching the sun come up; they all fell in love with each other in one form or another. Kerouac later recalled this period nostalgically in *Vanity of Duluoz*, all of it cast against "the war, the second front (which occurred just before this time), the poetry, the soft city evenings, the cries of "Rimbaud! New Vision!," the great Gotterdammerung, the love song 'You Always Hurt the One You Love,' the smell of beers and smoke in the West End Bar, the evenings we spent on the grass by the Hudson River on Riverside Drive at 116th Street watching the rose west, watching the freighters slide by."

That their bonding took place as the war raged only seemed to lend their ideas and pursuits a critical valence. During that initial conjunction of the group, as the conceptual groundwork for their use of drugs was being laid, the relationships that formed between them were supercharged with a special kind of electricity and urgency. Everything walked hand in hand with their experience of literature and poetry, with the New Vision.

As Rimbaud was calling them to "plunge to the bottom of the gulf," in that summer of 1944 the group plunged straight to hell. Lucien Carr had been followed to New York by another acquaintance of Burroughs from St. Louis, a tall, red-bearded teacher named David Kammerer who was obsessed with him and had dogged his path since his youth. Lucien had a kind of stoical acceptance of Kammerer's presence and the inconvenience of his obsession until it mounted in intensity and broke loose after a night of heavy drinking at the West End, when Kammerer threatened to assault him sexually on the narrow strip of grass between the West Side Highway and the river. In the struggle that followed, Carr whipped out his Boy Scout knife and plunged it twice into Kammerer's chest. Then he bound Kammerer's hands and feet with shoelaces, weighed his dead body down with stones, and pushed it down into the dark waters of the Hudson. He went to find Kerouac, and together they dropped the knife into a sewer and buried Kammerer's glasses in Morningside Heights.

So this is how David Kammerer ends, Burroughs thought after they told him what had happened, advising Lucien to find himself a good attorney. After Lucien turned himself in, Kerouac was arrested and held as a material witness. In the trial that followed, the newspapers called it an "honor slaying" and made much of the group's connection to literature. Lucien was sentenced to two years at Elmira Reformatory.

The episode only enhanced the growing social alienation they all felt. Columbia was scandalized, and all of their parents were duly mortified. Another layer of restraint seemed removed from them, submerged along with Kammerer's body in the brackish waters of the Hudson. Ginsberg would look back on the episode and see it as a turning point when he became more bold and honest about transgressive ideas and behaviors like drug-taking and homosexuality.

"Jack, you know I love you, and I want to sleep with you, and I really like men," he revealed to his friend.

"Ooooh, no," groaned Kerouac.

Fuck the Jews, Ginsberg wrote with his finger on his dirty window after Kerouac was discovered sleeping in his room in Hamilton Hall by the Irish cleaning woman. Nothing sexual had happened, but Kerouac was banished from the campus.

Kerouac felt that the entire affair was a demonstration of the truth of the New Vision. He renewed his vow to become a great writer but began to understand that in order to do so he'd have to break free from the rules he'd been bred to accept. He and Burroughs attempted to write a novel based on the affair entitled *And the Hippos Were Boiled in Their Tanks*, after a line that Burroughs had heard on the radio in a story about a fire that had broken out in a traveling circus. The novel was rejected, putting Burroughs off writing and causing him to turn his attention elsewhere—toward drugs, which would break out in their lives quite like the fire in that traveling circus.

2.

Having decided that Burroughs was "a great seeker of cities and souls," Kerouac and Ginsberg had, by the time of his introduction to the needle, already come to see him as a kind of mentor and considered themselves his apprentices. Burroughs was fearless, and yet, as detached as he could seem, he was also capable of great compassion. He seemed to make no moral judgments about things, only personal observations, and prided himself on his dispassionate ability to analyze the "facts." On a visit to Burroughs's apartment with Kerouac, Ginsberg recorded the titles of books in his collection: Rimbaud's *A Season in Hell,* Kafka's *The Castle,* Melville's *Moby Dick,* Cocteau's *Opium,* Céline's *Journey to the End of the Night,* Yeat's *A Vision,* Walter Van Tilburg Clark's *The Ox-Bow Incident,* volumes of Blake, Baudelaire, Gogol, Chandler, O'Hara, Hart Crane, Wilhelm Reich's *The Cancer Biopathy,* Korzybski's *Science and Sanity.*

"Burroughs was primarily a master of gnostic curiosities and in his approach to the mind he had the same Yankee practicality and inquisitiveness as his grandfather who had invented an adding machine," as Ginsberg noted. At the end of the visit, Burroughs had handed Kerouac his two-volume edition of Oswald Spengler's *The Decline of the West* with the words, "Edify yer mind, my boy, with the grand actuality of fact."

As they followed Burroughs into a period that Kerouac would later call in *Vanity of Duluoz* "a year of low, evil decadence," some of the books on Burroughs's shelf came to shape their whole approach to drug experimentation. Indeed, the whole notion of how drugs could be used to expand experience and consciousness—a concept that would form the entire countercultural paradigm for the use of drugs over the next quarter of a century in America—is traceable to books on Burroughs's shelves and to these three individuals at precisely this moment in their lives. It was a hodgepodge of influences. From Cocteau and others they took the scientific, personal approach to drugs and their effects, which involved extensive note-taking and discussion, and the acceptance of drug-taking as a legitimate avenue of self-expression. From French romantic writers and poets like Gautier, de Nerval, Victor Hugo, Honoré de Balzac, and others in the Paris of the 1840s, they adopted the idea of a society, the famous Club des Hashischins, revolving around the ingestion of hashish and its effect on their creative sensibilities. From Spengler, they took the idea of the ineluctable decay and demise of Western civilization in the grand cycle of history. In the existential emptiness of the Spenglerian world of postwar corruption and darkness, they came to see drugs as a potent method of cleansing the palate so that the world could be experienced anew. From Rimbaud, they appropriated the notion of "seasons" during which they would all go through a similar phase of development and experience, along with his "derangement of the senses"—after all, what could possibly be more deranging than the effects of mind-altering drugs? But perhaps no concept was more important than Blake's "the eye altering alters all": the notion that a change in consciousness was not only a means to an end but an end unto itself. As Allen Ginsberg would always emphasize, this was serious business—"the ancient heavenly connection," as he would later call it in *Howl*—not some frivolous party drug scene.

"It was aesthetic, more of a curiosity, as to the nature, the texture, of consciousness itself; and how that could be altered from the point of view of the Blake phrase, 'The eye altering alters all'—almost like an instant experience of Einsteinian relativity, that the measuring instrument would determine the appearance of the external universe, so that as the brain changes, the appearance of things change. It's a very Buddhist notion, actually, that the external universe is dependent on the perceiver."

The next important element in this equation of drugs was the idea of "kicks"—a word that would take on as many meanings in the post-nuclear underground as *cool* or *hip*. Today, along with "an instance of kicking," the *Oxford English Dictionary* defines it as "a thrill of pleasurable excitement" and cites *stimulation, tingle, frisson, charge, buzz,* and *high* as synonyms. Another definition is "the strong stimulating effect of alcohol or a drug." In the existential emptiness of the Spenglerian world, this little group of writers would come to view kicks as a potent and reliable substitute for the failed moralities and aesthetics they would reject. In the cultural etymology of kicks, nothing would have more of an effect on creating the drug connotations of this word than these individuals and how their ideas and lifestyle would resonate in the literature they produced.

As Allen Ginsberg found his fascination with mind-altering substances growing, he began his search for information about them. "There was really no place to even go to get any reliable information on drugs and their effects at the time," he noted. "The only place to look was in the foreign literature, in literary terms. But in terms of popular information? In America, there was nothing. It was really quite amazing."

The more personal experiences Ginsberg had with drugs, the more he realized how completely ignorant people really were about them.

When they had a narcotics bust, they would say that they had just seized drugs or narcotics, and there wouldn't be any account in the newspapers as to whether it was marijuana or cocaine or heroin. They obfuscated everything, and even the news reporters were snowed and just reported that dope was seized. So the common person, like my father or Lionel Trilling, whether a sophisticated intellectual or a high school teacher, thought that all narcotics were the same, and that all were habit-forming, and that all users would become dope fiends.

At that time one of Ginsberg's most important discoveries was the most obvious one: that all of the different substances had their own different effects. Of course he had heard about marijuana, but he could never seem to find any . . .

"I didn't know what it was. I heard it got you high. I had already had Benzedrine; I had already had morphine and heroin before I had grass. . . . I had found those quite delightful, taken in moderation, so I figured that grass must be awfully nice too, and not habit-forming, like everybody told me."

As Kerouac later described Ginsberg in *The Town and the City,* he was "an eager, intense, sharply intelligent boy of Russian-Jewish parentage who rushed around New York in a perpetual sweat of emotional activity, back and forth in the streets, from friend to friend, room to room, apartment to apartment. . . . He brimmed and flooded over day and night with a thousand different thoughts and conversations and small horrors, delights, perplexities, deities, discoveries, ecstasies, fears."

And now cannabis was about to be added to this mix. Ginsberg had just finished Rimbaud's *A Season in Hell* with its famous line "Now is the time of the hashischins" when he found a Puerto Rican sailor down on 105th Street who sold him twenty dollars' worth of grass—"and so I had the honor of bringing the first box of grass back to Burroughs and Kerouac and my circle of friends at Columbia."

3.

The first time he was ever really high on marijuana, Ginsberg was driving in a car with Walter Adams, a friend from Columbia, on the Upper

West Side. He began to realize how high he was because the streets and people were mutating into some vast robot megalopolis that seemed to be inside a great firmament of brilliant blinking lights, and he began to feel that he was floating in a boundless universe.

At first he was frightened by how fast and radical the changes were in his perception of space and time. He felt hopelessly lost in a place he knew well, and just parking the car seemed a titanic trial. When they finally got the car squared away and walked into an old-fashioned ice cream parlor at the corner of 91st and Broadway, they sat down at a table and he ordered a black-and-white sundae. When it suddenly appeared—"this great mound of snowlike ice cream but absolutely sweet and pure and clean and bright"—he couldn't quite believe his eyes, but as good as it looked, that was nothing compared to what happened when he took his spoon and put some into his mouth. The hot chocolate syrup had become a chewy candy in the ice-cold vanilla cream, and each and every delicious molecule of it seemed to detonate on his tongue.

"What an amazing taste it had! I don't think I ever truly appreciated what an outstanding invention a black and white ice cream sundae was—and how cheap it was, too!"

And then, as Ginsberg perceived the infinitude of the blue sky and looked outside the plate-glass window and saw the river of life flowing past—the people walking dogs, smiling, laughing, weeping—he experienced a moment of profound synchronicity and well-being, "everything just perfectly joyful and gay."

Marijuana had been way more fun and interesting than Ginsberg had ever expected, and he began to think about how he might apply the high to other experiences. At the time he was taking an art course at Columbia, and he became curious to see what would happen if he experienced the paintings of Paul Cézanne at the Metropolitan Museum of Art in that state of mind, so he arranged a special viewing and made sure to smoke a few "sticks" in the garden before going in. As he stood staring at the paintings, he noticed that he began to understand the artist's use of space and color in a way he hadn't before—the way the warmer colors seemed to advance toward him and the cooler colors receded. It was a new kind of funhouse "optical consciousness" that Ginsberg and Kerouac would later call "eyeball kicks."

"I would later come to understand it in Buddhist terms as *maya*, maya sensory space. Cézanne was very conscious of that optical space, and marijuana had sensitized me to that precise awareness or mindfulness, and so I'll always thank it for leading me to the paintings, into modern optics—the same eyeball experiments that led into cubism, or through Paul Klee into the magic squares."

These early experiences were as momentous and life-altering for Ginsberg as Mezz Mezzrow's first experience with marijuana had been as he played jazz in that Indiana Harbor roadhouse. For Ginsberg, it was "only the beginning of the exploration of the senses, the first scratchings of the Buddhist meditation exercises I would learn; the actual observation of how the senses operate, and the exploration of the wall of the senses of sight, smell, sound, taste, touch and mind."

One can easily recognize in Ginsberg's experience of that black-and-white sundae a foretaste of the gastronomic delight that millions would later discover after smoking and getting "the munchies" and reaching for that pint of ice cream, or, in his notion of "eyeball kicks," the aesthetic foundations for the psychedelic light shows of the sixties. But of course all of that was decades away. Very few people smoked marijuana at the time, and when Ginsberg would get high and walk around the Columbia campus by himself, he was always acutely and uncomfortably aware of being the only one in that population of twenty thousand "intelligent scholars" who happened to be in that particular state of consciousness. In addition to the "fear and trembling that would come just from the sense of being in awe of the great enormity I was in, just in smoking it and altering the mind and being in the universe," he began to understand the "just plain paranoia that was connected to exploring the illegal unknown. . . . Remember, there was always the association of what society was laying on you, the notion of the 'dope fiend.' If you altered consciousness, there was something wrong with you, and I would often find myself pondering the official terminologies and implications of just what it meant to be a fiend, which is a very strange, horrific, almost science fiction distortion of reality, wicked and diabolically cruel."

By far what disturbed Ginsberg the most was realizing how this substance that could expand his awareness and actually impart something educational had been so demonized by "this giant official government propaganda machine called the Federal Bureau of Narcotics, because you found it in the media everywhere you looked."

But as intensely aware as Ginsberg was of the kind of trouble he could get into, that wasn't about to stop him—"what it had to offer far outweighed the dangers, it seemed"—and that was when he and Burroughs and Kerouac began putting Benzedrine in their chewing gum, and smoking marijuana when they could get it, and going down to Times Square just to see what would happen.

4·

It was truly an odd and yet compelling destiny. As the war was ending and twelve million men and women in the US military were demobilizing and returning to their lives, Burroughs, Ginsberg, and Kerouac were perceiving and digesting the meaning and magnitude of the dropping of the atomic bomb and the uneasy peace that followed as they experimented with illicit drug-induced altered states of consciousness. They would station themselves underneath the great Pokerino sign, sublimely stoned, Ginsberg in a belted raincoat and a paisley scarf, Kerouac in his seaman's jacket, and Burroughs in his homburg, always looking like a bank president in his three-piece suit. The sign would cast a pulsing neon glow over the the multitiered labyrinth of elevated platforms and the arcades and the chop suey joints and the tropical fruit drink stands and the multitudes of people and cars, and Times Square would transmogrify before their eyes into what seemed a giant surreal room hanging in the space of a dying postnuclear world.

"All the characters that were asked to leave Bickfords and Horn and Hardart were falling into Pokerino; junkies from Dixon's on 8th Avenue, also," wrote Ginsberg in "A Version of the Apocalypse," his 1945 prose sketch of Times Square.

> Spades of all kinds; adorable sharpies and strange gargoyles, and also some pretty mad looking spade chicks were cutting in and falling into combinations around the Jukebox. Teaheads from everywhere, hustlers with pimples, queens with pompadours, lushes with green faces, fat dicks with clubs, cherubs with sychophants, wolves with adenoids, faces with blotches, noses with holes, eyebrows with

spangles, old men with the horrors, bums with the stumbles and sometimes squares with curiosity or just passing through to catch a bus; and not only these few but the unprotected, the unloved, the unkempt, the inept and sick. . . . Myself I am considered affected by the atmosphere—the wild, tremendous Jukebox, the weird overbrilliant lighting, the hundreds of slot machines that line the wall, the beat, absolutely beat characters but the plain fact is that it is not a matter of aesthetic taste. For Hipster or Square, aesthete or philistine, or anything, so to speak, mankind is as one in the Pokerino.

As Ginsberg concluded, "The time of grand molecular come-down is coming. Pokerino is a radioactive Rose."

Just as marijuana and amphetamine could enhance the neon glow over Times Square and stoke the paranoia of their apocalyptic perceptions to a ragged edge and make the little bugs that one can sometimes experience crawling under the skin during an amphetamine jag seem like the "enamel particles" and "little white hairs" of radiation poisoning, so could those substances deepen the religiosity of those perceptions. If the Pokerino sign in Times Square seemed radioactive when they were high, it was also supernal, holy. The junkies and prostitutes became "angels" to Ginsberg, and Kerouac began his search to "see God's face" as the next phase of the New Vision. All of them became "naked angels" in their search for "the Supreme Reality." It was at this point that they began referring to themselves as "ghosts"— "Hello, drunken ghost," or, "What have you got to say tonight, old phantom?" These shared visions of Times Square became spiritual tenets and artistic touchstones that would profoundly affect their lives and literature.

Ginsberg obviously found Benzedrine very interesting but quickly recognized the danger of abusing the substance. "From the beginning I was leery of amphetamines because after the sixth, seventh hour, there would be complete mental chaos. I quickly found out that I could hardly write under them because your mind got so tangled— those were the 'stanzas of gibberish' I later referred to in *Howl*—but Kerouac would find that he could write *whole novels* on them."

Sometimes their Benzedrine marathons would go on for days, the whole group of them gathered on a bed, wired and dry-mouthed but talking endlessly, the stream of consciousness leading them into the long improvisations that became routines.

Nobody took more Benzedrine than Joan Vollmer, who soon began to develop hollow eyes and sores on her body; nobody knew more about the "little white hairs that appear out of the eyes and nose and mouth and copulate like corkscrews in the middle of the air" than Joan, for she began to see them all over the place. She could hear people talking about her clear across the street, she claimed, not to mention from the apartment downstairs, where an old couple lived. Joan kept insisting that she heard the woman calling her a whore and the man calling them all a bunch of dope fiends and threatening to call the police on the whole group. One day Ginsberg found her hysterical after she started hearing the harrowing screams of the woman being murdered.

"Kerouac and I ran downstairs to rescue the lady and banged on the door and it turned out that nobody was home. She was experiencing Benzedrine hallucinations, and when we told her, she understood that it was a hallucination, finally. But she was the earliest case of amphetamine psychosis I ever saw."

As the French romanticists had believed in art for art's sake, the New Vision as Kerouac saw it clearly embraced the notion of drugs for art's sake. He began taking more and more Benzedrine, wandering around the city for days at a time, taking nonstop notes for his first novel, a tapestry that would contrast this life he had come to know in the city with the life of his boyhood in Lowell. There was never any doubt in his mind that the purpose of these substances was to help him understand people and himself and to see how he might use them for his writing. "Benny has made me see a lot," he wrote Ginsberg in November of 1945. "The process of intensifying awareness naturally leads to an overflow of old notions, and violà, new material wells up like water following its proper level, and makes itself evident at the brim of consciousness. Brand new water!"

Kerouac watched his hair fall out and his body turn flabby, but that didn't deter him. Plunging ever deeper into the new jazz, he also believed that the more he wired himself up on Benzedrine, the more he would be able to understand the new bebop—as if pushing his mind and nervous system to the absolute farthest limit would somehow bring him in tune with the essence of the music. His friend Seymour Wyse's brother was an editor at *DownBeat,* so he always knew what was going on in the jazz scene. It was the period of Kerouac's life when his relationship with the music and its folk tradition became sacramental.

"Night after night we'd go to the clubs," remembered Edie Kerouac-Parker. "All the musicians would be playing downtown in the hotels with the big bands, and then after midnight come up to Minton's, the little bar in the basement of the Cecil Hotel on 117th Street. It was just the beginning of bebop. Jazz was becoming a living language, we'd never heard music like that. Pot was very hard to find—who had it and who could afford it?—the guys who had it would come up from the South. All it ever did was choke me and make me want to eat, but Jack, my God, he loved it. Sometimes Billie Holiday would sit at the table with us and Jack would be glowing because her song 'I Cover the Waterfront' was his favorite. The musicians would be playing whatever came into their minds. It was almost like a feeling that was speaking to a part that was already deep inside you, the drums and rhythms. The place was filled with smoke, and there would be Jack, stoned on pot, his eyes closed, just completely gone into the music, and then he would open his eyes and look at me. He had the saddest, most beautiful blue eyes . . ."

At first Kerouac found it hard to let go of swing and was resistant to the new jazz, but he was soon deeply affected by the technical virtuosity of the musicians, the emotional textures of their music, their lives and private "kicks," and the experience of meeting black people and coming into contact with the richness and humanity of black culture. He was fascinated by how everything happened in the moment, by the infinite possibilities of pure improvisation, and by how the saxophone could seem like a human voice. It was only the beginning of his yearning to write a new kind of prose exactly the way a musician played jazz on his instrument—just like Charlie Parker.

14

Parker's Mood

Heroin was right there with Charlie Parker during those visionary mornings with Dizzy Gillespie and Thelonious Monk and Kenny Clarke in the basement of Minton's, as bebop was being invented moment to moment in jam sessions with the volatile unpredictability and impulsion of neurons firing back and forth across some new musical synapse. The habit followed him down to 52nd Street when Bird and Dizzy Gillespie moved to the Three Deuces to showcase the music for the first time and perform tunes like "Salt Peanuts," "Groovin' High," and "Dizzy Atmosphere." At the height of the run, Bird arrived late one night and locked himself in the john to fix, and Dizzy angrily told Max Roach that Bird was in the john with a needle in his arm—"Do you know what that muthafucka is doing? He's in there shooting shit"—and the microphone picked it up and everybody in the club heard him say it. The habit would soon enough follow him out to Los Angeles, with momentous consequences.

At the end of 1945, Bird went into the studio for Savoy with Gillespie and cut two blues, "Billie's Bounce" and "Now's the Time," along with "Ko Ko," a song as audaciously original and revolutionary as Louis Armstrong's "West End Blues" had been in 1928. The tremendous scrambling velocity and feel of his choruses on "Ko Ko" were seminal and would point the way for the entire evolution of jazz in the postwar era. By this time it was evident that Bird was an explosively gifted musician—the purest and most dazzling kind of artist. Much would be written about his incredible melodic lines, the complex rhythms and chords, his shadings, embellishments, phrasing, the light tone with almost no vibrato, the way he broke up time, his blues edge, how hard and fast he could play. Perhaps Dizzy put it best when he said that Bird could "run snakes" on his horn, which somehow seemed to say it all—there was just nobody like him. Later on Bird was asked how he was able to accomplish what he did during this period. "I lit my fire, I greased my skillet, and I cooked," was his simple response. Yes indeed, he cooked.

Bebop flouted convention and provoked instantaneous controversy everywhere, from the jazz establishment to police departments, and it seemed that Bird was always at the center of the storm. Servicemen taunted him; vice squad cops began tailing him; women flocked to him. Bird loved women and sex as much as music and drugs, and he could look out on the floor and provide a witty accompaniment to a woman as she sashayed to the powder room. It was uncanny how he could capture the attitudes, the expressions, the very emotions of women in the little phrases he blew—and the women responded as if being rendered by a great painter.

As Bird took up with Doris Sydnor, he quickly came to symbolize everything about 52nd Street that the vice cops loathed: drug use and integration. At the end of 1945 the local authorities cracked down hard on the street, shuttering clubs under the same pretext used to close down Storyville in New Orleans back in 1917: the corruption of American servicemen by sex, drugs, and jazz. As the clubs closed, musicians began scrambling, and Dizzy Gillespie struck a deal to bring his sextet out to Billy Berg's in Los Angeles. As Dizzy saw it, the engagement had the potential to be a groundbreaking showcase for the music, as well as for the genius of Charlie Parker.

As reefer was associated with swing, heroin marked the transition from swing to bop, and nobody was more upset by the arrival of dope on the scene than John Birks Gillespie, determined as he was to push jazz ahead creatively and dedicated from the very beginning to ensuring that the music attained its rightful place in the pantheon of American and international culture. Dizzy was also determined to move the country ahead racially as well as musically, and he was resolute in his deep conviction that jazz could play a key role in the racial progression of American society during the postwar era. Like Louis Armstrong, Gillespie was a man of great largesse and a congenial smoker of marijuana who frowned upon the use of hard drugs.

"Everybody at one time or another smoked marijuana," Gillespie recalled of the time,

> and then coke became popular—I tried that, too; but I never had any
> desire to use hard drugs, a drug that made you a slave. I always shied
> away from anything powerful enough to make me dependent, be-
> cause realizing that everything here comes and goes, why be depen-
> dent on one thing? I never even tried hard drugs. One time on 52nd
> Street a guy gave me something I took for coke and it turned out to
> be horse. I snorted it and puked up in the street. If I had found him,
> he would have suffered bodily harm, but I never saw him again. . . .
>
> The whole thing is that, like most Americans, we were really igno-
> rant about the helpful or deleterious effects of drugs on human be-
> ings, and before we concluded anything about drugs or used them
> and got snagged, we should have understood what we were doing.
> That holds true for the individuals or the society, I believe. The drug
> scourge of the forties victimized black musicians first, before hitting
> any other large segment of the black community.

No two musicians in the history of jazz ever played together more successfully, or significantly, than Bird and Diz—"like putting whipped cream on Jell-O . . . like putting salt on rice," is how Gillespie characterized it. Diz considered Bird "the architect of the new sound. Most of what I did was in the area of harmony and rhythm." But he stayed well away from Bird's lifestyle.

> We were pretty close philosophically, but my closeness to him was
> mostly musical. I didn't hang out with the same people he hung out
> with. I didn't do the same things he did, so I wasn't actually one of
> the crowd, one of the "deep in the hat" boys. Countless thousands
> of guys that were using shit were probably closer to his other life.
> Yard always denied the fact that he was using shit to me. I used to
> say, "Motherfucka, you're high." He'd be nodding. "Man, when you
> gonna come down off that shit?" "Oh, Diz," he'd say, "you know
> I ain't using nothing." Nodding all at the same time and talking
> about, "Man, I don't use no shit." And I never saw him use anything.
> All I saw were the symptoms.

In Los Angeles, the symptoms became worse than ever. Never had Bird seemed so dependent on the drug to Dizzy, and never had he seemed so close to cracking up. Completely snared in the vise of addiction, Bird was now in a city where he had no connections, where the drug was scarce and the cost high. There was a small group of musicians already attuned to the music on the West Coast, a beachhead that included Howard McGhee, Dexter Gordon, Art Pepper, Hampton Hawes, and Wardell Gray, but for the most part bebop left the audiences at Billy Berg's cold. The engagement did not go well, but that was a minor sideshow compared to Bird's larger problem. Eventually he found a heroin dealer named Emry Byrd, known along Central Avenue as Moose the Mooche—a paraplegic in a wheelchair. Bird got so strung out that Diz had to finally drop him and hire Lucky Thompson; he gave Bird the fare to get back to New York, but Bird spent the money on dope. Nevertheless Bird still managed to make history out on the West Coast. He arrived late for Norman Granz's "Jazz at the Philharmonic Concert" on January 28, 1946, because he had been scouring the town for drugs. Having found what he was looking for, he showed up twenty-eight choruses into "Sweet Georgia Brown" and stepped on the stage to play a chorus that brought the music to a whole new level and the audience to its feet, then he stayed on to play alongside Lester Young on "Oh, Lady Be Good." When Granz later released a record of the performance, Bird's choruses astounded musicians and jazz fans everywhere. Everything he played that night would become part of the basic syntax of modern jazz.

Bird then came up with a master plan to solve the problem of his unsteady supply of heroin. For his first solo recording session for Dial, while driving to the studio, he composed a piece dedicated to Moose the Mooche and planned to sign over half the royalties to the dealer. The tune was based on "I Got Rhythm" and was the first one recorded on March 28, 1946, at Radio Recorders alongside the teenaged Miles Davis on trumpet, Dodo Marmarosa on piano, Vic McMillan on bass, and Roy Porter on drums. That crucial bit of business taken care of, Bird went on to record "Yardbird Suite" and "A Night in Tunisia," during which he blew a solo that floored everybody in the room. He also recorded a song called "Ornithology"—a remarkably apt and witty title considering how the growing cult around him studied virtually everything he did.

All of the songs recorded that day would become bebop classics. Bird had been punctual, at his very best. Then everything changed and all it took was a single event: Moose the Mooche was busted in April and dispatched to San Quentin, wheelchair and all. The panic was on. Bird was not only broke but also strung out in a way he had never experienced before. When he couldn't get heroin he took virtually everything else he could get his hands on—goofballs, bennies, reefer—to stave off the horrible symptoms of withdrawal, particularly large quantities of whiskey, which only wreaked more havoc on him. He was soon living in the garage of trumpeter Howard McGhee, desperate for money. It was McGhee who finally went to Ross Russell of Dial on Bird's behalf and begged him for another recording date for Bird. As McGhee remembered, the problem was that "Bird couldn't find nobody with no shit, and he was trying to make it off alcohol." It was a recipe for disaster, and for a mythic recording session.

"He couldn't get started on anything," recalled the writer Elliot Grennard, who was present at the session at J. P. McGregor Studio in Hollywood on Monday, July 29, 1946. "They did two tunes, 'Bebop' and 'Lover Man.' He couldn't tune up. He could just fit the mouthpiece. 'Oh, Christ,' Russell said, 'I've just lost a thousand bucks tonight.' He kept recording the three other guys in the hopes of salvaging something out of the session. Parker curled up and took a nap. . . . He was staring into space."

It was the song "Lover Man," written by Roger "Ram" Ramirez and recorded by Billie Holiday in October of 1944, that would do more than any other to create the legend of Charlie Parker as both a genius and a righteous dope fiend. Somebody gave him a handful of Benzedrine tablets and Bird swallowed them like candy, thinking they were goofballs that would help ease his misery. Already at the breaking point, the pills put him over the edge, causing his limbs and muscles to jerk and twitch uncontrollably, but he played the song with everything he had left inside of him, and you can hear him breaking up inside. As Gary Giddins so eloquently describes it, "He founders in shallow waters, tossing in dilatory confusion as though the shore were always one stroke beyond his grasp."

There are those who thought Russell should never have proceeded with the session in the first place—the humane thing to do would have been to take Bird right to the hospital. Russell had a legitimate financial investment in the recording session, but he was also no doubt motivated by the sentiment of jazz fans who were already well aware of Bird's perilous lifestyle and obsessed with his appearances and recordings. "Catch him before he dies" is what people always said about Edgar, the character that John Clellon Holmes based partly on Bird in his novel *The Horn*. As Elliot Grennard expressed it in a story based on the "Lover Man" session called "Sparrow's Last Jump," "Yeah, Sparrow's last recording would sure make a collector's item. One buck, plus tax, is cheap enough for a record of a guy going nuts."

Bird tried to cut another song, "The Gypsy," but could go no further and crumpled into a chair. That night at the Cecil Hotel he came stumbling down through the lobby twice without his pants on and fell asleep holding a lit cigarette, which started a fire. The LAPD arrived along with the firemen at the hotel and dragged Bird away in handcuffs, but not before blackjacking him over the head.

Five days after the arrest, Ross Russell found Bird handcuffed to an iron cot in the psychiatric ward of the LA County jail. It was fortunate that Russell managed to have his sanity hearing transferred from the scheduled court to that of Stanley Mosk, a more liberal judge on the municipal bench in LA who later became attorney general of California. After Howard McGhee and Russell appeared on Bird's behalf, Mosk had him committed him to Camarillo State Mental Hospital.

According to Howard McGhee, at Camarillo Bird was treated by a Viennese psychiatrist, and apparently he had a good time putting the man on. "Bird used to tell me, 'I got this cat goin' around in circles . . . 'I know more than he does.'" He was kept in the institution for six months for his "cure." "He was out there," McGhee continued, "and they brought him down off the drugs, gradually brought him down, so when he came out, he didn't need it, but his capacity, his mind was the same."

A single story that McGhee tells about what happened the first night they opened the Hi-De-Ho Club is more than enough to illustrate the course that Bird's life would take. "Bird walked right up to the bar and said, 'Gimme eight doubles.' . . . The bartender looked at him like he was crazy, and he says 'Well, who's with ya?' Bird said, 'This is for me!' He say, 'I'll tell you what, if you drink 'em, I'll give 'em to ya.' So he said, 'Line 'em up!' An' he drank every one of 'em, went up to the bandstand and played like a champ."

And so it would go. Charlie Parker became famous as a man who was perfectly capable of spending a whole day in his hotel room, draining a fifth of whiskey as a reefer dangled from his lip, jacking heroin into a vein while a woman knelt between his legs fellating him—and then he would get on a stage and through some alchemical magic it all seemed to pass through his brain and nervous system and heart and soul and take transcendent flight in music of such natural originality and power that it would leave his fellow musicians dumbstruck with wonder. As the pianist Hampton Hawes so memorably put it, "Those of us who were affected the strongest felt we'd be willing to do anything to warm ourselves by that fire, get some of that grease pumping through our veins. He fucked up all our minds. It was where the ultimate truth was."

What people heard when Ross Russell released "Lover Man" was an artist looking into the abyss and turning his pain into the most authentic kind of musical truth. As Herbert Huncke expressed it, "Oh, the *pathos*—how does one even *speak* of it? You can literally hear him breaking down—the tone, he blows so piercingly on that sax, it's like he's *crying*. Oh, my, my—*yes*, man, you can hear his agony, one junkie to another. The people I was with felt the same way about it."

Even before he cut the songs "Relaxin' at Camarillo" and "Cool Blues" in California before coming back to New York in 1947 and appearing at the Royal Roost with the famous quintet of Miles Davis on trumpet, Duke Jordan on piano, Tommy Potter on bass, and Max Roach on drums, the strange and compelling myth was already spreading that heroin could make you play like Bird—and that somehow the heroin life could stir the creative growth of the music called bebop.

In Los Angeles, the first three notes from "Parker's Mood," whistled into the night, became the code signal among the musicians that they wanted to cop. When they heard the three notes whistled reassuringly back, they knew they were among their own kind, and that the coast was clear to proceed with the transaction.

The use of heroin would spread in direct proportion to the cult of Charlie Parker, and by 1947 Bird was at his most incandescent and awe-inspiring. When Miles Davis played with him at the Royal Roost, he remembered him playing "in short, hard bursts of breath. Hard as a mad man. . . . When Bird played like that, it was like hearing music for the first time. I'd never heard anybody play like that."

15

A Ghost in Daylight
on a Crowded Street

1.

William Burroughs was keeping an apartment on Henry Street as a kind of separate compartment of his life, an antechamber to the underworld of drugs and crime that he now immersed himself in. Herbert Huncke was allowed to stay there. As Burroughs's habit took hold, he and Huncke planned their routines for "making the croaker." Later he tried "working the hole" with the Sailor. The two of them would descend into the maze of the subways and, as Huncke explained it, "Bill acted as the shill. Phil was, of course, a highly qualified pickpocket. This was all very exciting to Bill, and he was a perfect shill. You couldn't have found a better shill to work with, from that standpoint, since no one would ever suspect him."

As the experience of addiction began to overtake him, Burroughs began frequenting 103rd Street and Broadway, where junk "haunts the cafeteria, roams up and down the block, sometimes half-crossing Broadway to rest on one of the island benches. A ghost in daylight on a crowded street." There he got to know the old-timers with their "thin sallow faces; bitter twisted mouths; stiff-fingered, stylized gestures."

For the first time Burroughs began selling heroin. His clientele consisted of "mooches, fags, four-flushers, stool pigeons, bums—unwilling to work, unable to steal, always short of money, always whining for credit."

Huncke was breaking into cars and leaving the stolen goods in the apartment at 115th Street, where things began to go haywire. Vicki Russell moved in; soon there were needles lying about.

"Things began to change the more the Times Square people came onto the scene," Edie Kerouac-Parker noted. "All of these characters that Jack would write about in *The Town and the City*, they were a very different crew from the Columbia crowd. They were interesting but all a bunch of gangsters and thieves. Our whole group, we were all so fascinated by Huncke. He talked so different. Burroughs was a sort of a strange father figure to us back then, and he played the role to the hilt, but I remember him with the strap around his arm, too, cooking up. He was very discreet; he didn't like to flaunt it in front of you. I thought it was sad, but we were all fascinated to watch him do it, shooting himself up in the arm, the legs."

Burroughs was coming to understand the "cellular equation" that would rule his life; he had picked up on "the silent frequency of junk" and viewed his addiction with clinical detachment. "As a habit takes hold, other interests lose importance to the user. Life telescopes down to junk, one fix and looking forward to the next, 'stashes' and 'scripts,' 'spikes' and 'droppers.' The addict himself often feels that he is leading a normal life and that junk is incidental. He does not realize that he is just going through the motions in his non-junk activities. It is not until his supply is cut off that he realizes what junk means to him."

It was during one of these early withdrawals that Burroughs experienced his own horrifying vision of the apocalypse. "Almost worse than the sickness is the depression that goes with it. One afternoon, I closed my eyes and saw New York in ruins. Huge centipedes and scorpions crawled in and out of empty bars and cafeterias and drugstores on Forty-Second Street. Weeds were growing up through the cracks and holes in the pavement. There was no one in sight."

The creativity of the group only seemed to flourish within this atmosphere of drug use, however. Oddly, Burroughs seemed quite undiminished by his addiction. In fact, to the rest of the group, it seemed that Burroughs had come to use drugs as only the next phase of a process of experience and self-discovery that had included Jungian and Reichian analysis, narcoanalysis, hypnoanalysis, and the methods of Karen Horney. Kerouac began to view him as a "great comic genius," though Burroughs was ill at ease and somehow pathetic as he acted out his routines. Hypnoanalysis had revealed many layers of Burroughs's character, which now became the basis of these routines. There he was, an English governess, shrieking and giggling, a kind of Edith Sitwell character who would dress up in one of Joan's dresses and invite everyone over for tea. Underneath that was old Luke, the psychotic southern sheriff with a shotgun across his knees. Then he would turn into a bald-skulled Chinese man, silent and inscrutable, starving by the banks of the Yangtze.

The group loved to goad Burroughs on and would interact with these characters as he took them farther and farther. Had the onset of his addiction not occurred in this environment with these people, had it not happened simultaneously with the development of a style of humor in which situations were extended and explored to their most surreal breaking point, Burroughs might never have turned out to be any kind of a writer at all; he might have turned out to be just another junkie, albeit it one from a privileged background. But Kerouac was forever trying to persuade Burroughs to think of himself as a writer. One day as Ginsberg was reading aloud from one of Burroughs passages and read "naked lunch" instead of "naked lust," Kerouac told him, "You should write a book with that title one day, Bill."

But then, as quickly as the season took flight, it all seemed to fall apart.

Perhaps it began unraveling on the night that Benzedrine caught up with Jack Kerouac. It was just before Christmas of 1945. He and Allen and Hal Chase had been up for five straight days taking benny when they decided to hike all the way down to the Brooklyn Bridge. In the brittle exhilaration of a clear and frigid morning, they undertook the trek like a great expedition and were approaching the bridge when Ginsberg, stretched to the limit of physical and mental exhaustion, was unable to take another step, and Kerouac then picked him up and nobly carried him on his back as Friar Tuck had carried Robin Hood. Allen was merrily humming a Bach toccata when Kerouac went buckling to the ground. They had to carry him to a cab, and he went home to Queens to collapse. Kerouac was hospitalized for thrombophlebitis, with blood clots in his legs from excessive Benzedrine use and drinking.

The year of "low, evil decadence" was now over for Kerouac, but the season of writing his first book was just beginning. As he portrayed it in *Vanity of Duluoz,* "I began to bethink myself in that hospital. . . . I began to get a new vision of my own of a truer darkness which just overshadowed all this overlaid mental garbage of 'existentialism' and 'hipsterism' and 'bourgeois decadence' and whatever names you want to give it. . . . So, partially well, I went home, and . . . I decided to become a writer, write a huge novel explaining everything to everyone." To write such a "huge" novel, however, Kerouac would once again come to use Benzedrine avidly, despite its hazards.

Then, like the final act of a play, William Burroughs took his first fall.

Things had been getting sloppy among the crew. Huncke stole a number of dresses with Phil White and Burroughs took one to a doctor and gave it to him in return for a morphine prescription; Bob Brandenburg was caught robbing a safe in a theater and dropped a matchbook with the Henry Street address; then Huncke was fingered by someone he had been using drugs with. Phil White then talked Burroughs into forging the name of a Dr. Greco on a script that Huncke used, and it was noticed by an inspector. It was only a matter of time; the trails were all leading back to Burroughs. Those moments of paranoia, and the feeling of being hunted like an animal, would remain forever burned in his mind—"I can feel the heat closing in, feel them out there making their moves, setting up their devil doll stool pigeons, crooning over my spoon and dropper I throw away at Washington Square Station, vault a turnstile and two flights down the iron stairs, catch an uptown A train."

When they picked him up, Burroughs was charged with violation of Public Health Law 334, obtaining narcotics through the use of fraud. He was taken to the Tombs, junk sick, bathed in sweat, too weak to move, and spent a horrendous night listening to the piteous voices of the prisoners in the neighboring cells ("Forty years! Man, I can't do no forty years!"). Joan bailed him out and called his psychiatrist, Dr. Wolberg, to sign his surety bond. Mortimer and Laura Burroughs then learned for the first time that their son was using drugs. His father attended the hearing of his case in June of 1946. Unlike Huncke, Burroughs was spared the grave detail on Hart's Island. Because it was his first offense and he was from such an upstanding family, Burroughs was given a suspended sentence. The judge admonished him with the following words: "Young man, I am going to inflict a terrible punishment on you. I am going to send you home to St. Louis for the summer."

No sooner had Burroughs left town than Joan Vollmer fell apart and suffered a nervous breakdown. She was picked up squatting on the pavement of Times Square with her daughter, Julie, by her side, after which she was taken to Bellevue. It was after Burroughs hurried back to the city to get her released that they conceived a son, William S. Burroughs Jr., in the neon glare of a Times Square hotel room.

The little libertine group had been forced to disband, but not before powerful bonds had been forged between all of them.

"More than anything else, the use of drugs that year had accelerated a process that had begun the year before, a process of cultural and personal deconditioning," Ginsberg reflected. "Boundaries began to dissolve between us. It definitely had a sexual impact, among many other things. All of us began to experiment sexually. Right around that time, I remember having my first serious homosexual encounters."

As Ginsberg looked back, he recognized that "it was only the beginning of the many entanglements between us—sexual, emotional, artistic, and spiritual—that would continue, really, for as long as any of us were going to breathe."

2.

In digesting that crucial year of 1945–46, during which the group had planted the seeds for an embryonic counterculture in America, Allen Ginsberg learned graphic lessons about drugs that would shape the course of his life and work. The lessons were many, and one of the first had to do with Burroughs and the nature of addiction.

"When I watched Burroughs get his habit, I realized that it was quite mechanical and cumulative, really. If you took dope every day several times a day over a period of weeks you could get quite a habit; so, consequently, I just didn't do that. Even though we were experimenting and exploring and had to find out about a lot of things about drugs for ourselves, I saw straightaway that there were most definitely intelligent choices to be made about drug use."

The next lesson was about Huncke.

"When I looked at Huncke, on the other hand, I saw someone who had a legitimate addiction, for which, at least in his case, there didn't seem to be a cure. Huncke was untrustworthy in some areas and something of a parasite, but here was a man who had found himself in a situation that he had virtually no control over. He had a metabolic habit, but instead of treating him medically he was being hounded, persecuted—really no different than a Jew had been in Nazi Germany."

Though these perceptions would shape Ginsberg's thinking about the use and politics of drugs in the years to come, by far the biggest lessons had to do with marijuana.

"The biggest impact was the realization of the enhancement of sensibility and consciousness directed at the awareness of what a whole scam the agenda of drug regulation was. People who smoked it were supposed to be like dogs frothing at the mouth, and once you smoked it you saw that the whole thing was some public hallucination that simply had no relationship to reality.

"We looked at it as a legitimate and valuable tool, and here was this great government plot to suppress it and make it seem as if it were something diabolic, satanic, full of hatred and fiendishness and madness."

When Mezz Mezzrow's autobiography, *Really the Blues,* was published in 1946, the book was like an epiphany for Ginsberg. Most of his historical references for cannabis had been European in origin, like the Club des Hashischins; nothing had ever provided such a clear context for the story of marijuana and its cultural lineage in America as Mezzrow's story. Ginsberg began to see himself as the logical descendent of the vipers, part of a significant cultural movement that was multicultural and interracial in origin. Harry Anslinger was duly horrified by the book, noting in an unpublished essay called "Marihuana and Musicians" that "in addition to deriding the dangerous aspects and being a glorification of marihuana smoking and other forms of drug indulgence, the book reeks of filth in general. It seems incredulous that such an advertisement for narcotic addiction could overnight become a sensational bestseller."

Moreover, it was through *Really the Blues* that Ginsberg and Burroughs first learned about the La Guardia Committee Report. Mezzrow had been arrested for marijuana in 1940 at the World's Fair and was sentenced to three years; while serving his sentence on Hart Island, he became aware of inmates from Hart and Rikers being "shipped over to the King's County Hospital, where they were used as guinea pigs by some city doctor's to find out what the score was with marijuana."

Commissioned by Mayor Fiorello La Guardia in 1938 to ascertain the truth about whether or not marijuana really did drive people to commit acts of crime, murder, and sexual deviance, as had been claimed by the Federal Bureau of Narcotics during the period of *Reefer Madness* and the evolution of the Marihuana Tax Act of 1937, the study was made with the full cooperation of the New York City Police Department. Published in 1944, it represented the most extensive and objective sociological study of marijuana-smoking in the history of the United States. According to the conclusions of the report, the practice of smoking marijuana "does not lead to addiction in the medical sense of the word"; "does not lead to morphine or heroin or cocaine addiction, and no effort is made to create a market for these narcotics by stimulating the practice of marijuana smoking"; "is not the determining factor in the commission of major crimes"; and "is not widespread among schoolchildren." Moreover, juvenile delinquency was "not associated with the practice of marijuana smoking." In summation, "the publicity concerning the catastrophic effects of marihuana-smoking in New York City is unfounded."

The conclusions of the report thus directly and unequivocally refuted every one of Harry Anslinger's claims about the great marijuana menace. Of course, Anslinger rejected the findings of the study out of hand and brought in the American Medical Association in a campaign to discredit its findings. In fact, so successful was the Bureau in rebutting and shunting aside the study that copies of it were almost impossible to find in any of the public libraries of New York, but Burroughs and Ginsberg got their hands on it and studied it very carefully. Consequently, of all the drugs he had tried, it was marijuana that shaped not only Ginsberg's aesthetic but political vision.

From then on, I realized that marijuana was going to be an enormous political catalyst, because anybody who got high would immediately see through the official hallucination that had been laid down and would begin questioning, "What is this *war*? What is the *military interest?*" It was instantaneous. It wasn't just grass. I remember Burroughs, his wife Joan, Kerouac and I sitting on the floor talking, listening to the radio, and I'll never forget Truman coming on after Roosevelt's death, and Joan Burroughs was mocking him, saying he sounded like a haberdasher, and how could this man possibly run the government?

The stark difference between the official story and Ginsberg's personal knowledge and experience of marijuana began to catalyze a complete reexamination of his consciousness in virtually every direction. As he saw it, the deduction was simple: "If one law was full of shit and error, then what of all those other laws?"

Within a year Kerouac would complete his first novel, *The Town and the City*. Burroughs emerges in the book as Dennison, "with his baby son in one hand and a hypo in another, a marvelous sight"— but it's the mad young poet, Levinsky, the character based on Allen Ginsberg—"one of the strangest and most curiously exalted youngsters" one could ever know—who stands in Times Square and predicts, "You'll see the great tycoons of industry suddenly falling apart and going mad, you'll see preachers in the pulpit suddenly exploding— there'll be marijuana fumes seeping out of the Stock Exchange!"

16

Ain't Nobody's Business If I Do

1.

On February 16, 1946, the Queen of Swing Street gave a concert at Town Hall in New York. For the first time, Billie Holiday appeared outside of a club setting, in a legitimate concert hall. She sang eighteen songs in a performance that displayed how truly stunning her artistry as a jazz singer had become. Leonard Feather raved in *Metronome* that her "dignified bearing and her wonderful poise helped to keep the large, quiet, intelligent audience enthralled."

Lady's Decca records were selling well, her audience was growing along with her fame and prestige, and she was making between $50,000 and $60,000 a year. People were just flat-out falling in love with her, from jazz fans to Hollywood stars like Orson Welles and Tallulah Bankhead. As her friend the actress Claire Lievenson described it, "She was so elegant. I don't give a damn if she was high, it was a gas to watch this bitch walk up to the microphone. She had a very feminine walk, short steps . . . and she just melted into the microphone. BOOM. And most times the eyes would be closed, and when she opened them, she was such a magnetic thing to look at and to hear, you were spellbound by her."

There would be much speculation about why Lady Day became a heroin addict just as her star was rising. From the outset, the entire progression of her addiction was tangled up in her relationships with the men in her life. Jimmy Monroe, her first husband, was a stylish bon vivant and playboy whose claim to fame was that he was the brother of Clark Monroe, who operated the Uptown House, the nightclub on 134th Street where Lady had a residence in 1937. He was also a hophead who introduced her to opium and cocaine. By the time her marriage to him was over, she had graduated to the needle and was addicted.

Enter Joe Guy, a twenty-five-year-old trumpet player from Birmingham who was both new on the scene and a heroin addict—"And he could be a big help to me. It wasn't long before I was one of the highest-paid slaves around." As *Lady Sings the Blues* would so famously put it, "I spent the rest of the war on 52nd Street and a few other streets. I had the white gowns and the white shoes. And every night they'd bring me the white gardenias and the white junk." Henceforth Lady would rely on the men who became her boyfriends—Guy, bassist John Simmons, John Levy, later husband Louis McKay—to score for her. Sadly, without exception, all were parasites who would make exorbitant profits from her addiction.

Various biographies and documentaries have purported to tell the truth about Billie Holiday's addiction—to reveal the "real Billie"—and some are no doubt more reliable than others. For the most part, what emerges is a narrative of addiction rooted in childhood, reared in the hardscrabble times of her youth, introduced and manipulated by the men she fell in love with. It was an addiction shaped by character and environment, fueled by fame, and driven by yearnings for glamour, adulation, and true love. By many accounts it was also exacerbated by her anger at the racism that always seemed to hang over her. In 1946, the woman who had stated that she would never be anybody's "damn maid" found herself playing one in her first movie, the independently produced *New Orleans*. Even though Louis Armstrong was in the movie, Lady wanted out. She had to wear a little white cap and "it was a real drag to go to Hollywood and end up as a make-believe maid." One day it got so bad that she cried on the set. She complained bitterly to her agent, Joe Glaser, who warned her that if she walked away she'd never work in Hollywood again. As it turned out, she never did.

Like any addict's, Lady's addiction was powered by family-of-origin issues and the deepest dynamics of her psychosexual being, but exactly how and to what degree her real feelings about her father and mother, the impact of rape and abuse, poverty and prostitution, sex and love, childlessness and romantic heartbreak may have actually factored into the equation of her addiction can ultimately never really be known. Everyone readily agrees that Lady had plenty of pain and problems, and it would be easy enough to attribute her addiction to a pressing desire for the sweet opiate oblivion of heroin—"Lady Day had an awful lot to forget," as pianist Mal Waldron would point out—along with the sheer metabolic compulsion that ensnares any heroin addict, but somehow it's never that simple. Billie Holiday was an enormously complex and contradictory person, and no sooner do you peel back a layer than you see the diametric opposite of what you thought you were seeing. There were many different versions of Lady Day, public and private, all mixing together. As John Szwed points out,

> We should not be shocked, then, to learn that, whereas onstage Billie Holiday projected a ladylike distance and grace, offstage her manner was sometimes rough, profane, caustic, and vengeful. Nor should we be surprised that she could be witty, kind, and perceptive; she could charm intellectuals, artists, and wealthy patrons, help younger singers with their careers, buy drinks for fans who could scarcely afford to see her perform, and dream of a house in the country with a white picket fence, children, and a dog.

Of course, all of this only hints at what makes any real understanding of Lady's drug use and addiction so tricky. Even some of the most basic facts of her addiction have been hotly contested by those closest to her. Nor should this be surprising, because it only makes sense that someone as multifarious as Billie Holiday would be every bit as changeable in her addiction. Lady has been depicted as everything from the most pathetic kind of hopelessly addicted junkie to someone who could stop and control it when she wanted and was able to go from shooting to snorting virtually at will—in other words, as someone who did exactly what she wanted to do. The different substances she used (marijuana, heroin, barbiturates, Benzedrine, alcohol) played different roles at different times in her life, whether as recreation, anesthesia, or adjunct to her professional and artistic life, but as a classic polydrug addict and alcoholic, she was perfectly capable of using them all at the same time—and often did. Yet even in her worst periods, she comes across as a person who never hurt a soul but herself—brashly honest and straight-talking, capable of great humor, generous to a fault, never self-pitying, and heartbreakingly vulnerable. Perhaps it was her friend, the singer and dancer Marie Bryant, who came closest to articulating this side of her: "This woman was only feelings. Billie was only quivering nerves, quivering emotions. That's why she couldn't make it in this world, she never could make it. She was just too gentle, too honest, too emotional—you know there wasn't a conniving bone in her body." Bryant would always see Billie and Lester Young as "people who couldn't play the game, couldn't make it on the terms of the world. They were pure: they were the real people, and the rest of the world were not."

Maybe this is the trait that U2's Bono was trying to express half a century later in the song "Angel of Harlem" when he wrote that "Lady Day has diamond eyes, she sees the truth behind the lies." After all, it can never be an easy thing to see the truth behind the lies.

2.

By 1946 Lady was using so much heroin that she needed a tuna-fish can to cook it up before shooting it. When she couldn't find a vein or her arm got infected, she would hit herself in the fingertips or the veins of her vagina. Such hard-core details would not be known for decades, and when they emerged, those who loved and revered her would find them sordid, voyeuristic, even pornographic.

One of the people who knew details of Lady's addiction was her agent and manager, Joe Glaser, who made it his business to know everything about his clients that might possibly affect his percentage of their incomes. Glaser was by all accounts a ruthless and crude Chicago character, a leftover from the days of Al Capone who had operated whorehouses and then muscled his way to the top of the business by booking the biggest name in jazz, Louis Armstrong, among others. As Glaser liked to tell people, at one time his relationship with Lady had been sexual—she was "his girl"—which made him all the more possessive and controlling. He would later claim that Lady's mother, Sadie, had come to him before she passed away in 1945 and complained that she was starving because Lady was spending all of her money on dope.

Glaser had already sent Lady to a New York sanitarium to be taken off heroin, but she had relapsed not long after leaving the clinic. Now he gave her an ultimatum to get clean, and when she did not comply, he decided that the only way he could save her was to force a reckoning with the law—in short, to set her up for arrest.

By the spring of 1947, Billie Holiday had already been watched for years by the Federal Bureau of Narcotics. Of course, she was exactly the kind of figure that Harry Anslinger wanted to make an example of. "She flaunted her way of living," observed Colonel George White, an agent of the FBN assigned to her case, "with her fancy coats and fancy automobiles and her jewelery and her gowns—she was the big lady wherever she went, and a good deal of resentment was generated."

And so it happened that Jimmy Fletcher, a graduate of Howard University and one of the few African Americans allowed to become an operating agent of the FBN, received a message from Anslinger to the effect that "Joe Glaser wants a colored agent to work on getting a case against Billie Holiday." When Fletcher met Glaser for lunch at the Palm Tavern on Fifth Avenue, Glaser told him that if he helped the Bureau bring Lady in, Anslinger had promised to "hook and crook" on Glaser's behalf and keep his name out of the entire affair.

Fletcher was one of the more interesting characters in the story of the FBN. A true believer in the war against narcotics, he moved with guile and ease in the drug underworld, effectively making cases and arrests. He knew that Joe Guy was buying two ounces a week and sometimes hiding an ounce in the collar of Lady's boxer, Mister, and that the pushers were taking advantage of her by selling her dope at vastly inflated rates when they knew she was sick and needed a fix. At the time, Lady was living with Guy in the Braddock Hotel, where Fletcher had already confronted her in a raid, but now when he arrived with a fellow agent named Cohen and knocked on her door, saying that they had a telegram, it was to bust her. When Lady let them in, Fletcher decided to level with her.

"Billie, why don't you make a short case of this, and if you've got anything, why don't you just turn it over to us? Then they won't be searching all around, pulling out your clothes and everything."

All they would find was a syringe outside the window on the ledge—hardly enough for a case against someone of her renown. Cohen wanted a policewoman to come up and do a body search.

"You don't have to do that," Billie said. "I'll strip. All that policewoman is going to do is look up my pussy!"

And strip she did, while they watched from the door of the bathroom. Putting a gown over her shoulders, Lady then went over to the toilet bowl, straddled it, and began urinating. She was staring at them as she did it.

"No, no, Billie," said Cohen, flustered, trying to close the door, "you don't have to do that!"—but Lady slammed it open and went right on, still staring at them. She was going to make them watch.

As Fletcher later recalled the incident, something happened to him at that moment: "She sealed our friendship. She sealed herself closer to me." Maybe it was her nakedness, but he felt himself feeling for her, somehow admiring her brazen defiance. It was the beginning of a curious relationship. They would meet again at different times, once in a bar where they talked intimately for hours, another time at the Club Ebony, where he danced with her—"She was the type that would make anyone sympathetic because she was the loving type." It would seem that the FBN agent sent to bust Billie Holiday was falling for her. By the time Fletcher was brought in for the next raid on her, he was seeing Lady's case as his "bad luck."

Lady was playing the final night of an engagement at the Royale in Philadelphia on a bill with Louis Armstrong and was staying at the Hotel Attucks when it all came down. The raid was led by an agent identified only as Max G. As soon as she and her driver arrived at the hotel in a green Cadillac and they saw the cops in the lobby, she knew something was up. As the driver already had a record, they didn't stay around long. Her autobiography would claim that even though she had never driven a car before, it was she who jumped behind the wheel and tore away from the hotel, tires screeching, as Max G. pulled out his .45 and started blasting away at their car, which swerved and went smashing into another car before they escaped. Although it was Jimmy Fletcher who found the green Cadillac with the telltale bullet holes back in New York and staked out the Grampion Hotel, where she was staying with Joe Guy, he was not involved in the raid that found sixteen capsules of heroin stashed in her stockings in their room.

On May 27, 1947, when Billie Holiday appeared before Judge J. Cullen Ganey in the district court for the Eastern District in Philadelphia facing charges for the use and possession of narcotics, she waived her right to an attorney on the advice of Joe Glaser and asked for treatment. In the trial that followed (*United States v. Billie Holiday*), US Attorney Joseph G. Hildenberger noted for the record that she had given "a full and complete statement and came in here last week with the booking agent and expressed a desire to be cured of this addiction." Indeed, in the early part of the trial Judge Ganey recognized that she had been exploited by drug dealers who "kept her under opiates, largely as a matter of persuasion and coercion and failing to exercise reasonable judgment on her own." It came as an enormous shock to Lady when the judge promised treatment but then issued a harsh reprimand—"you stand as a wrongdoer"—and sentenced her to a year and a day in the federal penitentiary. As *Lady Sings the Blues* would portray it, "It was all over in a matter of minutes; they gave me another shot to keep me from getting sick on the train, and at nine o'clock that night I was in an upper berth of a train headed for the Federal Women's Reformatory at Alderson, West Virginia, with two big fat white matrons guarding me."

There is no documented evidence that Harry Anslinger personally intervened in the case to ensure this outcome, but directly responsible or not, given his views and the fact that Billie Holiday was on his list of targets, he must have been delighted with the sentence.

Lady's decision to follow Glaser's advice and waive legal counsel would turn out to be disastrous. For one thing, it seemed obvious to everyone that good representation would have drastically diminished the likelihood that she would spend a single day behind bars. Furthermore, Lady now lost the all-important cabaret card that allowed her to perform in establishments that served liquor in New York, and that meant all of the jazz clubs where she made her living. As her autobiography put it, "I felt like the fool of all time."

There was no "cure" for heroin addiction at Alderson. "They don't cut you down slow, weaning you off the stuff gradually. They just throw you in the hospital by yourself, take you off cold turkey, and watch you suffer."

As her book tells the story, the suffering went on for nineteen days.

Although Lady had told people that she had a morbid fear of going to jail, she appears to have done her time well. Alderson was a much better place than Welfare Island. The women lived in dormitory-like cottages—fifty to sixty in each one, white girls segregated from black girls—and worked on a farm. Lady wasn't happy about being assigned to KP, but she accepted it and became a model inmate; she also picked vegetables, fed the pigs, and even took up knitting. Fans sent her thousands of letters, but she could not receive them until she left because they were not from immediate family. One couple in Switzerland sent her $1000 and invited her to come and live with them when she was released, telling her that America would "never accept her" now that she'd been arrested and incarcerated.

But Lady knew that there was no running away. She would have to find out for herself whether her public would accept her or not.

3.

Billie Holiday was released from prison on March 16, 1948, after serving eight months of her sentence. Her contract with Glaser had expired; while she was serving time, Ed Fishman was vying to become her new manager. It was Fishman who arranged for a concert at Carnegie Hall, to be held only ten days after her release.

The plan was for her to spend some time in Newark at the home of pianist Bobby Tucker's mother, who had taken Lady in after her previous stay in the New York clinic. That was to be her parole address, but when Tucker met her at the train station, it was clear to him "that she was completely out of it. She had changed trains in Washington and had already made a connection." All Tucker could say to her was, "Lady, how could you?"

But there was good news, too. Lady hadn't sung a note in ten months. She might have been back on dope, but when Tucker sat down at the piano back at the house, it was clear from the first notes she hit of "Night and Day" that she sounded magnificent, better than ever.

On the night of Saturday, March 27, three thousand people stood in a downpour waiting to get into Carnegie Hall. The demand for tickets had been so high that an extra six hundred were sold and people were seated on the stage and in the aisles. Lady was anxious. She had put on about twenty pounds at Alderson, but her real worry was whether or not her public would accept her now that she was a "jailbird."

The answer was obvious from the moment she walked out dressed all in black, with white fingerless gloves, her hair in a twisted, unbraided coronet with white gardenias, to what *DownBeat* called "one of the most thunderous ovations given a performer in this or any other concert hall." Lady smiled and eased right into "I Cover the Waterfront."

The photographer and novelist Carl Van Vechten later described the moment in a letter to his friend, the painter Karl Priebe: "She was nervous and perspiring freely, but her first tones were reassuring and rewarded with a whoop. . . . All with that seesaw motion of the arms, fingers always turned in, that swanlike twitching of the thighs, that tortured posture of the head, those inquiring wondering eyes, a little frightened at first and then as the applause increased they became grateful. The voice the same, in and out between notes, unbearably poignant, that blue voice."

The audience was rapt through twenty-one songs. When they shrieked for more, Lady gave them six encores. The two shows she did that night set a new house record for Carnegie Hall, and when another was scheduled for three weeks later, it sold out on announcement.

As Lady's autobiography recognized, "The Carnegie concert was the biggest thing that ever happened to me." But it was also the beginning of a gnawing insecurity that would only grow worse over time. She worried that people were really coming to see what a junkie felon looked like onstage. "They're all here to watch me fall on my ass" was her comment backstage before the show.

Billie Holiday was now the most famous heroin addict in America. She was hot copy for tabloid editors and reporters who recognized that voyeuristic and titillating articles about the excesses of a black female heroin addict with a racy reputation like hers would certainly sell newspapers. Lady knew they could write what they wanted about her and that there really wasn't much she could do about it, but worse than the press were the narcotics police, local and federal, always tailing her, watching her every move. The situation she found herself in was both strange and unprecedented. The Carnegie Hall shows and the promoters and out-of-town club owners who booked her after her release did very well, making it clear that her addiction and arrest were by no means career-ending catastrophes—paradoxically, her pain and problems could actually be *good* for business. But at the same time her position was fraught with stress and peril. There was only one public relations tool available to her, one way to exert at least some control of her public image. It was something that no public figure had ever really done before, and certainly not something she ever wanted to do, but she decided to talk about her addiction. For the most part, she was remarkably frank and honest, blaming nobody but herself for her troubles, but she also used the platform to talk about how she was being hassled by the police. "I came out expecting to to be allowed to go to work and to start with a clean slate," she told *Ebony* in July 1949. "But the police have been particularly vindictive, hounding, heckling and harassing me beyond endurance." She also made bold statements about how she thought that the problem of addiction should be taken away from the police and put into the hands of the doctors.

The headlines of articles over the years tell the story of the kind of game she had to play: "Don't Blame Show Biz—Billie," "Billie Holiday, Now Remarried, Finds Happiness, a New Sense of Security," "I'm Cured for Good Now," "Can a Dope Addict Come Back?," "How I Blew a Million Dollars," "Billie's Tragic Life."

It was a dance that Lady Day would do through three more arrests, virtually to her last breath. In the process, the sensation of her life would become one with her stage persona as a torch singer to create what Farrah Jasmin Griffin calls "a new image, that of the tragic, ever-suffering black woman singer who simply stands center stage and naturally sings of her woes." And thus was Billie Holiday's destiny sealed as Lady Day, the legendary tragic queen of jazz. Perhaps no one encapsulates exactly what followed better than Griffin: "There are images and myths that seem to swallow up individuals who are too complex to be explained by them, yet cannot escape their powerful hold."

There was one more important element that would mold and define this persona. On August 17, 1949, in a Decca recording session, Lady cut "Ain't Nobody's Business If I Do," her sassy, swinging update of the well-traveled standard by Porter Grainger and Everett Robbins about the freedom of choice and everything else be damned. The song had already been rendered by Anna Meyers, Sara Martin, Alberta Hunter, and Jimmy Witherspoon, but it was Bessie Smith's memorable 1923 version that no doubt drew Lady to it (both Grainger and Robbins had been accompanists for Smith), and from its very release the song would be forever hers. It became the theme song of the Billie Holiday persona. It was her statement about everything she was and everything she did: the girl who taunted the boys in Fell's Point to the point that they chased and beat her; the bold and defiant young singer who picked up and sang "Strange Fruit," no matter the consequences; the heroin addict who stood naked, urinating in front of agents of the Federal Bureau of Narcotics, and would not flinch . . .

Ain't nobody's business if I do.

17

The Sacralization of the Mundane

1.

"How did we get here, angels?" Allen Ginsberg asked blissfully one night in the West End. It was 1948 and they were all back in New York, young and in love with each other and very high.

Ginsberg had just gone to bed with Neal Cassady while Jack Kerouac splashed naked in a tub with LuAnne Henderson.

"This life is our last chance to be honest . . . really the Last Chance Saloon," Kerouac declared. Jack, Neal, and Allen then wrote a poem together called "Pull My Daisy" that seemed to capture all of it perfectly—

Pull my daisy
tip my cup
all the doors are open
Cut my thoughts
for coconuts
all my eggs are broken

So much had happened in the two years since the twenty-year-old Neal Cassady and his sexy teenaged bride, LuAnne Henderson, had bolted from Colorado like a couple of wild horses racing for open pasture, showing up in New York in December of 1946.

Kerouac first saw him standing buck naked in a doorway—"a young Gene Autry—trim, thin-hipped, blue eyed with a real Oklahoma accent—a sideburned hero of the snowy West," as hc'd later portray the moment in *On the Road.*

Allen Ginsberg had encountered him in the West End when he first arrived. Cassady hadn't made that much of an impression on that occasion, but the second time, when Kerouac brought Cassady over to Vicky Russell's apartment in Spanish Harlem to smoke pot for the first time on January 10, 1947, was very different indeed. Several things happened that night as they all got "frantic high." Ginsberg fell madly in love with Cassady. Cassady fell madly in love with marijuana. And Kerouac fell madly in love with the *idea* of Cassady, for Neal seemed to be the very incarnation of the Rimbaudian adventurer of the New Vision.

That first night of smoking marijuana together would resonate in one of the most celebrated passages of *On the Road,* as Sal Paradise and Carlo Marx meet Dean Moriarty and they "rush down the street together, digging everything in the early way they had, which later became so much sadder and perceptive and blank," and Sal Paradise goes shambling after them because "the only people for me are the mad ones, the ones who are mad to live, mad to talk, mad to be saved, desirous of everything at the same time, the ones who never yawn or say a commonplace thing, but burn, burn, burn, like fabulous yellow roman candles exploding like spiders across the stars and in the middle you see the centerlight pop and everybody goes 'Awww'!"

The scene as Kerouac renders it in the novel does not explicitly include marijuana at all, but in fact the weed is right there at the very beginning of their story—at the moment when the "whole mad swirl" of everything that is going to happen begins.

2.

The man who became the spark plug in the engine that would drive the Beat Generation to life was born, fittingly, en route. Neal Cassady came into the world on February 8, 1926, in a charity hospital in Salt Lake City, where his parents had stopped on their way from Iowa to Hollywood. He was on his own almost from the beginning of his life. After his parents split up, he grew up with his father in skid row flophouses and condemned buildings on the corner of 16th and Market

Streets in Denver, in the company of drunks and thieves and whores, sleeping on filthy mattresses, eating breakfast at the Citizen's Mission as his father slept off a drunk. His favorite toys were a ball that he bounced along the roads and alleyways and a homemade dart that he made from a sewing needle and could throw with great skill and accuracy, the way he could also skip stones along the South Platte River. He learned to take care of himself, doing whatever he had to do to get by, and toward that end, the avocation he cultivated to the level of a spoken improvisational art form was talking. Kerouac might have been known as the Great Rememberer during his youth, but Neal Cassady was "the great experiencer and Midwest driver and talker," as Allen Ginsberg called him.

When Cassady went to live with his mother after he started school, his bully of a half brother would make him lie on a Murphy bed and then close it, but rather than finding the experience of being entombed in this "mattress'd jail" of darkness frightening, Neal would experience an acceleration of image and thought and time—"simply an awareness that time, in my head, had gradually apexed to about triple its ordinary speed of passage," as he described it in *The First Third*—in short, cultivating the sensation of the feeling. It was only one early example of how his nervous system and brain seemed to operate at a much higher octane level than the normal human being's and how he had a natural squint for mind-altering experiences of any kind, whether marijuana, Benzedrine, women, cars, spirituality, or life itself.

Like Charlie Parker, Cassady was a ravenous autodidact and passionate about anything he did. The obsessions of his youth and adolescence were athletics, cars, driving, and sex—not necessarily in that order—all of which became pursuits of herculean proportions. He could throw a football seventy yards, do fifty chin-ups, and masturbate seven times a day. He has always been described as the sort of person whose every relationship was supercharged with an erotic electricity. He used sex as a form of currency as well as communication, but he was never cynical about it—he was honest, quite sincere about the fact that he liked to screw women of all ages—in dangerous places, if possible—and proud of his considerably large penis (not for nothing would Ginsberg later call him the "cocksman of Denver" in *Howl*). He could include men in his palette of sexual experience but never as a mainstay or prime focus, as Allen Ginsberg would soon enough learn to his consternation. Labels like *bisexual* seem far too limiting for him. It would be more accurate to say that Neal Cassady's sexuality was simply, at any given moment, natural, unpredictably volatile, and omnidirectional. He was an example of what sociologists would call a juvenile delinquent during the 1950s, albeit a kind-hearted and gentle one who abhorred violence. The focus of his criminal activity then was stealing cars, and he claimed to have stolen five hundred during his adolescence, but he liked to do it for the pure thrill rather than any kind of profit. He stole them to go joyriding, and his exploits became feats of legend around Denver. By the time he arrived in New York—"a young jailkid hung-up on the wonderful possibilities of becoming a real intellectual"—he had been arrested ten times, with six convictions, and had served fifteen months in reform school. He had also spent innumerable hours in libraries reading Schopenhauer, Nietzsche, Proust, Shakespeare, and Dostoyevsky.

Casssady had a restless, brilliant but undisciplined mind that never stopped. He had come to town much like a jazz musician looking to jam, only what Cassady had to blow were words and modes of being. Hungry for the interplay and development that could only come from butting up against other minds of similar quality, he knew that he was in the right place from that first great all-night mind-bending marijuana rap with Ginsberg and Kerouac.

Reams would be written about Cassady's impact on Kerouac, by Kerouac himself and many others—how Cassady looked like Kerouac and represented his long-lost brother, how each possessed qualities that the other admired but did not have himself. From the outset Kerouac perceived in Cassady "a kind of holy lightning . . . flashing from his excitement and visions." Perhaps the most profound effect Neal had on Jack was the most obvious one. Whereas Kerouac was essentially an observer, mired in guilt and forever attached to his mother, Cassady was an absolute force of nature, and what made his impact on Kerouac so galvanic was his natural ability to live completely and unselfconsciously in the moment, where he seemed to burn radiantly with the sheer ecstasy of life.

"Yes! That's Right! Wow! Man!" he'd exhort as he stood over Kerouac's shoulder and watched him work on *The Town and the City*, egging him on just like the hipsters in the clubs egged on Charlie Parker.

"Man, wow, there's so many things to do, so many things to write!" Dean Moriarty exclaims to Sal Paradise, wiping his face with a handkerchief. "How to even begin to get it all down and without modified restraints and all hung-up on like literary inhibitions and grammatical fears . . ."

In a way the whole impact of jazz and mind-altering substances—especially marijuana—on the evolution of Kerouac's style is contained in this question about writing asked by Cassady/Moriarty at this moment in the tale. Sal Paradise tells Dean that he can't really tell him how to become a writer "except you've got to stick to it with the energy of a benny addict." Cassady would never become the writer he wanted to be, but in becoming Dean Moriarty and "that wow-mad Cody" of *Visions of Cody*, he would succeed in unleashing Kerouac's spirit and creativity, becoming both muse and catalyst for his breakthrough.

They all had their own reasons for going on the road. Ginsberg was in pursuit of sexual and emotional love and poetic inspiration. Kerouac went off in search of "America" and spiritual epiphany, to fulfill his destiny as a great writer. Cassady was always chasing the next sensation, the next girl of the moment, always in motion to see what might lie just beyond the next horizon, down the highway. For Burroughs, it was always about the next place with less regulation that seemed more hospitable to his habit. In an age of loveless materialism, when the greatest disease afflicting man seemed to them the barrenness of the heart, all of them were opting out of conventional life and into something else—a vision of life in which everything was "holy." In doing so they cultivated what Kerouac biographer Gerald Nicosia calls their propensity to "sacralize the mundane." Perhaps no better phrase exists to describe the role that marijuana and other substances played in accentuating not only what happened on the road but in the whole evolution of the Beat Generation and the counterculture that subsequently derived from it. They even brought forth a new phrase for it—"to elitch"—deriving the verb from the Elitch Gardens, an amusement park in New York where the hipsters would congregate on the lawn to "blast."

They elitched whenever possible. As Kerouac and Cassady crossed the country and went wailing down into Mexico, they elitched. As Ginsberg followed them to Denver and was rejected by Cassady and returned to New York, they elitched. As Burroughs moved first to New Orleans and then to Waverly, Texas, where he attempted to become a marijuana farmer, then became an exile in Mexico City after still another narcotics bust, they elitched. As Cassady married Carolyn Robinson and shared her with Jack, they elitched.

While these and other events became the early plot points in the gestation of the Beat Generation, what was really happening during these peregrinations was an unraveling of their minds, a journey across the landscape of their souls, but as they poured out their innermost thoughts and feelings to each other, Neal and Jack and Allen and Bill elitched together as often as possible because they were certain that the weed was invaluable to the entire endeavor, and when they ran out they would search and search until they could elitch once more.

By 1948, Ginsberg was seeing a Reichian therapist in New York who strongly disapproved of marijuana. It isn't hard to understand why he refused to comply when the therapist insisted that he stop smoking it, which led to his dismissal. After all, Reichian therapy paled in comparison to the sacralization of the mundane.

3.

The events and conversations of that season of 1948 would later be chronicled by John Clellon Holmes almost verbatim in his roman à clef, *Go*. Holmes had come to know Kerouac during the summer of 1948, when Kerouac was twenty-six and Holmes was an aspiring novelist of twenty-two. The two of them would go out and listen to jazz and walk around the city. Bird was flying high, and the nights of bop at the Royal Roost were luminous; the clubs were teeming with a new breed of underground habitué called hipsters.

Many writers of the time expounded on the hipster but all could agree on only one thing: Charlie Parker seemed the living validation of their philosophy. As jazz impresario Robert Reisner stated, "Bird was the supreme hipster. He made his own laws. His arrogance was enormous, his humility profound." According to Reisner, the hipster

is to the Second World War what the Dadaist was to the First. He is amoral, anarchistic, gentle, and over-civilized to the point of decadence. He is always ten steps ahead of the game because of his awareness, an example of which would be meeting a girl and reject-ing her, because he knows they will date, hold hands, kiss, neck, pet, fornicate, perhaps marry, divorce—so why start the whole thing? He knows the hypocrisy of bureaucracy, the hatred implicit in reli-gions—so what values are left for him?—except to go through life avoiding pain, keep his emotions in check, and after that, "be cool" and look for kicks. He is looking for something that transcends all this bullshit and finds it in jazz.

John Holmes was an intellectual—an industrious New England Yan-kee struggling with a bad marriage. Like Jack, he'd fallen head over heels in love with jazz and was looking for a subject to write about that he hoped would resonate with the times. A powerful bond would form between them that would last the rest of their lives.

During the fall of that year, Kerouac and Holmes had many dis-cussions about their generation. Both of them were seeking a concise epithet for it, like "Lost Generation," which had been applied to the generation of the 1930s. As Holmes later recalled in *Nothing More to Declare,* one evening the two of them were walking through Times Square and Kerouac was describing "the way the young hipsters of Times Square walked down the street—watchful, cat-like, inquisitive, close to the buildings, *in* the street but not of it—I interrupted him to say that I thought we *all* walked like that, but what was the peculiar quality of mind behind it?"

"It's sort of a furtiveness," Kerouac explained. "Like we were a gen-eration of furtives. You know, with an inner knowledge there's no use flaunting on that level, the level of the 'public' kind of beatness—I mean, being right down to it, to ourselves, because we all really know where we are—and a weariness with all the forms, all the conventions of the world. . . . It's something like that. *So* I guess you might say we're a *beat generation.*"

Kerouac then laughed a "conspiratorial, the-Shadow-knows kind of laugh" at his own words, and at the look on Holmes's face. Kerouac's use of "beat" had evolved from its original usage by Huncke to refer to the "wiped out" or "beaten down" world of the hustler and junkie. It now meant "upbeat," and as time went on he would use it more and more in the sense of "beatific." Kerouac also made prognostications during their conversations and in letters about how "all America would be picking up"—in other words, getting high—"changing, becoming sweeter, no more wars, sweet presidents."

Tranquility would be found in a gentle tolerance of one's neighbors, Kerouac predicted—"a sort of revolution of the soul"—what Ginsberg would call a condition of "tender-heartedness." Kerouac envisioned this future as a time of vision-questing and great optimism and hope. "Something will come of it," he would always say. Four years later, Holmes would attribute the coining of the phrase to Kerouac in his essay for the *New York Times Magazine*, "This Is the Beat Generation."

January of 1949 was a season of "mad, vast" parties for this "generation of furtives" in New York. John Holmes found himself pulled into a world of

> dingy backstairs "pads," Times Square cafeterias, bebop joints, night-long wanderings, meetings on street corners, hitchhiking, a myriad of "hip" bars all over the city, and the streets themselves. It was inhabited by people "hungup" with drugs and other habits, searching out a new degree of craziness; and connected by the invisible threads of need, petty crimes of long ago, or a strange recognition of affinity. They kept going all the time, living by night, rushing around to "make contact," suddenly disappearing into jail or on the road only to turn up again and search one another out. They had a view of life that was underground, mysterious, and they seemed unaware of anything outside the realities of deals, a pad to stay in, "digging the frantic jazz," and keeping everything going.

Ginsberg would refer to the season as "the year of consciousness that runs through everything that followed." It was the time of his visions, when he was studying the relationship between mysticism and modern artistic expression, and one night in his apartment in Harlem he heard a voice reciting William Blake's "Ah! Sunflower." The experience was like a "crack in his consciousness" that provoked in him "the impression of the entire universe as filled with poetry and light and intelligence and communication and signals. Kind of like the top of my head coming off, letting in the rest of the universe connected to my own brain."

Ginsberg's perception was so quickly and radically altered during this experience that he found himself projected into a visionary state in which, like Blake, he was capable of seeing the world in a grain of sand, or the timelessness of the graying sky outside—as if Blake's very mind had traveled to him through the centuries to speak directly to him. He was so ecstatic that he crawled out on the fire escape and tapped on the window, alarming the two women inside—"I've seen God!" They banged the window shut in his face.

Over the following days, Ginsberg remained in this elated state of mind, feeling a confirmation of his purpose in life as a poet, but also becoming frightened as the presence of it took on the hellish dimension of a "giant octopus serpent-monster consciousness" poised to devour him.

These were no mere "eyeball kicks" but full-blown visionary experiences. It was four years before Ginsberg would take peyote and ten years before he would know LSD, but he had already experienced the manifestations of heaven and hell that would later define his most important psychedelic experiences. While the visions provided both context and direction for the development of his poetic voice, they also initiated a period of committed experimentation with mind-altering drugs that would last for the next fifteen years.

"I thought for many years that my obligation was to annihilate my ordinary consciousness and expand my mystic consciousness," Ginberg later explained. "The remarkable thing is, I stupefied myself from 1948 to 1963. A long time. That's fifteen years preoccupied with one single thought."

4.

One freezing morning in February of 1949, Herbert Huncke showed up at Ginsberg's flat on York Avenue. He was starving, just out of jail, emaciated, delirious, his feet horribly blistered and bloody in his cracked shoes. It was like something right out of Dostoyevsky. In an act of compassion Ginsberg washed his bloody feet and invited him to stay until he recovered, but as the saying goes, no good deed goes unpunished. Huncke's crew of Vicky Russell and Little Jack Melody gradually started filling the place up with stolen merchandise, including a rather conspicuous cigarette machine in the kitchen. Ginsberg got increasingly irritated and nervous, until he could take no more and told them it was time to go, but not before they all piled into a stolen car and headed out to Queens to fence the stuff. When they passed a police car, Little Jack panicked because he was out on parole and driving a stolen car. The high-speed chase that followed ended when the car overturned, Ginsberg tumbled out onto the pavement, and they were all arrested.

Louis Ginsberg persuaded his son that he was in dire need of serious help and arranged for him to enter the Columbia Presbyterian Psychiatric Institute. He was on his way to the "bughouse" for eight months. Herbert Huncke was on his way to Sing Sing for five years.

That year Ginsberg wrote a poem called "Bop Lyrics" that seemed to sum up his life and the lives of his friends in a single line—"Smart went crazy." It was a theme that began laying the track for one of the most provocative poems of the twentieth century.

18

That Was Our Badge

1.

During the day, you could see them all hanging around down on the little square on St. Nicholas and 149th Street. The core of the group was right from the neighborhood: Jackie McLean, Arthur Taylor, Walter Bishop Jr., Kenny Drew, Connie Henry, Arthur Phipps. There was also Theodore Walter Rollins—called "Newk" because of his resemblance to pitcher Don Newcombe of the Brooklyn Dodgers, soon to be called "Sonny" by Clifford Brown—tall and intense, spare and goateed, who lived over on Edgecombe Avenue. They all had a certain look that consisted of dark wraparound shades and Mephistophelian-looking goatees and dark berets and dark suits with white-on-white shirts and silk ties and marcelled hair with double-dip pompadours. You had to look "clean," as Miles Davis liked to say. "Clean as a motherfucker. . . . Cleaner than a *broke dick dog*."

At night the young men of the Sugar Hill crowd could be found in their cleanest threads, hanging out at any number of places that included Sugar Ray Robinson's nightclub, Smalls Paradise, the Club Lido, Monroe's Uptown House, the Showman Bar, Club Harlem, the Baby Grand, the Rio, the Diamond, or Sterling LeVant's pool hall. Everywhere they went, they were noticed, admired, perhaps none more so than Miles with his marcelled hair and sharp Brooks Brothers suits. Having played second horn to Charlie Parker on his historic Savoy and Dial recordings, he was at the center of the group, one of the youngest stars of the bebop scene. Heroin had arrived in his life at a very vulnerable moment, after his return from Europe, where he had gone to perform at the International Jazz Festival of 1949, returning in a depression after a torrid affair with the French actress Juliette Gréco. He was living in the Hotel America down on 48th Street, "getting famous at exactly the same time I was getting hooked," as his autobiography so colorfully related it. "I didn't know it was going to hit me like that. I was so depressed when I got back that before I knew it, I had a heroin habit that took me four years to kick and I found myself for the first time out of control and sinking faster than a motherfucker toward death." (As with *Lady Sings the Blues*, the reliability of Miles's very readable and entertaining autobiography has been called into question by jazz scholars, again putting one in the paradoxical position of having to evaluate just where and how or whether or not to even use it at all; and as with Billie and her autobiography, the myths about drugs in Miles's life would become as much a part of his story as the truth.)

The son of a hardworking dentist with a very successful practice in East St. Louis, Miles grew up in an affluent upper-middle-class family, privileged, ambitious, but alienated and angered by the racism around him. He was sullenly hip and handsome, shy but arrogant, hot-blooded, prone to melancholy, and very droll if he was in the mood. Above all else Miles was an audaciously gifted and passionate musician, but as he was overtaken by his habit, he was growing ever more passive and remote. The nonet that had produced the *Birth of the Cool* sessions of 1949 represented the end of his first creative peak. Capitol Records had recently dropped his contract, and Miles had entered a period of his life when he would be forced to do anything to make money for dope: transcribe lead sheets, pawn his trumpet, cheat, lie, get money any place he could get it. He scraped by during this period by getting involved with a stable of uptown whores who were quite taken with him and were giving him money—"If it hadn't been for the women who supported me, I don't know how I would have made it without stealing like a lot of junkies were doing." He and Jackie McLean became roommates for the next couple of years. They liked to hang out at Stillman's Gym and sip cocktails at Bell's on Broadway. They would ride the subways together "higher than a motherfucker, laughing at the corny shoes and clothes people were wearing."

All of the Sugar Hill group had a deep musical connection to Charlie Parker, but none more so than Jackie McLean, the youngest member of the group. The Sugar Hill that McLean had grown up in, home to luminaries like Duke Ellington and Don Redman, was a neighborhood that was steeped in jazz like a rich roast simmering in a delicious gravy. McLean's stepfather owned a record shop that always carried all the latest sides, and from the age of fifteen, he knew that he would play an alto saxophone for the rest of his life. McLean was in the audience at Smalls Paradise on that night in February of 1947 after Bird returned from California, when Dizzy Gillespie had organized a welcome home celebration and Bird walked in with his wife, Doris, but without a horn, when suddenly an alto sax came sliding across the floor, glistening in the lights, and in one graceful motion Bird scooped the horn up and started playing "Cool Blues." It was a moment McLean would never forget. After that he would go down to 52nd Street whenever he could, looking for Bird exactly the same way that Bird had looked for Lester Young back in 1936 in Kansas City. He was too young to get into the clubs, but he would wait doggedly for any fleeting glimpse of Bird he could get, strain outside the doors to hear every note that he possibly could. One night Bird came out, smiled at him, and asked him what he'd like him to play. "A Night in Tunisia!" Bird went right in and played it for him. McLean was ecstatic. It was enough to make him go home and practice for a month.

It was right around the time of Bird's return that McLean first became aware of heroin in his neighborhood. "I would go to a party, and I would see some of my friends nodding. I had one friend, Richie Huggins. Someone said to me, 'He's *bangin.*' I said, "What do you mean?' 'Well, you know, man, that was what was wrong with Bird when he made the record, 'Lover Man.' And all of a sudden it began to register. That's when I first started seeing it in my neighborhood. And from the very beginning, in the neighborhood, and in my own mind, it was associated with Bird." McLean had just turned sixteen when he took his first snort of heroin at a Sunday afternoon cocktail sip he was playing at Bell's. As with so many others, snorting led him to his first shot—"taking skin," as they called it—"and then, finally, one day I was gone, man, just gone."

Since Bird's return from California, McLean had watched other musicians and kids in the neighborhood pick up heroin as Bird had plucked up that horn sliding so splendidly across the floor that night in Smalls Paradise, and now here they all were—the best and brightest modern jazz musicians of their generation—all stone hard-core junkies just like Bird.

Nowadays the group's ranks included plenty of out-of-towners. There was long tall Dexter Gordon, the son of a doctor, all the way from Central Avenue, hip and raspy-voiced, a veteran of Billy Eckstine's and Dizzy Gillespie's seminal bebop big bands, who carried his tenor in a sack under his arm. From Philadelphia came the hard-driving drummer, Joseph Rudolph Jones—"Philly Joe"—who would become to dope what W. C. Fields was to booze—the junkie's junkie. Philly Joe was an ex–truck driver, tap dancer, and the first black trolley driver in the history of Philadelphia. Nobody would exceed the sheer junkiedom of Philly Joe Jones, a man perfectly capable of locking himself in a hotel bathroom for three days and kicking cold turkey for the express purpose of getting his habit down, only he never did it for moral reasons or because be wanted to be a clean citizen or anything like that—he did it just to reduce his economic load, just so he could start shooting dope all over again.

Also from Philadelphia came John Coltrane, a very different kind of junkie than Philly Joe. The shy and introverted grandson of ministers, Coltrane had a heroin habit that had grown in stark and painful contrast to his strong Christian background. He was unpredictable, wildly creative, but saturnine, his head always off in the clouds, and his addiction had already by this time gotten him in trouble. He had already been fired from Dizzy Gillespie's and Johnny Hodges's bands, but his talent was simply too singular and overarching to keep him out of work for too long. Dope for Coltrane was an unfathomable thing, medication for all kinds of pain, beginning with the bad dental problems he had developed from a lifelong addiction to sweets, but his worst pain seemed to come, paradoxically, from what he loved the most. The exhibitionism of walking the bar with his saxophone in Philly clubs like the Musical Bar and the Zanzibar, being forced to play music he did not really want to play just to make a living during his early years, was a uniquely excruciating experience for him. Among many other things, dope was anesthesia for the pain of not being able to play the kind of music that he kept hearing in his head—music he was always changing his reed, adjusting his mouthpiece, doing everything possible to find.

When they had money for dope and weren't practicing, their days were easy, filled with the indolent pleasures of musicians. The group of them would cop their dope around 110th, 111th, and 116th Streets; they would get high at Bishop's, or at Jackie's parents' place, or at Sonny Rollins's place, which overlooked Yankee Stadium and where they would watch the sunset. Sometimes they would fall by Bud Powell's place. Like Art Blakey, Powell had also had his head cracked open, by a bouncer with a pistol at the Savoy. He was never the same, especially after the shock treatments he received when his mother sent him to Bellevue in 1946. Bud Powell was like a heartbreakingly lost child who wandered around in some tragic state of grace; he was mentally ill, but he played beautifully. His apartment had always been a kind of bebop salon, and just sitting there and watching him play, a big smile spread across his face, was for many of them a bittersweet kind of joy that seemed to mix perfectly with the heroin that coursed through their veins.

Of course, there were plenty of white boys, too: J. R. Monterose, the tenor player; Gerry Mulligan, the baritone player and arranger; Red Rodney, the trumpet player who had taken Miles's place on the stand with Bird and had gotten hooked. There was a downtown crowd that included Zoot Simms and Al Cohn. There was a whole other crew out on the West Coast: Art Pepper, Chet Baker, Stan Getz, Anita O'Day. The list goes on and on: Tadd Dameron, Sonny Stitt, Gene Ammons, James Moody, J. J. Johnson, Hampton Hawes . . .

The amazing diversity and number of musicians who became addicted to the drug during that time was a phenomenon unlike anything that had ever happened before. Jazz historian James Lincoln Collier estimates that as many as 75 percent of jazz musicians used heroin during the forties and fifties.

"There were a lot of tasters, who were just social users, who controlled the situation," observed Orrin Keepnews, who began running Riverside Records in the early 1950s and recorded scores of heroin-addicted musicians, including Bill Evans. "And then there were those for whom the most amazing thing got to be how such a creative artist was able to maintain such an unquestionably high level of performance despite a pretty overwhelming drug problem."

Forty years later, it was still difficult for Keepnews to visualize these artists as heroin addicts.

> So many men of great intelligence and spirit and passion and talent—Coltrane, Sonny Rollins, Max Roach—became drug addicts during that time, that it can only be understood as a very complex phenomenon. You can look at people who grew up in exactly the same musical environment, who went through many of the same experiences, and you have such incredible variety. Some, like Clifford Brown, were great players who never had any drug involvement; some had a deep drug involvement and made a decision to get out and did; others spent their whole lives chippying in one way or another. Which only goes to show that, in my opinion, it had a hell of a lot less to do with any kind of cultural universalities than it had to do with individual temperament.

2.

The dynamics of the presence and use of heroin, like the complexities and dimensions of its effects—on the lives of the musicians, the music itself, and the culture at large—would only become apparent with the passing of time.

The experience of the drug for each musician was as different as their psyches and backgrounds, every bit as individualized as their fingerprints, but once an individual was addicted, the drug preyed upon all the frailties and vulnerabilities of the human condition.

Dealing with heroin addiction would have been difficult enough under any circumstances, but it quickly became clear that the set and setting of the jazz scene itself, not to mention the life of criminality around heroin, only compounded those difficulties. Doubtless many individuals would never have conceived of taking heroin had they not made contact with the drug within the context of the jazz scene.

Others were drug addicts just waiting to happen, like land mines waiting to detonate. For these individuals, heroin quickly came to mean much more than just insulation against anxiety or rationalization for failure when things went wrong. From the very first contact, the drug appeared like the materialization of fate, and they become instantly dependent on the drug not just to face the rigors and challenges of a jazz career but to face life itself.

The life around jazz had always been a difficult one, teeming with every temptation of the night. "It would take a very unique individual to resist those strains and insecurities," commented Keepnews. "The real wonder is that everybody didn't go down the tubes."

Into this crucible was thrown a group of young, highly sensitive artists, whose youth and immaturity made them particularly susceptible to the lure of the drug. The pressures of being a young musician in the burgeoning bebop scene were particularly weighty. Each time a musician appeared in public he knew he was being closely scrutinized, judged by the quality of his ear, his capacity to improvise, the personal texture of his sound and style. As if this weren't nerve-racking enough, jobs were scarce and competition fierce, which played posthaste into the syndrome of heroin addiction.

Like Miles Davis, Jackie McLean was considered a prodigy, and it was Bud Powell who took him under wing and introduced him to Davis. McLean found the experience of performing with Miles's group at the age of eighteen absolutely harrowing at first. "That first night he was so scared and high that after playing about seven or eight bars of his solo, he suddenly ran off the stage and out the back door," Davis recalled of McLean's first gig with his band at Birdland. He followed him out back and found Jackie "puking his brains out in a garbage can, vomit all over his mouth." Club owner Oscar Goodstein offered him an handkerchief—"Here, kid, wipe your face"—and then "Jackie went back in there and played his ass off. I mean he was something that night."

"Bud Powell and those guys had kind of babied me," McLean explained. "They let me play by ear. But when I got with Miles, he wouldn't accept that. 'What, you don't know *this*, you don't know *that*, you gotta *learn* this! Come on, let's get busy!' It was rough for me because I was used to being spoiled. Bird said this about me, Bud said that, and his attitude was, 'I don't care about any of that cutesy stuff from two years ago. You're eighteen now and I'm taking you out here. You don't know how to play ''Round Midnight,' then learn it!' It was rough, but it was great, too. But in terms of my heroin use it was a bad time because I was strung out, and I had to learn everything the hard way, on the bandstand, embarrassed by playing the wrong changes and everything."

McLean would always view playing with Miles's band as his most emotionally challenging but musically important learning experience. "It consisted of the front line of Miles and Sonny Rollins, two of the brightest musicians of that time, and I was an add-on. Sonny and Miles were just incredible. I was afraid to play behind both of them! One night I remember feeling, I won't play behind Sonny tonight because he's playing too much, I'll play behind Miles . . . and then Miles would play more than Sonny! There was no soft spot for me, no easy cushion. If I played first, I felt it was trite compared to what would come later; and if I played in between them, I felt like I would get squashed! The heroin played a major role in keeping all of those feelings of insecurity about the music at bay, in a place where I could at least deal with it."

From the beginning there was the notion that heroin was a "working drug" when it came to the creation of jazz. "The thing I liked about it was that it relaxed me, as all opiates do," McLean acknowledged. "I understand that now. No stage fright; just go on and play. And of course when you're relaxed you play better."

Beyond this sedative kind of relaxation came a detached lucidity, and beyond that was the stimulation and challenge and concentrating power that came naturally from a lifestyle of constant danger and risk—the creative impetus of life on the edge. Scores of musicians who were addicts have talked about how the distance and detachment experienced while under the influence of the drug allowed them to mask out all other distractions and concentrate for extremely long periods of time, whether for purposes of writing or playing. Heroin took everything in life and reduced it to one very basic and simplified issue. Charlie Parker once depicted it as "a loan. You consolidate all your loans into one payment; that's a junkie. All of life's problems are one problem."

That the use of the drug had a profound impact on the music itself is indisputable. As John Szwed observes, like driving a fast car, "heroin narrowed the emotional and visual fields to only the moment. It gave a crystalline vision of the music, slowing the music down as well, stopping and holding to the light those beautiful bop melodies that otherwise could fly by so fast that they left nothing but vapor trails."

In *Swing to Bop*, Ira Gitler writes about noting in an earlier book, *Jazz Masters of the Forties*, that "in spite (or because?)" of the use of the drug, "a great music was made. . . . Drugs do not necessarily help musicians play better, but the music could not have been the same without everything that went into it. Now I would take the question mark off 'because.'"

Gitler was criticized for his opinion, which is not surprising considering heroin's dark and misapprehended history and that people in the jazz community were concerned about its public image, but his point is well-taken. Heroin was so prevalent at the time and became such a consequential part of the lives of so many musicians that regardless of its negative properties, it simply had to have been an essential ingredient in the great cultural and musical mixture that became bebop. As Dexter Gordon pointed out to him, "That's what you were playing—your lifestyle."

Red Rodney described to Gitler how various important experimental aspects of the music were clearly impacted by the effects of the drug—"the tempos for one thing. The tunes with the great changes in it. The intellectual part of it. Guys were always experimenting and the drugs had something to do with that, too. When a guy is loaded and at peace, he shuts everything else out except what he's interested in . . . he could tune out the honking of the world. And, 'Hey man, I just figured this out,' and it was great."

Rodney also made it very clear that the negative aspects of heroin were reflected in the music as well. "Hostility, pettiness, a lot of us became thieves, even though we didn't want to be. Our embarrassment showed. Our being ashamed of people that we liked knowing that we were hooked. Everything showed."

3.

Heroin may have served the functional and emotional needs of the musician, but there were other needs that were more psychological, symbolic, cultural, racial, and these were far-reaching. By 1948, the needle marks on one's arm had also become a declaration of hipness, an insignia of rebellion. Both were powerful elements in what was becoming a whole cultural sensibility coalescing around bebop, but to grasp the relationship between these attitudes and the use of heroin requires looking beyond the world of jazz and into the entire postwar temper and direction of hip black urban culture, and the white response to it.

As music mostly created by avant-garde African American artists in the wake of the Second World War, bebop was music of great hope and optimism, the heartcry of musicians striving to create an entirely new aesthetic, but it was also music of social upheaval, resentment, alienation, isolation, and nonconformism. Bebop became the soundtrack of resentment for a generation of black servicemen who returned from the war after risking their lives for their country only to find out that they were still very much second-class citizens. As drummer Kenny Clarke bluntly put it, "If America wouldn't honor its constitution and respect us as men, we couldn't give a shit about the American way."

The inner nucleus of musicians who created the music consisted of an artistic elite of spectacularly talented and accomplished individuals who deserved to be among the most venerated members of society and yet found themselves among the most denigrated. The music they created was not only outside of the mainstream of American culture but outside of the mainstream of the culture of jazz as well. The bebop tradition that developed froze out the outsiders with inside jokes and hip lingo, creating a distance from which one could gaze with blatant irony at "square" America—"birding the outsiders," as Coleridge Goode called it. Consequently, bebop provoked attacks from not only the jazz establishment but also from social critics across the cultural spectrum.

"For the first time critics and commentators on jazz, as well as critics in other fields, attacked a whole mode of Afro-American music," observed Amiri Baraka (then still LeRoi Jones) in his classic work *Blues People*. He asserted that heroin played an obvious role in fomenting this cultural stance of isolation and distance: "Narcotics users, especially those addicted to heroin, isolate themselves and are an isolated group in society. They are also the most securely self-assured in-group extant in the society, with the possible exception of homosexuals. Heroin is the most popular addictive drug used by Negroes

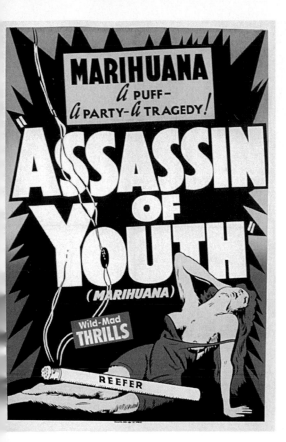

Perhaps nothing expresses the hysteria inherent in the history of drug prohibition in America more than "Marihuana: Assassin of Youth," the centerpiece of Harry Anslinger's antimarijuana campaign in 1936. *(Everett Collection)*

Louis Armstrong appearing in *Every Day's a Holiday* (1937), a title that nicely sums up his philosophy of life. Pops was the first in a line of powerful jazz innovators and improvisers who would become renowned for the use of a particular substance; his marijuana smoking would always be identified with his genial, generous, live-and-let-live nature. *(© AGIP/RDA/Everett Collection)*

The Savoy Ballroom,
circa 1940. One of the
few places in America
where whites and blacks
could mingle and dance
together in freedom,
it became the nexus of
viper culture as well.
(Everett Collection)

Harry J. Anslinger, head
of the Federal Bureau of
Narcotics—a complex
blend of cop, crusader,
bureaucrat, propagan-
dist, xenophobe, and
racist—in G-man fedora.
(Everett Collection)

Promotional shot of
Billie Holiday, circa 1936.
(*Underwood Archives/UIG/
Everett Collection*)

The quintessential Lady Day, a singer capable of transforming popular ballads into intensely personal and poignant works of art. The problems of her life became one with her stage persona as a torch singer to create a myth that ultimately over-shadowed her musical genius. *(CSU Archives/Everett Collection)*

(Facing page, top) Lester Young, the "President of the Tenors," in his trademark porkpie hat in the early 1940s. To a significant degree, the modern version of "cool" began as a way of looking at the world through the dark glasses that he wore onstage at the Savoy, hiding his stoned, heavy-lidded green eyes as he came to define the very essence of it. *(Everett Collection)*

Mezz Mezzrow in
1946, signing copies
of *Really the Blues,* a
book that the young
Allen Ginsberg stud-
ied in the Columbia
University bookstore
as if it were the
Rosetta Stone.
(Library of Congress)

Charlie Parker—the iconic Bird—after his return to New York from his breakdown on the West Coast. The use of heroin spread in direct proportion to the
cult of Charlie Parker, and by 1948 Bird was at his most dazzling. *(Everett Collection)*

Fifty-Second Street in 1949, when the doorman at the Royal Roost was the heroin connection. *(Everett Collection)*

Self-portrait of Allen Ginsberg in 1949, when he was twenty-three, before his seven-month stay at the Columbia Presbyterian Psychiatric Institute.
(© *Allen Ginsberg LLC*)

Portrait of two sphinxes: William Burroughs visiting the American Museum of Natural History in 1953, the year he published *Junky* and traveled to the Amazon to ingest yage.
(© *Allen Ginsberg LLC*)

(*Top*) Burroughs and Kerouac in Ginsberg's apartment, 206 East 7th Street, in the fall of 1953, as Bill lectured Jack about his mother: "But Jack, I've told you over and over, if you continue your present pattern of living with your memere, you'll be wound closer and closer in her apron strings till you're an old man." (*© Allen Ginsberg LLC*)

Herbert Huncke: hustler, petty thief, jailbird, raconteur, writer, lifelong drug *addict*, and the man who first put the word *beat* in the "Beat Generation," photographed by Allen Ginsberg in the Hotel Elite before Christmas of 1953. According to Ginsberg's handwritten caption, "He fixed at the sink." (*© Allen Ginsberg LLC*)

(Facing page) Neal Cassady, Dean Moriarty himself—"that wow-mad Cody"—
"the great Midwest driver and experiencer and talker"—in San Francisco in the
spring of 1955, helping Ginsberg and Peter Orlovsky purchase a used car.
(© Allen Ginsberg LLC)

(Facing page) Miles Davis and Stan Getz in 1951. By this time Miles was a full-blown
heroin addict doing anything he could to survive and feed his habit.
(© AGIP/RDA/Everett Collection)

(Above) Bird and Dizzy Gillespie at Birdland in March of 1951, with John Coltrane
and Tommy Potter on bass. Like Louis Armstrong, Diz always set clear-cut boundaries
and never touched hard drugs, whereas Bird was the exact opposite, grasping at life,
music, and drugs with a reckless, insatiable hunger.
(© AGIP/RDA/Everett Collection)

(Above) The brilliant John Coltrane in the mid-1950s. Though he was trapped in the routines of drug addiction and alcoholism, his playing was the one thing that was never the same, and his breakout from heroin and booze would unleash a creative surge that would have major repercussions on the entire direction of jazz. *(Everett Collection)*

(Facing page) Studio session for *Miles '58* on May 26, 1958. L to R: John Coltrane, Cannonball Adderley, Miles, and Bill Evans. Trane had been clean for a year and Miles for four years, but Bill Evans was a heavy junkie. *(© AGIP/RDA/Everett Collection)*

Jack Kerouac, the Great Rememberer. His life became his work and the substances he used became inseparable from his creative process as he searched for "the wild form that can grow with my wild heart." *(Everett Collection)*

(*Above*) The Lady of CBS's "Sound of Jazz," in the studio in 1957, "in full control of the tart, penetrating, sinuously swinging instrument which was her voice." Despite everything she'd been through, it was uncanny how she appeared more luminous, more beautiful with each passing moment of the broadcast.
(© *AGIP/RDA/Everett Collection*)

(*Facing page*) Jackie McLean, one of Charlie Parker's protégés, performing in *The Connection* at the Living Theatre—a play that mirrored the predicament of his life as a heroin addict so closely that there was virtually no transition as he stepped from street to stage.
(*Mary Evans/Ronald Grant/Everett Collection*)

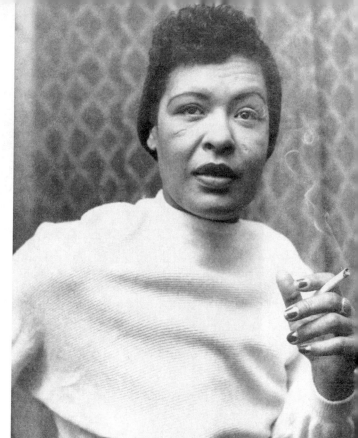

Lady, as the problems closed in.
(©Mirrorpix/Everett Collection)

Allen Ginsberg at a LEMAR demonstration in the winter of 1964, sending his message to the world and making good on his vow to challenge Harry Anslinger and the regime of marijuana prohibition. *(CSU Archives/Everett Collection)*

because, it seems to me, the drug itself transforms the Negro's normal separation from the mainstream of the society into an advantage (which, I have been saying, I think it is anyway). It is one-upsmanship of the highest order."

As Baraka viewed it, heroin served to enhance and anesthetize the isolation of the black jazz musician from society and "the horror, etc." of racism. For this reason the equation of heroin and hipness could mean very different things to whites and blacks. If a *hep cat,* as derived from the Molof *hipicat,* was defined as "a man who has his eyes open," what the white hep cat became aware of, instead of racism, was usually the suffocating squareness and soul-murdering rigidity of the straight white world. For white hipsters like the painter Larry Rivers, dope could facilitate the expression of a cool existentialism, a flight from conventional white society, an identification with the dangers of hip black culture. "I just knew that Parker did it and a lot of the guys I knew started trying it," Rivers related. "I didn't really understand it beyond that. You knew you could go to jail; you knew that it was serious stuff, way more serious than pot. You knew you could *die*—and you knew people who already *had* died. You were living right there on the edge in common with guys like Charlie Parker, who were black and definitely lived outside the law. I always compared it to getting on a motorcycle and going very fast. You knew you could get killed but somehow felt that the odds were with you."

For the black musicians, on the other hand, the element of hipness as it related to heroin was more uniquely and purely concerned with an awareness of racial oppression and isolation from society. Culturally, it was a matter of the difference between people using a drug to *become* outsiders and people using a drug precisely because they *were* outsiders. Thus, for black jazz musicians, dope only served to enhance a process of out-casting that had already existed for centuries, and their isolation from society was only exacerbated by the oppression they experienced within the business of jazz itself—by the element of racism inherent in the system and the sense of exploitation and rage that resulted from it.

Nobody experienced this exploitation and rage more acutely than the great bassist, composer, and bandleader Charles Mingus. "Aw, they own us, Mingus," expounds Fats Navarro in a telling passage of

Mingus's autobiography, *Beneath the Underdog: His World as Composed by Mingus*. "If they don't own us, they push us off the scene. Jazz is big business to the white man and you can't move without him. We just work-ants. He owns the magazines, agencies, record companies and all the joints that sell jazz to the public. If you won't sell out and you try to fight they won't hire you and they give a bad picture of you with that false publicity." Navarro then refers to the plight of "King Spook" as an example of this exploitation—obviously a reference to Charlie Parker: "King Spook don't even own fifty percent of himself! His agent gets fifty-one, forty-nine goes to a corporation set up in his name that he don't control and he draws five hundred a week and don't say nothing—but he's famous, Mingus, hear, he's famous!"

Though Mingus would fight this system his whole life and would never become a drug addict himself, from this perspective it was no wonder that so many, like Billie Holiday, became junkies:

> Oh, it's a hard wrinkle, Mingus. Haw haw! I'm thinking when Peggy Lee be appearing in some east side club. Her biggest applause comes when she says, "Now I'm going to do the great Billie Holiday," and Billie be out on the street and they all be saying she's a junkie. They had Billie so hung up they wouldn't pay the right way, they just put a little money in her hand every night after work, just enough so she come back tomorrow. They drives ya to it, Mingus. They got you down and they don't let you up.

No single artist reflected this experience in all of its complexity and bitter irony more than Charlie Parker—the "King Spook" of Mingus's *Beneath the Underdog*. Perhaps the most famous story of how Bird was "bugged by the fact that, being a Negro, he could go just so far and no farther" was related by Duke Jordan and took place during the celebrated Royal Roost engagements of 1948.

> Once he finished a set to great acclaim, ducked out and went quietly to a bar around the corner on Sixth Avenue between 51st and 52nd Street, called McGuire's. The paradox of his life was brought into focus when the bartender asked what he wanted and addressed him as "nigger." Parker vaulted over the bar to teach the fellow

manners. The man picked up a bottle and broke it over Bird's head. It cut his dome and he always had a little scar; but it did not prevent Charlie from blackening both the guy's eyes and knocking a few of his teeth out.

Such incidents were painfully ubiquitous occurrences at the time, commonplace in the lives of black jazz musicians everywhere, and were no doubt what prompted Hampton Hawes to characterize Bird as "the first jazz musician I have ever met who understood what was happening to his people. He couldn't come up with an answer. So he stayed high."

The theme of heroin as an anodyne for the frustration and pain of racism in the lives of musicians comes up over and over again. Certainly, in the world inhabited by these musicians during the period 1945–1965, racism was as real as the scar on Charlie Parker's head, and Bird could easily cite the existence of such racism, along with the exploitation of the music business, as an excuse for his continuing use of drugs. "Wait until everybody gets rich off your style and you don't have any bread," Bird once told Babs Gonzales when Gonzales tried to tell him to get off drugs, "then lecture me about drugs."

Moreover, that Bird presented a powerful paradigm of rebellion—a newfangled kind of integrity and courage—by using drugs in the face of this predicament of racism and exploitation was also undeniable. Max Roach would liken it to "a young Buddhist monk pouring oil on himself and lighting a match. 'Sure, I got a lotta talent, but I'm not gonna let you exploit it.' . . . 'Kiss my ass!' is the way Bird perceived it within himself, I believe, just from knowing him."

If bebop represented what Jackie McLean called "the first time the black ego was expressed in America with assurance," heroin constituted its greatest liability. By 1950, it was becoming apparent that heroin was especially disastrous for jazz musicians even beyond its damaging effects on the lives of the individual musicians who used it, for the simple reason that it only made them more vulnerable to exploitation and presented the police with the most convenient tool of repression possible. One of the most painful paradoxes of the use of heroin was doubtless to be found in the fact that here was a group of supremely gifted African American artists—extraordinary men of fierce pride and courage and dignity who were seeking autonomy and freedom, rebelliously asserting their manhood through a music that had ignited a revolutionary cultural movement—who at the same time were making themselves ever more vulnerable through their dependence on heroin.

Yes, drugs had quickly become a convenient reason to close down places like the Spotlight because, in the view of Miles Davis, "they didn't like all them black men being with all them rich, fine, white women," but now drugs also made advancement more difficult for these musicians within their own industry. Whatever aspirations these artists had to change the system that exploited them would certainly never be fulfilled by individuals desperate for a fix, who were willing to agree to virtually any term set by a club owner or record company executive or lowly pawnshop clerk just so they could get their hands on any sum of money for drugs. This held especially true for their relationships with the small independent labels that recorded jazz during the forties and fifties. Some labels, like Prestige, became known as "the junkies' label" and "the plantation" simply because the musicians knew they could get quick money for a recording date—and most were happy to know it was there when they were dope sick. Did the independent record companies and club owners knowingly take advantage of musicians who were strung out on dope?

"Are you kidding? To the point of death," Jackie McLean rejoined. "It was terrible. We were helpless. If I could go up to an office and get twenty-five dollars every day because of my addiction, that was it, I'd do it. I'd sign anything to just keep getting the money. Some of the labels were terribly exploitative. They took advantage of all of us, Miles included. . . . I never read the contracts because I was always strung out. 'When is the date?' That's all I wanted to know. We paid for the whole date. All the music went into their publishing company, so they made a killing there. The recording contract you signed said that you paid for everything eventually: sandwiches, cabs, Rudy Van Gelder, studio time, the pressing of the records, the design, everything. You got no royalties until that nut was met, plus your three-hundred-dollar advance as a bandleader. And so when the royalty statements would come, Dolly, my wife, would look at it and say, 'I don't understand this, look at this!

We owe the company fifty-four thousand dollars, how can this be?' And that sum you owed them would only gradually diminish over the years, slowly, over all those albums."

On the other side were men like Orrin Keepnews of Riverside Records, who loved jazz and respected the artists and tried to do the right thing but found themselves caught in the middle. "There were people who used to say, 'I could just look into somebody's eyes and know if they were straight or not.' Well, I don't know about that, but I could tell by looking in my checkbook. The guy that came in to hit me up for a ten- or fifteen-dollar draw two or three times a week, chances are he didn't need that to get his laundry out. . . . I lived with that aspect of it a lot. There were guys I was close to, but I was a record company—that's how I got into the business. 'Can I have a draw against next week's record date?' After a while it was, 'Can I have a draw against *next year's* record date?' I was always having to balance emotions and practicalities, between my compassion for them as people and the hard requirements of running a business. And there was always the question of whether I was doing them any fucking favor by giving them any money for dope in the first place. . . . It became a pretty consistent part of my life, and you ended up dealing with it in the fashion of most people: you didn't form some sort of ironclad set of standards. You did what you felt you had to do from day to day, and it varied tremendously."

More than anything, dope was a whole way of life, like living in a world of your own construction, inside a walled city with those of your own kind, where you could make up your own language, create your own set of rules.

"That's right, and you didn't have to be a musician to be in that club, either," McLean pointed out. "I had plenty of buddies who followed the music, and they ended up getting strung out, too. In the end it was us against the world, and it had no racial lines."

Perhaps nobody elucidated the phenomenon more vividly or succinctly than Red Rodney.

"That was our badge. It was the thing that made us different from the rest of the world. It was the thing that said, 'We know, you don't know.' It was the thing that gave us membership in a unique club, and for this membership, we gave up everything else in the world. Every ambition. Every desire. Everything. It ruined most of the people. It turned out that the drugs had to be done away with and if it had to kill many of us, it was a lesson."

The lessons were very hard ones to learn, and for many, would be a long time coming. But despite and through all of it, they created a classic American music.

19

Blues for a Junkie Whore

1.

Ruby Rosano's first arrest came at the end of November, 1955: loitering for the purposes of prostitution.

Ruby had hung out in a bar called Grenado's in the Village on Third and MacDougal ever since she had run away from the Bronx, and one night she was in there with Terry, one of the lesbians who frequented the place. Ruby wasn't even working that night when some guy came in wearing one of those stupid loud Hawaiian shirts that were the most obvious thing that vice cops ever used to wear to make themselves look hip and inconspicuous. He was flashing a lot of dough and acting drunk. Ruby was standing with Terry over by the jukebox, and Tony, the bar pimp, told them, "See that guy over there, all he wants is a show," which meant that he wanted to watch two women make love. Ruby was so fucked up at the time that she went against her hunch about the guy, but that, in a nutshell, was always her problem in life: being far too fucked up at any given time. The plan was to take this guy to one of the cheap little hooker hotels in the Village, like the Marlton on 8th Street, and just wait until he passed out and take his money and run. They had gotten into a cab with him when he grabbed each door handle and held the doors closed so that they couldn't escape. "Freeze!" he shouted at them as a patrol car came screeching up alongside them. "You whores are under arrest!"

It was perfectly true that Ruby Rosano was a whore, but what they didn't know when they dragged her into the Women's House of D at

10th Street and Sixth Avenue for the first time was that she was a junkie whore. Oh, they would find out soon enough, of course. When she got picked up she had the worst oil burner of a heroin habit she had ever had in her life up to that point, and you couldn't hide such a thing for too long in a place like that. Nobody at Grenado's would put up a red cent to bail her out, despite the fact that she had been working out of there for years, and she was so furious that she gave the whole place up, told the police everything that was happening there, and they promptly got a court order and shut the place down. There would be a lot of people pissed off at her when she got out but she didn't give a damn, and this was another of her problems: there were always a lot of people pissed off at Ruby; somebody was always after her and punching her in the face or taking a shot at her out on the streets. She was notorious throughout the Village as "Ruby the crazy Italian," and what they said about her was, "Ruby is crazy, she doesn't give a shit if she lives or dies, but if you fuck with her she'll take you with her," and they had fucked with her by not bailing her out.

When they appeared before the judge, Terry's lawyer said his client couldn't possibly be a prostitute because she was a lesbian and a virgin, and the judge went for it and cut her loose. Ruby was flabbergasted by Terry's good fortune, which mystified her because Ruby never seemed to have any. Worse, the judge was a guy who hated whores, and all it took was one look for him to hate her even more.

It's not hard to imagine the way Ruby looked in those days because by that time there was a whole genre of pulp fiction about juvenile delinquents and drug addicts. Ruby looked exactly like one of the girls painted on the covers of lurid paperbacks that sold for a quarter, like *Dope, Inc.* or *Reefer Girl* or *Sin Hipster* or *Narco Nympho*. She could have easily posed for one of the covers that featured girls in a state of wanton, drug-induced sexual languor, lips parted in erotic supplication, poised on the verge of an orgasm you knew would never be enough to satisfy them. She was always dressed completely in black, from head to toe. Everything was always skintight, and she wore black spike heels. She had raven hair hanging down to her ass and pale skin that never saw the light of day. With the heavy, dramatic, kohl-black eye makeup she got up at Stein's in Times Square, she looked like an Italian version of Morticia Addams, and she had a Morticia Addams body too, tight-assed and small-waisted with beautiful, ripe, upthrust pointed breasts that were always being shown off by plunging necklines and push-up brassieres.

But she also had large mannish hands for a girl her size and broad Joan Crawford shoulders, so she could go the other way, too. The lesbians of the Village all said she was really a dyke and that was why she dressed so feminine; the gay guys would insist she was really a fag in drag ("Oh, Mary," they always said to her, "who are *you* trying to kid?"); and straight men who saw her, well, they wanted her for the same reason men always wanted girls like her: they wanted to use, possess, ravage, and degrade her. For that reason Ruby never knew whom she would attract, and the truth was, she liked it that way. She liked never knowing whom she would go home with on any night.

"I know this is your first arrest, but I know you've been on the streets for a long time, and I'm gonna make sure the streets are at least safe from the likes of you for the holidays," the judge proclaimed sternly. Then he slapped her with forty-five days and gave her "spite time," which meant that she couldn't get any time off for good behavior. He banged the gavel down hard, and the next thing she knew she was in a cell, puking into a tin can.

The first couple of days she thought she might die. The story that was going around the jail was that if you were a junkie and died there, they would ship your ass over to Bellevue and shoot you full of morphine and say that you had come in that way, just OD'd and died, and there would be no questions asked. If you got too dehydrated while you were kicking, they would drag you upstairs and stick needles in you and run sugar water into your body, but that was even worse. Your legs would blow up like balloons so that finally the pain got worse than the pain of constant vomiting, and you would just rip the IV tubes out and go back down to your cell and cold turkey it, and that's what Ruby did, puked her guts out, chills, sweats, diarrhea, but that wasn't the worst part. The worst part was that she had finally been arrested. That was the ultimate disgrace. To come from an old-world Roman Catholic Italian family and be arrested like that—it was like dirt that wouldn't wash off. They had put that number around her neck and taken her mug shot and fingerprinted her and stuck their fingers in every hole that she had. She was finished; she had gone down as far as she could go. *Oh, you've hit bottom now, Ruby,* she kept telling herself, *you worthless piece of shit. Every possibility of you ever changing, of ever living a decent life, is finished.*

Then one day in her cell she made a resolution: *That's it, I'm never stickin' another needle in my arm,* she vowed, *'cause I'm* never *going to jail again.* She really meant it, but on her first day out she stopped in the bar to wash the taste of the prison out of her mouth, and everybody had forgiven her by that time and was glad to see her and started geezing her up with all kinds of free booze, free pot, free pills, and before she knew it she was slogged silly, but none of it got her where she really wanted to go. It never did . . .

Ruby was on her way to 116th and Lenox. She was in the same shooting gallery, the little basement apartment, where Bird and Lady sometimes came to get straight. You waited there while the dealer went and got the stuff, so there was never too much on the premises. She used someone else's works. The only problem was, she forgot. She cooked up as much dope as she had been using before she went to jail. She couldn't wait. The moment it was ready she popped that spike in. One push and the darkness came rushing in on her like a great terrible wind that came out of nowhere and she was going down, being washed away in a tidal wave; she was caught in a swirling vortex pulling her swiftly down into a deep dark drain, and her last drowning thought was, *Please, dear God, I know I deserve it, but if I'm going please don't let it be to hell . . .*

Imagine her, coming to in a bathtub. Imagine her surprise to discover that she was naked in a tub full of ice. Four strange black men were standing over her. They had concerned looks on their faces. One of them was sticking a pin in her big toe, studying her reaction. She looked up at them, and all she said was, "Which *one* of you motherfuckers has my dope?" And they just looked down at her and shook their heads sadly. "Baby, you were blue," one of them said back to her. "You were *dead.* If you hadn't opened up your eyes we were gonna dump you out in the alley with the rest of the garbage, and that's all you can think to say?"

"I was a junkie and I was a whore and I did what I had to do to survive," Ruby Rosano said later by way of simple explanation. It was about forty years after this incident occurred, and she was recounting the story of her life in her apartment on the Upper West Side of Manhattan. As surely as addiction was a by-product of the drug culture of the time, her story belongs in this narrative. In fact, Ruby had been one of those very benighted and degraded "angels" that Kerouac and Ginsberg were sketching as they hung out in Times Square, stoned on pot and buzzing on bennies and contemplating the Great Molecular Comedown.

"We were a new kind of prostitute—the heroin-addicted kind. We were members of a strange, sad, and very fucked up sorority. And we have our own story to tell."

And quite a story it was.

2.

"From the time I was five I felt destined for terrible things," Ruby acknowledged. "Through most of my journey through life, I felt crushed by defeat and humiliation. Most of my life I have felt completely alone. By the age of nineteen, I believed I would be dead before I reached my twenty-fifth birthday, and that I would die violently."

She came from an Italian immigrant family on the Lower East Side of New York. Her mother had been abandoned by her first husband with two babies to raise alone in the new country and suffered a nervous breakdown after performing an illegal abortion on herself. The alcoholic and gambler her mother then married became Ruby's father. One day her father attempted suicide by jumping into the East River, and then after returning from the hospital he just disappeared, never to return.

The only person who paid any attention to her was her grandfather, who started molesting her when she was eleven, sometime after they moved to the Bronx. He would take her to the cellar and fondle her, exposing himself. He would lift her up and place his penis between her legs. To the end of her days Ruby still tried to block out the specific acts, but images came back to her in horrific stroboscopic flashes. Her grandmother's room. Being placed on the folded-over mattress. She could still see the flickering vigil candles on the top of the dresser, surrounded by the statues of the Virgin Mary and the infant Jesus. How scared she was of those statues! He must have been trying to penetrate her because she remembered that it hurt so bad that she went to her mother and told her. *Please, Mama, make him stop. Make him stop because it hurts.* Instead her mother blamed her, accused her of doing something to lead him on; and later, after her grandmother died and her grandfather got drunk and stabbed her uncle in a quarrel over the funeral, the whole story came out, and Ruby had to tell it over and over again in the judge's chambers.

Her grandfather was dragged away to jail, but then everybody in the neighborhood knew what had happened. Now the boys in St. Mary's Park began circling her like vultures. They told her that they wanted to play with her. She was desperate for attention because she always thought she was so ugly and unpopular, and she followed them back to the empty part of the school yard where nobody ever went. Two of them pinned her down hard by the shoulders and one held her feet apart. She couldn't move. One of them climbed on top of her and started raping her. Then they took turns. There was nothing that she could do and no power on earth that could stop it, and she ran home crying hysterically and told her mother, who didn't know what to do so she did nothing. It happened again. And again.

As she told the story, Ruby could still see their faces in the late-afternoon sunlight, these rough Italian boys from the neighborhood who did this to her. She hated them with all her soul but she hated her mother even more, and every man who would ever leave her alone to fend for herself in this great big cold hard sick rotten fucking world. Mostly, of course, she hated herself. Ruby grew up with the most embittered unremitting kind of self-hatred imaginable. "If someone could only know, if someone could taste my heart, I would sometimes say, it would poison them. I'd been taught that God is vengeful and punishing, and if such things were happening to me, then it must certainly be my fault. Something must be terribly, dreadfully wrong with me. What happened is that something in me just hardened. I remember the day it happened, the day I promised myself that no matter what, no one would ever make me cry again."

The day after Pearl Harbor was bombed, Ruby gleefully hopped on a subway down to Times Square. She was fourteen. Everyone might have been scared about the war but not Ruby—she felt perfectly comfortable with the chaos and fear.

Times Square was electric, thrilling, suddenly filled with handsome men in uniform. She discovered the Paramount and Frank Sinatra and Tommy Dorsey. Sinatra had those blue eyes, and Ruby became one of the thousands of screaming, squealing teenagers in bobby sox waiting on line with her lunch, sitting through every one of his shows from morning until closing. Lionel Hampton was playing at the Strand and she learned how to lindy hop with the best of them. Ruby became a big band fanatic, and one night she got drunk on a neighborhood stoop and a couple of friends asked her if she wanted to go down to the Square.

"I went roller-skating at the Roxy with the sailors, and the whole place seemed magic to me, and everything changed. It's such an old story, right? Like Cinderella. I was transformed from this horrible ugly duckling into a beautiful, exciting princess, capable and fearless, and I had fun maybe for the first time in my life, talking to the sailors. They had their arms around my waist, and I actually liked the way it felt, and I wasn't afraid of them like the boys up in my neighborhood, and with each turn of that skating rink, it seemed that my life in the Bronx started to recede."

This is how Ruby spent the war years, reveling in Times Square, skating and dancing and drinking. Her sex life began in earnest when she stared making out with sailors in the backs of cabs and one of them taught her how to give him a hand job, and when another one wanted her to give him a blow job, she didn't know how but she was willing to learn, and he was only too willing to teach her. "You see, a blow job is a real art," he explained, "and not every woman is good at it," but she found that she was quite good indeed.

Ruby was working in a factory in the Bronx, and coming out of the subway one day she got picked up by this redheaded Jewish hipster named Allen Schwartz, who turned her on to marijuana. She found her true home on the day Schwartz took her to Café Society downtown. "He knew a lot of people there, where all the jazz musicians went when they finished their gigs up on 52nd Street, and as soon as I walked in I knew I was home; this whole other world opened up. It was like heaven. It was a world where nobody cared what you did. Nobody gave a damn. It was much more exciting than Times Square. There were no fingers pointed—it didn't matter how outrageous you were. That's what the Village was all about, and I fell completely in love with it."

Ruby smoked pot whenever she could find it but soon found bennies and barbs too and became what would later become known as your classic garbage head. She liked the danger and excitement of throwing down anything that you put in her hand, just to see what would happen. She started dressing wild, and more people in the neighborhood started noticing her. She discovered that one of her friends from elementary school was a lesbian—and she liked the idea. She also liked the idea of having sex with all the jazz musicians she started hanging out with at the clubs in the Village, especially the black ones, because what could possibly be more wicked than that? She became a kind of camp follower, an early form of what would later become known as a groupie. She started waiting for them outside stage doors, following them around. She still adored Lionel Hampton, and the guys in his band started having a lot of fun with her. One night she got really high and let it all go, and before it was over she managed to break every rule; she got passed from one to another daisy-chain style and in every conceivable combination acted out every single sexual scenario and violated every taboo that people like Harry Anslinger and the other guardians of American civilization had always feared would happen to Caucasian girls with black men when they smoked marijuana together. She had become exactly like the girls in books like *The Golden Spike* who smoked reefer and became instantly corrupted, and became junkies and had wild perverse sex with black jazz musicians, and she loved every minute of it. Much later in life she would encounter the phrase "acting out" and of course realize that was exactly what she was doing. And then came the red-letter day when she just left Arthur Avenue forever and moved to the Village.

"I went down to the Village and went to Grenado's and said, 'I need a place to hang out until can get a pad.' I had nowhere to turn, no money, no education, no skills. I had nothing but my resentment, my bitterness, my hatred of the world, and my enormous terror, but I could push that away with alcohol and pot. I quickly became more sexually active with women and had more anger toward men, which made it easier because I made my living as a con, pulling the 'key trick.' I used to promise guys I would fuck them if they would give me money in advance. Then I would give them the key to my house and tell them I would meet them there, and I would give them the address of the Women's House of Detention. Oh, I loved it!—I had a wicked sense of humor and I wanted to get over on those bozos. It was now 1949, 1950, and I started hanging out with a jazz musician who lived right over Café Society, and who shall go unnamed. This guy really fell in love with me but he was much too nice; he bored the hell out of me. I had my own table right downstairs. Fifty-Second Street was really hoppin' and the Metropole was at its height, and there was Jimmy Ryan's, and I adored all those sleazy little strip joints. . . .

"Things were going along and then I pulled the key trick one too many times. I was getting out of a cab and going into my apartment and some guy started shooting at me right there on the street! I dropped to the ground and crawled into my house and stayed in there, trembling, for a whole day. Some guy had obviously taken a bit of umbrage at my having taken his money and not put out. So I went to Grenado's and there were women hookin' out of there, and this girl said, 'Look, I work for this high-class madam uptown, do you want to meet her?' I didn't know what else to do. I was a high school dropout, but I wasn't about to work in a factory. The only thing I could think of was to be a waitress, but I was afraid that if somebody ever gave me any shit I would just pull out a knife, stab them in the heart. She took me uptown to meet this madam. Terri. Big, tough woman. And she sent me on my first trick."

Terri decided that Ruby ought to have it easy for her first time.

"This guy only saw a woman once. He had this special thing. I smoked opium for hours and hours before I went to his house, so the whole thing happened in a kind of dream. A butler greeted you at the door. He would tell you to strip, and you'd go to a room and there were black heels of all sizes, long, dangling earrings, black stockings, garter belts, and he handed you a drink and said, 'When you're ready, when you're naked, come out and stand in front of the drapes, please'—all very proper. I had been warned what to expect, of course. The drapes were pulled back, and this guy, this old turkey, would be laying in a coffin in his living room with a candelabra on both sides of the coffin. He would be dressed in a tuxedo, and all that would be moving would be his hand on his prick, and when the curtains got ripped back, you would scream, and the moment you screamed, he came. I guess he got off on women being scared out of their skulls, so when it happened I shrieked really well. What can I say, I was a really talented screamer. . . . The butler handed me two one-hundred-dollar bills, and I got a fifty-dollar tip, I was so good. That was a lot of money in those days."

And so began Ruby Rosano's illustrious career as a bebop hooker.

3.

Ruby fell into the life quickly. As she became a fixture in the Village, she loved hanging out with the homos on 8th Street. Club 81 had the best transvestite show in town. The waiters were all lesbian dolls in tuxedos. But most of all, she loved the jazz scene, getting high and diggin' Dizz, Bird, Stan Getz, and especially Billie Holiday. When Ruby encountered Lady in the clubs of Harlem, 52nd Street, and the Village, she felt that it was destiny. In fact, Ruby was in the Carnegie Hall audience on that unforgettable night in March of 1948 when Lady Day had made her triumphant return from Alderson.

"She couldn't sing in the clubs anymore but I would see her around and I knew her music very well, and God, how I adored her. I would hear so much about her along that drug grapevine of the jazz scene. I mean, the parallels between us were pretty obvious. I heard that there was sexual abuse in her childhood. I knew she'd been a prostitute. I heard she liked girls, too. High-class white girls. And it was also obvious that she'd get bored by the guys who were sweet and caring and that she was hung up on a certain kind of pimp-like rough guy and that beating the crap out of each other along with the sex was just a natural part of the deal, and I was exactly the same way. . . . She didn't give a damn what anybody thought of her—and neither did I. And from the first time Billie ever looked into my eyes, it was like she was seeing right into my soul and she just knew exactly who I was and everything I'd been through. And then when I became a heroin addict, I felt even closer to her."

Being a high-priced whore was fun for Ruby—glamorous, at least for awhile.

"You wouldn't believe the wild showbiz parties at the Warwick in the big suite Jackie Gleason kept for his show. Delmonico's. The Hotel Pierre. The Chateau Madrid. Going to El Morocco, where all the gangsters hung out. I would tell people I was an actress waiting to be discovered. My clients included a famous New York City disc jockey, who dedicated songs to me on the radio, and a famous cartoonist for the *Daily Mirror*—and Herb Purdy, a real estate magnate who became my steady Friday night trick for five years. What a kinky fuck!"

Herb Purdy would take her to the Latin Quarter and they would have dinner and he would get loaded, and at a certain point in the show he would give Ruby a shot glass and she would have to take it into the bathroom and dutifully urinate in it and bring it back and place it on the table, and Herb would put ice and scotch in it and tell her that he loved her and drink it while looking deeply into her eyes. What can you say about Herb Purdy? He kept a suite in the Delmonico with two bathrooms, but he preferred to pee in a corner. There were hundreds of dirty photos pinned up on the walls, and they would walk around the room together and he would masturbate while she stood behind him, playing with his nipples. Sure, Herb Purdy was off his nut, but Ruby loved him because he paid promptly in cash and always took care of her. For years she called him her "boss." Sometimes he would buy another woman for the night to watch them together and Ruby would get to choose her, but by that time he'd be so out of his gourd that Ruby and the other girl would go into the bathroom and just shoot up together and pretend they were making love. They would just make the sounds and he would lay there on his bed trying to whack off. And then one day Herb Purdy just dropped dead, and that was the end of her financial stability. That was when things began to change for the worse.

"What was heroin like? Well, it was like being back in your mother's womb. Like being in this place where nothing could ever touch you. This warm, wonderful place where you really feel like you're floating. Almost in a liquid. It's a weightless condition. Everything is very far away. There's this very nice voice whispering in your ear, *Nothing matters. Everything's fine.* Someone could say to you, 'Hey, Ruby, you're gonna die right now'—and the voice whispers, *Wow—that'd be weird, where's the needle?*"

4.

Nothing went better together than dope and the world's oldest profession. They were like love and marriage. Peanut butter and chocolate. Pretzels and beer. Prostitution and narcotics had always been cozy partners, walking hand in hand since Lucky Luciano began organizing and amalgamating all of the mob rackets in the 1930s—hookers and heroin in close proximity—and Ruby's experience perfectly illustrates how it had always worked. To get money for dope you had to sell your body, and because you sold your body you then had to run to the spike. Heroin was the best assuager of guilt and shame that God ever invented for whores, but then of course you had all that guilt and shame from being a dope fiend, too, and it just went back and forth, on and on, ad infinitum, deeper and deeper, this great waggle dance of self-destruction, host and parasite sucking each other to death, only you never knew which was which, you only kept craving the pure nepenthean propitiation of the heroin more and more; and the fact is, you *needed* it, you needed that distance from everything, you needed that numbness, you needed to be out of your skull, because you never knew what they'd want in bed or what they would do. You never knew which one would want you to take a shit on them, and you'd have to be stoned because no matter how low you'd sunk, you were still a person who had been trained to defecate in a toilet!

Some of them liked to hurt you. Yes, some of them did. One night a john just started whaling on her, out of nowhere. It felt like he broke her nose, she was choking on the blood, and all she could do was try to kick him in the nuts before she went running naked and bloody down the hallway of the hotel. At that point in time the place she always ran to was the little shooting gallery in the basement apartment of a building on 116th Street. There was dope down on the Lower East Side, but she always went up to Harlem. Everybody knew that anybody up there with a white face was probably there for only one thing, but she didn't care; the people up there accepted her for what she was.

It wasn't a bad little place as far as shooting galleries went, much nicer than the abandoned buildings of future generations. A little couch, a bed, some old rugs, some chairs, threadbare curtains, low lights. Jazz musicians would sometimes fall by to get straight, and that was where Ruby would sometimes run into Billie Holiday. Everyone would get real quiet when Lady was there. People would start whispering, like a famous patient was convalescing in a hospital: "Shhh, don't go in there, Lady is nodding." Besides the physical compulsion, Ruby always felt that she and Lady went there for the same reason: to block any bad memories from consciousness. As time went on there was more and more of a need.

Like the night there was a lightning bolt outside the window of the hotel, illuminating the face of the guy on top of her. Usually it was dark and she did not have to see their faces, but she caught a glimpse and he had a very strange look in his eye. The clap of thunder that came at that moment enveloped and shook the hotel, and at that moment he looked up at the ceiling and said, "Yes, Lord, I hear you." Then he calmly looked down at her and placed his hands around her throat and told her that the Lord wanted her dead because she was a woman of sin, and he started strangling her. The first thing that flashed in her mind was that it was true and this must be the vengeance of the Lord and the saints and all the nuns and her mother coming for her, and she started to cry and beg for her life: "Please mister, I have a sick mother who needs an operation to save her life, I have no choice, I can't let her die, this is the only way I can make money, do you think I *like* this kind of life?"

And he slowly unwrapped his fingers from her throat and let go, but he kept staring at her as she got dressed. She had no idea what was going to happen and was whimpering with fear. Then he reached into his wallet and pulled out $200 for the operation she had lied about. "Promise me you'll stop this," he said. "I promise I'll stop," she said back to him, "I promise to God." And he made her get on her knees with him and pray right there, where she had knelt sucking his dick and where he had almost strangled her to death, and the moment was so surreal and terrifying that as soon as she could get out she went running down the street and hopped on the A train, and nothing mattered except getting uptown.

Charlie Parker and Billie Holiday were there that night, along with five or six others. As soon as Lady saw her, she just shook her head and said, "Oh, honey," with such compassion in her eyes that Ruby couldn't help herself, she began to weep. With her $200, Ruby had plenty of dough in hand and she knew that she was going to get good and high, and that she could buy a taste for everyone there too, but her arm was shaking very badly.

"Here, baby, let me," said Lady.

Ruby just held out her arm and let Lady tie her off, and as soon as Lady pumped a shot of shit into her veins it all just drifted away. . . . It didn't matter that she was losing all of this weight and had no idea how in God's name was she ever going to get out of this life . . .

That's when she heard the music.

Bird had a horn to his lips and was blowing a slow blues. Everything just stopped, and Lady was smiling. The music filled the room and just seemed to seep into Ruby's heart and pierce her soul. Feeling no pain now, she watched him for as long as she could, slumped against the wall, about to nod, but she couldn't let go, she wanted to stay with it for as long as possible because Charlie Parker was blowing. She couldn't believe it. Imagine it. Right there. Sitting there like a dusky god in the dim light of a dope dream. Like he was playing just for her. Charlie Parker. Blowing so beautiful and lonely. Blues for a junkie whore.

20

Wild Form, Man, Wild Form . . .

1.

Charlie Parker was watching jugglers on the Dorsey variety show in the Stanhope Hotel suite of the Baroness Pannonica de Koenigswarter when he keeled over and his pulse stopped. Nica, known as the "jazz baroness," was a great patron of the musicians, especially Monk and Bird, and when Bird had arrived at her suite instead of going up to Boston to play Storyville, she was knew something was very wrong when she offered him a drink and he said no. When he vomited up blood, she called a doctor, who insisted he go to a hospital, but Bird had refused. At the moment of his passing, Nica claimed that she heard "a tremendous clap of thunder. I didn't think about it at the time, but I've thought about it often since; how strange it was."

The unspoken implication of her remark about the thunder was that somehow it was the heavens themselves acknowledging the departure of a great soul. The death of Charlie Parker only fed the pyres of his lionization. There were those who contended that they actually observed a golden nimbus around his head as he lay in his coffin before his burial back in Kansas City. But nothing illustrated the power of Bird's myth more than the spreading of the slogan BIRD LIVES. It was the work of poet Ted Joans, an ex-roommate of Bird's who lived above the San Remo Café in the Village and who, after Bird's death, set out with three of his friends in four different directions, like disciples spreading the gospel after the crucifixion, inscribing BIRD LIVES everywhere they went. The mainstream press seemed more interested in the fact that Charlie Parker had used drugs and died in the hotel suite of a wealthy white woman, but Ted Joans and so many others whose lives had been deeply touched by Bird needed to mark the passing of one of the great artists of the twentieth century. The slogan went from the subterranean johns of clubs and bars in the Village, up to Harlem, out to the other boroughs, and then out to other cities across the country—BIRD LIVES!—a new mantra for an alternative culture that had coalesced around jazz and sought to resurrect Bird's spirit and claim his true meaning from the moment of his passing.

Everyone who knew Bird had some searing memory of his final years that were like epiphanies of his helplessness and deterioration as he suffered a series of professional and personal reverses. There was the drinking as he tried and failed to get clean, and the terrible ulcers, and a suicide attempt in which he drank iodine. In March of 1954, on a visit to California, he learned that his daughter Pree had died from congenital heart failure. Something gave way inside of him after the event, like the earth shifting irreversibly along some deep fault line; he broke down and was never able to climb out of the abyss again. "Diz, why don't you save me?" he stammered the last time Dizzy Gillespie saw him play Birdland. Thirty years later, Gillespie was still haunted by the moment. "It was the worst feeling in the world, man. As different as we were, Charlie Parker was my brother, and I was no more able to help him in 1955 than I could in 1945."

As Bird collapsed and found himself reduced to playing in dives and storefronts, the community of musicians who had become accustomed to the relentless brilliance and unsurpassed vitality of his music and the seeming indestructibility of his constitution found his downfall particularly hard to abide, or even acknowledge. If people ran into him wandering around the city at dawn, shabby and broke, sleepless and alone, they could only stare and hope that it wasn't really happening. As Nica remembered, "For all the adulation heaped upon him by fans and musicians, he was lonely. I saw him standing in front of Birdland in a pouring rain. I was horrified and I asked him why, and he said he just had no place to go."

And yet even these agonizing moments and images would become as much a part of Charlie Parker's mythology as the expression of his genius. As Ralph Ellison wrote in *Shadow and Act*, "In attempting to escape the role, at once sub- and super-human, in which he found himself, he sought to outrage his public into an awareness of his most human pain. Instead, he made himself notorious and in the end became unsure whether his fans came to enjoy his art or to be entertained by 'the world's greatest junky,' the 'supreme hipster.'"

"Music is your own experience, your thoughts, your wisdom," Bird had declared. "If you don't live it, it won't come out of your horn. They teach you there's a boundary line to music. But man, there's no boundary line to art."

Charlie Parker had lived and died by this creed, and to many there seemed a shamanic element of self-sacrifice in his journey—the feeling that his flight through the night skies of America had been undertaken on the behalf of others who would be lifted by it. He may have been a junkie, but in the end his addiction and ruinous lifestyle were really quite irrelevant, because by his death he'd long since become an icon of freedom and creativity. Good or bad, all of it would now be woven into the tapestry of his music and myth, which would live on.

Even at this embryonic stage of the drug culture, a young poet like Diane di Prima living in Greenwich Village could recognize that there were those in the New Bohemia who were destined to go down just like Bird, but that even in one's downfall there could still be a sublime beauty.

"For us, who had replaced religion, family, society, ethics with Beauty, who saw ourselves as in the service of Beauty, no warnings were understood, no traps anticipated. To go down, in the service of That— that was the ultimate grace."

2.

Jack Kerouac had always felt like Bird's brother in spirit. One night in 1948, he saw Bird strolling down Eighth Avenue with Babs Gonzales and a beautiful girl—Charlie Parker, the preeminent jazz musician of his day, just walking down the street and digging life with the openness of a child—and he was struck by Bird's innocence and vulnerability. He had watched Bird play like some beautiful, demented angel on the bandstands of jazz clubs and had always been astonished at how the breadth of his experience could rush, all in the course of a single evening, from sullen loneliness and brooding despair to the great lucent, transcendental peaks of his playing. Bird happened to die on Kerouac's thirty-third birthday, March 12, 1955. Kerouac was only a year younger than Bird, and like others, he would try to digest the meaning of his passage into the American cultural imagination. He saw a snapshot of Bird in his coffin that remained emblazoned in his mind like a shimmering mandala, and now as he composed the "sensory meditations" that became *Mexico City Blues* over the summer of 1955, Bird inspired the final choruses. "Charley Parker Looked like Buddha," Kerouac wrote, and in death as in life, his expression was "as calm, beautiful and profound" as the Buddha's, and what Bird was really saying as he played was exactly what the Buddha was saying: *All is Well.*

Kerouac loved the Mexican summers, loved the country from the very first time he experienced it with Neal Cassady on their wild maiden voyage together in the summer of 1950. The last time he had been in Mexico City was in 1952, when he lived with Burroughs in this very same spot, 212 Orizaba Street, right near the Cine Mexico and the verdant park with the beautiful fountain. At that time, he proclaimed in a letter to John Holmes that someday he was going to write "a huge Dostoyevskyan novel about all of us," going on to tell Holmes that

> if I could only stick to novels long enough to tell a few good big stories, what I am beginning to discover now is something beyond the novel and beyond the arbitrary confines of the story . . . into the realms of revealed Picture . . . revealed whatever . . . revelated prose . . . wild form, man, wild form . . . Wild Form's the only form that holds what I have to say—my mind is exploding to say something about every image and every memory in it . . . at this time in my life I'm making myself sick to find the wild form that can grow with my wild heart.

The central role that jazz and mind-altering substances played in Kerouac's discovery of this "wild form" began almost as soon as he returned from that first trip to Mexico. As Cassady went home to wife and kids in California and began work as a brakeman for the Southern Pacific, Kerouac holed up in his mother's apartment in Richmond

Hill and they began exchanging letters. High on marijuana, Kerouac described himself as "wrapped in wild observation of everything" as he considered his life, but lamented that they no longer had access to the potent marijuana they'd smoked in Mexico—"I tell you, nothing beats the Mexican t, and I'm frankly spoiled now."

Kerouac's first novel, *The Town and the City*, had been published to mixed reviews and disappointing sales, and he yearned to break free from the ossified conventions of traditional fiction and the over-arching influence of Thomas Wolfe. "What is my own voice? Because I am an artist no one ever hears it nor my ideas either."

He was cognizant that somehow the answer to finding the kind of truth and authenticity he wanted to achieve in his fiction lay in the way a musician played jazz—free form improvisation, completely in the moment, nothing held back—telling Cassady, "You, man, must write exactly as everything rushes into your head, and AT ONCE."

The "road novel" he was wrestling with had been marinating, through several unsuccessful attempts, before Cassady took his advice and turned the key that unlocked the door. That key had arrived in December of 1950 in the form of a twenty-three-thousand-word letter from Cassady about a sexual encounter he'd had five years earlier in Denver, written while high on Benzedrine and marijuana, that was virtually one long unpunctuated sentence. "The Joan Anderson letter," as it would be called in Beat lore and literature, was a massive outpouring about girls and loneliness and suicidal thoughts and poolrooms and jails that reaches a crescendo when Neal is trapped in Cherry Mary's apartment as her parents come home—"here I was, nude, no clothes, and all exits blocked"—and had to make a hair-raising escape out the bathroom window—"I almost tore off my pride and joy as I wiggled out into the cold November air."

The letter was like an epiphany for Kerouac. It was an exact literary rendition of how Cassady's mind had unfolded in their car along the road and the way he would talk, and it proved beyond any doubt to Kerouac that fiction didn't have to be false—that he could embrace the exact truth of their experiences together and render it in the form of a novel. Perhaps the most remarkable thing about the writing was that for all of its detail and carnality, ultimately its real power was spiritual, about the impact of these events on Neal's soul. Kerouac raved to Cassady that "You gather together all the best styles . . . of Joyce, Celine, Dosty & Proust . . . and utilize them in a muscular rush of your own narrative style & excitement." Virtually from this moment on, Kerouac let go of Thomas Wolfe as his primary inspiration and stylistic paradigm and replaced him with Neal Cassady—the "Colossus risen to destroy Denver," as Allen Ginsberg called him after reading the letter.

After Cassady attempted to "proceed into the actual truth" of his life in the "Joan Anderson letter," the subsequent letters that Kerouac exchanged with Cassady and others during this period would form the very aesthetic infrastructure of the books that followed. "I want to fish as deep as possible into my own subconscious in the belief that once that far down, everyone will understand because they are the same that far down." He began to see that the truth existed only "from moment to moment, incomprehensible, ungraspable yet terribly clear," and that his purpose as a writer was "to catch the fresh dream" like "a fisherman of the deep with old partially useful nets."

What emerges in these letters is an intuitive awareness on Kerouac's part that craft and revision, two foundational principles of good writing, were somehow the mortal enemies of spontanaiety—the first thought was always the best thought—and that marijuana, which sharpens sensitivity and can increase awareness of all the "excruciating details" usually filtered out by the conscious mind, could function in part as those "nets," helping him to capture the stream of his consciousness by removing self-censorship or judgment of any kind.

Cassady agreed. "Now, eyeball kicks are among the world's greatest, second to none actually in terms of abstract thought, because it is thru the way you handle the kicks that is what determines your particular conclusion (in abstraction of the mind) to each moment's outlook." He told Kerouac that he could now recall this state of mind and apply it to whatever he was regarding at the moment, in effect conceptualizing reality "as one looks into a picture." The implication was that the intensified perception and panoramic consciousness of marijuana could be utilized without even having to smoke it because once known, it created a mindfulness that could frame the whole act of writing. But of course they would smoke as much as they could get their hands on.

Different descriptions began to attach to this developing notion of spontaneous prose. Kerouac began calling it "kick writing"—"You must and will go on at all costs including comfort & health & kicks; but keep it kick writing at all costs, that is, write only what keep you overtime and awake from sheer mad joy." He told Cassady that "you and I will be the two most important writers in America in 20 years at the least. . . . That's why I see no harm in addressing my next ten novels & possible lifework to you and you alone."

Keoruac was back in New York, working as a freelance reader of scripts and in the middle of his short-lived second marriage, to Joan Haverty, living in a big loft at 121 West Twenty-First Street, when the the breakthrough ocurred. After several abortive attempts at beginning, Jack had returned from a stroll along the Chelsea waterfront with John Holmes. According to Haverty, a tired young waitress sick of hearing about Jack's literary frustrations and all the stories about Cassady, it was she who asked him, "What was it like, Jack? What really happened on the road?"

The book that Kerouac produced would become mythical for story and style and cultural impact, but as time went on those epic qualities became inextricable from the unique mode of its creation. When he sat down at his typewriter on April 2, 1951, he wanted to be able to tell the whole story as though spinning the yarn in a single sitting, barely pausing for breath—exactly as he and Cassady had gone blazing across the country and into a Chicago jazz club and down into Mexico. He could type one hundred words a minute, and the writing method he now improvised allowed him to take full advantage of this skill. The rolls of tracing paper he found were left in the loft by Bill Cannastra, Joan's previous husband. (Cannastra, perhaps the most wild and reckless member of their whole bohemian crowd, had been killed trying to climb out of a subway train leaving the Bleecker Street station, his head crushed against a pillar—nobody could tell if it was an accident or a suicide.) Kerouac took the rolls and carefully trimmed the width of them with a ruler and attached them to form one single roll of 120 feet that could be fed continuously into his typewriter. It was an innovation that would now enable him to write without the distraction of having to stop and thereby sustain a completely free flow of words.

For the next three weeks, Kerouac slept and ate very little, existing only on pea soup. Given his extensive experience with Benzedrine up to this point and how much he would use it for later books like *The*

Subterraneans, it seems logical that he must have used it, but accounts vary. The pioneering Kerouac scholar Ann Charters states in an early biography and in her introduction to *On the Road* that he did, but according to Kerouac himself, he produced the entire 125,000-word manuscript scroll on cup after cup of coffee—"Benny tea, anything I KNOW none as good as coffee for real mental power kicks." Subsequent biographies by Ellis Amburn and Joyce Johnson adhere to this conclusion.

What is certain is that he listened to jazz constantly, smoking cigarette after cigarette, sweating so much that he soaked through T-shirt after T-shirt, getting up to change the shirts and hang them out to dry. The piece he listened to over and over again was "The Hunt," which he and Cassady had gone wild over around the time of their voyages. It was the B-side of a Savoy release that featured Wardell Gray and Dexter Gordon blowing in a wild bout of dueling tenor saxophones, with Al Killian on trumpet and Trummy Young on trombone, recorded live in Los Angeles on July 6, 1948—a "wild, rompin', stompin', jumpin', wailin', roaring balling session," as it was described by an unknown writer in the original Savoy liner notes—and as Dexter blew on his tenor and Connie Kay pounded the skins, the floodgates opened, and Jack Kerouac let it rip.

If bebop was really lifestyle as music, as Dexter Gordon has suggested, what emerged on Kerouac's roll of paper can surely be described as "lifestyle as literature," as John Clellon Holmes has called it. Kerouac narrates the story as Sal Paradise and Neal Cassady (Dean Moriarty) is the hero, with a supporting cast that includes Huncke (Elmo Hassel), Ginsberg (Carlo Marx), and Burroughs (Old Bull Lee). The setting of the book is "the dawn of jazz in America" as the chill of the Cold War settles over the country. The backdrop of the work is an American patchwork quilt of freight trains, hobos, plains, cities, states, rivers, floods, and highways; the ambiance of the novel is decidedly neon, as seen from the window of a cheap motel room. But the real subjects are God, the brotherhood of man, devils, saints, freedom, love, loss, loneliness, ecstasy, transcendence, and those great cosmic moments when "you know everything and all is decided forever." And throughout, Kerouac writes about drugs—Benzedrine, morphine, but mostly marijuana—in the authentic language of those who used them as a way of life.

When the story was finished, it was one uninterrupted paragraph that went on for 250 feet—"rolled it out on the floor and it looks like the road," as Jack described it to Neal. "I've told all the road now. Went fast because road is fast." In the future he was going to "write all my books in twenty days." Kerouac was certain that he'd broken through to a new form of writing. No sooner had he finished the last sentence than he called Robert Giroux, who'd edited *The Town and the City,* and he showed up at Giroux's office a half hour later with the scroll under his arm. As Giroux told biographer Joyce Johnson, "He was in a funny state. I was too dumb to realize he was drunk or on drugs." As Johnson puts it, "The strangeness Giroux attributed to drugs may have been another kind of high entirely—the dream trance in which Jack had just written his last lines, from which he had not yet emerged." Kerouac unrolled the scroll and "tossed it across the office like a piece of celebration confetti" and told Giroux that "the Holy Ghost wrote it." When Giroux complained about how difficult it would be to edit this new work in its present form, Kerouac's exaltation turned to rage. Refusing to change a single word, he called Giroux "a crass idiot" and stormed out.

It was a pivotal moment. Everything unique about the book worked against it and made it unpublishable. For the next five years, the book that he called *On the Road* and *Road* and *The Daybreak Boys* and *On the Road* again met a similar response everywhere it was submitted, regardless of revisions or title. Kerouac was crushed. The rejection consigned him to a life of penury and the shame of having to live off his mother. A melancholy more profound than any he'd known before seized his soul. Perhaps most fatefully, there were more and more drunken nights as he poured booze over his disappointment and bitterness.

But even as Kerouac became "the loneliest writer in America" and his career seemingly stood still, the story of his life and the lives of the others went on exactly as if the roll of paper had never stopped its incessant feed into his typewriter. During the next five years, it was his work that held him together. He worked along roadsides, in skid row hotels in San Francisco, on freight trains and ships, in the stick huts and on the adobe rooftops of Mexico, and at his rolltop desk in his mother's house, always moving more and more into the style of the new writing, purifying it, pushing its boundaries, and the substances he used became more than ever inseparable from his creative process. "I'm afraid I need Miss Green to write; can't whip up interest in anything otherwise," he told Neal and Carolyn in a 1952 letter. "Still, what's the sense of living if you can't get what you need. And I need food, rest, girls, dope, wine, beer and Old Grandad."

The experience of writing *On the Road* was like woodshedding for Kerouac—the beginning of the discocvery of his true voice as a writer. "Why don't you just sketch in the streets like a painter but with words?" suggested his friend Ed White. "Sketching" was the next step in the evolution of his new spontaneous style, and it worked perfectly with the trance-like associative effects of marijuana. As 1951 turned into 1952, Kerouac reworked the road material into *Visions of Cody* while living in the Cassadys' attic at 29 Russell Street in Russian Hill, turning the conventional linear narrative of *On the Road* into "a big multidimensional conscious and subconscious character invocation of Neal in his whirlwinds." He described sketching as "everything activates in front of you in myriad profusion, you just have to purify your mind and let it pour the words . . . and write with 100% personal honesty both psychic and social etc. and slap it all down shameless, willynilly, rapidly until somethines I get so inspired I lost consciousness I was writing." His model was "Yeats's trance writing. It's the *only way to write.*"

As the writing became even more marijuana-induced and experimental, so did their relationship. As Neal went off to work during the day, Carolyn seduced Jack with her husband's blessing and they began an affair. When Neal returned at night, he and Jack would smoke together and talk as if their conversation was the most consequential event in the universe. They would listen to jazz and assess its importance to their generation, and trace the story of how the group had first met back in the forties, and then they would tape-record their exchange as they shared these "real teahead goof kicks," as Ginsberg later explained it, and then smoke even more, and then talk about the tape, and then smoke and talk some more, exploring "the mind blanks & impressions that tea creates. . . . The halts, switches, emptiness, quixotic chatters, conversations, meaninglessness, occasionally summary piths."

"I'm sorry, but we gotta get a renewal of the supply of the material which makes it possible for us to *be* this way," Cody says at one point in the tape.

"War will be impossible when marijuana becomes legal," Kerouac pronounces in the book. Later, he writes, "High, I'm telling you, high. What's the law against being high? What's the use of not being high? You gonna be low?"

Kerouac held to the belief that marijuana was a valuable tool that could collapse space and time and render memory and feeling as synesthesia or heartbeat itself. Although it wouldn't be published until 1973, *Visons of Cody* contains some of his best work. As John Clellon Holmes observed, "He'd blast, get high, and he'd write all night. And the reason why those sentences are so long and exfoliating and so incredible is because of pot."

As the months went by and Jack's affair with Carolyn became complicated and bittersweet, Neal began to withdraw more and more. When Neal immersed himself in the teachings of Edgar Cayce, Jack countered by plunging into the Noble Truths of Buddhism. They quarreled over philosophy and eventually wrangled bitterly over the division of a pound of weed before parting angrily. Time would reconcile them, but they would never be as close again.

As important as marijuana was to them, both Kerouac and Cassady came to know the downside of the substance. Before Jack's arrival, Neal had been smoking so much marijuana that his mind would go "utterly blank; can't think of a thing to say," as he described it to Kerouac in a letter, explaining why he had ceased his writing. "It's really a form of exhaustion brought on the steady use of t, which with its enormous number of images, contents the brain with just thoughts— terrifying tho they now are—so no can write." Jack also experienced what it was like to stupefy oneself on the weed by smoking too much— it could ossify him to the degree that he was unable to write so much as a clear sentence. Paranoia was another negative aspect. When John Holmes's article "This Is the Beat Generation," which mentioned Kerouac by name, appeared in the *New York Times Magazine* in November of 1952, Kerouac worried that it would make people think of him as a "dope addict," even though Holmes's view of the Beat Generation was life-affirming: "They drink to 'come down' or 'get high,' not to illustrate anything. Their excursions into drugs or promiscuity come out of curiosity, rather than disillusionment." On the way back to New York Kerouac even threw his stash of weed off the ship in "a fit of fear."

In a single year, Kerouac produced three major works: *Visions of Cody, Dr. Sax,* and *The Subterraneans,* the latter over three successive nights on Benzedrine. Burroughs and Ginsberg were astoinished by this feat, and when they suggested that he sit down to codify his style and working methods in a "list of essentials" one particular element spoke volumes about his working method—"Like Proust be an old tea-head of time."

3.

Just before Kerouac's trip to Mexico in the summer of 1955, he learned that Keith Jennison of Viking had expressed interest in publishing *On the Road.* Suddenly there was hope that everything was going to turn around.

Over that summer Allen Ginsberg started a long poem in San Francisco that embraced Kerouac's technique. "I realize how right you are, that was the first time I sat down to blow, it came out in your method, sounding like you, an imitation practically," Ginsberg explained in a letter on August 25, sending along some pages of the poem. "How far advanced you are on this. I don't know what I'm doing with poetry. I need years of isolation and constant everyday writing to attain your volume and freedom and knowledge of the form."

Ginsberg was calling the poem "Strophes" but across the top had scrawled the legend, "Howl For Carl Solomon." When Kerouac read it, he suggested Ginsberg just call it "Howl." He also criticized Ginsberg for revising his words. As Ginsberg later summarized Kerouac's letter, "He said Anything is good because it is everything. And things are said in time, and time is of the essence, and when you change yr mind even for an instant and muss up with the x-marks (as in the 'original' ms of 'Howl') you lie. He wrote that the truth *is already there.* He was not interested in what I had to hide i.e. my 'craft,' he was interested in what I had to show, i.e., blow."

Kerouac started *Mexico City Blues* to show Allen how he could adapt his spontaneous style to poetry. And so all through that summer he blasted with Miss Green and sketched "the flow that already exists intact in the mind," living and breathing his literary technique more purely than ever before.

The building he was living in was dirty and run-down, with creaking metal stairs and crumbling stucco walls, but it was teeming with the loud, rich, Fellaheen lives of the Mexican families packed into the small apartments. Kerouac would perch himself on the slippery red adobe roof and fire up a giant bomber of tea, no mere joint but a veritable burrito of the stuff, like the one he had smoked on that first trip with Neal and a Mexican named Victor in Gregoria. He found the rooftop apartment on Orizaba Street "a perfect place to write, think, blast, think, fresh air, sun, moon, stars, the Roof of the City." He had written *Dr. Sax* there in 1952, "high on tea without pausing to think, sometimes Bill would come in the room and so the chapter ended there, one time he yelled at me with his long gray face because he could smell smoke in the yard."

Burroughs had gone to Tangier, but Old Bill Garver, whom Burroughs had known as an overcoat thief back in the old days in Manhattan, was downstairs in a room with barred windows facing Orizaba Street. Garver was now a sixty-year-old junkie living on a trust fund, smoking opium in his purple pajamas, who liked to talk and was happy for Jack's company. Kerouac liked talking to him for the same reason he always liked talking to Huncke—he viewed him as some kind of unique anthropologist of the underworld—and every afternoon he would launch himself into T-consciousness with Miss Green and sit in Garver's big easy chair with his little sketching notebook, and Garver would ramble on about Minoan civilizations and his experiences in China and drugs like sodium amytal and heroin, and Kerouac would let his mind drain out into poems that could only be as long as one notebook page, each one its own chorus, freely associating words for their sound values, all of it flowing out with complete spontaneity.

What streamed forth mixed his earliest memories of Lowell with all the crazy people he had known and cooking bacon and eggs with Garver and Sanskrit terms for states of consciousness and the philosophy of the Surangama and the Lankavatara Sutras of Buddhism and the Eternal Slowdown of Charlie Parker and the beatitude of loneliness and melancholy and down-and-outness and the pure luxuriant freedom of the writing itself. Kerouac might have become a mad hermit—a "Zen lunatic," as Allen Ginsberg later called him—but he was writing from the realm of pure consciousness and sound—

Charley Parker, forgive me—
Forgive me for not answering your eyes—

By this time Kerouac had become exactly like a Perfect Musician himself—"a jazz poet blowing a long blues in an afternoon jam session on Sunday. I take 242 choruses; my ideas vary and sometimes roll from chorus to chorus or from halfway through a chorus to halfway into the next"—achieving with words what Bud Powell and Miles and Bird had accomplished on their respective instruments. Buddha was a bop musician, and Bird was Buddha; Jack was a bop musician, too, and as he got high and blew on his visions they were Buddha together, and all of it was the absolute apotheosis of wild form.

Charley Parker, lay the bane,
off me, and every body

It was a kind of poetry that had never been written before. Like Charlie Parker, Jack Kerouac had become a pioneer of the New Reality Jam Session.

With the poems finished, Kerouac prepared to depart Mexico and meet his destiny. He packed the dog-eared typescripts that he always carried in his duffel bag along with his dime-store notebooks and dirty underwear and towels and his old lantern. Before leaving he declared in his letters to Ginsberg that when he arrived, they would shout their poetry in the San Francisco streets together—

"PREDICT EARTHQUAKES!"

Concerned about the possibility of being arrested at the border, Kerouac left his supply of Miss Green behind, but what he carried across—*On the Road, Visions of Cody, Dr. Sax, Maggie Cassidy, The Subterraneans, San Francisco Blues, Some of the Dharma, Book of Dreams, Mexico City Blues,* sketches, stories like "October in the Railroad Earth"—represented a remarkable body of work, a "spontaneous bop prosody and original classic literature," as Ginsberg would later call it—an achievement that would be likened to Proust's and Melville's and Shakespeare's.

21

Trust the Germans to Concoct
Some Really Evil Shit

1.

The journey inaugurated by the box of morphine syrettes that William Burroughs used in 1945 reached a frightful crescendo in Tangier in 1954 with dihydrohydroxycodeinone hydrochloride, a strong German-made combination synthetic narcotic analgesic and hypnotic manufactured by Merck during the war as a painkiller under the brand name of Eukodal.

Burroughs had never heard of the concoction before, but it was love at first encounter, bait that he couldn't resist—"the best junk kick I ever had," as he declared in a letter to Allen Ginsberg not long after arriving in Tangier. "I am hooked. Met a doctor's son, he needed money, and the old man's script pad right there. . . . Start dolly cure in a few days now."

After Mexico and South America, Tangier was the next logical stop on the journey of William Burroughs. The city was an international free zone, cosmopolitan but provincial, a mecca of unregulated tastes and enterprises, loaded with expatriates, spies, smugglers, spongers, exiles, outcasts, black-market schemers, the stranded and the lost from every corner of the earth. With the Mediterranean on one side and the Atlantic on the other, with its low sand hills and dark streets and blind alleys and crowded, dirty native quarter, the place projected an exotic quality of decadence and exemption from morals and laws, what Burroughs described upon his arrival in January of 1954 as "an end-of-the-world feeling . . . with its glut of nylon shirts, Swiss watches, Scotch and sex and opiates sold across the counter." At the same time, he detected "something sinister in complete laissez-faire."

The man who arrived in Tangier had become accustomed to recognizing the sinister. After being busted in New Orleans in 1949, Burroughs was thrown junk sick into a Second Precinct cell where he lay tumescent on a narrow wooden bench when there was "a sudden rush of blood to my genitals at the slippery contact. Sparks exploded behind my eyes; my legs twitched—the orgasm of a hanged man when the neck snaps." With his narcotics case hanging over his head, he quickly slipped across the border with his family to Mexico City, where he planned to wait for his case to be canceled when the statute of limitations ran out after five years. There he went to work on a book he was calling *Junky*, which would play a critical role in the development of his voice as a writer.

Utilizing his nearly photographic memory, he crafted the book to proceed exactly like a diary, beginning in New York with what he portrayed as his first shot in the apartment on Henry Street, continuing through four increasingly traumatizing attempts at withdrawal, and ending with his experiences in Mexico City.

For the uninitiated reader, here was everything you could possibly want to know about being a junkie, graphically delineated as never before, nakedly reduced to its purest and most organic cellular and metabolic equation—the "algebra of need." *Junky* mixed the style of the hard-boiled detective fiction of Raymond Chandler and Dashiell Hammett with the disturbing shadowy ambience of a film noir movie, but it was rendered in language that blended the detached cool of the hipster underground with the concise and elevated syntax of his Harvard education. Published in 1953 with a glossary of drug user slang, *Junky* was the first truly authentic documentary portrait of the emergent subculture of drug users in America after 1945—"the first intelligent modern confession on drugs," as Kerouac called it. It was also the first book critical of the Federal Bureau of Narcotics; the first to characterize the entire climate in the United States regarding drug use as a "nationwide hysteria" and "a paranoid obsession, like anti-Semitism under the Nazis"; the first to call the narcotic laws "police-state legislation penalizing a state of being."

At a time when drug addiction represented the ultimate evil of American society and when few books on the subject even existed beyond the most luridly sensationalized dime-store novels or outdated medical tracts, here was a cold, hard, gritty, thoroughly unromanticized account of drug use and addiction, but written as an adventure story, exactly like episodic pulp fiction or a movie matinee cliffhanger. As a comprehensive compendium of information, it was also a how-to manual of sorts—the World of Illicit Psychoactive Drugs, Complete, according to William Lee, Master Addict. But perhaps the most subversive characteristic of the book was embodied in a single word of its subtitle—"unredeemed"—a word that denoted the exact opposite of the familiar genre of drug addict confessional in which the principal character is recovered from a life of depravity to live a shining new life of moral rectitude and spiritual awakening. William Lee did not care a whit about redemption. There were no apologies for the life he led or any moral judgments made about it, and certainly no heartfelt wishes to go "straight" in the future. In fact, at the end, the author hears about still another new drug experience and sets off in search of what he hopes might be the ultimate drug kick of all: yage, *Banisteriopsis caapi*, the ayahuasca vine of South America. Burroughs then set about writing a kind of companion volume about his homosexual experiences called *Queer*, but tragedy struck before either book was published.

Burroughs would always remember the knife sharpener's whistle down on the street, and how he took the knife he'd bought in Quito down to have it sharpened, and how he was overcome by a feeling of dread and foreboding and a sense of depression and loss so powerful and dark that tears began to stream down his face. He'd been drinking heavily since morning on that day, September 6, 1951, as had Joan. He was smarting from his rejection by Lewis Marker, who'd accompanied him on his recent trip to South America—an impossible infatuation with an unobtainable man that drove Burroughs mad with the frustration of unrequited lust and his unfulfilled desire to possess and completely inhabit another human being. Needing money, he had decided to sell his .380 automatic pistol, and a friend, John Healey, had found a buyer for the gun. Everyone had gone to the potential buyer's apartment above a bar called the Bounty. They were sipping *limonada* and gin when Burroughs pulled the .380 out of the bag and said to Joan the words that would change his life forever . . .

"I guess it's time for our William Tell act."

Joan balanced her highball glass on her head, turned to the side, and giggled. "I can't watch this. You know I can't stand the sight of blood."

Burroughs was about six feet away when he pulled the trigger. As Joan's head rolled to the side, blood began spurting from a hole in her temple about an inch below the hairline. As soon as she toppled, the still-intact glass rolling on the floor, Burroughs began moaning "*Joan, Joan,*" and rushed to her side as the others ran out to get help.

"Why I did it, I don't know, something took over," Burroughs later told the police in his deposition. "It was an utterly and completely insane thing to do. Suppose I had succeeded in shooting the glass off her head, there was a danger of glass splinters flying out and hitting other people."

Burroughs spent thirteen days in Lecumberri Prison. There was no form of capital punishment in Mexico, and Bernabé Jurado, a defense attorney highly adept at employing the bribery and perjury that formed the pillars of the Mexican criminal justice system, promised that he would not stay in jail, and he delivered on the promise. At a pretrial hearing Burroughs was charged with *imprudencia criminal*—criminal negligence. Pleading guilty to the charge, Burroughs was released on bail until his sentencing in a year's time—it carried a maximum sentence of five years—but by then he would be long gone. Julie, Joan's daughter from her first marriage, was sent to live with the Vollmers; Billy went to live with the Burroughs family in St. Louis. Kerouac described Burroughs as "a mad genius in littered rooms" when he arrived at his apartment to spend that summer with him and found him writing. "He looked wild, but his eyes innocent and blue and beautiful. . . . Misses Joan terribly. Joan made him great, lives on in him like mad, vibrating."

When the summer was over, Burroughs left Mexico for the jungles of South America, but not before Kerouac had sketched his departure.

Burroughs is gone at last—3 years in Mexico—lost everything, his wife, his children, his patrimony—I saw him pack his moldy room where he'd shot M all this time—Sad moldy leather cases—old holsters, old daggers—a snapshot of Huncke—a derringer pistol, which he gave to old dying Garver—medicines, drugs—the last of Joan's spices, marjoram, now mold since she died & stopped cooking—little Willie's shoes—& Julie's moldy school case—all lost, dust, & thin tragic Bill hurries off into the night solitaire—ah Soul—throwing in his bag, at last, picture of Lucien & Allen—Smiled, & Left.

Not a single day of his life would pass without Burroughs thinking about what had happened. As much as he would have to wrestle with the ghastly fact of his responsibility for the death of his wife and the pain he had inflicted on his children and all who knew her, he would also have to reckon with the question of Joan's acquiescence, which over time would become a conception equally horrifying to him. He communicated to Allen Ginsberg his reluctance to write about the incident, not because he was worried that it might be in "bad taste" but because he was "afraid. . . . Not exactly to discover unconscious intent. It's more complex, more basic and more horrible, as if the brain *drew* the bullet toward it." For Burroughs, who believed increasingly in the forces of a magical universe, there was no such thing as an accident. Bad things were caused by sinister forces, what he would later call an "Ugly Spirit." The notion of diabolical insinuation would weigh upon him as much as the reality of his own guilt and the possibility of his wife's complicity in her death, and it became still another unsettling element in the geography of his life and work and the mythology they would construct. The story of the freakish killing would become such a staple of Burroughs's story, such an essential ingredient of his shadowy legend, that David Cronenberg would skillfully weave it into his imaginative 1991 movie version of *Naked Lunch*.

A different kind of symbolism would attach to Joan Vollmer Burroughs. With the passing of time, many would come to view this sharp-witted woman who had rebelled so fiercely against the convention and smugness and hypocrisy of the middle-class American way of life as an early casualty of the counterculture—a person who had found herself at the vanguard of a new way of life whose perils had yet to be fully gauged. Similarly, it's easy to view her marriage to Burroughs as an example of two addicts living together, helpless to prevent the calamitous consequences of their own and each other's addictions. By the end she was a gaunt, ashen, spiritless shell of a human being with sores on her arms, compulsively sweeping lizards off the tree in the yard with a broom, and Burroughs had also become skeletal, with bad teeth, yellow fingers, dead-looking eyes. But as with all such events and complicated personalities and circumstances, this version of Joan Burroughs and her marriage to Bill Burroughs is only useful as the roughest of sketches. Whatever the personal, psychological, or cultural interpretations, the death of Joan Burroughs was a tragedy that shattered everyone who knew them both.

More than anything, the death of Joan committed Burroughs to the life of a writer. "I am forced to the appalling conclusion that I would never have become a writer but for Joan's death," he later wrote in his introduction to *Queer,* "and to a realization of the extent to which this event has motivated and formulated my writing. I live with the constant threat of possession, and a constant need to escape from possession, from Control. So the death of Joan brought me into contact with the invader, the Ugly Spirit, and maneuvered me into a lifelong struggle, in which I have had no choice but to write my way out."

As Burroughs turned forty years old on the fifth of February, 1954, there were few bright spots on the horizon. He had arrived in Tangier lovesick for Allen Ginsberg and deeply troubled by the memory of his dead wife, but more determined than ever to write his way out.

2.

At first, Burroughs was not wild about Tangier with its Islamic culture. He found the local queens and aristocrats irritatingly snobbish and writers like Paul Bowles, whose books, including *The Sheltering Sky,* had attracted him to the city in the first place, standoffish. The drunks and expatriates were tiresome and, perhaps worst of all, the stool pigeons far too numerous for his taste.

But Tangier was also not without its charms and amusements. The place was a "desert of beautiful boys who look at me with soft brown eyes like a puzzled deer," as available in the Socco Chico as the kief being smoked in clay pipes and the hashish being eaten with the tea. There were other curiosities as well: "vicious, purple-assed baboons in the mountains a few miles out of town. (Paul Bowles was set upon by enraged baboons and forced to flee for his life.) I intend to organize baboon sticks from motorcycles. A sport geared to modern times."

It didn't take Burroughs long to find a handsome Spanish boy named Kiki along with the Eukodal. The boy would turn out to be pleasing and harmless enough; the drug was quite a different matter. That spring and summer, as he made the first attempts at planning and organizing a novel-length work of fiction that he planned to call *Naked Lunch*—a title suggested by Jack Kerouac nine years before—William Burroughs developed the most vicious habit of his life. While the un-limited hashish and things like purple-assed baboons would certainly become important ingredients in the novel, it was the habit that would become the most essential element in the invention of its universe.

Production of Eukodal had been discontinued by Merck, but a sur-plus of the drug had accumulated in local pharmacies, making it very hard to resist. With his doctor's prescription, Burroughs had no trou-ble getting as much of it as he wanted at first. The habit grabbed hold fast and hard and wouldn't let go; his first attempt at a Dolophine cure was a dismal failure.

"Trying to write novel," he announced to Ginsberg in a letter dated March 7, two months after he arrived. "Attempt to organize material is more painful than anything I ever experienced. Shooting every four hours. Some semi-synthetic stuff called Eukodol. God knows what kind of habit I am getting. When I kick this habit I expect fuses will blow out in my brain from overcharge and black sooty blood will run out my eyes, ears and nose while staggering around the room acting out routines like Roman Emperor routine in a bloody sheet."

By the summer, as the habit tightened around his neck like a noose, Burroughs's worst fears about how hard it would be to kick the drug were being confirmed.

When the druggist sells me my daily box of Eukodol ampules he smirks like I had picked up the bait to a trap. The whole town is a trap and someday it will close. . . . Allen, I never had a habit like this before. Shooting every *two hours*. Maybe it is the Eukodol, which is semi-synthetic. Trust the Germans to concoct some really evil shit. It acts direct on nerve centers. This stuff is more like coke than morphine. A shot of Eukodol hits the head first with a rush of pleasure. Ten minutes later you want another shot. Between shots you are just killing time.

In the darkened seclusion of his shuttered room, laying immobile on his bed, staring at his big toe for eight hours at a stretch, Burroughs began to experience addiction on a level he had never known before. It was a passage of his life that would produce some of the most disturbingly graphic descriptions of his drug use in *Naked Lunch*: "I have an open sore where I can slip a needle right into a vein, it stays open like a red, festering mouth, swollen and obscene, gathers a slow drop of blood and pus after the shot."

After a German tourist overdosed in a ditch and the police clamped down, his supply was suddenly interrupted, and he spent four desperate hours trying to score two boxes of ampules. From that day on his desire to get off the drug began to escalate.

The first method he tried was one he had learned from his readings of De Quincey and Coleridge. He paid an Englishman named Eric Gifford fifty dollars to take his clothes away and dole out his drugs on a reduction schedule and bring him food, but that only worked until the second day, after which Burroughs stole the clothes of another boarder in the house, "sneaked out, and bought some Eukodol ampules, and glutted myself." The boarder began locking his room and Gifford took away his money, but eventually Burroughs had to give the job to the Spanish boy, Kiki, whose presence in his life at that point was the only thing that seemed to mitigate the obsession of the habit.

Kiki has confiscated all my clothes and intends to cure me of the habit . . . spontaneous orgasm being one of the few agreeable features of the withdrawal syndrome. And not limited to single orgasm, one can continue, with adolescent ardor, through three or four climaxes. . . . He is a sweet kid, and it is so pleasant to loll about in the afternoon smoking tea, sleeping and having sex with no hurry, running leisurely hands over his lean, hard body, and finally we doze off, all wrapped around each other, into the delicious sleep of a hot afternoon in a cool, darkened room.

With the approach of the new year, Burroughs wanted to concentrate on his writing more than ever. Though he had published *Junky* in 1953, he believed that his talent as a writer was only marginal, but he began to realize that Tangier could serve as the perfect setting for what he wanted to write: a book based on his most outrageous routines, as spoken and included in his letters to Ginsberg. Certain that what he would produce would be unpublishable, Burroughs felt utterly compelled by forces that he associated with the death of his wife and his own survival to go ahead and write the book anyway. But he also knew he could never even begin to create the book with any kind of consistency and discipline unless he could somehow get clean—"Once I get off junk, anything is possible."

By this time in his life, his pronouncements about how he was going to get off narcotics and his mounting despair at being unable to do so had become a cruel comedy, the reprise of a pathetic, tired song that he had sung for years as he relocated from place to place. He tried a two-week cold-turkey sleep cure at a clinic run by a doctor from Strasbourg named Appfel, who prescribed chloral hydrate, barbiturates, and Thorazine. He tried rapid reductions, correspondence cures, codeinettas, paregoric, goofballs—nobody was more adept or informed about all the theories and modalities of withdrawal from narcotics circulating around the underground like folklore or within the tiny faction of the medical community venturing into the uncharted waters of addiction throughout the forties and fifties than Burroughs—but nothing broke the vise of the synthetic habit. Each day, Burroughs got up determined to kick, and each day he found himself automatically returning to the pharmacy for still one more box of ampules, and plunging into complete despair.

In September he entered the Benchimol Hospital for a cure. Dolophine was administered once every four hours, but the psychological temptation to use Eukodal again soon began to play havoc with his mind and became stronger than ever. As Burroughs described it in *Naked Lunch*, "The critical point of withdrawal is not the early phase of acute sickness, but the final step free from the medium of junk. . . . There is a nightmare interlude of cellular panic, life suspended between two ways of being."

All the while, Burroughs was "strangled with routines, drowning in routines," the material for the book fading in and out of his consciousness during the discontinuous interludes between fixes. Sometimes when he sat down and smoked some tea it all come out of him like a great "glob of spit"—

> The incredibly obscene, thinly disguised references and situations that slip by in Grade B movies; the double entendres, perversion, sadism of popular songs; poltergeist knockings and mutterings of America's putrefying unconscious, boils that swell until they burst with a fart noise as if the body had put out an auxiliary asshole with a stupid belligerent Bronx cheer. . . .
>
> Did I ever tell you about the man who taught his asshole to talk? His whole abdomen would move up and down, you dig, farting out the words. It was unlike anything I ever heard (being a decent girl and don't you forget it, Mister).

Tangier began to transmute into Interzone, the setting for the novel, whose "space-time location is at a point where three-dimensional fact merges into dream, and dreams erupt into the real world. . . . The very exaggeration of routines is intended to create this feeling."

But Burroughs could make no significant progress with the actual writing of the book. At the start of 1956, he began to feel that he was facing a "vast, Kafkian conspiracy to prevent me from ever getting off junk." He had reached a condition of cellular and psychic obsession and imprisonment that he now described as "biostasis": "I just experienced indescribable, nightmare flash of physical helplessness: wherever I go and whatever I do, I am always in the straitjacket of junk, unable to move a finger to free myself, like I was paralyzed by an anesthetic, and suddenly realized that my will had no power over my body."

By February, Burroughs had reached the unmitigated nadir of the habit. Waiting desperately for a check from his family, he planned to use the money to take the first plane out of what he now called this "sneak preview of Hell." The political unrest that was growing in the city may have been disquieting, but it was nothing compared to what was taking place inside his body and mind. He would "simply not travel with this Chinaman any longer," he pronounced. "Taking so much I keep going on the nod. Last night I woke up with someone squeezing my hand. It was my other hand." His veins had all but disappeared, and when he could find one with the hypodermic, he "kissed the vein, calling it my 'sweet little needle sucker,' and talked baby talk to it."

There was a "croaker" Burroughs had heard about in England, Dr. John Yerbury Dent, author of *Anxiety and Its Treatment,* a pioneer in the use of a substance called apomorphine to treat narcotic addiction, who operated a clinic at 44 Egerton Gardens in London. When he received a $500 check from his father in April, he immediately boarded a plane for Britain. What William Burroughs left behind in Tangier was a reputation, the beginning of a dark legend that would only grow with the writing and publication of his book, and would follow him for the rest of his days.

"The days glide by strung on a syringe with a long thread of blood. . . . I am forgetting sex and all sharp pleasures of the body—a grey, junk-bound ghost. The Spanish boys call me El Hombre Invisible—the Invisible Man."

22

Holy the Bop Apocalypse!

1.

Almost four decades after writing *Howl,* Allen Ginsberg was giving a poetry reading at the Cooper Square bookshop in New York with Gregory Corso and Peter Orlovsky. In the middle of the reading Corso wanted to light up a cigarette and a bookstore employee stopped him, informing him that smoking was not permitted in the store and he would have to go out into the stairwell. Corso appeared completely dumbfounded by the reprimand, as if the moment exemplified something comically incongruous about how the times had changed. After all, here he was, *Gregory Corso,* reading his *poetry* in the Village, the very place where he had been reading his poetry since the fifties, during those fervent days of the San Francisco Renaissance and the Black Mountain poets and scores of small, independently published magazines of poetry and underground culture with names like *Yugen* and *Beatitude* and *Big Table* and *The Floating Bear,* which seemed to be proliferating like rabbits, when poetry meant everything and to be a poet reading your work at places like the Gaslight was to be at the revolutionary crossroads of the universe, and now he couldn't even light up a lousy *cigarette*?

Corso stared out at the audience for a moment, which was packed with poetry lovers and Beat Generation aficionados, because he knew that these people would appreciate the great irony of it all. At a reading after the publication of *Howl,* Ginsberg had courageously ripped off his clothes to challenge a heckler, proclaiming, "Nakedness . . . The poet stands naked before the world!" Burroughs had always used the notorious maxim of Hassan-i Sabbah, "Nothing is forbidden, everything is permitted," to delineate their artistic ethos. And here it was, the 1990s, and Corso wasn't even permitted to smoke a cigarette at a poetry reading in the Village. "Oh, *wow*," he whined petulantly, "we used to be able to do *anything*, man," and the people laughed because even at the age of sixty, Gregory Corso was still very much the curly-headed, mischievous street imp of Beat poesy, and because they knew exactly what he was talking about. Implicit in his reaction was the recognition that if he and his handful of coconspirators in literary and cultural sedition had ever fully complied with the rules and mores of the time of McCarthy and Eisenhower, had they not purposefully set out to violate every conceivable boundary of taste and behavior and attitude, they might never have created the literature being read and celebrated on this occasion in the first place. What Corso was conveying was that every component of that sensibility and lifestyle had been integral and interrelated, bleeding into a new consciousness. There was the pure freedom, wild form, and Dionysian spirit of art. There were all of those great orgies, which helped free the body. And of course there was the taking of mind-altering substances . . .

"It is hard, in our present era of self-righteousness, to even begin to imagine what drugs and the taking of drugs meant to us," writes poet Diane DiPrima. "How special and indeed precious it was—what promise it held. . . . Consciousness itself was a good. And anything that took us *outside*—that gave us the dimensions of the box we were caught in, an aerial view as it were—showed us the exact arrangement of the maze we were walking, was a blessing."

During that historic breakthrough season of the Angel in Moloch, curiosity about mind-altering substances of any kind had been surging in North Beach—pot, bennies, goofballs, mushrooms, junk. As poet Michael McClure remembered it, "There was a mystery about drugs, and they were taken for joy, for consciousness, for spiritual elevation, or what the Romantic poet Keats had called 'Soul-making.' He expressed it in the phrase, 'Call the world if you please the Vale of Soul-Making.'"

Soon everyone would be talking about *Lophophora williamsii*—the little round, dark-green, pincushion-like cactus that grows wild in the Rio Grande Valley better known as peyote.

2.

On September 5, 1939, Count Basie and the Kansas City 7 recorded for Vocalion "Lester Leaps In," a song based on Prez's head arrangement for the chord progression of "I Got Rhythm." Of course Prez could never have imagined that sixteen years later his riffs would inspire Allen Ginsberg's head arrangement for the most avant-garde and notorious American poem of the twentieth century.

Howl began with a single line from Ginsberg's notebook in August of 1955—*I saw the best mind angel headed hipster damned.* As he sat at the typewriter by the first-floor window of his apartment facing Montgomery Street—"not with the idea of writing a formal poem, but stating my imaginative sympathies"—he reached for the long saxophone line as modeled by Prez and utilized by Kerouac in *Mexico City Blues,* and the whole first part of the poem came pouring out of him in a catharsis of seven single-spaced pages.

> *I saw the best minds of my generation*
> *generation destroyed by madness*
> *starving, mystical, naked,*

The next pivotal moment came when Ginsberg changed the word *mystical* to *hysterical,* which altered the whole tone of the poem. It was an apt change of words, considering the life he'd led since his days as a college student. "It was a line that could never have been written without having encountered Carl Solomon on my first day at the Columbia Presbyterian Psychiatric Institute, where I'd been admitted in 1949, anxiously clutching my copy of the *Bhagavad-Gita,* in lieu of a jail sentence after being implicated in the larcenies of Herbert Hunckc and his band of fellow junkie burglars."

"One of the accused, Allen Ginsberg, 21 years old, of 1401 York Avenue, told the police he was a copy boy for a news service who had 'tied in' with the gang, all with police records, to obtain 'realism' he needed to write a story," the *New York Times* had reported in a story on April 23, 1949.

Six years later, as Ginsberg sat writing, it was clear that the *Times* story hadn't been at all far from the truth—he *had* been doing a kind of research. The first line of *Howl* was infused with this experience, along with virtually everything that had happened in Ginsberg's life since. In a single line he was able to draw upon those feelings and attach them to all the broken and disaffected spirits he had ever known, from his own mother to Joan Burroughs, but extrapolated in a way that presented them as metaphor for a spiritual malaise afflicting his generation. But if the first line was autobiography that would serve as generational metaphor, the second—

dragging themselves through the negro streets at dawn
looking for an angry fix,

—belongs to Herbert Huncke, and it introduces the first drug reference of the poem. *Howl* is a perfect storm of many factors and ideas. It is an emotional, spiritual, and artistic catharsis; "a lament for the lamb in America"; "a tragic custard-pie comedy of wild phrasing, meaningless images for the beauty of abstract poetry of mind running along making awkward combinations like Charlie Chaplin's walk." But it is also a definitive cataloguing of every drug used in every set and setting that Ginsberg had ever observed or experienced them in. The next lines, included in the second draft, form the cultural nexus of the poem—

angelheaded hipsters burning for the ancient heavenly
connection to the starry dynamo
in the machinery of night,

who poverty and tatters and hollow-eyed and high sat up smoking in the
supernatural darkness of cold-water flats floating across the tops of
cities contemplating jazz,

This is the circle of teahead subterraneans of the San Remo bar in Greenwich Village—Bill Keck, Anton Rosenberg, Mason Hoffman, Stanley Gould, Larry Rivers, Philip Lamantia, Julian Beck, and Judith Malina of the Living Theatre, and others also portrayed by Kerouac in *The Subterraneans* ("They are hip without being slick," explains Adam Moorad, the Ginsberg character, "they are intelligent without being corny, they are intellectual as hell and know all about Pound without being pretentious or talking too much about it, they are very Christ-like"). Here Ginsberg links this small enclave of alienated, jazz-loving, drug-experimenting bohemians to a spiritual quest for experience and wisdom as old as humankind itself.

For the rest of the first part of the poem, Ginsberg rides this anaphoric "who" as a base beat at the beginning of each verse, returning to it exactly as Prez would circle back to the same note at the beginning of another chorus. Prez's saxophone line allows Ginsberg to keep blowing for as long as the ideas keep coming—seven single-spaced pages that break the poet loose. But the influence of jazz is hardly limited to Lester Young. Biographer Michael Schumacher observes that jazz clearly shapes the structure of the rest of the poem into "three distinct musical movements: the first part with its hot saxophonic expressions, reminiscent of the jazz lines of Charlie Parker and Lester Young; the second part with short 'squawks' or statements, not unlike those played by Miles Davis; and the third part, with a cool bluesy and lyrical feeling similar to the moody music played by John Coltrane."

One could quibble with Schumacher's choice of artists as stylistic paradigms (especially as Coltrane had not yet come into prominence at the time Ginsberg wrote the poem) but his point is well taken: *Howl* could no more have been written without jazz than it could have been written without mind-altering substances, especially marijuana.

Exactly like Kerouac in works like *Visions of Cody* and *Mexico City Blues*, Ginsberg incorporates the consciousness of marijuana into the style of the writing itself, into what he later called "the mechanisms of surrealist or ideogrammatic method, the juxtaposition of disparate images to create a gap of understanding which the mind fills in with a flash of recognition of the unstated relationship (as in 'hydrogen jukebox')." Having observed that "the line . . . could be governed by breath measures, images or thought" and that "the poet's decision about where to break the line would have great bearing on his ability to coax the reader into the level of consciousness that he desired," he was writing poetry based on the "eyeball kicks" that he'd first remarked on when he had gone to the museum as a college student to study Cézanne's painting after smoking marijuana and experiencing Cézanne's "petit sensation" of space on a flat canvas by interlocking squares, cubes, and triangles of "hot" colors advancing and "cold" colors retreating in the optical field.

The poetics of *Howl* were only part of the reason why Allen Ginsberg would always claim that marijuana could offer the possibility of an "educational experience," but it's another substance that cracks open the central metaphor of the entire poem.

3.

As they went out into the San Francisco night after having eaten the peyote buttons and effects of the cactus began to overtake them, there came a wrenching moment when Allen Ginsberg looked into Peter Orlovsky's face and was horrified to see nothing but vacancy in his lover's eyes—"two phantom ghosts with empty eyes, laughing fiendishly. I got scared, thinking 'Oh, oh, it's all empty.'"

Orlovsky was Ginsberg's new lover, this "eternal boy" he'd met shortly after moving to San Francisco. It was his first relationship with a man who Ginsberg felt truly accepted him as friend and lover and offered the reciprocity of love—"the fulfillment of all my desires since I was nine." The two of them hopped on the clanging Powell Street trolley, and it was then that the Sir Francis Drake Hotel appeared before him as a dark tower in the night, a smoking death's head in the red glare of the city. All at once the metaphor came to him and the building became Moloch, the ancient Canaanite fire god.

"Moloch! Moloch!" Ginsberg intoned, completely overwhelmed by the image of parents burning their children in ritual sacrifice to the horned beast. He and Peter got off the trolley and wandered down Powell Street, and when they went into the cafeteria at the foot of the hotel, Ginsberg got out his pen and began jotting furiously in his journal—

Moloch! Molock! Whose hand ripped out their brains and scattered their minds on the wheels of subways?

The conduit directly responsible for bringing peyote into Ginsberg's life was Antonin Artaud, the French dramatist, poet, essayist, actor, and theater director, widely recognized as one of the major figures of twentieth-century theater and the European avant-garde. In 1936, Artaud had traveled to northern Mexico to experience the peyote rite of the Tarahumara Indians. It would take him the next twelve years to piece together his experiences and the images he brought back with him—the signs and crosses, the movements of the peyote dance, and the ritual slaughter of the bull and the drinking of its blood—into a book that documented his struggle to integrate what had been for him an overwhelming mystical experience into his own being. *The Peyote Dance* was not translated into English until the 1970s, but it had already become the stuff of bohemian folklore in New York by the early 1950s, when peyote buttons became available via COD shipments from Smith's Cactus Ranch in East Texas for eight dollars for a hundred buttons, and a certain store opened on East 2nd Street in New York that sold them. It was Bill Keck, one of the subterraneans hanging around the San Remo, who gave Ginsberg his first peyote buttons in April of 1952, which he took in his father's backyard in Paterson, New Jersey. By that time, Ginsberg had become thoroughly intrigued by the substance.

"The legend of peyote was that its very use was a prayer, that it contained the whole universe," Ginsberg explained, "that it could show you everything there was to see—all the people in the world, all the different animals, everything that was in the sky, everything under the earth. It was said that peyote could turn your eyes into X-rays so that you could see the insides of things. It was like telepathy, like electricity, and those who took it believed they could send their thoughts to loved ones twenty miles away."

The first time he took it, Ginsberg sat in his father's backyard and, after gagging down a second chunk, he noticed a "metallic imaginary aftertaste & feeling of stomach sickness." It was a flawlessly beautiful day—"The sky is a solid light blue"—and he found himself pondering a cherry tree in bloom. "The great mystery is that of being," he recorded in his journal, noting the flies and butterflies and how "space is a solid." He found himself "grinning idiotically at people" and was astounded to be actually "in the literal presence of one's father." And then this: "A bird just shat on me! It must have been on purpose." Notwithstanding the bird shit, it was a relatively pleasant experience—"Peyote is not God—but is a powerful force"—but the next time Ginsberg took it, in October of 1954, was very different indeed.

He was staring out the window of his Nob Hill apartment at the Sir Francis Drake Hotel when the building began to transform into what seemed a giant cyclops rising wickedly out of the "timeless city gloom." The more Ginsberg stared at the hotel in that state of consciousness, the more it looked like the skull face of a robot, with the powerful searchlight on top of the concrete structure beaming intrusively into his window. The image stayed with him—"This is deep-gong religious," he wrote in his journal.

The "deep-gong" religiousness of Ginsberg's vision was perfectly in keeping with the legends and traditions of peyote-eating, the origins of which are shrouded in antiquity. Nobody knows when it was first discovered that the fleshy top of the cactus contains an alkaloid that is one of the strangest and most intriguing substances in pharmacology. The Aztecs worshipped it as *peyotl,* a divine substance, "flesh of the gods." The Spaniards who conquered them demonized it as *raiz diabolica,* the "diabolical root," the direct invention of the devil, and for three hundred years Spanish priests tried to persecute all who used it, at times torturing its users by gouging out their eyeballs and cutting crucifixes into their bellies and loosing ravenous dogs on them. But peyote never died out among the native peoples of Mexico. By the end of the nineteenth century it had spread north to more than fifty tribes in the United States. As the buffalo were disappearing and the tribes were being herded onto reservations and their cultures were being shattered, these tribes evolved a form of peyote use that emphasized singing and chanting, meditation and prayer.

"What I had heard about peyote was that it was a medicine which could sustain an otherwise troubled people by making every one of its users a shaman who could find salvation through the natural elements of a God-given world," Ginsberg related. "Peyote was regarded by Native Americans as the vegetable incarnation of a deity, as the means of ascending towards God, a panacea in medicine, a key which could open to them all the glories of another world."

The fleshy slices of the cactus called mescal buttons were dried in the sun until they looked like brittle little wrinkled brown discs, then crushed and boiled in water or eaten raw. The stomach-turning taste of the substance made purgative vomiting an important part of the ritual, which began at sundown on a Saturday night inside a tepee, around a fire in front of a crescent moon altar to "father peyote." As the night wore on the drum would start to sound like it was coming from inside the soul. Voices would begin to speak out of the rattle. Thoughts would burst loose like a stampeding herd of horses. Visions would begin dancing in the fire. And now, like a vision escaping from his soul and dancing in the fire of a teepee, the Sir Francis Drake Hotel had turned into Moloch, and Allen Ginsberg had turned into a shaman poet raging against Moloch, the destroyer of the human spirit. It was a metaphor that allowed him to vent his most visceral feelings of rage, and the very sound of the word itself became the basis of the ranting exclamatory bursts that ignited the second part of the poem—

> *Moloch! Filth! Ugliness! Ashcans and unobtainable dollars! Beauties dying in lofts! Harpsichords unbuilt! Children screaming under stairways! old men weeping in parks!*

4.

Perhaps only San Francisco could have given birth to *Howl,* and nobody describes the set and setting of its arrival and the immediate impact of the poem better than Michael McClure. "The world that we tremblingly stepped out into in that decade was a gray, bitter one," he observes in *Scratching the Beat Surface,* his collection of essays about the poets of the San Francisco Renaissance.

> But San Francisco was a special place. Rexroth said it was to the arts what Barcelona was to Spanish Anarchism. Still, there was no way, even in San Francisco, to escape the pressures of the war culture. We were locked in the Cold War and the first Asian debacle—the Korean War. . . . My self-image in those years was in finding myself—young, high, a little crazed, needing a haircut, on an elevator with burly, crew-cutted square-jawed eminences, staring at me like I was misplaced cannon fodder. We hated the war and the inhumanity and the coldness. The country had the feeling of martial law. . . . As artists we were oppressed and indeed the people of the nation were oppressed.

McClure had always been interested in nature and the intensity of experience. Born in Kansas City on October 20, 1932, he grew up in Seattle with his grandparents, on the beaches and in the forests of the Pacific Northwest, in love with the fog, tide pools, animals, and trees. He started writing poetry at fourteen and had become interested in art by the time he returned to Wichita, Kansas, for high school; and it was there, at the age of seventeen, in an "aura of jazz, William Blake, Swedenborg, and the Visionary Surrealists," that he met a bebopper from Kansas City named Don and was taken to the jazz clubs along 13th Street and smoked pot for the first time. As he recalled it, "The first time I got high I was listening to Thelonious Monk, probably 'Misterioso,' and I had this incredible sense of elegance, something akin to a state of grace that was utterly different in the sense that I felt it was a black man's state of grace."

After a brief spell at college in Arizona, McClure arrived in San Francisco in 1954 with his wife, Joanna, and their infant daughter, Janie, and they found a home on the "reservation" of poets and artists in North Beach, which by that time had become a hothouse of the arts and an oasis of free thinking and eccentricity that was thriving amid the stultifying conservatism of the era. McClure was attending Robert Duncan's poetry workshop when he was invited to organize a poetry reading at the Six Gallery, but he was too busy, so Ginsberg volunteered to do it. It was Ginsberg himself who wrote and distributed the handbills announcing the event: "Six poets at the Six Gallery, Kenneth Rexroth, MC. Remarkable collection of angels all gathered at once in the same spot. Wine, music, dancing girls, serious poetry, free satori. Small collection for wine and postcards. Charming event."

The Six Gallery was an old garage at Union and Fillmore that had been converted into an art gallery and at the time was filled with the sculptures of Fred Martin—"pieces of orange crates that had been swathed in muslin and dipped in plaster of paris to make splintered, sweeping shapes like pieces of surrealist furniture."

On the night of Thursday, October 13, 1955, the space was packed with 150 fervent people. Nakedness was in the air as Robert Duncan had recently read his play *Faust Foutu* ("Faust Fucked") there, stripping off his clothes at the end. Jack Kerouac had arrived in town only a few days earlier and followed "the whole gang of howling poets" to the gallery. Neal Cassady showed up in his brakeman's uniform. "It was a mad night. And I was the one who got things jumping by going around collecting dimes and quarters from the rather stiff audience standing around in the gallery and coming back with three huge gallon jugs of California burgundy."

The MC for the evening was the distinguished but prickly poet and critic Kenneth Rexroth, who'd recently criticized one of Ginsberg's poems as academic and stilted. Seated behind the bow-tied Rexroth, in a semicircle, was an uncommon group of charismatic young poets; Kerouac would sketch all of them in *The Dharma Bums*.

First to read was the surrealist Philip Lamantia, an "out-of-this-world genteel-looking Renaissance Italian" who "looked like a young priest" and read the poetry of his friend John Hoffman, a peyotist who had gone to Mexico and had died of mononucleosis. Lamantia himself had participated in the peyote rites of the Warschau Indians. Lamantia believed fervently that drug-taking was a sacrament—that human beings had an absolute right to take any drug they desired, including narcotics, and he later expressed that opinion in a book called *Narcotica*.

Then came the "delicate pale handsome" Michael McClure, who read "For the Death of 100 Whales" and "Point Lobos Animism," his poem about Antonin Artaud and his deep desire to unite himself viscerally with nature. All of the poets who read that night were peyotists with the exception of McClure, who would avidly become one two years later and record his experience in one of the most elegant and lucid essays ever written on the substance.

Next up was Philip Whalen, who wrote poetry but had no plans of actually having a career as a poet before being asked to read that night—"a hundred and eighty pounds of poet meat, who was advertised by Japhy (privately in my ear) as being more than meets the eye." Whalen had taken peyote earlier that year, and the experience had broken him free from the imagist and formal academic poetry of Wallace Stevens and T. S. Eliot.

And finally there was Gary Snyder, who would become "Japhy Ryder," the central character of *The Dharma Bums*, the earnest woodsman and mountain climber from Oregon, devoted scholar of Zen Buddhism and Asian languages and Native American myths and texts—a "truly illuminated intelligence" with his background "in Oriental scholarship, Pound, taking peyote and seeing visions, his mountain climbing and bhikkuing, wow, Japhy Ryder is a great new hero of American culture."

Bearded and rugged in his lumberjack boots, Snyder's voice was "deep and resonant and somehow brave, like the voice of oldtime American heroes and orators" as he read "A Berry Feast," which made everybody "howl with joy, it was so pure, fuck being a dirty word that comes out clean. And he had his tender lyrical lines, like the ones about bears eating berries, showing his love of animals, and great mystery lines about oxen on the Mongolian Road showing his knowledge of Oriental literature." Later in the novel it's Japhy Ryder who gives voice and vision to the "rucksack revolution"—

> a world full of rucksack wanderers, Dharma Bums refusing to subscribe to the general demand that they consume production and therefore have to work for the privilege of consuming, all that crap they didn't want anyway such as refrigerators, TV sets, cars, at least new fancy cars, certain hair oils and deodorants and general junk you finally always see a week later in the garbage anyway, all of them imprisoned in a system of work, produce, consume, work, produce, consume, I see a vision of a great rucksack revolution, thousands or even millions of young Americans wandering around with rucksacks, going up to mountains to pray, making children laugh and old men glad, making young girls happy and old girls happier, all of 'em Zen Lunatics who go about writing poems that happen to appear in their heads and also by being kind and also by strange unexpected acts keep giving visions of eternal freedom to everybody and to all living creatures.

The "rucksack revolution" offers a prescient vision, just as many of the themes conveyed in the poems read at this legendary event—the spiritual emptiness of materialism, the sacred beauty of nature, artistic freedom, love, visionary transcendentalism, pacifism, veneration of Eastern and Native American wisdom traditions—would all resonate in the counterculture of the next decade.

The penultimate poet of the evening had never read his poetry before in public. Ginsberg is described by Kerouac as a "hornrimmed intellectual hepcat with wild black hair" dressed in a gray suit and tie. He was nipping freely from one of the big jugs of wine, and by all accounts was quite buzzed by the time he faced the audience.

"Allen began in a small and intensely lucid voice," McClure recounted. "At some point Jack Kerouac began shouting 'GO' in cadence as Allen read it."

As Ginsberg read on, he seemed transported, swaying to the incantatory rhythm and cadence of his own words, more exalted and impassioned with each line. The enthusiastic audience was riveted, hanging on his every word, exhorting him on with their cheers, and by the time he came to the end—

Holy forgiveness! mercy! charity! faith! Holy! Ours! bodies! suffering!
magnanimity!
Holy the supernatural extra brilliant intelligent kindness of the soul!

—Ginsberg was in tears, and the audience was shell-shocked.

At that moment Michael McClure sensed that something elemental had shifted with the mere reading of the poem. "In all our memories no one had been so outspoken in poetry before—we had gone beyond a point of no return—and we were ready for it, for a point of no return. None of us wanted to go back to the gray, shrill, militaristic silence, to the intellective void—to the land without poetry—to the spiritual drabness."

Also present at the reading was Lawrence Ferlinghetti, the poet and publisher and proprietor of the three-year-old City Lights, an independent bookstore and press, who also immediately recognized that the poem would become a vehicle for a whole paradigm shift in not only American poetry but also American consciousness: "I knew the world had been waiting for this poem, for this apocalyptic message to be articulated. It was in the air, waiting to be captured in speech. The repressive, conformist, racist, homophobic world of the 1950s cried out for it."

"Ginsberg, this poem will make you famous in San Francisco," Kerouac declared after the reading.

Kenneth Rexroth, who had sat in tears during Ginsberg's reading, corrected Kerouac. "No, this poem will make you famous bridge to bridge."

Of course it was Rexroth's prediction that would turn out to be more accurate. That night, as the poets and their girlfriends and boyfriends went to a Chinese restaurant and celebrated the reading with an orgy, Ferlinghetti typed out a telegram to Ginsberg that echoed Ralph Waldo Emerson's response to Walt Whitman's *Leaves of Grass* and set in motion what became known as the San Francisco Renaissance—"I greet you at the beginning of a great career. When do I get the manuscript?"

Howl and Other Poems was published in October of 1956 as Number Four of Ferlinghetti's small, square-format City Lights Pocket Poets series. The poem is a rich and provocative cultural tapestry that is woven with the consciousness of illicit drugs, containing no fewer than twelve explicit references to the use of such substances, proclaiming them holy. Ginsberg had sat on a San Francisco bus, weeping, as he wrote what became the "Footnote," the coda and final movement of the poem—the spiritual counterpoint to the fiery indignation of the Moloch section. Before the poem was over he proclaimed everything holy in a series of remarkable exclamatory lines—Peter, Allen himself, Kerouac, Huncke, the hipsters, the junkies and criminals, the damned and the saved, every private part of the body, every conceivable sex act, the middle class, cities, visions, time, eternity, the soul, his mother in the insane asylum, his father's cock, the "cocks of the grandfathers of Kansas," the heavens, the cafeterias, the rivers, the pavement, the sea, the desert, the very shit in the toilet, the typewriter, poetry, the voice, heaven, ecstasy, "the unknown buggered and suffering beggars," "the hideous human angels," the Fifth International, the abyss, the Angel in Moloch, Everyman was holy, Everything was holy . . . Before the poem ends Ginsberg also returns to the theme of jazz and drugs with epochal fanfare, using yet another juxtaposition of "disparate images" that condenses the entire era into two indelible words—*bop apocalypse*—providing its perfect metaphor.

> *Holy the groaning saxophone! Holy the bop apocalypse! Holy the jazzbands marijuana hipsters peace & junk & drums!*

The notoriety of the work was all but guaranteed on March 23, when the San Francisco office of US Customs, under the direction of Chester McPhee, seized 520 copies of the second, three-thousand-copy shipment of the book, which had arrived from its British printer, calling it "obscene." As Ginsberg described it, "I may have conjured the pleasure of a 'teahead joyride,' but what really summoned down the fury of Moloch was writing about the 'cocks of the grandfathers of Kansas.'"

By the time the celebrated trial on the legality of the seizure was over and the book had prevailed, there were ten thousand copies in print. It would always strike Ginsberg as the ultimate irony that in the end, it was the conservative advocates of censorship who succeeded in doing more than anyone else to spread the news of the poem about "peyote solidities of halls."

Perhaps it was Gary Snyder who came closest to predicting what was going to happen when he wrote Ginsberg from Japan, where he was studying. Snyder requested four additional copies of the poem from City Lights and was "carefully figgering where to place these bombs."

By the time of Snyder's letter, Ginsberg was already in Tangier with William Burroughs, helping him with the manuscript of *Naked Lunch*. He had cited the book on the dedication page of *Howl*, calling it "an endless novel which will drive everybody mad."

23

'Round Midnight

1.

Every night after the gig with the Miles Davis Quintet at the Café Bohemia was exactly the same for John Coltrane. He and Elvin Jones would be hanging out together and they would get into the same cab and share it up to the same dealer's apartment in Harlem. The same cab driver would always wait for them because he was a junkie, too. They would all get straight together and sit around listening to music until eight or so in the morning, then they'd cop the same five or six bags of dope and walk out completely insulated against the jarring blare of the morning and everything else on God's earth, and the cabbie would drive them down to Times Square and drop them off right in front of the same all-day triple-feature movie house.

It was the same scene on the street; the people rushing past them, clutching briefcases on their way to work, would always seem a part of some faraway square existence while they would stand, blank and ossified, at the counter of the same coffee and donut stand to get their containers of coffee and the same selection of donuts: a dozen glazed and a dozen plain. They would always ask for the same two containers of water. Going into the theater, they'd see the same painted hookers and freaks of indeterminate sexuality who also had no place to go, and they'd pay off the same usher and head up to the same seats in the balcony. They would settle in and take out the same tarnished bent spoon and begin cooking up the same breakfast of champions.

After hitting up, they would slump back in the seats with their sunglasses on and recede into the same place of mummified sequestration where the outside world had absolutely no corporeal existence whatsoever, where there was nothing but spoon and spike and bag and point of contact and the push that sent the ebb tide of dope in their veins flowing out to every filament of being, cresting in the viscera like a wave of warm sunshine, leaving them awash in a surreal world of disembodied celluloid and light flickering through the darkness and reflecting in the lenses of their glasses.

A bite of donut might be followed by a sip of coffee, but such bodily necessities as hunger and thirst were of very little consequence in this world because the whole of the universe was completely decocted down to the next shot of dope. The movies they watched over and over were usually a main feature followed by two B films, and after five or six hours of running dialogue from something like *The Girl He Left Behind,* with Tab Hunter and Natalie Wood, they would have absorbed every bit of dialogue by heart and have enough to serve all of their conversational needs for that evening.

At eight or nine o'clock they would take their last shot, after which they would pull themselves together and go shambling out, bedraggled and dope-dimmed, into the rush and bustle and glare of the Times Square night, as if they had just crawled sluggishly out of the wet soil from underneath a newly overturned stone. Hailing a cab, they would head downtown along Seventh Avenue, rolling down the windows and letting the brisk air revivify them for the big scene. Pulling up to the curb in front of the Café Bohemia, it would seem as if it was all happening in a continuum, as if they had never left, and they would issue forth into the hip sidewalk throng trying to get inside.

2.

The engagement of the Miles Davis Quintet at the Café Bohemia in the spring of 1956 signaled the arrival of the cutting edge of jazz in the Village. The Miles Davis Quintet was a statement of many things: that Miles was once again bestriding the world of jazz like a colossus; that he was the anointed one who was bearing the standard since the flame of Charlie Parker had flickered out. But the group was also a showcase for the emerging brilliance of John Coltrane. Word quickly spread that Miles had found a sax player whose every appearance with the group was an adventure. The club quickly become a mecca of the new underground. Every night the sidewalk outside on Barrow Street was backed up with people seeking admittance to the dark cavern downstairs, like pilgrims seeking a new meaning. Just to be inside the club was thrilling, filled with every possibility and adventure of the night.

Trane and Elvin always had their shades on as they went sauntering past the onlookers, and once inside the club they would make their way to the bar or backstage. They would say very little, but what they would say would be communicated in nothing but snatches of dialogue from the three movies they had seen that day. People would look at them and scratch their heads. The two of them thought it was very funny, some new innovation in the art of hip modern living, how they could hold an entire conversation and never have to use anything that was not a part of the dialogue of those movies, which had been looped through their consciousness over and over again through nods and junk dreams, but to anyone else it seemed as if they were talking in some kind of postmodern cabalistic code. People were completely unable to fathom what they were talking about but absolutely certain that what they said was unequivocally hip. They were like members of some strange underground society, speaking a language and doing things that nobody else could possibly understand, but talking was something that was completely beside the point at the club anyway.

What people at the Café Bohemia were coming to understand was that John Coltrane made his statements with his horn. Everything else in his life may have been flattened by the routines of addiction, but his playing was the one thing that was never the same. As soon as he stepped on the stand, he was constantly probing, penetrating, reaching for the outer edge, sometimes completely changing directions in the middle of his solos. Coltrane was slipping into ever-deeper levels of heroin addiction, but his playing was becoming characterized by a nightly exploration that barraged the audience as he kept stretching for advanced harmonics and sought to take the music further and further out, beyond what he later described to composer David Amram as "the 32-bar song form, improvising on a simple line the way an Indian musician would do with a raga."

There were those at the club who could not understand or hated Coltrane's obsessive experimentalism, who hooted and whistled during his solos and wanted Miles to fire him—they kept saying that Trane wasn't really playing anything, that he was only "playing scales." Miles's brother Vernon had warned him about playing with Coltrane: "You can't use that boy . . . everything he plays is unresolved." "If he plays with me, he'll resolve things," was Miles's response, but it didn't quite happen that way. There was sometimes tension between the two of them. Miles didn't like to talk about music or direct his musicians, and Coltrane interpreted his brooding silences as license to do what he wanted to do. Miles asked him, "Can't you play twenty-seven choruses instead of twenty-eight?" And when Coltrane tried to explain that he couldn't find a way to stop, Miles's rejoinder was dripping with sarcasm: "You might try taking the horn out of your mouth." But underneath the tension, Miles understood the fury of Coltrane's obsession to find something new. He instinctively understood that what Trane was doing was taking a musical idea and trying to explain it five different ways at once. Nobody understood and appreciated the importance of freedom like Miles Davis, in jazz and everything else, and as much as the denizens of jazz may have been buzzing with the tidings of Trane's coming, it was Miles Davis who was always at the center of attention at the Café Bohemia.

Miles himself had only recently emerged from his own addiction to lead what many were claiming was the greatest quintet in the history of jazz: Coltrane on tenor saxophone, Philly Joe Jones on drums, Paul Chambers on bass, and Red Garland on piano. Since his reemergence it had seemed as if Miles's talent had only been tempered and deepened by what he had gone through, as if he had passed through a trial of fire and darkness and had emerged from the ordeal, purified and strong. It was much more than the fact that he had once again become a creative cynosure of the music after a four-year period of artistic decline. There was a feeling of survival about him. Of defiance. Of the reassertion of manhood and genius. He would arrive at the club in his sports car like a sleek black underground movie star. He was never more sharply togged out, never more poised or self-assured or intense, never more charismatic, but he was removed, forbiddingly aloof. "Miles had an aura," was how the engineer and producer Lewis Merenstein recalled his appearances at the club. "He didn't even have to put the horn to his lips. He could just stand there and look at you, and you would feel like you were experiencing something powerful about his being."

Up on the stand Miles sometimes turned his back on the audience. He rarely talked, and when he did, what he had to say was often surly and caustic. Sometimes he'd respond with nothing but a single raspy-voiced phrase that, more than any other, seemed to express not only his quiet, seething cool but also his world-weary disdain for everything—"*So what?*"—a phrase he would later use for the name of a song on his 1959 masterpiece, *Kind of Blue.* Smiles were even more infrequent than conversation. He often played with his eyes closed, lost in his own private meaning, and when he opened them, they seemed to burn with passion and anger, feelings that issued forth bitingly from the lustrous trumpet at his lips. But mostly there was a mood of stark melancholy and isolation that struck people, a tone subtly delineated by the Harmon mute he now used on "'Round Midnight," the Thelonious Monk composition that had signaled his comeback. Miles had played the song after kicking heroin at the end of the first Newport Jazz Festival in 1955, in the aftermath of Bird's death, during a tribute that included "Now's the Time." He had come out in a white seersucker jacket and bow tie and played the piece with the mute, and the people had loved it. The song now had the same effect when he played it at the Bohemia. Something about the way he played it and what he had gone through had fashioned it as a statement of not only his own life and exactly where jazz had come to, but also of the whole emerging hip subculture that was drawn to the frenetic creativity of jazz during the mid-1950s from every corner of the arts, all of it fermenting together. Actors from the Living Theatre and the Actor's Studio and the modern dancers. Writers like Norman Mailer and Ralph Ellison, and a whole new generation of poets like Allen Ginsberg. The expressionist painters all hanging around the Cedar Tavern. The hip kids all over the West Village who were now moving over to the Lower

East Side. The jet-setters like the Rothschild baroness, Pannonica de Koenigswarter, whose gleaming Bentley was always parked underneath a street lamp on Barrow Street. All of them were drawn to jazz and found some kind of definition in this theme, which became one of the most striking ballad performances in all of jazz.

As word about the Miles Davis Quintet spread among the hip cognoscenti in the spring of 1956, each performance of the group took on the electricity of an event, and each performance of "'Round Midnight" became the emotional crescendo of that event. Gil Evans had helped Miles arrange his version of the song in three movements. Miles led the group into the tune with his muted solo of Monk's melody, escorted by Trane's obbligatos. There was a lonesome, aching poignancy to Miles's playing, followed by a trumpet-saxophone fanfare that introduced Trane's middle movements, with Trane bursting in double-time for two choruses in a beautiful overlapping profusion of notes that he sprayed out like brilliant soulful drips of color on a Jackson Pollack canvas. They offset each other, Miles and Trane, their musical counterpoint as conspicuous as the differences in their physicality and appearance: Miles tight and slim, elegant, cool and restrained; Trane large and bearish, with his luminous, melancholy eyes, disordered but seeking some kind of profound release. It was music that inspired the writers in the club to inscribe memorable words. Coltrane had "a dry, unplaned tone that sets Davis off like a rough mounting for a fine stone," as critic Whitney Balliett wrote. The poet Langston Hughes rendered Miles and his music as "honey mixed with liquid fire."

The Miles Davis Quintet may have represented the resurgence and creative rebirth of a man who himself had beaten the odds and left his heroin habit behind in what seemed a monumental act of will, but it was also a stark reminder that the history of jazz was still being written to a significant degree by the comings and goings of junkies. Coltrane might never have had the opportunity to join the band had not a slot for a saxophone opened after the great Sonny Rollins bottomed out on heroin. Rollins had been arrested and remanded to the Federal Narcotics Prison and Hospital at Lexington. When he got out, he had entered a period of crisis and relapse and had left New York, completely disappearing in Chicago. Sonny had completely withdrawn from the scene, giving up music while he worked in a factory and tried desperately to kick his habit. During his absence Coltrane had been invited to join the group and had thus garnered his growing notoriety. It was only one more instance of how the private habits of the musicians were shaping the music.

There was a dark, seductive, outlaw beauty not only to the music but to the scene itself, all of it accentuated by the attitude of the musicians on the stand—a subtext of people walking the jagged improvisational edge of life as well as music. Thelonious Monk had written "'Round Midnight" back in the mid-1940s, during the birth of bebop, at a time when the first wave of musicians were "getting on" to dope. Thelonious himself had never been a heroin addict, but when he was arrested holding Bud Powell's dope in a car, he refused to roll over on Bud and served sixty days for it, losing his cabaret card in the process. By the time the Miles Davis version of the song became celebrated, many of the musicians who had come to heroin were hitting bottom. The piece now resonated with the long and arduous journeys of scores of musicians who had been caught in the vise of addiction for years and were coming to the grim reckoning that they now had to somehow change their lives. For those who played it in Miles's band and so many others, "'Round Midnight" became a set piece about heroin, as evocative of a time and place in their experience as Charlie Parker's "Lover Man" had been during the period of getting on, because it would oftentimes be right around midnight when the jones would begin to set in and the men on the stand would begin thinking about how long it had been since their last shot, and how long it would be to the next. Here was jazz that smoldered with the pathos and dark romanticism of life around heroin. The constant pawning of wristwatches and instruments. Spot checks for needle marks and strip searches at bus and railway stations and in alleys outside of clubs. Being thrown junk sick into kick tanks and jail cells. Salt shots and ice cubes on testicles after near-fatal overdoses. Rooftop nods and dope-sick dawns. Bad counts and rip-offs and the desperation of dope panics. Relapses and the frantic despair of loved ones. Perhaps most of all, it resonated with what William Burroughs called "the algebra of need"—that feeling of being completely powerless over the cellular certainty that at the end of the last song of the last set, Trane and his cohorts would pack up their instruments and head out into the night with only one thing on their minds. And so it would go, day after day, night after night . . .

"'Round Midnight" became a soundtrack for all of it.

3.

The Miles Davis Quintet was becoming known as the "D&D band"—the dope and drunk band—for very good reason. As Miles was the only one clean, he had to play nursemaid to them, watching over them, making sure they ate something, sobering them up, trying to keep them out of trouble with the police. He even kept a secret stash of heroin in the event of a dire emergency. It was tiresome and nerve-racking; the only one who seemed like he could keep it together was Philly Joe, who could use use dope like nobody else. Philly Joe's biggest problem was the fact of a finite income against the magnitude of his habit, not the impairment of his ability to function.

John Coltrane was another story. The dope he copped uptown in New York was of a much better quality than the dope he was used to in Philadelphia, and since spending more and more time in New York, he had fallen prey to the increased availability of supply as well as the increased quality. Despite his recent marriage to Naima Grubbs, a woman clearly devoted to him, Coltrane displayed a complete inability to resist spending virtually every penny of his earnings on dope. He also drank copiously and compulsively. Heroin addiction and alcohol-ism had always been a double whammy for Trane. When combined with long hours and lack of sleep, he would lose control and begin nodding out on the stand, which both embarrassed and infuriated Miles Davis.

When it started happening more frequently at the Café Bohemia, Miles began warning Trane to get himself together. He cared about Trane, but he also cared that people might think that Miles was back on dope. He understood the internal rhythms and needs of a junkie very well, but as much as he could sympathize with the problems of addiction, he could simply not abide such a breach of professional-ism by one of his musicians at a club date where Miles was command-ing $1,250 a night and setting the jazz world on its ear, even one as gifted as John Coltrane. The warnings continued. Miles hoped that the increasing attention being paid to Coltrane would pull him out of it. He told Trane that there were record producers and executives coming around, people who wanted to give him contracts but who were afraid to because of how strung out he was. It didn't seem to matter. By October of 1956 it was getting very bad. Trane was spiraling down fast. He started coming in late. Then later. A few times he didn't show at all. According to Miles's autobiography, everything came to a head one night backstage—"One night I got so mad I slapped him upside his head and punched him in the stomach in the dressing room." Thelonious Monk was in the club that night and walked into the room just in time to witness the violent scene. "When he saw that Trane didn't do nothing but sit there like a big baby, Monk got hot under the collar. He told Trane, 'Man, as much as you play on saxophone, you don't have to take nothing like that.' . . . I was so mad I didn't care what the fuck Monk was talking about, because in the first place, it wasn't none of his business. I fired Trane that night, and he went back to Philadelphia to try and kick his habit. I felt bad about letting him go."

Coltrane was soon replaced by Sonny Rollins, who had returned to New York and had made a quantum leap in his musical abilities after freeing himself from the fetters of his own addiction. Trane's dismissal was an event that set him on the path to a final confrontation with the demons of his addiction, and with the deepest truth of himself. Like so many others', his struggle was characterized by false starts and relapses. For a period he would wander, suffering terribly, helplessly lost in an urban wilderness of booze and dope, and then return to the Quintet, only to fall back into dope and be dismissed again. Jackie McLean was witness to several of Coltrane's unsuccessful attempts at kicking his habit. Trane was still playing with the Miles Davis Quintet and McLean was playing in the great Charles Mingus Jazz Workshop around the time the group produced the Mingus classic, *Pithecanthropus Erectus*.

"We were getting high together, copping from the same dealer every night in the club. He'd cop for me and vice versa. One night I came to work and came down and he was in the basement practicing his horn. 'Hey John, I spoke to Shorty. He'll be here around eleven o'clock. If I'm on, get me five bags.' He said, 'No, I'm not doing that anymore!' So he left the club, and when he came back he was in the same shirt, and his collar was all twisted up, and he got up on that bandstand next to Miles, and he looked horrible, man, like a real der-elict. He had just gone home and laid in bed in his clothes in complete agony. I watched him do this from Tuesday night to Sunday night, with those same clothes on every night, sweating, smelling bad. But I saw him kick that habit on that bandstand every night, and I *heard* him kick it, because you could hear it all coming through his horn, all the feel-ings of it. What sounds, my God, what notes he was playing! I watched it happen, and by the second week, he was still drinking too much, but his playing was just incredible. After playing I'd just pack up my horn and sit out there in the front row and just marvel, and Mingus would get mad at me. He'd say, 'Man, would you come on, don't go sit in the front row like a fan, man. You're playing with *me*, and as soon as you get off the stage you can't wait to go sit down and listen to *him*, how do you think that makes me feel?' And all I could say was, 'Charlie, I'm just listening to Trane, man, he's playing *so much*, man!'"

4.

The experience of breaking free from heroin became watershed events in the lives of Miles Davis and John Coltrane. Both are the stuff of leg-end, but they are very different stories indeed.

What happened to Miles presents the example of a man emerging from the wasteland of addiction to reclaim his manhood and assert his independence. His long descent included two arrests and two unsuc-cessful attempts to quit cold turkey. Miles hit rock bottom one night in the summer of 1953 when he was in very bad shape and just hap-pened to meet Max Roach in the street outside of Birdland. Max had been clean for years by that time and looked so proud and dignified, and Miles was badly strung out. "What's happening?" asked Max, but the question was rhetorical—he knew very well what was happening—and before Miles could turn to walk away, Max slipped $200 into his pocket. It was a act of compassion, but Miles was deeply humiliated by it. His shame became so intolerable that he called his father and asked for the money to come home. That fall Miles withdrew to his father's 650-acre farm in Millstadt, Illinois, where he locked himself into the guest house. As the experience would later be dramatized in Miles's autobiography, for the next eight days he threw up everything he ate, sweating so much that he smelled like chicken soup, wanting to die. He had been a junkie for four years, and the physical pain and discomfort of withdrawal got so bad that he actually contemplated throwing himself out of the upstairs window of the house, just to get relief by knocking himself unconscious on the ground below. "Then one day it was over, just like that. Over. Finally over. I felt better, good and pure. I walked outside into the clean, sweet air over to my father's house and when he saw me he had this big smile on his face and we just hugged each other and cried."

It's this portrayal that formed the legend of his withdrawal. The truth is that even after this experience, whether accurately depicted in his autobiography or not, there was one more relapse, still one more stumble into the pits of dope, but Miles was somehow able to emerge from that one free and clean of the drug for good.

When Miles returned to New York he adopted Sugar Ray Robinson as his role model, resolving that not only did he have to stay clean, he had to pursue his career like a boxer training for a fight. As a boxing aficionado who had once entertained the notion of becoming a boxer himself, Miles admired Sugar Ray because he was the most forceful fighter he had ever seen—and yet Sugar Ray was precise, measured, calculating, ruthless. Miles pursued his career and the growth of his artistry with the same discipline, focus, and energy. He signed the most lucrative jazz contract in the history of Columbia Records, changing the very terms under which club owners did business with jazz musicians. His comeback presented a paradigm of freedom and self-regeneration at a time when many musicians were finding it almost impossible to get off dope. He became a powerful model of self-confidence and hope for the community of musicians who now began looking to him and beheld a man of furious pride, towering self-regard, and steel-willed resolve. To the inner community, the kicking of his habit quickly became the powerful stuff of legend, like a modern jazz version of Booker T. Washington's *Up from Slavery*.

What was much less apparent was the damage that had been done. The needle marks on his arms healed over, but the wounds of his addiction remained fresh and raw on the inside. Miles was haunted by the years of his heroin addiction and from this time forth would become physically ill in the presence of someone shooting up. His newfound self-assertion was the legitimate expression of a healthy artistic ego, and his need for self-protection reflected the hard realities of the music business, but they were also the products of a lingering emotional legacy of bitterness and embarrassment from his most desperate days as a junkie and could become toxic in the flash of an eye. Miles covered his shame with smoldering anger and moodiness and the distance that he put between himself and almost everyone. And no sooner had Miles kicked heroin than he began using cocaine more often—a drug that would play a heavy role in his life for years to come. No, peace of mind would never come easily to Miles Davis, which meant it would never be easy to be his associate, friend, or lover. What he fiercely demanded, what most obsessed and drove him, was the need to be on top again, to always be right on the creative cutting edge of music and style. It was a pressing need that had always been deep inside of him, but one that had been painfully deferred by his experience of addiction. His exit from heroin allowed him to tap deeply into his unique powers of self-transformation. He became a supreme creative changeling in the process, complex, driven—"one of the quintessential heroes of the jazz life," as Nat Hentoff calls him—Sugar Ray in a smoky club spotlight, taking on all comers with his blazing trumpet. Before the end of the decade he would produce *Kind of Blue*, arguably the greatest and certainly the best-known album in the history of jazz.

What happened to John Coltrane seems almost biblical by comparison, the parable of a man emerging after a long exile in a desert to become what can only be called a channel of God. As Miles had retired to the seclusion of his father's farm in Millstadt and Sonny Rollins had sought refuge in the anonymity of Chicago, Coltrane returned to his mother's house in Philadelphia. One morning after returning home, he awoke and informed his wife that he was forever through with putting poisons in his body. He told his family that he would only walk back among them again when he was completely clean, purged of all the impurities, and withdrew into a room. For two weeks his family prayed for him and brought him water, and he never left the room except to go to the bathroom. Sometime during the worst part of the experience, Coltrane had what he later described as a spiritual awakening. As the agony of his withdrawal from heroin and alcohol worsened, he prayed fervently, asking God to take the weight of his addiction from him so that he could devote his life and music to His glory. At that moment the worst of the misery lifted, and for the first time in his life he knew what he later described as a kind of profound inner peace.

"During the year 1957, I experienced by the grace of God, a spiritual awakening which was to lead me to a richer, fuller, more productive life," Coltrane wrote in the liner notes of *A Love Supreme* in 1964. "At that time, in gratitude, I humbly asked to be given the means and privilege to make others happy through music. I feel that this has been granted through his grace. ALL PRAISE TO GOD."

The fact that Coltrane had sought the help of a Higher Power, a "God of his understanding," to help him through the experience of withdrawal is not surprising considering his strong Christian upbringing in Hamlet, North Carolina. After all, both of his grandfathers had been ministers, and his wife was a devout Muslim. Perhaps more than anything else, Coltrane's experience was an example of the kind of spiritual awakening that Bill Wilson, the founder of Alcoholics Anonymous, experienced when he lay in Towns Hospital in New York on December 11, 1934, at the very end of his long years of drinking, looked into the abyss of insanity and death that awaited him, and cried out in his powerlessness and anguish, "If there be a God let Him show himself!"—and his room blazed with "an indescribable white light," as he later put it. "I was seized with an ecstasy beyond description. Every joy I had known was pale by comparison. The light, the ecstasy—I was conscious of nothing else for a time." This, Wilson realized, must be "the God of the preachers."

In *The Varieties of Religious Experience*, his seminal work about the psychology of the religious experience, William James theorizes that "the sway of alcohol over mankind is unquestionably due to its power to stimulate the mystical faculties of human nature, usually crushed to earth by the cold facts and dry criticisms of the sober hour. . . . Not through mere perversity do men run after it. The drunken consciousness is one bit of the mystic consciousness, and our total opinion of it must find its place in our opinion of that larger whole."

As Bill Wilson corresponded with Carl Jung, the great Swiss psychiatrist also advanced the theory that the spiritual awakening was the most effective antidote to alcoholism. Jung based his conclusion on his experience with the alcoholic known as Rowland H., who had seemingly been beyond all hope, recognizing that Rowland's craving for alcohol was "the equivalent on a low level of the spiritual thirst of our being for wholeness . . . expressed in medieval language: the union with God. . . . The only right and legitimate way to such an experience is that it happens to you in reality, and it can only happen to you when you walk a path which leads you to a higher understanding."

Coltrane never became a member of Alcoholics Anonymous, but it is hard to deny the significance of his use of the phrases "by the grace of God" and "spiritual awakening"—his experience seems the embodiment of what Wilson, James, and Jung were writing about. If using drugs and alcohol had been the equivalent of a low-level search for God, as Jung suggests, in his sobriety Coltrane's spiritual quest ascended to the highest level and he created music that was truly imbued with what William James calls "mystic consciousness." His breakout from heroin and alcohol unleashed a creative surge that would have major repercussions on the entire direction of jazz. "Live right," he told his musical colleagues as he delved into vegetarianism and weight lifting along with the Koran, the Kabbalah, and the works of Krishnamurti and Paramahansa Yogananda. By the end of the decade, with his famous quartet of McCoy Tyner on piano, Elvin Jones on drums, and Jimmy Garrison on bass, Coltrane would take "My Favorite Things," the Richard Rodgers composition from *The Sound of Music,* and transform it into one of the most uniquely lyrical and spiritually uplifting statements in the history of jazz. He began to visualize his music as the act of opening his arms wide in an embracing gesture and suffusing his audience with the radiance of his love, using jazz as a means to create awareness of the sacred interconnectedness of all living things—all of which reached a spiritual and creative crescendo in his 1964 masterpiece, *A Love Supreme.* It was precisely this quality of Coltrane's music that has made Carlos Santana and so many others view him as no mere jazz artist but a spiritual guide—"I heard the Supreme One playing music through John Coltrane's mind." It isn't hard to understand why Coltrane became one of the only musicians in the history of jazz whose music has been incorporated into the worship services of churches in Philadelphia and San Francisco, exactly as other churches use Bach's *St. Matthew Passion* or Handel's *Messiah.*

But just as Miles Davis had to deal with the addictions of Coltrane and others in the wake of his own withdrawal, so Coltrane had to continually contend with the heroin-related troubles of his extraordinary drummer, Elvin Jones. More important was the physical damage that Coltrane may have suffered as a result of his addictions. An emotionally complex and driven man who practiced compulsively and sometimes fell asleep with the reed in his mouth, Coltrane approached music as if privy to the knowledge that his days were numbered, that every moment was precious. One cannot help but think that the liver cancer that would tragically take him in July of 1967 at the young age of forty may very well have been related to the heavy drinking and the drugs he shot into his body during the years of his addiction.

"The etiology of liver cancer is still basically unknown," observes one of Coltrane's biographers, Eric Nisenson, "and there is no reason to believe that alcohol or drugs had anything to do with Coltrane's illness."

Nor, for that matter, is there any reason to believe that alcohol or drugs had nothing to do with it.

5.

Sometimes for Jackie McLean, the endless waiting was even worse than getting sick or trying to kick, because there was so much anxiety about the simple act of scoring, and as McLean waited for the dope man named Shorty out there on Barrow Street outside the Café Bohemia, he couldn't help it: he found himself pondering all of the imponderables. Would Shorty show? How long would it take him to show? Would he be holding? Would it be good dope, a good count? Was he being watched? As more junkies were being taken down in and around the jazz scene and turned by the police, some would roll over on other junkies. Would the buy turn out to be some kind of a setup?

In these moments McLean often thought about his beautiful wife, Dolly, who was always worrying about him, always trying to help him find a way out of the endless maze of his addiction. He would think about the baby and the rent being late. Everyone who knew McLean during these years always said that he was an intelligent, enormously likable, and talented man—a man with a good heart and a fine wife who loved him and beautiful kids—but a man who suffered from a seemingly insoluble problem called heroin addiction. He continued to try everything. He tried Lexington twice, to no avail. He tried large doses of Dexedrine and Nembutal because he was told they would relieve the symptoms of withdrawal. It was the same technique that Charlie Parker once tried so disastrously in Los Angeles, and the results were distressingly similar: he had a nervous breakdown, ending up in Bellevue exactly as Bird had crashed at Camarillo.

Inevitably, at these times when he was waiting for his connection, he would also think about Bird. Because he was such an obvious example of everything that Bird represented musically, the years of Bird's decline had been particularly difficult for him. Not only was their relationship emotionally charged by their strong mentor-protégé bond, but they were also fellow addicts at a time when Bird was slipping away and McLean's own addiction was only hardening. He was particularly haunted by the last time he saw Bird alive. When McLean was playing the Montmartre and got sick and Ahmed Basheer offered to take him home, Bird told him that he would mind his alto and took the horn and went right out and hocked it. It wasn't the first time it had happened, of course, but even though Bird had it back to him in time for his next gig at the Open Door, McLean refused talk to him. At the end of the night of that gig, Bird approached him. "Going uptown? I'll get a cab for us." "I'll get my own, Bird," McLean said, and turned angrily away. McLean was on an uptown bus when he learned about Bird's death from a newspaper. He just got off the bus and went down the street, weeping inconsolably, and now he was filled with remorse. *If only I had known*, he would think. *If only I had known it would be the last time I would ever see him, I would have shared that cab with Bird to the ends of the earth.*

Sometime after McLean moved down to the Village, the sculptor Harvey Cropper showed him the work of Hieronymus Bosch, and McLean instantly recognized something elemental about the life of the modern urban junkie in the infernal visions of the gothic Dutch painter. He felt the horror especially when he was junk sick. At least he'd been very fortunate in one regard: seven years of heroin addiction had led to no serious degradation of his talent. He'd written songs like "Dr. Jackle" and "Little Melonae." The hard bop style that he had come to exemplify was a response to the West Coast "cool school" of Chet Baker—less technically dazzling than the bebop of the forties but more organically open to the black popular traditions of blues and gospel. It was hard, fast, expressive, sometimes bleak and tormented, and few played it as piercingly as McLean. It had gotten him notice and a contract with Prestige. There were great artists who always seemed interested in working with him, like Charles Mingus and Art Blakey, but mostly what he thought about out there on Barrow Street, leaning against the cold wall, was how long it would take Shorty to show and where he could get some more money, because he needed to get straight, his bones were just starting to ache, and if he didn't cop soon it wouldn't be long before he started to shiver. These were the most pressing issues of the moment, and Jackie McLean was pondering all of them when Miles Davis pulled up. As Miles got out of the car and saw Jackie waiting there, he motioned the other people with him into the club and walked over alone.

"Hey, Jackie, how you doin', you got yourself together? You told me you was gonna get yourself together."

Miles was togged out in a beautiful suit and a very expensive-looking cashmere overcoat. He was not only "cleaner than a broke dick dog" in the sartorial sense, he was also completely clean of heroin—and had been so for over a year now. He was back on top, bigger than ever, and there were projects that he was interested in talking to Jackie about, but Jackie also knew that Miles was concerned about his addiction.

"Yeah, yeah. I got myself together."

"Now, you're not usin' *nothing*?"

Miles was checking him out, studying him intently, looking for those telltale signs of an itchy nose or red, runny, heavy-lidded eyes.

"No, man. I'm not."

Miles nodded. "I'll see you later," he said, and went into the club.

Ten minutes later, Shorty still hadn't showed, and Miles popped his head out of the door. He looked at Jackie, still waiting, and walked slowly back over, glancing furtively around the street. "Hey, Jackie," he said in that lowered raspy voice, "you know where I can get somethin'?"

"What do you mean?"

"Man, you know, where I can get some *smack*."

It was the look on Miles's face that got to Jackie, that old conspiratorial look that he had known so well when they had been roommates
and had used together, when they would ride the subways together
high as hell, laughing at the clothes that all the straight people wore,
hanging around down on 42nd Street, going to the gym and watching
the boxers train. The feeling that Jackie got when he saw that look was
hard to explain. It had to do with how sometimes junkies can like the
idea of another person using again, especially an old buddy. It seems
perverse, but it had little to do with satisfaction. It would be far more
accurate to say that it made him feel a little less alone, a little better
about himself and his own inability to stop, and it would never have
occurred to Jackie that Miles was testing him, trying to see if Jackie was
being straight with him, maybe trying in his own gruff way to get him
to take a hard look at himself and make a stand—the same way that
Max Roach had once gotten Miles to take stock of himself by giving
him that money outside of Birdland.

"Yeah," Jackie told Miles, falling right into the trap. "I know where
you can get something."

Miles's eyes flashed with anger. "You *jive motherfucker*," he said before
turning away, leaving Jackie out there alone on the street.

In all the years of his addiction, Jackie McLean never felt more
alone than at that moment. But far worse than any shame he may have
felt was the fear of not scoring—and then he saw Shorty coming toward him out of the night, and everything went out of his mind, as it
always did.

24

Why Are All These Young Boys Being Hanged in Limestone Caves, Bill?

1.

Like Burroughs, Dr. Dent believed that drug addiction was a metabolic illness and that the control of addiction began with the cells. At his small clinic he used a morphine derivative called apomorphine, which was made by boiling morphine with hydrochloric acid, to regulate the addict's metabolism, treating only two patients at a time and monitoring them very closely.

The treatment was designed to last fourteen days. First, the patient was given two and a half grains of apomorphine, which produced vomiting in two minutes, then one-twentieth of a grain every two hours, day and night, for six days. During this time Burroughs was still getting morphine in decreasing amounts. By the sixth day, he was getting apomorphine shots every four hours and morphine every twelve hours. By the seventh day, Dr. Dent had taken him down from thirty grains of pure morphine a day to no morphine at all. The effect on the metabolism was the cellular equivalent of a deep-sea diver suffering from a bad case of the bends, with the apomorphine acting as a kind of decompression chamber as the doctor tried to stabilize his patient.

At first there was no sleep at all. Burroughs would walk for miles and come in "stumbling with fatigue," but still he couldn't sleep. There were no sleeping pills or sedatives administered during the cure. The thought of sex gave him the "horrors." During the worst of it, Dent would visit Burroughs at two in the morning and stay until five, fascinated by his insomnia-driven monologues about Mayan archaeology and yage and scores of other subjects that Burroughs would expound upon.

With the habit finally broken, Burroughs resolved that he could no longer take so much as "one shot or paregoric or codeine or demorol or junk in any form. Not now or never." Dr. Dent gave him three tubes of apomorphine in case he might ever have to take a narcotic for "intense pain" and sent him on his way. Burroughs was now more convinced than ever that addiction was a metabolic illness, an actual disease, and that the reason junkies relapsed was that they were not "metabolically cured."

Burroughs was soon on his way to Venice, feeling "sexy as an eighteen-year-old and healthy as a rat," formulating theories about schizophrenia in his letters to Ginsberg that it was a "drug psychosis" and a possible means of treating schizophrenics might involve getting them addicted to heroin so that they could then be taken off with apomorphine. The theory was an indication of the direction of his thinking. Burroughs would remain deeply immersed in the emerging medical literature of addiction and in the process become a highly knowledgeable addictionologist himself.

The Tangier that William Burroughs returned to in September of 1956 was about to become independent. He took a small whitewashed room with a view of the harbor and a private entrance opening to a walled garden at the Hotel Muniria at 1 Calle Magallanes. He was soon into a new health regimen, rowing on the bay every morning. Finally free from the straitjacket of junk, Burroughs entered "a period of change more drastic than adolescence or early childhood. I live in a constant state of routine. I'm getting so far out one day I won't come back at all."

Burroughs began to experience a rebirth, a creative surge. What he started writing was "a straight continuation of Interzone," but he was now increasingly viewing addiction as a general condition not limited to drugs. Politics, religion, the family, and love were all forms of addiction, Burroughs theorized. In the post-bomb society, when all the mainstays of the social order had lost their meaning, the bankrupt nation states were being run by "control addicts." These power addicts

entrenched themselves in self-perpetuating hierarchies using sophisticated control methods. Bureaucracy was their primary instrument,
as well as corruption. The theme of control in this general theory of
addiction formed the basis of the political landscape of the novel, with
its Liquefactionists, Divisionists, and Senders all attempting to control the world through parasitic possession, each party infiltrated by
agents of the other. The Factualists were the only party opposed to the
use of control techniques, and the only ones who opposed "atomic
war, the use of such knowledge to control, coerce, debase, exploit or
annihilate the individuality of another living creature." The theme
took on the form of routine itself and became the creative engine
which drove the work to life:

> Fuck your nabor. He may like it. And I want you fellows to control
> your basest instinct which is the yen to control, coerce, violate, in-
> vade, annihilate, by any means whatsoever, anybody else's physical
> or psychical person. . . . Anybody wants to climb into somebody else
> and take over is no better than a fuckin' control addict. He should
> kick his noisome habit instead of skulking around with his bare ass
> hanging out lousing up the universe. Be it known that such name-
> less assholes will suffer a painful doom. And remember, when the
> control yen rips through your bones like a great black wind, you
> have connected for Pure Evil.

That the world had already "connected for Pure Evil" was a fore-
gone conclusion to Burroughs, who also felt that one of the worst
forms of addiction was addiction to rightness, precisely because such
notions were always used to justify mankind's most heinous behavior.
The evidence of these addictions in recent history was monstrously obvious. The twentieth century had already witnessed mass slaughter fests
like the rape of Nanking and the dropping of the atomic bomb, and
had brought forth horrors like the torture chambers of the Gestapo
and the crematoria of Auschwitz, always in the name of social control
systems and a higher good. As Burroughs saw it, those who would be
shocked and repelled by the hanging scenes and the "sexual obscenity" in *Naked Lunch* after its publication in the United States had no
moral basis for judging him because they lived in a country where the

lynching of blacks had been commonplace for a century; moreover, it was a society that used hanging as a form of capital punishment. And did not the United States government support the greatest obscenity of all, a nuclear arsenal capable of reducing the entire world to an ash heap?

What Burroughs set himself to writing was a catalog of sexual fantasies and perversions that were meant to revolt as the planet drifted to what Burroughs called its "random insect doom." In this respect Burroughs came to view his work less as a form of satire and more as an accurate report of reality as he viewed it, but it was always the perception of this reality as deconstructed and filtered through the distorted universe of a kicking junkie in a jail cell that would create the uniquely surreal platform of *Naked Lunch*.

2.

Soon after returning to Tangier, Burroughs was working on the book every day, rowing in the morning and writing by noon in his white-washed room, with one wall covered with photos from his 1953 yage expedition, another filled with bullet holes from target practice, and his trusty orgone box in the corner. Junk may have formed the contextual underpinning of the book, permeating the consciousness of everything that began to emerge, but another substance now began to figure prominently in the arena of the writing itself.

Every other day, Burroughs took majoun, a local mixture of ground kief, honey, cinnamon, caraway seeds, and ground nutmeg—a sticky, gooey, powerfully psychoactive candy that Burroughs had learned how to make himself, described in *Naked Lunch* as having the taste of "gritty plum pudding." On the days when he didn't take majoun he smoked lots of kief, sometimes having several joints burning in different ashtrays at the same time, which unleashed his unconscious and gave free vent to the profusion of associations and images as he typed away. His room was soon covered with hundreds of yellow pages, many with his heel marks on them, covered with rat droppings and bits of cheese sandwiches.

Paul Bowles visited Burroughs and saw him write a page and just let it drop to the floor; sometimes the loose pages would be blown by the breezes out into the garden. Such were his working methods. He would sleep and begin jotting immediately upon waking, sometimes transcribing whole dreams for the book. As the ballast tanks of his psyche and subconscious mind were blown, images and characters began jumping right out of his head onto the pages. The sadistic Dr. Benway had been around since his Harvard days and had long been a staple in his repertoire of routines but now began evolving into a tour de force character.

Others personages began emerging as bit players making cameo appearances: A. J., the Gimp, the Vigilante, the Paregoric Kid, the Rube, Pantopon Rose, Clem Snide the Private Asshole, Clem and Jody. Burroughs jumped from place to place, the writing always taking the form of a routine, the only consistency being the point of view of Burroughs's antihero and alter ego and narrator, William Lee, as an addict, with junk a constant presence and metaphor for control, relief, pleasure, fear, magic, sociology, politics, self-loathing, imprisonment, self-release, life and death itself.

"I will send along about 100 pages of Interzone," Burroughs wrote Ginsberg on December 20, 1956. "It is coming so fast I can hardly get it down, and shakes me like a great black wind through the bones." The following month he told Allen he was "hitting the majoun pretty heavy of late. . . . All the etiology of my homosex and practically everything spill right out of me."

In February he described the creation of the book as "almost automatic writing. I often sit high on hash for as long as six hours typing at top speed." The manuscript "does not hold together as a novel for the simple reason that it is not a novel," Burroughs observed in September. "It is a number of connected—by theme—and separate short pieces. My feeling is that it will eventually grow into several novels all interlocking and taking place simultaneously in a majoun dream."

Kerouac arrived late that winter and found Burroughs so deeply involved in the work that he was speaking in routines like some mad George Sanders character. He began typing the many fragments into a manuscript, but the recurring images of talking assholes and spurting hard-ons as the hanged man's neck snapped, vast paranoiac theories of agents and psychic senders taking over the world in bureaucratic conspiracies, began to induce nightmares of "great long baloneys" flying out of his mouth. One day he looked up from the pages and asked, "Why are all these young boys being hanged in lime-stone caves, Bill?"

"Don't ask me," Burroughs told him. "I get these messages from other planets. I'm apparently some kind of agent from another planet but I haven't got my order clearly decoded yet. I'm shitting out my ed-ucated Midwest background once and for all. It's a matter of catharsis, where I say the most horrible things I can think of. Realize that—the most horrible slimy niggardliest posture possible."

The "catharsis" now included scenes like the infamous "Hassan's Rumpus Room," always presented as little self-contained movies within the novel. Burroughs always fades into these scenes cinemat-ically—"Gilt and red plush. Rococo bar backed by pink shell. The air is cloyed with sweet evil substance like decayed honey. Men and women in evening dress sip pousse-cafés through alabaster tubes. Near East Mugwump sits naked on a bar stool covered in pink silk. He licks honey from crystal goblet with a long black tongue" as the slender blond youth is pulled to a couch and "stripped expertly," with brutal acts of sodomy and hanging and ejaculation to follow; the scene ends with the dead boy impaled on the Mugwump's cock "like a speared fish" and the Mugwump falling to the floor "with a fluid, sated plop."

These passages are often as extravagantly comical as they are hor-rifying, of course, at times causing Burroughs to cackle aloud in his room as he smoked his kief and typed his scenes of naked Mugwumps twanging lutes as Greek boys fornicate doggy-style on the porticos of great golden temples. The world of Williams Burroughs was a place of purple-assed baboons being led around on a gold chains; of "anal tech-nicians" mixing bicarbonates of soda and pulling switches that reduce the earth to cosmic dust—

"Belch . . . They'll hear this fart on Jupiter."

Some who have analyzed the fiction of William Burroughs have traced the origins of his literary aesthetic all the way back to his very first morphine experience, and his description of it as "floating with-out outlines," and a series of pictures passing through his mind as if on a screen. Such scenes are always graphically depicted in "precise, clinically observed and unemotionally rendered details," as John Tytell notes in *Naked Angels,* his classic critical analysis of Beat literature, with all the speed of the motion picture lens, and all transitions, even the formalities of infinitives, prepositions and definite articles are omitted for the sake of increased tempo. . . . The rapidity of shifts of points of view and transformations of character creates an exceptional momentum that leaves the reader in the center of a maelstrom, caught in an exhilarating dance of desperation that invariably leads to death and obliteration—through the addict's needle, etc.

As Burroughs wrote about things that seemed like a sick dream at the time but became a literal account of what came to pass, the visionary component of his writing also has come to be strongly identified with a drug-induced sensibility. His hypothesis of an addicting venereal virus that originates in Africa and is passed from person to person in sexual contact turned out to be an uncanny prediction of the AIDS virus, of course, just as his ghostly image of a deserted city evokes the Cambodian capital of Phenom Penh after Pol Pot forced its inhabitants to relocate. The Swarm Bar, where "huntsmen strut about with imbecile narcissism in black leather jackets and studded belts, flexing their muscles for the fags to feel" presents a vision that came to pass in the gay leather bars of the 1970s. Burroughs's extraordinary foresight extends all the way to the present day with the "Jihad Jitters," his comical expression of paranoia about Islamic fanaticism. The Dream Police, brain rape, "addicts of drugs not yet synthesized"—all are presented as signals of apocalyptic disaster and warning, what John Tytell calls "a future possibility far more dismal and terrifying than Orwell's *1984* or Huxley's *Brave New World*, a dystopia where technology strangles all vestiges of freedom, a police state where the human attributes of love and community are stripped away and defiled." In Tytell's interpretation, with the passing of time Burroughs came to seem more and more like some receiver tuning his antennae psychically toward the "strange circuits revealing the future," speculating about things like the future of biocontrol, systems of bioelectric signals injected into the nervous system that would telepathically regulate physical movement, mental processes, emotional reactions, and sensory impressions. "According to the new physics that seems to have informed Burroughs's world, as well as the possibility of telepathy induced by the drug experience,

Burroughs may be introducing us to a futuristic vision of the cybernetic reality slowly replacing human perspectives in the West."

The process of editing the book was every bit as postmodern as the writing. "Me and Peter Orlovsky arrived not long after Kerouac departed—just as the work most needed editing," Ginsberg recalled. "We settled into a pretty steady schedule of typing and editing. For six hours a day we worked on the text. Of course some of it was completely disorganized. I had three years of his letters and they were a great source; sometimes we just took things right from his letters and flew them right into the text."

Poet Alan Ansen also became part of this collective effort, and after two months, they had organized the material into a two-hundred-page manuscript, but as Ginsberg remembered it, "that was when Burroughs began changing it around, constantly experimenting with the sequential order of the material and the effects of its reordering. That was a game-changer on top of all the other game-changers involved in the work."

In this manner, the influence of these drug experiences, which had already served to recontextualize and deconstruct Burroughs's perceptions of Tangier as Interzone and scores of other things he wrote about, now also became an important ingredient in the editorial process itself. Burroughs was "interested in a form that reproduced his experiences both of Tangier and his work's composition," Oliver Harris explains in his introduction to the volume of Burroughs's collected letters that he edited, noting how Burroughs's "drug-induced sensitivity to the place's strange collage of histories and cultures resulted in sudden, heightened intersections of dream and reality; and this corresponded to the fusions of reversals of past and future, fact and fantasy, that came from the transcribing, cutting, and selecting from a mass of fragmentary material drawn from his letters."

The juxtapositions of segments of material, and the synchronicity of the combinations themselves, now began to take on cryptic significance. It was an aspect of the creative process of the book that continued to the last days of its editing in Paris, as Burroughs and painter and performance artist Brion Gysin walked the finalized sections of the manuscript from the Beat Hotel at 9 rue Gît-le-Coeur to the offices of Maurice Girodias's Olympia Press in July of 1959, and thereafter into

Burroughs's experimental cut-ups of text and images with Gysin as a way of objectively reproducing the process of his own consciousness.

All of this makes *Naked Lunch* as unlike a conventional linear narrative as one of Dr. Benway's exchanges is unrecognizable from the typical palaver between doctor and nurse in the operating room of the average American hospital—

NURSE: Adrenalin, doctor?
DR. BENWAY: The night porter shot it all up for kicks.

25

The Empirical Soul of Jazz

1.

During the sound check, producer Robert Herridge received a note from the sponsor's representative making it very clear that they wanted Billie Holiday off the show: "We must not put into America's homes, especially on Sunday, someone who's been imprisoned for drug use."

Herridge didn't know what to do. It wasn't as if Lady and her story had never been on television. Four years earlier, in 1953, she had appeared on ABC's *The Comeback Story*. Hosted by Georgie Jessel, the series presented half-hour episodes about people triumphing over great obstacles, infirmities, and afflictions—in Lady's case, racism, poverty, and heroin addiction. It was a precursor of reality television that sometimes featured cheesy reenactments, but Lady's story had allowed ABC to deal with a subject matter that was generally forbidden on national television. John Hammond had declined to be on the show because he thought it was in bad taste, but Artie Shaw, Louis Armstrong, Count Basie, and others had participated. The show ended with her singing "God Bless the Child."

This show was a very different matter. For a special production of CBS's *The Seven Lively Arts* series called "The Sound of Jazz," Herridge had asked jazz critics Nat Hentoff and Whitney Balliett to put together a stellar cast of the greatest jazz musicians of the era to appear on a live show due for broadcast on December 8, 1957. The format and production of the show had been left completely up to Herridge and his associates and was designed to be as freewheeling and improvisational as jazz itself. As Lady was slated to be the swan song of the whole production, the sponsor's demand presented a serious dilemma for Herridge, Balliett, and Hentoff, who huddled together to discuss the matter.

Certainly, by the end of 1957, the American public was more steeped in the life, legend, and troubles of Billie Holiday than ever before. In February of 1956, as her autobiography was being edited and checked for libel, Lady and her second husband, Louis McKay, were arrested at the Radnor Hotel in Philadelphia, where she was appearing at the Showboat. Police claimed they found an ounce and a half of heroin and an unlicensed gun; Lady said there were no drugs and McKay claimed that the police had tried to plant the evidence. The judge mandated that Lady be sent to a sanitarium for a cure after finishing her engagement and the case was later dropped, but not before a lot of publicity.

Then, in July of 1956, Doubleday released *Lady Sings the Blues*.

That Lady had needed money was obvious to all around her. She still did not have her cabaret card back, she owed money to the record company, the IRS was after her, and Louis McKay was copping large amounts of heroin for her, not to mention fleecing her blind. But there were motivations other than financial for doing the book. People had approached Lady to do a book before, and she was interested in telling her side of things, in a book as well as a movie. Any portrayal of narcotics had been banned by the Motion Picture Production Code of 1930 and no major studio would go near the subject. In 1948, restrictions were relaxed for Columbia to produce *To the Ends of the Earth*, a dramatization of the FBN's worldwide efforts to combat the smuggling of narcotics—in which Harry Anslinger, never one to miss an opportunity for publicity and self-promotion, makes a cameo appearance as himself. But after Frank Sinatra broke through the code with his portrayal of the heroin-addicted jazz drummer Frankie Machine in Otto Preminger's 1956 film of *The Man with the Golden Arm*, Lady felt that perhaps the time had arrived for her to tell her story. She liked the idea of Dorothy Dandridge playing her in a movie after they sold her book to Hollywood.

The man whom Lady had chosen as her collaborator on the book—William Dufty, the husband of her friend Maely Dufty—had the credentials for such a venture. As a columnist for the *New York Post,* he did a series on heroin addiction called "Drugs USA" and had once taken on no less a figure than J. Edgar Hoover in a column. Lee Barker of Doubleday thought that Dufty captured Lady's voice so authentically that he'd bought the book on the basis of a single chapter, which began with the famous opening lines—"Mom and Pop were just a couple of kids when they got married. He was eighteen, she was sixteen, and I was three"—and stated that Lady had been born in Baltimore on Wednesday, April 7, 1915. Of course, Clarence and Sadie were never married at all, and Lady had really been born in Philadelphia. But while such errors would later cast doubts on the entire enterprise in the eyes of critics and biographers, it was certainly a provocative opening that grabbed the reader right by the lapels. Dufty worked mostly off of old articles that were already full of dramatic self-embroidery and took selective liberties with the details and dates of her life, but in other respects the book is remarkably frank about her early years in Baltimore and her time as a prostitute. It is also replete with information about her life with drugs and history of addiction. "I've had my troubles with the habit for fifteen years on and off. I've been on and I've been off. As I said before, when I was really on, nobody bothered me. I got in trouble both times I tried to get off. I've spent a small fortune on stuff. I've kicked and stayed clean; and I've had my setbacks and had to fight all over again to get straight."

Some of the statements about drugs in the book were candid and true and others were no doubt disingenuous, which is hardly surprising considering that Billie Holiday was in the unusual position of being a felon publishing a book about a subject for which she had been convicted and served time and that she had just recently been arrested for drug use once again—and of course, she was still using drugs. The book concludes with a chapter entirely about narcotics, added by Dufty when Doubleday asked him to update the book with a final chapter on Lady's most recent troubles with the law. It ends with a passage as memorable as the opening lines of the book, with a final sentence that would turn out to be eerily prescient: "I knew when I started to work on this book that I couldn't expect to tell the truth in it unless I was straight when it came out. I didn't try and hide anything. Doubleday carried an item in their winter catalogue that I was writing about my fight with dope and that I knew it wasn't over yet. There isn't a soul on this earth who can say that their fight with dope is over until they're dead."

Future biographers and critics would argue interminably about *Lady Sings the Blues*. Julia Blackburn, for example, insists that Dufty had "a lot to answer for. When he was drawing up his contract for the book he agreed with the publishers that narcotics would be what they called 'the gimmick' that would sell it. And he did everything he could to give prominence to Billie's drug addiction."

Depending on one's point of view, Dufty was either a crass opportunist doing everything possible to capitalize on the most salacious aspects of Billie Holiday's life, or a skilled journalist weaving a very compelling story out of whatever materials he had to work with. Of course the truth probably lies somewhere in the middle. There can be no doubt that Dufty always had genuine respect and admiration for his subject (they became close friends for the rest of her life) but whatever the motivations for doing the book and however accurate it may be, *Lady Sings the Blues* was really the first significant celebrity dope confessional of the modern age. And it is not the story of a victim. Nowhere does the book blame anyone other than Lady for her own weaknesses and the bad choices that led to her addiction. What also makes the book noteworthy are its outspoken views about how addiction should be treated as a purely medical problem as in Britain, rather than a criminal one, as in the United States. "Well, let me tell you, in America if they haven't got government interference in medicine I don't know what it is. If you're on and you get a doctor to help, he can't because the government has passed regulations saying, in effect, that if he does he will go to jail along with you. If you go to the doctor, he's liable to slam the door in your face and call the cops."

Not only did the book criticize the entire punitive and absolutist approach to the treatment of drug addiction as formulated by Harry Anslinger and the Federal Bureau of Narcotics, it also bluntly pointed out its racial ramifications. "On a recent Sunday, Judge Jonah Goldstein talked about the narcotics problem in New York. He told the people the same thing I've been trying to tell them; that narcotics has to be taken out of the hands of the police and turned over to the doctors.

He said that in all his years on the bench he'd never seen anybody but poor people brought before him for violations of the dope laws."

While reviews were mixed, most of the mainstream press lauded the book's "authenticity." *The New York Herald Tribune* called it "a hard, bitter and unsentimental book, written with brutal honesty and having much to say not only about Billie Holiday, the person, but what it means to be poor and black in America." *Time* declared that the book "has the tone of truth. . . . The book's deadpan manner is a little chilling. No matter how it is told, hers is a chilling story. Billie sings a sad, sad song."

Lady's feelings about the book were as mixed as the reviews—at first she denied even reading it. "I can't help it," she later commented. "I just told what happened to me. A lot of my life has been bitter. You ought to read what they left out of the book."

Lady Sings the Blues sold twelve thousand copies in its first year and has never gone out of print. While it can never be viewed as the truth of Billie Holiday's life, it has other undeniable value. As Farah Jasmine Griffin observes, the book is not so much an autobiography as the story of her stage persona: "Readers who had seen Lady in concert received a prose version of those live, dramatic performances. In many ways, this is not the life story of Eleanora Fagan, or maybe not even the story of Billie Holiday, but it is the story of Lady Day. And that story is filled with subtle allusions to the life stories of the other two."

The publicity around the book focused on exactly this aspect, further burnishing the legend of Billie Holiday as the great American junkie/jazz songstress of sorrow, and more than ever turning it into her brand. When *Ebony* excerpted the book, it appeared with a staged photo essay that actually featured a reenactment of her arrest with McKay in their Philadelphia hotel room. Then, in November of 1956, Lady did a special concert at Carnegie Hall that included readings of passages from the book by Gilbert Millstein of the *New York Times*. That same month she sat down with Mike Wallace for a radio interview. Art Tatum had just died, and Wallace asked her for her thoughts about "why so many jazz greats seemed to die early—Bix Beiderbecke, Fats Waller, Charlie Christian, Charlie Parker?"

"The only way I can answer that question, Mike, is that we try to live a hundred days in one day," Lady responded, "and that we try to please so many people. Like myself, I want to bend this note, bend that note, sing this way, sing that way, and get all the feeling, eat all the good foods, and travel all over in one day, and you can't do it."

Perhaps nobody had ever described the fundamental spirit and sensibility of the jazz life of the time better or more honestly: "to live a hundred days in one day." Lady had put her finger on the very romantic but enigmatic life force that drove jazz and produced some of its greatest artistic breakthroughs and triumphs at the same time that it seemed to engender the kind of addiction and alcoholism that would consume some of its greatest artists. And nobody personified that spirit and sensibility more than Billie Holiday.

When Herridge, Balliett, and Hentoff contemplated doing a show without her, they simply could not abide the prospect. Herridge delivered the message that if Billie Holiday was not allowed to appear, they would all walk off the show. The gambit worked, and on December 8, 1957, the segment was introduced by host John Crosby: "Billie Holiday is one of a handful of really great jazz singers. Her blues are poetic, highly intense. . . . Playing with her here today are some of the musicians who accompanied her back in the thirties on some of the greatest jazz records ever made."

And there they were, all arranged in a semicircle around a stool in the center of Studio 58: Roy Eldridge and Doc Cheatham on trumpets; Lester Young, Ben Webster, and Coleman Hawkins—three of the greatest tenor sax players in the history of jazz; Gerry Mulligan, the youngster of the group, on baritone saxophone; Mal Waldron on piano; Milt Hinton on bass; Vic Dickenson on trombone; and Ossie Johnson on drums.

"There's two kinds of blues—there's happy blues and sad blues," Lady remarked in a voice-over that was heard as she walked to her stool and settled down in front of the mike. "I don't know, the blues is a sort of mixed-up thing, you just have to feel it. Anything . . . I *do* sing, it's a part of my life."

Although she was often referred to as a blues singer, Lady had in fact only recorded three songs in the traditional twelve-bar blues format, and the band now broke into one of them, "Fine and Mellow," the B-side of the 1939 release of "Strange Fruit." Like the others, it was a blues that she had penned herself, and no sooner did she open her mouth than the studio was suffused with magic.

> *My man don't love me*
> *Treats me oh so mean*

Lady was dressed simply in a pale woolen dress that just covered her knees, her hair pulled tightly back into a ponytail that revealed a pair of earrings, which glimmered in the studio lights. She looked quite thin compared to the once ample figure of her youth—"She was just a little bitty woman," as Roy Eldridge remarked, shocked by how much she'd changed—and yet, despite everything she'd been through, it was uncanny how she appeared more luminous, more beautiful with each passing moment.

Ben Webster took the first solo. Like others in the room, he had his own special connection to Lady—"a little light housekeeping," as Roy Eldridge put it. In Webster's case it was a dalliance back in the thirties that had ended when he gave Lady a black eye. Billie's mother, Sadie, had gotten so angry when she saw her daughter's black eye that she had chased Webster all the way down from their apartment to a cab on the street, drubbing him with an umbrella.

Lester Young was the next to blow—the man who had been her dearest friend. From the moment Prez had arrived for rehearsal two days earlier, it was sadly obvious to all that he was deteriorating. He'd kept quietly to himself the whole time, wearing carpet slippers because his feet hurt so much, and when Lady had invited all the musicians back to her apartment for ribs and greens, Prez hadn't even come. Twenty years had passed since they had shared their first joint together, when he played so brilliantly behind her on "I Must Have That Man," the song that began their musical romance. Their relationship had had its ups and downs over the years, leading to a lingering estrangement that saddened both of them. At the age of forty-eight Prez looked haggard, his deep-set green eyes laden with melancholy, but as he raised the horn to his lips and played with everything he had left, you could once again hear the love he had for her. As Nat Hentoff describes it, "He blew the sparest, purest blues chorus I had ever heard. Billie, smiling, nodding to the beat, looked into Prez's eyes and he into hers. She was looking back, with the gentlest of regrets for their past. Prez was remembering too. Whatever had blighted their relationship was forgotten in the communion of the music. Sitting in the control room I felt tears, and saw tears on the faces of most of the others there." Watching and listening, Hentoff was stunned. Instead of the "cracked husk of what she had been before," Lady was "in full control of the tart, penetrating, sinuously swinging instrument which was her voice."

Then Lady traded lines with gorgeous solos by Mulligan, Hawk, Dickenson, and Eldridge. "Love is just like a faucet, it turns off and on," she sang with a wistful smile, bringing the song home, leaving no doubt that she was telling the story of her life—as she always did. "Sometimes when you think it's on, baby, it has turned off and gone."

And with that, the Lady who wanted to live a hundred days in one day was gone herself.

"The rest of the program was all right," recalled Hentoff, "but this had been its climax—the empirical soul of jazz."

It is a performance that stands as perhaps the greatest moment of jazz ever captured on film. Everything about it is redolent of their love for the music and each other and the great musical legacy they had all shared during an era that was fading away, along with their lives.

2.

As soon as Ruby Rosano heard that Billie Holiday had published her autobiography she couldn't wait to read it. It was the summer of 1956. Even in her worst days as a heroin-addicted prostitute, Ruby always tried to keep up with anything that Lady ever did. She felt bonded to Lady from their days in the little subbasement on West 116th Street where they used heroin. But her reading of the book would have to wait. By that time, the mob had a contract out on her and she was running for her life. It was not exactly a situation conducive to any casual pleasure reading.

"They held this private party at Grenado's Restaurant," Ruby related, "and the place was closed down for about thirty people, including me and couple of other women of ill repute. Later, we were taken to this fabulous penthouse on Sheridan Square and told that we were to make the men happy and do whatever they wished. We were each given two hundred dollars and told that we could accept tips and not to aggravate them—or we would be sorry. Everything went fine until I went into one of the bedrooms with a guy who was drunk, and as soon as he got into bed he passed out. I started to leave the room and then spotted his wallet on the floor. It was just bulging with money, so of course I couldn't resist picking it up and looking inside. . . . I almost choked, there was about ten thousand dollars in it! I had never seen that much money in my life! My heart was pounding. I hesitated for about a second, and then took some of of it . . . Well, okay, *most* of it. I put the wallet back in his pants and crept out, and everyone had gone to other rooms, and I grabbed my clothes and went down the stairs dressing as fast as I could, and there I was out on the street, running my ass off."

The next day, Ruby was informed by one of the neighborhood cops that the "family" had learned that she was Italian and was especially enraged by the fact that one of their own had done such a thing, and was determined to make an example of her. Ruby was now terrified that not only was she going to die, she was going to die a slow, agonizing death.

"I blew the money really fast, and for the next nine months, I lived in the Times Square area, hiding, hustling as best as I could. Hustling was radically different there. No subtleties or niceties. You strolled the street and risked your life daily. I was like a fish out of water up there, and I lived in fear that I would be found and killed. Every smiling stranger that passed me could have turned out to be the man that was going to kill me, and I could only make this possibility more tolerable by increasing my drug intake. Finally, word got to me that the neighborhood cop had interceded for me, this cop who was a really good guy and always looked out for me on 3rd Street."

What had happened was that the family had done some research on her and had heard all the stories in the neighborhood about Ruby the Crazy Italian. They heard about how she would wear these black patches over an eye that had been blackened badly after a fight and would paint gold glitter in the shape of an eye on the patch like it was some kind of a fashion statement, or wear her hair down over her black eyes like a battered Veronica Lake. They learned that the guy she had been living with—a dangerous, violent man named David—was a drug dealer, drunk, pill-head, and would-be pimp who was also known for being a necrophiliac. David liked to get his women stoned and then have sex with them when they were unconscious, and he had a particular fascination for Ruby, who spent much more time unconscious than the average person. And, Ruby being Ruby, she stole from this guy all the time. She would do things like take all his money except for a dollar, or take all his clothes and sell them, or clean out all the food from his refrigerator and leave. Then, like a good masochist, she would come back and this guy David would beat her from one end of the apartment to the other. Then she would be too messed up to leave, and he would keep her there until she healed, all the while giving her pills until she passed out cold and then having sex with her. She would get better, then just steal from him again and run away—and then when she came back the whole cycle would start all over again.

By now Ruby was a legend at the emergency room of St. Vincent's Hospital. She was always in a cast for one thing or another or going around with a broken nose. The word was that she overdosed a lot, too. She was always coming out of an overdose to find herself stuffed in the hallway closet or naked on a roof after being stripped clean. She would come to and find herself being walked around and around after someone had shot her full of salt, or being held under an ice-cold shower to keep her from dying, or having fallen asleep with a cigarette and started a fire. One time the fire department had to be called to her apartment in the Village and arrived to find her lying on the mattress with her hair just beginning to crackle with flames. Ruby was so out of it that they couldn't even get her to stand up out of the bed, so they just hosed her down along with the mattress and then rolled her singed carcass right onto the floor, and she went on nodding as if nothing had happened.

When the family heard all these stories about Ruby the Crazy Italian, somebody evidently decided that she was such a poor, pitiful broken-down junkie whore that she wasn't even worth the effort of killing. Whacking somebody like that might actually make them look bad. They figured she would probably be dead in a few months anyway, so why the hell bother?

It was November when Ruby heard that Lady was going to do a staged musical presentation of *Lady Sings the Blues* at Carnegie Hall. It was a good thing that the heat from the mob was off her and she could appear in public again. Ruby Rosano was an unholy mess, but she was not about to miss it, especially after seeing Lady on the cover of *Ebony* at a newsstand. When she picked up the magazine and hurriedly thumbed through it, she was amazed to see a photo of Lady's latest bust in Philadelphia. Was it real? No, it couldn't be. In the photo, Lady and her husband, Louis McKay, were in a bed in a hotel room, feigning shock as the police were bursting in on them. Ruby laughed and wondered if Lady's show was going to be like this.

"I pulled myself together as best as I could and put on my best dress. What I remember most about walking into Carnegie Hall with all of those people for the midnight show was how god-awful I felt, but then when I saw Lady up on the stage with the musicians, somehow that didn't matter anymore. Just to be in that room with her was everything."

Lady was backed by Carl Drinkard, Roy Eldridge, and Coleman Hawkins, among others. The music of the evening was fittingly magnificent, but it was the four long passages from the autobiography read by Gilbert Millstein interspersed with the songs that Ruby would always remember. There were those in the audience who found the readings dull and Millstein's rendering of them flat and tolerated them as a means to the music, but not Ruby. From the moment Millstein said the words, "This is Billie Holiday's story," she was swept into it, hanging on every word. There was so much in the readings that moved her, but it was the last lines of the final reading that got to her the most: "Who can tell what detours are ahead? Another trial? Sure. Another jail? Maybe. But if you beat the habit again and kicked TV, no jail on earth can worry you too much. Tired? You bet. But all that I'll soon forget with my man."

And then Lady sang "My Man" and brought down the house. There would be bottoms in the two years ahead for Ruby Rosano, and bottoms to those bottoms, and trap doors to those bottoms that she would fall through to even lower depths, but she would never forget this night at Carnegie Hall.

"I don't know what anyone else was seeing there that night, what anyone else might have thought about her or her book. I assumed it was all true but it wouldn't have mattered to me if it wasn't. Who the fuck cared? All I could see up there was someone like me—a drug addict and an alcoholic—who was actually *owning* their own story. *That* was what was so powerful. It wasn't the cops, it wasn't the press—it was *her*, and it just blew me away. I'd never known any addict who had ever done that before, and for her to be the one to do it . . . That to me was an unbelievable triumph, and as low as I'd gone, it made me feel some kind of hope."

26

Peyote Solidities of Halls

1.

For Peter Berg, it all began at the little bar called the Gatorland at the University of Florida, where students drank pitchers of beer. Someone had gotten a copy of *Howl* and jumped up on a chair and started declaiming it loudly and very theatrically. The reading of the poem at a place like this was unusual enough—it could actually lead to fistfights—but when the guy reading got to the part about "peyote solidities of halls," someone else said, "Hey, I know what peyote is, it's a *cactus*, I bet I could find out where you could actually *get* peyote!"

"This fellow was vaguely related to somebody from Texas, and that was how we found out about the cactus ranch that sold fifty peyote buttons for five dollars through the mail," Berg recalled upstairs above the office of the Planet Drum Foundation in San Francisco, remembering the first time he took peyote. "The next question was, who was going to be fool enough to go pick it up at the post office when it arrived, and that was when I volunteered."

That Berg had volunteered for this bold and risky undertaking speaks volumes about him. He was the son of an alcoholic, but the sort of an alcoholic who would go into a bar with a copy of Spengler's *Decline of the West* and lecture the people about it. Originally from New York, he was sent to Florida after his parents divorced, and he grew up alienated on the outskirts of Miami in a strange world of Cuban émigrés and redneck kids who looked like the young Montgomery Clift drag racing in pale green Chevrolet sedans with Thunderbird belts and wolf's-head rings that would leave deep indentations if you were punched in the face by them, as Berg had been. When he later became one of the central figures in the Diggers during the 1960s, he described his youth to Leonard Wolfe as something that seemed right out of Nathanael West, but with his 160 IQ he was given a working scholarship to the University of Florida at the age of sixteen, and he was sweeping floors in the union to make ends meet when he fell in with a tiny enclave of subterraneans.

"This was a segregated college, and these were the people that would have belonged to, you know, the French film club. There were some Korean vets in the group and some pretty wild women—pre-feminist liberated types who wore black berets and smoked with cigarette holders—you know, that kind of damsel."

Berg paused, then digressed.

"To really set the scene here, I should talk a little about the times . . . Oh, the fifties were very impressive, let me tell you. Very impressive, indeed! Anybody ever tells you they were like *Ozzie and Harriet* or *Father Knows Best,* they're automatically full of shit. The editor of the college newspaper at Gainesville had secretly interviewed something like two hundred and fifty college professors just so he could find out which ones would invite him to their homes and put their hands on his leg, just so he could expose them and get those 'faggots' out of the University of Florida—and it was all done as a community service, of course. I was constantly called a 'Yankee nigger-lovin' Jew motherfucker,' all in one phrase—always an odd experience for me, I should add, because I'm from a German Protestant background."

And sex?

"It was the most furtive thing in the world, practically unknown. It was like climbing Mount Everest to get laid in the fifties. That's why it was so shocking when all of these girls started taking off their bras and panties at Elvis Presley concerts and peeing in their pants. . . . The landlord of this shed I lived in when I had a girl in there one night came and pounded on the door and stood five feet back, and was shouting, 'I know you're fuckin' in there, Berg! Come on out, I know you're fuckin' in there!' Can you *imagine* it? People who look back and long nostalgically for that time as some halcyon era of wonderful family values before everything went haywire in America are yearning for a myth, something that never really existed in the first place. The fifties were terrible. Gary Snyder, in one of his essays, writes, 'In the 1950s, you would drive a thousand miles just to have a conversation with a friend.' That really sums it up. . . . When I read *Howl* I knew I didn't have anything to lose. That's what did it. That's what sent people out in search of experience."

On the day Berg picked up the package with the peyote at the post office, everybody in the tiny underground at the university assembled in his little cabin for the big event.

"We knew so little about it. This one person said, 'I know you're supposed to pull the cotton off the top and use the buttons,' so we cut it up and that's what we were going to do, just eat them, until somebody tasted it. My God, have you ever *tasted* it? I mean, it set the standard for incredibly disgusting. You could compare things like brake fluid to peyote, and you still wouldn't get close. Of course, not knowing what to do, and being college kids in the fifties, we knew we had to devise a method for downing the stuff, and what we decided to do was to cut it into sections and put it into a meat grinder, then squeeze it through cheesecloth into shot glasses, and just drink these shots and chase it with Coke, just like it was alcohol."

Berg would remember the vomiting that followed for the rest of his days.

"It came out in a straight line, right through the air. Today they would call this projectile vomiting. Back then there was no name for it except vomit without precedent. *WHAM!*—it came right out of the stomach in one big cataclysmic wave and went whapping against the wall—*RING-POW!*—and I thought, *Oh, God, I'm gonna* die."

Apparently everyone else did too. People were lying about on the floor, moaning. They had put some jazz records on, but everyone started to disperse one by one. Berg spent the next two days alone, just wandering around, completely out of his head.

"I heard and saw unbelievable things. I heard crickets screaming in my ears so loud it sounded like the ocean pounding and locomotives roaring . . . I saw microscopic red bugs on Spanish moss, these practically invisible red bugs, but I saw them by the millions in the moonlight of the humid Florida night. My senses peeled completely away. . . . Good Lord, it was a deep, true virgin psychedelic experience—the benchmark that I would measure everything else against."

Sometime at the end of the two days Peter found himself at the Sunoco station in the middle of the town. At the time Sunoco still had these industrial pumps from the 1930s, yellow pumps for regular and purple for ethyl, and as he stood there this purple pump would go shooting way up into the sky and become a hoop way off on the horizon, and then come flying all the way back down to the ground and land like a flying saucer, and that was when Peter found himself being interrupted by the gasoline attendant as he had his arms around the base of that purple pump saying, "Poor pump, *poor little pump*," because this pump was obviously completely out of control shooting off into the sky and becoming a purple hoop like that, so Peter had decided to comfort it, of course, *poor little pump,* and that was where he was when the police arrived and picked him up.

"The policeman said, 'Boy, what in the world you been *drinkin*? You ain't actin' *regluh*. We better git you home,' and they actually dropped me home. . . . They didn't know what drugs were. Oh, they might have heard about them, but they had about as much familiarity with any mind-altering substances other than alcohol as they had with Russian spies, which they might have also heard about."

Peter Berg knew that he had crossed some kind of a threshold, though he did not as yet fully understand its implications.

"How did it change me? Initially, I suppose the impact had something to do with the fact that I didn't finish college. I wanted to spend all my time reading novels. Didn't care about getting a degree anymore. Wanted to come to San Francisco. Wanted to come and meet Allen Ginsberg and these wondrous old men like Henry Miller and Kenneth Rexroth. . . . So I came out here, and when you got to North Beach you saw that it was a liberated territory. The police were very upset about it. There were squad cars everywhere to pick up these young people sitting around on street corners playing bongo drums, but it was very innocent compared to what happened later in the sixties. . . . The thing the Beats were establishing was the reality of small groups of kindred turned-on people. The fifties were cabalistic times and they were celebrating their cabal. Theirs was a small cabal, but it was the only life-affirming cabal that seemed available at the time."

2.

"We were not taking peyote to get high, we were taking it for personal and alchemical reasons," Michael McClure emphasized, looking back on the period from his East Bay living room. "We were damned serious. Remember, it was a different time, a quite desperate time. You knew you were an outlaw and you saw people dying of pain. I'm talking about just plain, decent, slightly more liberal people—just dying of pain. Thorazine eased so much pain at the time. In the late fifties all these classes of drugs were being discovered and brought out, like Miltown and Thorazine, and these twisted grieved spirits walking around in intense psychic pain were given merciful solace by this first generation of antidepressants. My image of the fifties was always of a dark street, not a lot of traffic on it, with a few lone street lamps and some people sitting on the curb with their heads in their hands because they were in such psychic pain."

Two years had passed since the reading at the Six Gallery when the artist Wallace Berman gave McClure his first peyote. "They were five beautiful buds. Wallace's idea was that you didn't drink or eat meat the day before or while you were taking it, and then when the high was over you'd have a feast. I did all that was supposed to be done, burrowed out the middle and all the little seeds and brought it over that morning. . . . I had an even more profound experience than I would have imagined; more open, clear, more in touch with the substance of reality as I came to believe it must truly be, but not filtered through the practicality of my nervous system. I sat listening to Segovia play the guitar and took notes on the experience, and I saw the army of the world go by, walk across my lap singing siren songs, saw the history of the universe move over my body, and saw the luminosity of the real non-universe shining."

McClure took pen in hand and wrote his "Peyote Poem"—Allen Ginsberg later called it the first psychedelic poem in America. It was only the beginning of his interest in the substance. "It was a profound and moving experience. It was like there was a fence between you and another reality and every once in a while there was a board missing in the fence. Mescaline was one board, peyote was another, psilocybin another . . . Very different experiences, and we became very interested in analyzing them. We believed it would bring us in touch with our own hero-hood, our own divinity and physical immortality and liberation. Oh, we were fascinated!"

As McClure saw it, to experience and write about these substances was truly a new frontier—"It seemed greater than exploring Siberia might have been to Kropotkin. I mean the bounds of the mind seemed so small, and then you'd take peyote and all of this illumination would take place about things I had not been aware of, and it just seemed so wonderful. I wanted to tell people what it was really like, and I felt challenged to describe a peyote experience accurately."

McClure would write about all of the substances with tremendous clarity and insight in his book *Meat Science Essays,* but the level of his prose reached its zenith in his essay about peyote:

> All things beam inner light and color like a pear or shell. All men are strange beast-animals with their mysterious histories upon their faces as they stare outward from the wall of their skin—their hair is fur—secretly far beneath they are animals and they know it. Far far underneath the actions they make, their animal actions are being performed as they walk and smile—and each one so different! There are wolf men and young fox kings and otter women. They have totems that they do not know. Buildings lean and shake and tremble and the movement of a cloud before the sun changes the colors of air. Dark spaces are secrets. Light is eternity. Breathing is music made in space and it looms like a physical object. Creakings and rustlings are Noh plays. Walls are partitions of space in vast eternity. The crisp edge and light on all things is vast and true. Colors are all bright and are new in Timelessness.

Along with the insights, however, McClure advised extreme caution. There could be "extreme fright and demon-seeing," and everyone should be very careful about "repeated and extensive use"— "it can cause, depending on flesh and temperament, an almost unending estrangement and alienation and ceaseless visions of nearly unendurable nature. You can spend days or months afterwards walking numbly through life and sitting in a room watching the play of lights on woodwork."

The warnings were well-founded. As McClure took more peyote he began suffering from not being able to return to a normal state of consciousness. "It backfired on me. Time ceased to exist to the point where it was frightening. I would have visions when I wasn't on peyote. These things would be flying through my head. Eagles and wolves riding eagles and flocks of wolves riding eagles would go through my head and disappear in the windows of cathedrals. I felt as if my eyes were spreading and dissolving into space . . . I was in serious grief, probably institutional. Joanna, my wife, and Janie, my daughter, somehow managed to hold me together."

McClure refers to the period from 1957 to the autumn of 1963 as the "dark night of my soul"—a foreshadowing of the acid bummers and psychedelic dislocations of the sixties. Finding it difficult to sleep, he began writing constantly in "an intensively turned on, visionary state." His work during this period—*The New Book/A Book of Torture, The Book of Poetry, Hymns to St. Geryon,* his early plays, *Meat Science Essays,* the spontaneous beast-sound poems called *Ghost Tantras,* which he would destroy and then later act out onstage naked but for a lion's head (GOOOOOOOOOR! *GOOOOOOOOOOOOO!*)—were all written during the time of his journey through peyote and made his reputation. It was the period in his life when McClure walked around with an American kestrel perched on his shoulder, when Henry Miller met him and called him an "arrogant and supercilious young man" ("And I probably was"), and Jack Kerouac portrayed him as Pat McClear in *Big Sur*—"one of THE most handsome men I've ever seen."

All the while McClure felt like he was losing his mind. It wasn't until he was flying to a poetry festival in Vancouver five years after first taking peyote that he looked out of the window and realized the symptoms had passed. "I didn't feel like I was floating in timelessness and nothing glowed, and I wasn't having visions, and I said, 'I'm gonna be okay. I'm gonna make it.'"

But even if the "fear, horror and self-blockading" had continued, it was a price McClure had been more than willing to pay, as he made quite clear in his essay.

"To walk a hundred yards in freedom is to live forever in eternity—freedom for an instant is beyond measure and is immortality. Huge and free."

27

A Readily Recognizable Stigmata

1.

On July 16, 1957, Major John Glenn Jr. established a transcontinental speed record when he piloted a jet from California to New York in 3 hours, 23 minutes, and 8.4 seconds. As the nation placed the highest value on its accomplishments in science and technology during the fifties, the feat assured Glenn's notoriety as an American hero and his future as an astronaut.

On September 5, 1957, a review appeared in the *New York Times* of a novel called *On the Road* by an author named Jack Kerouac, which featured a character named Dean Moriarty who appeared to set transcontinental speed records of a very different nature, also guaranteeing the character's notoriety as a very different kind of hero, one might say, as well as his future as quite another type of astronaut.

On the Road was "an authentic work of art," Gilbert Millstein pronounced in his *New York Times* review, "a major novel," and he compared the quality of the writing to Thomas Wolfe's. Millstein declared that, as Hemingway's *The Sun Also Rises* came to be "regarded as the testament of the 'Lost Generation,' so it seem[ed] certain that *On the Road* [would] come to be known as the 'Beat Generation.'" The Beat Generation "was born disillusioned," Millstein concluded; "it takes for granted the imminence of war, the barrenness of politics and the hostility of the rest of society. . . . It does not know what refuge it is seeking, but it is seeking."

With regard to the element of drug-taking and "kicks" in the novel, Millstein also noted, significantly, that they were both a "readily recognizable stigmata" within the phenomenon that Kerouac had written about, describing it as "the frenzied pursuit of every possible sensory impression, an extreme exacerbation of the nerves, a constant outraging of the body. (One gets 'kicks'; one 'digs' everything, whether it be drink, drugs, sexual promiscuity, driving at high speeds or absorbing Zen Buddhism.) Inwardly, these excesses are made to serve a spiritual purpose, the purpose of an affirmation still unfocused, still to be defined, unsystematic."

That Millstein even came to write this critical review in the first place was a fluke in itself. Orville Prescott, the paper's daily book reviewer, a conservative, establishment-oriented literary critic, was on vacation; Millstein was the one who had originally suggested that John Clellon Holmes write an essay about the Beat Generation for the paper's Sunday magazine five years earlier, after the publication of Holmes's novel *Go*. In fact, when Prescott returned and read Millstein's review of the book, "he was enraged," Millstein recalled. "He hated the book. He hated to even *look* at it. That was the end of me in daily book reviewing for the *Times*."

On the Sunday after Millstein's review appeared, in an article called "In Pursuit of Kicks" that would set the tone for the rest of the press's response to the book, David Dempsey went much farther than to call the element of drug-taking in the book "a readily recognizable stigmata." Outraged by the criminality and dope-taking because it was rendered from a "morally neutral" point of view, Dempsey panned the book in the *New York Times Sunday Book Review*. But it was too late; the proverbial cat was out of the bag, and word about the almost completely unknown author and his book about a new generation of rootless young people driving to the coast and looking for kicks was already spreading like wildfire. Kerouac was soon appearing on John Wingate's *Nightbeat*, where forty million viewers heard Wingate ask him, "Do you smoke dope?" and listened as Kerouac explained that what he was really doing was "waiting for God to show his face."

The attacks began to intensify. Herbert Gold called the book nothing but a bunch of "hooey" in *The Nation*, "proof of illness rather than a creation of art," but nothing could stop the book from taking off. Few novels in the history of American culture have seemed more pertinent at the moment of publication than *On the Road*. It was a book that the age seemed to demand, with a ready-made audience of high school and college students who seemed to know exactly what it was about before even opening its cover.

If the death of Senator Joe McCarthy and the persisting phenomenon of rock and roll seemed to signal the beginning of a cultural thaw, the opposite was also true. America was still an overwhelmingly conservative place in 1957. Songs like "Jailhouse Rock" were counterbalanced on the charts by immensely popular hits like "Love Letters in the Sand" and "April Love" by the squeaky-clean and lily-white Pat Boone, a straight-A student and paragon of family values who was happily married with two children and attended church regularly. Billy Graham, appearing on television for the first time, drew record crowds to Yankee Stadium; Art Linkletter topped the nonfiction best-seller list with *Kids Say the Darndest Things!* The three top box office stars in the country were, in descending order, Rock Hudson, John Wayne, and Pat Boone. Social critics and pundits thundered that juvenile delinquency was reaching "epidemic proportions" as studies were released showing that 50 percent of those arrested for robbery and 60 percent of those arrested for burglary in New York were under the age of twenty-one; sociologists raced to analyze the phenomenon, blaming it on everything from postwar entropy, materialism, and a decline in corporal punishment to a rise in "broken homes" and an increasing number of working moms. As the economy surged and the Cold War and space race heated up, the phenomenon that Eisenhower would call "the military-industrial complex" became more prevalent and powerful than ever. The prevailing social climate was hardly receptive to the kind of "kicks" that Millstein had identified as "the frenzied pursuit of every possible sensory impression, an extreme exacerbation of the nerves, a constant outraging of the body."

On the Road contained explicit descriptive writing about drugs like Benzedrine and morphine, and aspects of drug consciousness are implicit in the entire inner journey of the book, but it was really Kerouac's portrayal of marijuana that was so controversial and subversive.

The exuberant use of the weed becomes most explicit at the end, when Sal and Dean travel to Mexico and meet the Mexican named Victor—

> "Ask him if we can get any tea. Hey kid, you got ma-ree-wa-na?"
> The kid nodded gravely. "Sho, onnytime, mon. Come with me."
> "Hee! Whee! Hoo!" yelled Dean.

From this point on, the potent Mexican marijuana imparts mystical, dreamlike qualities of revelation and becomes inseparable from the vision quest of the narrative itself—"Somewhere along the way I knew there'd be girls, visions, everything; somewhere along the line the pearl would be handed to me." It transfigures both landscape and perception, catapulting the whole excursion to the level of pure spiritual transcendence. The "pearls" begin appearing on the way to Victor's. Sal thinks Dean can understand Victor's Spanish telepathically, "by sheer wild insight and sudden revelatory genius inconceivably associated with his glowing happiness." "In myriad pricklings of heavenly radiation" Sal has his vision of Dean as Franklin Delano Roosevelt and then as God. The magical otherworldliness continues in the whorehouse of Gregoria as they cavort madly and the mambo "flared in the golden mysterious afternoon like the sounds you expect to hear on the last of the world and Second Coming." In his stoned soul delirium, Dean delves so deeply into the raw ecstasy of the place that it becomes "like a long, spectral Arabian dream in the afternoon in another life— Ali Baba and the alleys and the courtesans."

Perhaps no one in America since Mezz Mezzrow had described the marijuana high and its state of "amazed somnolency" more lyrically or powerfully than Kerouac, but the subversion hardly ends there. Kerouac's association of marijuana consciousness with the "Fellaheen" culture of Mexico was radical in itself. By presenting the dirty evil weed of the Mexicans as something not only desirable but morally good— mystical medicine for a spiritually bankrupt American culture— Kerouac takes Harry Anslinger's nightmare of marijuana as the "killer weed" and "the assassin of youth" and turns it upside down. To his young audience, it was as if Jack Kerouac had written a hipster version of *Huckleberry Finn* and had sent Huck and Jim down the river with a great big bomber of *Cannabis sativa*. As a result, the book infused the idea of marijuana with spiritual questing, Eastern religion and philosophies, and great sensory exploration, imbuing it with a numinous romanticism and a new kind of untamed cultural freedom.

2.

As the Beat Generation began emerging as a cultural movement that transcended literature, the viciousness and sanctimonious bombast of the attacks only drew more readers to it. What the Beat Generation really represented, warned Norman Podhoretz in *Esquire*, was nothing less than "a conspiracy to overthrow civilization." In a scathing essay called "The Know-Nothing Bohemians," Podhoretz, later to become one of the nations's leading neoconservatives, claimed in *The Partisan Review* that Kerouac's "love for Negroes and other dark-skinned people" was "tied up with a primitivism," and that the "primitivism of the beat generation is a cover" for a bitter anti-intellectualism. According to Podhoretz, "The notion that to be hopped up is the best of all human emotions lies at the heart of the Beat Generaton Ethos."

"Nothing gave the Beat scene the image of cool more than the media rap," acknowledged Ed Sanders, who grew up in Missouri and encountered a seventy-five-cent copy of *Howl* at the bookshop on a state university campus in 1957 before coming to New York to attend NYU, becoming a writer and poet and proprietor of the Peace Eye Bookstore in the East Village. "Societally, the Beats weren't important at all in the Midwest, but they were important to me personally. In a story I later wrote about it, this kid in Missouri reads *Howl* and it 'rips through his mind like the tornado that had uprooted the cherry tree in his backyard when he was a child'; that was how the poem had really affected me. . . . I was aware of *On the Road* when it came out, but I was more interested in poetry, and then the great big splash about Kerouac happened, and the book started attracting a much broader spectrum of kids interested in prose writers as opposed to poets."

The Beats were easy targets and the media had a field day excoriating them as deviants, dropouts, homosexuals, drunkards, pill-takers, junkies, and convicts. Their criminal activities and use of drugs made them a menace to society, and their moral decadence undermined not only law and order but national security. Drugs were always hot copy and the press had always been a willing tool in Harry Anslinger's antidrug crusades, playing fast and loose with the facts in the process of rousing public opinion. At the same time, the effect of the press coverage of drug use in America had also been, ironically, to call attention to it and give it an ever-growing outlaw magnetism.

Now, as the press trained their sights on Ginsberg, Kerouac, and later Burroughs, the latest villains of this saga became the New Bohemians with their marijuana, which represented a significant historical departure because for the first time the culprits were for the most part the white and educated refugees of the American middle class. In San Francisco, where poetry readings were booming at places like the Co-Existence Bagel Shop, the hungry i, the Gas Haven, and the Place, these young people were derisively labeled as "beatniks" by *San Francisco Chronicle* columnist Herb Caen because, like *Sputnik* orbiting the Earth, they were so "far out." When Caen intimated that the smell of marijuana was becoming stronger than the smell of garlic in the North Beach area, police began harassing people around the galleries and poetry readings. By the summer of 1958—the "beatnik summer" of conga drumming in North Beach previously referenced by Peter Berg—the police and the media uproar had charged the scene with excitement.

At the same time, a pervasive media stereotype of the beatnik began to emerge. Beatniks were dirty and wore black. The men had goatees and the women were always in leotards. They also wore sandals and played bongos and snapped their fingers at poetry readings and said things like "That's cool, Daddy!" They lived in subterranean pads and drank espresso and despised work. They were obsessed with jazz and intermingled freely with Negroes. Sometimes they had orgies— sometimes even with Negroes! And worst of all, they were lefties—yes, actual Commie sympathizers—who smoked pot. It was an image that became so emblazoned in the public mind that within a few years, no less a personage than the redoubtable J. Edgar Hoover would be proclaiming in a speech that "beatniks" were one of the "greatest threats" facing America, equating them with "Communists and eggheads." Hoover's diatribe was itself a reflection of another time-honored tradition: the vilification of the drug user for political purposes. But as people like Ed Sanders readily point out, the immediate result of all the media attacks was simply to load up the beatnik scene with the romance of a righteous insurgency and to call a disproportionate amount of attention to the element of drug use in the writing itself. As Sanders expressed it, "If the medium is the message, as Marshall McLuhan would so famously later claim, the message of the media rap went something like this: Beatniks smoke *pot*. Beatniks are *bad*. Pot is *very* bad. . . . So, therefore, if you wanna be bad, be a beatnik; and if you wanna be a beatnik, well, then you gotta smoke pot."

3.

"Suddenly he would go to all these literary parties," recalled the novelist and editor Joyce Johnson, Jack Kerouac's girlfriend at the time of the publication of *On the Road*, later to win the National Book Critics Circle Award for her memoir of the period, *Minor Characters*. "He was to be on the radio. He was to be on television. Appearances on campuses. It was heavy, and it went on for months. And he would make these appearances and be interviewed, and the tone of the interviewing would often be extremely hostile. You know, 'You say this about the Beat Generation . . . These are terribly immoral people. They take *drugs*. What are you talking about? These people are *awful*.'"

The questions and answers are typified by Mike Wallace's interview of Kerouac for the *New York Post*:

Q. What is the Beat Generation?

A: Well, actually it's just an old phrase. I knocked it off one day and they made a big fuss about it. It's not really a generation at all.

Q: Is it a type of person?

A: Yeah. It starts with rock 'n' roll teenagers and runs up to sixty-year-old junkies, old characters in the street. . . . It really began in 1910.

Q: Well, what links the junkie and the fourteen-year-old and Jack Kerouac? What is it to be Beat?

A: Well, it's hipness. It's twentieth century hipness.

Q. Hip to what?

A: To life.

As gamely as Kerouac attempted to respond in these situations, he could no more explain what "hip to life" meant to the American mass media of 1957–58 than rationalize what a sixty-year-old junkie might possibly have had to do with a rock-and-roll teenager, and he gave up trying. Instead, he drank copiously and, in the wake of the book's publication, more or less constantly. Before the publication of the book Kerouac drank to medicate his depression over his lack of success and fame; now he drank to numb the bitter disappointment and emptiness of the very things he had wanted, to blast himself away from everything.

"Well, how do you like fame?" asked Irene May, one of Kerouac's friends.

"It's like old newspapers blowing down Bleecker Street" was his disconsolate reply.

In the interim between the writing of *On the Road* and its publication, Kerouac had produced his most ambitious work, but in forums or on talk shows, he was constantly queried about drugs, kicks, promiscuity; few openly acknowledged the deep spiritual underpinnings of *On the Road*. As he wrote *The Dharma Bums*, Grove released *The Subterraneans*. The reviews weren't all bad, but for the most part the press savaged the book like a pack of salivating jackals. *Time* ventured that Kerouac was far from Rimbaud, only "a kind of latrine laureate of Hobohemia . . . ambisextrous and hipsterical." Similarly, when *The Dharma Bums* was released, the component of its spiritual journey was almost completely overlooked or dismissed. All that J. Donald Adams in the *Times* could see in the book was a world of "drugs, drunkenness, and aimless wandering."

The reviews plunged Kerouac into the blackest depression of his life. When he would insist that his work really constituted a lifelong effort to force God to pull back the veil and reveal himself, interviewers would stare blankly or roll their eyes. Worse than the outright attacks were the parodies, an endless barrage of articles and commentaries and shows that trivialized and ridiculed him. Kerouac's response was to go on a six-day binge, lurching from bar to bar, making a spectacle of himself, getting himself thrown out of one place after another.

At readings and events like his appearance at the Hunter College Playhouse, where he gave a speech entitled "Is There a Beat

Generation?," the "King of the Beats" behaved like a drunken Zen lunatic in his trademark baggy pants and checkered shirt with the tails hanging out. For the next three years Kerouac would watch, drunk and brokenhearted, suffering a kind of nervous breakdown, as the media force-fed their stereotypical images of the beatnik to the public, turning the Beat Generation into television fare like the character Maynard G. Krebs on *The Many Loves of Dobie Gillis.*

"What's goin' on, Allen?" he asked Ginsberg mournfully. "It's not money I'm worried about anymore, but the perversion of our teaching which began under the Brooklyn Bridge so long ago."

As much as the response to his work desolated him, Kerouac was equally annoyed by the increasing number of teenagers and college students showing up at his mother's home in Northport, Long Island, where he was writing *Desolation Angels* in the basement, who wanted to go carousing with him and always seemed to know where he was.

"Just like in New York or Frisco or anywhere there they all are hunching around in marijuana smoke, talking, the cool girls with long thin legs in skirts, the men with goatees, all an enormous drag after all and at the time (1957) not even started yet officially with the name of the 'Beat Generation,'" Kerouac wrote about these kids who were becoming known as "beatniks," lamenting his accidental creation of the phenomenon. "To think that I had so much to do with it, too, in fact at that very moment the manuscript of Road was being linotyped for imminent publication and I was already sick of the whole subject. . . . But all I could do was sit on the edge of the bed in despair like Lazarus listening to their awful 'likes' and 'like you know' and 'wow crazy' and 'a wig, man,' 'a real gas'—All this was about to sprout out all over America even down to the high school level and be attributed in part to my own doing!"

As fame and alcoholism overtook him, Kerouac became less and less the protean seeker who had shared the road with Cassady and Ginsberg; he grew ever more embittered and reactionary, regressing to the rigid political and social opinions of his father, Leo Kerouac. There would still be moments of great inspired writing in his work—passages of *Big Sur* that contain some of the most shatteringly truthful and evocative descriptions of the ravages of alcoholism on the soul and the yearning for redemption ever put to paper—but his greatest work was behind him. If marijuana had effectuated creative breakthroughs and had been an important factor in his life and work and the lives and work of those he'd written about, it had also turned into a ready-made form of ammunition for those seeking to attack and discredit him. He became increasingly paranoid, afraid that cops would catch him associating with drug users and throw him in jail. It was a fear not without foundation, as was harshly demonstrated by the fate of Neal Cassady.

4.

From North Beach to Los Gatos, everybody knew about Dean Moriarty, and everybody knew that Neal Cassady was Kerouac's "Holy Goof . . . He was beat—the root, the soul of beatific."

In the wake of the publication of *On the Road,* as Jack Kerouac fell apart in New York, Cassady became an instantaneous cult figure in the thriving North Beach bars and coffeehouses, a character imprisoned by the myth created by the outsized hero of Kerouac's novel who seemed to live the very stereotype that *Time* magazine had used to characterize the Beats: "Excitement and movement mean everything. Steady jobs and homes in the suburbs are for squares."

Ironically, by this time, Neal Cassady was trying his best to live exactly this kind of square life in the suburbs. By now he'd been working steadily as a brakeman for the Southern Pacific for ten years, and Carolyn Cassady had once again taken him back. But even as Cassady once more attempted to live the kind of middle-class existence of family and home that had always divided him, his life was more than ever a nightly nonstop whirlwind that lasted until dawn, driven by the imperatives of his super-octane nervous system, the wild, freely associative patterns of his mind, and the Dionysian appetites of his body. After the publication of *On the Road,* the very air around Cassady seemed charged with electrical energy. People wanted to be around him for the same reason they liked to watch a dangerous storm blazing across the night skies. They could see that Cassady really was the untamed free spirit that Kerouac had written about—the guy who had "the tremendous energy of a new kind of American saint," who stood as naked to the world as Dean Moriarty had when he ran yipping and naked though the sage of the orange-rocked Pecos Canyon country in the novel. Just to be in a car with Cassady while he was driving was an experience that people began seeking out. Women wanted to lie down with him; men wanted to rap with him about life; everybody wanted to get high with him and absorb the greased lightning of his magic; and he was always ready to oblige. Nowhere was the stigmata of dope and kicks more recognizable than around Neal Cassady.

"He became kind of a Johnny Appleseed of grass around San Francisco," related Allen Ginsberg, "turning on everybody he could and consuming as much as he could get his hands on, to the point that me and his wife Carolyn got worried about it. He was just so in love with it."

For Carolyn Cassady, life with Neal was no easier since his return, especially with all the publicity from *On the Road*. He had moved out late in 1955 to live in San Francisco with his girlfriend, Natalie Jackson, and Neal and Natalie had forged Carolyn's signature and blown $10,000 of the money that the railroad had paid him in compensation for a foot injury, trying to prove a "system" he had developed for winning at the racetrack. The episode ended tragically only six weeks after the Six Gallery reading when Natalie, unhinged by the affair, climbed to the roof of their building in San Francisco after slashing her wrist with glass from a broken skylight and fell three flights to her death as police attempted to restrain her. Carolyn once again took Neal back after he returned home devastated and guilt-ridden, opening her arms and her heart and her home. Neal always did his best to be a good father and husband, but when the night beckoned, his best was never good enough. And then in April of 1958 he found himself suddenly entrapped and imprisoned by other forces outside of his control—forces directly related to Kerouac's novel.

"I was at a party at Ferguson's apartment," Neal told Carolyn about what had happened.

When I said I had to go to work, a couple of guys offered to drive me to the depot. When we got there, I offered them a couple of joints in return and went to my locker to get them. I gave them three. Then, on my way home, it hit me: something told me they were narcs, and now I'm positive they were. . . . I think it's a trap. You see, a couple of months ago two other guys asked me to buy 'em some pot. They gave me forty dollars, and I said I'd try. I was sure they were agents, so I took the money to the racetrack. This, of course, told them I knew who they were. Somehow I think it's all connected.

Cassady was right; the narcotics squad was definitely gunning for "Dean Moriarty." When several weeks went by and nothing happened, Carolyn assumed they were in the clear and breathed a huge sigh of relief, but on the morning of April 5, she was shocked to see "two stony monsters standing at the bathroom door" while Neal was shaving.

"You're Neal Cassady? We have a warrant for your arrest. You'll have to come along with us."

Carolyn was enraged at the intrusion into their home. "How is it possible that you people can walk in unannounced, and snatch a man away from his home, his family, his job—just like that?" she protested, of course to no avail. "How can you do it? How do you support your own families by destroying another's? How can you sleep nights?"

As they took Neal away, Carolyn worried that her outburst would backfire.

Suddenly I was afraid I'd gone too far, and they'd take me, too— why not? They didn't care. . . . Through the window I saw them walk to the waiting police car, and the final hideous sight was branded on my memory forever: the man I loved, the father of my children, a man I knew to be gentle and kind, shackled in steel chains and being hauled off by other men as though he were a dangerous beast. "He's a *man*," I wanted to scream, "a son of God, whether you *like* him or not." How was it possible? He looked so forlorn, humble, and defenseless. Neal, Neal—no one could be so evil as to deserve such humiliation. I sobbed and moaned, but it was only the beginning.

Cassady was taken to San Francisco and held for a week in the city jail, but the grand jury had to throw out the case for lack of evidence. He was ebullient as he returned home, certain that he'd beat the rap, but while in jail "they wanted me to tell them everybody I knew who smoked marijuana and where they got it." When he refused, they beat him in the stomach, and when they found out that they had to release him, they told him, "We'll see you in San Quentin, Cassady, if it's the last thing we do."

The narcs wouldn't have to wait long. The morning after his release he was rearrested and put in the San Bruno jail. This time the district attorney called for a special meeting of the grand jury at midnight and changed the cast of collaborators, including the public defender Cassady had been assigned the first time and who was sympathetic to him. Meanwhile a news item had appeared in the *San Jose Mercury News* that identified Cassady as the leader of a gang of marijuana smugglers that brought large quantities up from Mexico—a family man who led a "double life." The article was complete guesswork and sensationalism without any concern for the truth on the part of the paper, but that was certainly not uncommon when it came to news coverage about illicit drugs and the dastardly individuals involved with them. The reporter had even neglected to find out that the trains of the Southern Pacific didn't even go as far south as Los Angeles, let alone Mexico. The article also noted that Cassady was a friend of "the controversial Allen Ginsberg," whose poem was "almost banned." Though the article was later retracted, it cost Cassady his railroad job for the rest of his life, but the damage was hardly limited to the loss of his employment by Southern Pacific.

Cassady would now be tried as a smuggler, and every Anslinger-driven, Hearst-circulated myth about the evils of the weed and the people who used and sold it now worked to implicate him, and his associations with such subversive characters as Allen Ginsberg and Jack Kerouac did little to help his cause. If Cassady had been buoyant and confident the first time in jail, now his mood turned savagely dark. The first time in jail he'd courageously separated two thugs sharing his tiny cell with him to prevent them from fighting—"I stepped right in between them and stopped the fight! Gad, when I sat down I nearly passed out. . . . they could have killed me on the spot." He had felt that his first arrest and release were metaphysical proof of the universal truth he had been learning and attempting to practice, but now he was furious at the injustice of his treatment and seething with a defiant anger that he could barely contain.

What made things worse was that the only way Carolyn could have raised the bail money was by selling the house. It isn't hard to understand her reluctance to do so. Her husband had lost his job and had a track record of desertion, and she had three children with no visible means of support. When she refused to put the house up for sale, Cassady was incensed and then crushed. As he began to realize that Carolyn was not going to change her mind, he resigned himself to the trial and sentencing that awaited him.

On July 3, Cassady was brought before Judge Walter Carpanetti of the district court. The previous case that day had involved a man who had been apprehended with a car full of marijuana and had accepted money from a narcotics agent for his sale. This man was "treated with respect bordering on the friendly," Carolyn Cassady reported. "Later we learned he had cooperated and implicated several other people. He was sentenced to one count of five years to life."

In Cassady's case, the rap was three marijuana cigarettes. When Cassady at first denied smoking marijuana, the judge told him, "In that case I must assume your connection with marijuana is as a dealer." Infuriated by Cassady's cool and composed demeanor, the judge began to berate him, "practically screaming insults at Neal for leading a 'double life.' . . . There stood Neal, his head bowed, poised, cool, and respectful, and there screeched this man who believed himself worthy to judge his fellow man, absolutely hysterical with vindictive rage."

When Cassady's attorney attempted to defend him—"But your honor, we haven't any *proof*!"—referring to the smuggling charges—Carpanetti's reaction personified the wrathfulness building up against marijuana and beatniks and everything they had come to represent: "Yes, well, I *don't care!* I don't like his *attitude!*"

Twenty years had passed since the Marihuana Tax Act had set the tone for marijuana prosecutions in the criminal justice system. With no hesitation, and even though he had a wife and three children who depended on him for support and he had never been convicted of any violent crime, Carpanetti sentenced Cassady to two terms of five years to life, to run concurrently, in San Quentin for possession and sale of three joints, not to include the three months he had already spent in jail.

In essence, the "readily recognizable stigmata" of drug use had only been a part of it—Neal Cassady was also guilty of his "attitude," convicted for the example of his untamed, recalcitrant life.

To Carolyn Cassady, the trial was surreal, Kafkaesque, like "something out of *Alice in Wonderland*." She was shaken by the sentencing for such a minute amount, but also greatly moved by her husband's fortitude.

"In my disillusionment, Neal looked even more the martyr to me. No one knew his weaknesses better than I, but now I was proud of his integrity in sticking to his own principles, especially in the face of the judge's display of passion and prejudice."

The sentence was to begin on Independence Day, 1958. Cassady's first stop was the medical facility in Vacaville. He had already set his mind toward whatever redemptive value he might possibly gain from the experience that awaited him. He immersed himself deeply in the Bible, Thomas Merton, other works of religious literature, and books endorsed by Edgar Cayce, and began to consider prison "an unparalleled opportunity to attain greater grace & I'm sensing this purging in ever greater amounts as I persevere in prayer and meditation." He told people that he hoped to emulate the "splendid rebirth" of Saint Paul.

After three months at Vacaville, dressed in snowy white pajamas, Cassady was put in leg irons and bussed to San Quentin, and placed in a 4½-by-7½-by-9½-foot cell, where he would lie encaged for the next two years among five thousand other felons. As when he had been involuntarily immured by his sadistic older half brother in the Murphy bed for so many hours, his inner life apexed and hurtled faster in prison, but he was sustained by his spiritual pursuits and devotional habits. He composed prayers, recited litanies, learned the names of every one of the 262 popes, from Peter to Pius XII, and lived more than ever with the knowledge that his every word and act were freighted with karmic significance. His job in the prison was sweeping out the constantly collecting flug in the textile mill, where he worked each day, shouting his prayers into the deafening roar of the high-speed looms. Cassady's letters to his wife and friends from prison were long and recondite. He took a course in comparative religion taught by Gavin Arthur, the grandson of the twentieth president, who picked him out of the other inmates on the first day of class and found him "shining with earthly fire."

28

Goodbye Pork Pie Hat

1.

Lester Young was sitting in the chair in his room on the fourth floor of the Alvin Hotel, looking out the window, as he always did. It was Saturday, March 14, 1959. The whole way home from Paris his ulcers had been so bad that he'd bitten his lip bloody from the pain. After he vomited up blood, Elaine Swain, the young woman devoted to taking care of him, tried to get him to go to the hospital, but Prez was terrified of doctors. He chose not to go home to his wife, Mary, and his kids, Lester Jr. and Yvette, in St. Albans because he was separated from his wife and wanted to be here, where he could drink in peace in the room rented for him by Max Roach and Sonny Rollins and Miles Davis and Jo Jones and the others who venerated him and wanted to help him. And here he would sit, hour after hour, fingering his horn, surrounded by his records, bottles of Gordon's gin lined up on his dresser, peering down at Birdland on the corner of 52nd Street and Broadway, watching his old friends come and go, seeing all the young cats with their horns who were copping his style. "They're picking the bones while the body is still warm," he once said of them. "When they come off and I go on, what can I play? Must I copy *them?*"

The previous two years had been a hard slog for Prez, but somehow he'd gotten up there and done it. It was Marshall Stearns who'd arranged for Birdland to celebrate his birthday in 1958 with "Thirty Years in Show Business." Prez had appeared, backed by Doug Watkins,

Willie Jones, Nat Pierce, and Curtis Fuller. Critic Dan Morgenstern was there to cover the performance: "The downbeat is soft, the tempo medium," he wrote. "'Pennies From Heaven' is a haunted song. Not a mild summer rain this but a gray November drizzle. The pennies are few and worn, thin and smooth. The tone is choked, the phrasing halting . . . not from inability but from pain. The last note dies and Lester looks up from a troubled sleep. Silence. The faces of the musicians who have backed him, so gently, so sympathetically, are intent and serious."

Then came the applause, and with each successive song Prez seemed to become more animated—"The master begins softly," Morgenstern continues, "gaining in volume and heat with each successive chorus (can one speak of choruses where there is unbroken continuity?), coming up shouting like the old Prez (did they say he was no more?) and suddenly there is a new astonishing Prez as well"—and that's how it seemed to go in the following months: the Newport Jazz Festival, engagements at the Five Spot. Prez may not have made a good soldier in the army but he soldiered bravely on with his horn even as he was faltering, and then came the invitation for him to go to Paris and play an extended engagement at the Blue Note. Billie Holiday was in Paris playing at L'Olympia, and one night she made it over and got on stage and did a set with him—their last. The author James Jones, who was there with his wife and found his music "great as ever"—"'The Pres' still wore his celebrated pork pie hats, and when he dressed, slowly and carefully, to go out into the streets after his last set, it was always something of a major performance. Framed by the big fur collar of the long coat he loved to wear, his long gaunt face with deep, purple, sick-looking hollows under the eyes would look out at you with a sort of princely helplessness."

While in Paris Prez gave several interviews, one to journalist François Postif, another to writer Chris Albertson. He was shocked that the racism that had so offended him his whole life had followed him there. Something hurtful had been said to him—he wouldn't say what in the Postif interview—by "somebody you wouldn't believe, too, a great person," and Prez made a remark about it that seemed to sum up his life: "You just fight for your life, that's all. Until death do you part. And then you got it made." Looking back, he talked about music and his signature style: "It's got to be sweetness man, you dig? Sweetness can be funky, filthy, or anything—but which part do you want?" When asked about Billie Holiday he simply said, "She's still my Lady Day." He was also angry about rumors that he was a homosexual or a drug addict and made it clear that his lifestyle was his own business: "Why you envy them because they enjoy themselves? Fuck it, you dig? All I do is smoke some New Orleans cigarettes; that's perfect. No sniff, no shit in my nose and nothing, no, I'll drink and I'll smoke."

And drink he did. Some said it was to palliate the symptoms of untreated syphilis, or the terrible dental pain that came from a lifetime of neglecting his teeth because he feared going to the dentist—or maybe it was just the sad, existential ache of life that he'd always felt so acutely. When Budd Johnson watched him buy six bottles of booze at a time at the liquor store and asked, "How can you drink like that?," his answer was telling: "Well, I never want to lose that feeling. This is the feeling I had when I made it with the horn, all the records with Basie and everything."

The doctors had long warned Prez about the drinking, but he'd ignored them. When Marshall Stearns brought his friend, the psychiatrist Dr. Luther Cloud, up to Prez's room at the Alvin, Cloud decided that he was "definitely schizophrenic"—"Yet, in a kind of partly arrested, semicontrolled way. Alcohol, for example, dissociated him and yet gave him the minimum comfort he needed to survive at all. And of course, pot and alky together are A-1 schizo triggers. One quickens time and one slows it. One widens space and one narrows it."

Cloud did his best. He wanted to give Prez injections of heavily concentrated vitamins, but Prez was "scared to death of the needle and of hard dope."

Of course, nobody could help him.

Coming home on the flight from Paris, Prez had been bleeding internally from a classic alcoholic condition called esophageal varices—varicose veins in the esophagus. As he sat in his chair that afternoon and into the evening, watching the comings and goings from Birdland, he finished a bottle of vodka and was working his way through a bottle of bourbon without having eaten a thing. It was an hour after midnight and he was dozing, moving his mouth as if playing the saxophone, when Elaine called the doctor, who arrived twenty minutes later.

Lester Young, the shy and gentle "President of the Tenors," whose singular talent and being had changed jazz and defined cool—"the greatness of America in a single Negro musician," as Jack Kerouac called him, who had so altered Kerouac's life by turning him on to his "New Orleans cigarettes" and had then inspired the breakthrough long saxophone lines of Allen Ginsberg's *Howl* with his playing on "Lester Leaps In"—died around 3 a.m. on Sunday, March 15. He was forty-nine. The whole jazz world turned out for the funeral at Universal Chapel on the corner of 52nd Street and Lexington Avenue. Nobody was surprised; everyone was devastated.

By the time of Prez's death, there were more and more white middle-class exiles like Paul Rothchild seeking new identities in places like Greenwich Village, imbibing the very notion of cool that had been handed down from Lester Young through a whole generation of jazz musicians. "So much of my roots, my definition of hipness, was to take on the speech, dress, attributes and mores of the black musical culture," acknowledged Rothchild, later to become the producer of Paul Butterfield, the Doors, and Janis Joplin. "It was a complete role reversal. The blacks had tried to integrate into white society and now this small group of whites was trying to integrate into black society and was finding out how hard it really was to exist in it. But we were learning new ways of walking, talking, thinking, being."

"The black musicians seem to be the ones who suffer the most for their art," remarked the trumpeter, bandleader, and composer Thad Jones many years later about Prez's passing to one of his biographers. "Maybe that's why the music comes out the way it does. Without that the music would be ordinary. Maybe without the pain and the humiliation, the rejection, the constant struggle, the music itself will be without vitality. Who knows? I would hate to think that that would be it. I would like to think that it was because of the love that the person has in him that creates this very unusual, this very vital, this very beautiful expression."

Perhaps the greatest tribute to Lester Young involved no words at all but was evoked by the sublimely sad and soulful beauty of the Charles Mingus composition that memorialized him, the title of which seemed to say it all—

"Goodbye Pork Pie Hat."

2.

Billie Holiday took the death of Lester Young badly. She wanted to sing at the funeral but Prez's wife, Mary, ruled it out because she was worried that Lady's own condition would create too much of a distraction. Instead Lady just stood there weeping as trombonist Tyree Glenn played a beautiful, muted "Just A-Wearyin' for You" before the coffin was borne out by Illinois Jacquet, Budd Johnson, Jimmy Rushing, and the others.

In the weeks after the death, Elaine Swain, who had been barred from the funeral by Prez's wife, went to see Lady, and Lady summoned Bill Dufty. She wanted Dufty to write a book about Elaine and Prez because she thought it was "a beautiful fuckin' love story." As Dufty saw it, "here was a man who had found a woman to take care of him, be a buffer for him, which was incredible, something [Billie] had never found, and she was in awe of this. She said this bitterly crying."

It was the reaction of a profoundly lonely woman. The last of her men, Louis McKay, was gone. Theirs had been a violent relationship, but it seemed that was the only kind Lady had ever known. She gave as good as she got in these brawls, once bashing John Levy over the head with a portable TV, another time getting cracked over the head by McKay with a telephone. It would remain a subject of ineffable sorrow to all who loved her that at every turn, when Lady could have been with someone who truly wanted to love and protect her—the kind of man who might have given her security and even children—she seemed to only want a man who would abuse her and steal her money, humiliate and discard her. When her piano players who adored her would see her go off with these men time and again, it would make them cry. From the standpoint of modern recovery, such behavior would immediately be identified as the classic acting-out and self-sabotage of an addict/alcoholic who had been a victim of sexual abuse, but of course such notions had yet to enter the mainstream of psychology, let alone the cultural vernacular. McKay had used drugs with her and had shared her life as an addict and, like others, had come to understand very well how to use her habit to control her. It would be easy to vilify him as just another in a long line of smooth-talking well-dressed players and hustlers and pimps like John Levy who had bled her dry, but he was her husband, and Lady had been devoted to him at least for a time. McKay at the very least had allowed her to maintain the fantasy of a life of normalcy, and when they separated, she felt more alone than ever.

The publication of Lady's autobiography and the attendant publicity assured that the downward spiral of her final two years would be public—a "triumphant decline," to use the phrase of biographer Donald Clarke—but that final year seemed more and more like a long, sad blues in the night. Despite it all, she would sing to the very end. She continued to perform to sold-out clubs and record, releasing *Lady in Satin,* an easy-listening album produced by Ray Ellis on which she is backed by strings and a chorus. Lady needed to be propped up at times in the studio by her assistant, Alice Vrbsky, in order to record it, and when the project was all over, a despondent Ray Ellis remembered taking the album home to listen to. "It was so sad. It didn't matter whether she sang the right note or the wrong note, because she sang twenty thousand wrong notes on that thing. But she poured her heart out." Depending on one's point of view, *Lady in Satin* was either her greatest album—Miles Davis certainly thought so, and Lady loved it—or the worst of her career, a sad parody of herself. For this reason, many fans and critics and even biographers would have trouble so much as acknowledging its existence.

Biographer Stuart Nicholson states that after 1957 Lady's use of heroin was largely "incidental" and that she used booze to suppress her urges for narcotics, but depending on who saw what and when, Lady was on dope and off dope, on dope and off dope. After McKay's departure it was procured for her by a tall, skinny, good-looking kid from Philadelphia named Frankie Freedom, who also did her hair and made meals for her. Carl Drinkard described him as "a hip little dude . . . and a shrewd son of a bitch. If you didn't watch out, he'd take your fuckin' socks off your feet without removin' your shoes."

When she was on, Lady's tolerance level was high and she needed a lot. Her audience would have to watch as she carried a kerchief onstage to cover the needle marks on her hands and wore long gloves to cover her hands and arms. She would spend a lot of time in her bathroom, legs crossed as she cooked up and tied up with a silk stocking and probed for a vein. When she was off, she was drinking heavily, gin and 7Up. And as she was oftentimes trying to stay off, she was drinking prodigiously. Most people who knew her well agree that it was the booze that ravaged her the most during those last years.

"Faults? Well, of course, she drank too much," pianist Mal Waldron commented. "She always carried a small bottle of gin with her and somehow it never seemed to get empty even though she was drinking all the time. When we played in a dry town she'd be under a terrible strain. She wouldn't stop drinking and she never really did kick the dope habit. But Lady Day had an awful lot to forget."

If Lady was in bad shape, everyone suffered, audience and musicians alike. Critic Ralph Gleason would remember her sitting stiffly in the lobby of the San Carlos Hotel in Monterey after the finale of the jazz festival, numbed, muttering rather than talking. "She looked totally wasted, shrunken to the bone. She couldn't even sing off key. It was painful to see and hear her at that time, even though she could still move an audience. . . . Finally, in that hoarse whisper that could still (after thirty years of terrifying abuse) send shivers down your spine, she asked, 'Where are you boys goin'?' And when no one answered, she answered herself, 'They got me openin' in Vegas tonight.'"

As she deteriorated, many who had often come around to Lady's basement apartment at 26 West 87th Street came around less and less, and their absence became painfully conspicuous. Lady hated solitude most of all, and her final year was the loneliest of her life. "She who had always been the center of attention sat alone most nights, and not by choice," recalled Annie Ross. "She thrived on company, yet there she was. She sat alone watching television every night. She sat in an armchair puffing away at a marijuana joint, hour after hour, just staring at the screen, shuffling the pages of the papers."

Perhaps the most unendurable loneliness of all was her childlessness. Dufty would tell the story about being with Lady in a Chinese restaurant when the waiter brought mustard to the table and Lady said, "Ask him to take away that damn mustard," revealing to him that she'd once sat in a bathtub full of hot water and mustard for eighteen hours as a means of aborting a baby so that her mother wouldn't have to be worried that she was a "bad girl"—"God will punish her, the kids used to say. He damned well did, too. The only thing I ever wanted is that baby." It was obvious from her relationships with godchildren like Bevan Dufty how much she loved children. She was also godmother to children of Leonard Feather, Mike Gould, Dorothy Winston, Rosemary Clooney, and others ("It takes a very bad woman to be a good godmother," Lady told Clooney when she became godmother to her daughter). She dreamed of buying land and establishing a home for orphan children and was trying to adopt her own, but with her drug conviction she knew she did not stand a chance. The lawyer Earle Zaidans was trying to help her by collecting affidavits from people who would swear that she would be a reliable parent. When her application was turned down not once but twice, she "cried and cried for days."

Even though Lady could still pull together a performance, the series of appearances that turned out to be her last broke the hearts of everyone around her. When she appeared at George Wein's Storyville in Boston, a local critic wrote that her voice "cuts through like a painful knife. But there is a ripe, mature beauty." Wein remembered her singing as "fantastic. . . . She had a lightness to her voice that I hadn't heard in years. . . . She said, 'George, I'm straight now. You gotta help me.' I said, 'Let's do it.'"

It never happened. Lady wasn't straight, nor could she maintain consistency in her performances. By the time of her appearance at a benefit for the Phoenix Theater on May 25, she was in shambles. Steve Allen, slated to appear in the show, barely recognized her when he got lost backstage after arriving—"and I just walked into a room, and there was this little old Negro lady sitting there on a cot or something, and just to be polite I said, 'Hello, how are you?' She said, 'Fine, how's it going?' something like that. It was a very old theater, there was a single light bulb in the room, very poor lighting. . . . And since I didn't know her I just looked at my fingernails for moment, and suddenly I had a creepy feeling and did a slow double take, and the little old lady was Billie, looking forty years older than I expected to see her."

Leonard Feather, the English-born jazz critic who had known and loved Lady since John Hammond first introduced them in 1936, was stunned when he saw her backstage in her dressing room. She was drooling, with spittle on her chin.

"What's the matter, Leonard?" she asked. "You seen a ghost or something?"

Feather was afraid that, yes, he was indeed looking at a ghost. He was certain that if Lady wasn't hospitalized immediately, she would be dead within weeks.

29

It's All a Part of Their Poetic—
No, Their Metaphysical—Education

Allen Ginsberg and Jack Kerouac reacted to Neal Cassady's arrest in very different ways.

Though he felt partly responsible due to the publicity unleashed by his novel, Kerouac distanced himself almost immediately. He was angry at Neal for not taking greater care about his marijuana-smoking, and concerned about his mother's feelings and his own reputation. When Kerouac wrote Burroughs about the affair, explaining his feelings and justifying his reluctance to get involved, Burroughs was infuriated by his "weak and cowardly letter." He found Kerouac's letter to be "like some cat explaining to a former friend how he 'can't have him to the house anymore because the little woman don't like Jews, and after all I'm out of 'all that now.'" Kerouac had "reaped fame and money telling Neal's story," Burroughs pointed out in a letter to Ginsberg from Paris after Cassady's sentencing, "recording his conversation, representing himself as Neal's life-long friend. Maybe the fuzz got onto Neal through Jack's book. In any case he had sold Neal's blood and made money. Now he will not lift a dollar to help. I don't see it, Allen."

In the eyes of William Burroughs, Jack Kerouac was behaving much more like a Shit than a Johnson. And as Cassady had refused to name the names of his fellow marijuana users, it was Neal who was the Johnson.

As Kerouac turned away, Ginsberg was galvanized into action by the arrest. Leaping to Carolyn Cassady's aid and visiting Neal in prison, Ginsberg tried to help them take on the California penal system, organizing people to attest to the fact that Cassady was a talented writer and a valuable member of society who had been victimized by the "evil laws" that caused the police to entrap citizens simply because they smoked marijuana. Ginsberg viewed the arrest as nothing less than a "crucifixion" and Neal as a martyr given a bad deal by evil laws.

"To me, Neal's arrest was the most graphic proof I'd ever had of how the whole phenomenon of the Beat Generation could be stigmatized because of the use of these substances. It was becoming clear to me that the only way people like Neal and myself who smoked marijuana as part of a way of life would ever be safe was when the laws were changed."

In the rapid metamorphosis of *Howl* from poem to event to cultural phenomenon, history had conferred upon Ginsberg a pivotal role as an ambassador of the cultural changes it would unleash, including the use of drugs. By now Ginsberg was firmly convinced that the literature of the Beat Generation could alter the cultural landscape of the nation as surely as the substances of the illicit pharmacopoeia had altered the minds of those who produced it.

"I knew that the fundamental issues of drug use in America in our time were going to become inextricable from issues of free speech and First Amendment rights and obscenity laws. The scenario would soon enough repeat itself with Burroughs and *Naked Lunch*."

Naked Lunch began appearing in America for the first time when editor Irving Rosenthal published a nine-page excerpt in the autumn 1958 issue of the *Chicago Review*, which quickly prompted a thunderous condemnation in the *Chicago Daily News* by Jack Mabley called "Filthy Writing on the Midway." Mabley called the issue "one of the foulest collections of printed filth I've seen publically circulated," which quickly persuaded Chancellor Lawrence A. Kimpton of the University of Chicago that something had to be done because Rosenthal was planning to publish more of the novel in the winter issue.

When Rosenthal went to the University of Chicago Press in November, he was told by the shop supervisor that he had been denied permission to set the copy in type for the winter issue. Outraged that the work had been suppressed, Rosenthal tried to drum up support at the university, but nobody would support him—not David Riesman, not Phillip Roth, not even Nelson Algren. Rosenthal and six members of the staff then resigned in protest.

Allen Ginsberg's prediction that *Naked Lunch* was a novel "that would drive everyone in America crazy" now seemed like a prophecy coming true, and it was only the beginning.

"In the end I knew you couldn't have it both ways: you couldn't have a society that allowed free and unfettered creative expression, that also might incorporate material about the use of consciousness-altering substances, without a significant segment of the population becoming interested in their use as well."

Neal Cassady's arrest and the suppression of *Naked Lunch* were clarion calls that foreshadowed all of Ginsberg's activism of the sixties. Before the arrest he had only written about drugs; now he began speaking out about them publicly, using his fame as a poet to publicize his views. He also recognized the necessity of informing his opinions with fact and began compiling his legendary drug files: "I began the files when the Beat Generation first started becoming a public matter—and that included the aspect of drugs and the distortions of the drug story as well as the distortion of the Beat Generation."

Besides Cassady's arrest, the other event that turned Ginsberg into "the original culture warrior for cannabis," as Martin Lee calls him— "a one-man anti-reefer madness wrecking crew determined to shake the foundations of pot prohibition"—was his 1961 appearance on the John Crosby talk show on CBS, along with guests Ashley Montagu and Norman Mailer.

"We were going to discuss the modern sensibility and maybe a touch of 'beat' or 'hip' and what it meant on television. I had lunch with Mailer before and said that I'd like to bring up the subject of the decriminalization or legalization of marijuana. He said that it would be foolish because we'd never get anywhere with that; it would just be considered shocking. But I did say something about it when it came up on the program, and when I did Ashley Montagu added that he thought I was right, there was no great danger with marijuana, and that he thought the government's story about it was wrong. So then Mailer chimed in that he had 'tried it somewhere' and that it was all right; and then Crosby, the host, added that he had tried it in Africa safely, and we all came to this consensus."

The FCC immediately intervened and forced Crosby and CBS to run a seven-minute refutation from the Narcotics Bureau that denounced the guests for their views. Both Ginsberg and Crosby were enraged by the disavowal, which was run by the network as a public service announcement. Did not a citizen's right of free speech also apply to the kind of public discussion of marijuana on television he had engaged in?

"What outraged me most was, first of all, the presumption of the government to take over the airwaves like that—they couldn't do that now. What right did the FCC have to be opposing our suggestions about the change of a law? But in those days, people were scared to death of the very subject, which is why Mailer had been so hesitant and dubious about even bringing it up. He smoked marijuana and had a lot to lose by the scrutiny of that aspect of his life—just like the rest of us—so it wasn't only a matter of censorship; it was a matter of the kind of fear which produced self-censorship, and it was enormous. It was censorship to the extent that you couldn't even open up your mouth on television without being refuted by the government."

What Ginsberg did next would have an important impact on his life for years to come. "I wrote a long, long letter to Anslinger, vowing to get him. I called him a disgrace and presented a long catalog of the duplicity and lies that they had been promoting for so many years."

In essence, the letter was an audacious declaration by Ginsberg of his passionate intention to pursue through political means the legalization of marijuana in the United States. Nobody knows exactly how Anslinger reacted to the missive, or whether or not it caused the FBI to open its long file on Ginsberg. Doubtless the Federal Bureau of Narcotics was not receiving many such letters in those days, and to send one like it was not only a bold but a reckless thing to do, especially if one happened to be a gay Beat poet who smoked marijuana, as Allen Ginsberg did. From that moment on, the Bureau and local narcotics police in New York would look for a way to set the poet up for a marijuana bust.

"When I got my Freedom of Information Act material so many years later, I found out that as of the date of the John Crosby broadcast, from then on, any suggestion that marijuana be legalized—by anybody—went into my file. For about three or four years, right around the beginning of the sixties, if anyone expressed such a notion in public, in any form, it went into my file. So, yes, I had quite a big file. It was quite amazing."

Ginsberg was already well aware that any organized effort to legalize marijuana in the United States would be a difficult struggle that would have to be waged on many levels. On the one hand, it would have to confront all the scientific and medical and sociological myths regarding the effects of the weed that had been built up since the thirties, which had become so deeply ingrained in the public mind that they were blindly accepted as truth by an overwhelming majority of the American population. On the other hand, it would also have to counter what the weed had come to represent in the public mind, and in this regard it would have to deal with an image. This part of the campaign would have to be, in effect, a public relations campaign designed to counter what Ginsberg believed was thirty years of disinformation, to remove precisely what Gilbert Millstein had called its "readily recognizable stigmata" and thereby make its decriminalization and legalization more plausible.

As Ginsberg viewed it, as surely as Gandhi had had to confront the British imperialist mindset in order to bring about the independence of India, such a movement would run headlong into the ramparts of some of the basic premises of American culture and society and politics. Already, by the late fifties and the coming of the Beat Generation, the notion was being circulated that marijuana was not only harmful in itself and would lead to harder drugs, but that it could induce a "defeatist" sensibility in the population regarding the Cold War. People all across the political spectrum believed that marijuana could sap the will of the people to resist communism as easily as it could devitalize the will and ability of Americans to work and produce and consume goods and services, which in a rapidly expanding economy of automobiles and household products would be equally catastrophic—the true undoing of the American way of life.

That was a stereotype that was introduced into circulation by the FBI, the CIA, and the Treasury Department. The notion that marijuana makes you dopey and retreatist and defeatist and all that was a critical notion introduced into modern letters, literary criticism, through the following route. Beginning with Norman Podhoretz's article called "The Know-Nothing Bohemians," or some similar article by him or somebody like that, then reinforced by the *Partisan*

Review.... It was picked up and magnified more in the sociological essays in *Encounter* magazine and in the circles around the Congress for Cultural Freedom, then was picked up from them bodily, like trench mouth, and put into *Time* magazine and *Life* magazine and spread nationally. The places where it first surfaced were the intellectual circles that were later connected with the CIA. . . . They turned into cold-war intellectuals and into paranoids, most of them. Then all of a sudden comes up a whole generation of people who are all anarchists, all sort of cheerful about Communism, who think McCarthyism is a big joke, don't take the cold-war Stalinism fight seriously, want to smoke grass and look at Cézanne, and realize that the government is a hallucination run by a bunch of dopes.

The files that Ginsberg began compiling, which would eventually become a significant part of his personal archive in the Butler Library of Columbia University, were composed of innumerable yellowed clippings of newspaper articles and carbon copies of reports and dog-eared, underlined studies and oral testimonies—anything he could get his hands on having to do with not only the culture of marijuana but all the drugs of the illicit pharmacopoeia. If he saw a newspaper article about somebody, like Cassady, given an outrageously draconian prison sentence for a tiny amount of marijuana, he clipped it; any information he could find, any evidence about the skullduggery of the government, the corruption of the police, the machinations of politicians, the inaccuracies of the media, the manipulations of scientists and researchers, was gleaned and gathered, organized and filed. He was particularly interested in people speaking truthfully about their marijuana experiences—people who could tell the true story of its underground use and culture, as Mezz Mezzrow had done, and could describe the short- and long-term effects.

Nothing like an independently compiled sociological record of marijuana use had existed in the United States since the La Guardia Committee Report of 1944, which had become almost impossible to locate. Little else existed apart from isolated fragments about cannabis in the scholarly and medical literature in some university libraries, information compiled on individuals by narcotics squads, some intelligence about smuggling and records of arrests in police departments, and the self-serving statistical data of the Federal Bureau of Narcotics.

What began to accrue in Ginsberg's East Village pad toward the end of the fifties, first in manila folders, then in cardboard boxes, eventually in big iron filing cabinets, was a remarkable record of a government's suppression of a part of its population that would only grow progressively larger with the years—the counterweight to the lies and myths that Harry Anslinger had compiled to launch the crusade against marijuana in the 1930s.

With the approaching sixties, as the files grew ever larger and more newspapers and magazines became interested in the phenomenon of growing numbers of middle-class American kids smoking marijuana, more and more reporters heard about Allen Ginsberg's remarkable archive.

"I'd been commissioned to write a serious, no-holds-barred report on marijuana," Dan Wakefield recalled. "It was moving from the back rooms of the jazz bars and cold-water pads of hipsters in Harlem and the East Village, seeping through the walls of college dormitories and into middle-class consciousness."

When Helen Weaver at Farrar, Straus told him, "You've got to see Allen. Allen knows everything about it, and he keeps these incredible files." Wakefield, like many others, found himself visiting Ginsberg's flat in the East Village, where Allen showed him "a big file cabinet and pulled out reports for me to read on the medical, legal, and historical aspects of *Cannabis sativa*. He was eager to help anyone who would write objectively about this drug he believed should be legalized, offering facts and opinions and background information, all in a friendly, matter-of-fact manner."

"Almost everyone has experimented with it and tried writing something on it," Ginsberg told him. "It's all part of their poetic—no, their metaphysical—education."

Allen Ginsberg would say the same thing for the next forty years. As he saw it, drugs were going to be "a cutting-edge issue—one of the fundamental ways we defined ourselves as a people in the second half of the twentieth century."

30

Let Lady Live

1.

Frankie Freedom was cooking oatmeal and custard for Lady in her apartment on May 31, 1959, when she collapsed. He called her Viennese physician, Dr. Eric Caminer, and she was rushed by ambulance to Knickerbocker Hospital.

No sooner did an orderly smell Lady's breath and see the old track marks on her arms than her case was diagnosed as "drug addiction and alcoholism" and she was moved to Metropolitan Hospital because it was a city institution. Lady was registered as Eleanora McKay and placed in a public ward, but word soon got out that it was Billie Holiday, and when the reporters and photographers began showing up she was moved to a private room. As the news spread, it seemed everybody in the hospital wanted signed copies of records and books.

The main problem was advanced cirrhosis of the liver but her heart, kidneys, and other organs had been compromised by an infection related to the cirrhosis, all of which was complicated by conditions like malnourishment. Lady was put in an oxygen tent. As they began feeding her intravenously, she began to rally. For the next ten days she put on some weight and showed signs of improvement. Soon her room was filled with visitors: the Duftys, Earle Zaidans, and then Louis McKay showed up broke, having flown in from California.

Was Lady on dope at the time of her admittance? The question would become a hornet's nest of controversy and discrepancy. There are those, like Earle Zaidans, who maintained that she was completely clean when she entered the hospital, and the fact that she did not appear to suffer any withdrawal symptoms for the first seventy-two hours seems to corroborate this. But according to William Dufty, "There were no withdrawal symptoms because she had drugs on her." For Dufty and many others who knew her, the real fear was what was going to happen when she would not be able to get any heroin. These people reckoned that after fifteen years of on-and-off addiction, Billie Holiday could no more do without heroin than a diabetic could do without insulin; they were afraid that she would never be able to suffer withdrawal symptoms at the same time she was trying to recover from all of her other conditions. That Lady was also thinking about it herself became obvious when she said to Maely Dufty, "You watch, baby, they're going to arrest me in this damn bed."

How painfully correct she turned out to be in her prediction.

Accounts vary as to exactly where the dope they found in her room was. It was widely reported that a nurse named Figueroa caught Lady with heroin in her hand and powder flecks on her nose.

"What's that?" the nurse reportedly asked.

"Mind your own damn business" was Lady's response.

Maely Dufty later claimed that the nurse had found heroin in Billie's handbag, "which was hanging on a nail on the wall—six feet away from the bottom of her bed. It was virtually impossible for Billie—with hundreds of pounds of equipment strapped to her arms and legs for transfusions—to have moved one inch towards that wall." The implication of her statement was that there was some foul play involved in what happened, perhaps a setup. William Dufty reported that the dope was found in a box of tissues at bedside. Lady herself claimed she'd brought the dope along with her in her handbag.

Whatever actually transpired on June 12, the result was Lady's arrest, along with the arrest of Frankie Freedom, who subsequently disappeared. Lady was charged with possession. Her radio, record player, flowers, and telephone were immediately confiscated—presumably an attempt to make it feel less like a hospital room and more like a jail cell. Lady was interrogated on her bed by detectives who neglected to even inform a lawyer first, which amounted to imprisonment without bail or hearing. Maely Dufty also maintained that the police threatened to throw her in jail regardless of her condition, and when Maely protested that they couldn't arrest anyone on the critical list, the police responded that they would deal with that by simply removing her from the critical list.

What developed over the successive weeks was a raging legal and ethical confrontation that turned Lady's hospital room into a battlefield and her situation into an angry vortex of debate in which all of the evolving attitudes and opposing viewpoints regarding the issues of drug addiction and criminality and the role of the medical establishment in the treatment of addiction converged in a single tragic setting. It was a conflict perfectly encapsulated by the exchange between attorney Donald Wilkes and assistant district attorney Irving Lang when Wilkes applied for a writ of habeas corpus against Stephen Kennedy, police commissioner of New York, and they argued the matter before Judge H. Epstein in the New York State Supreme Court on June 16.

"Far from attempting to deprive the petitioner of any constitutional or statutory rights, I think the police department has been extremely solicitous of the condition of this petitioner," offered Lang, asserting that the police were behaving properly and humanely and that Lady would have already been arraigned "if not for the fact that hospital authorities thought it would be detrimental to her health."

"Your Honour, I must say that the interrogation of a witness, who is classified by the hospital as terminal, by three detectives, hardly appears to be an act of solicitude for her welfare," countered Wilkes.

"If, your Honour, this drug which is slowly killing, I believe, this defendant, if the detectives had prevented her from jumping off a bridge, they would be considered great heroes," Lang rejoined.

When the writ was granted and Lady was paroled into Wilkes's custody pending arraignment, the fight was carried into the newspapers as Dufty, who found Lady's treatment a "horrifying outrage," began writing about it and drafted a petition to be sent to the mayor's office that Lady be allowed to die in dignity and peace, without police harassment. Working with press agent Dorothy Ross, Dufty and others sympathetic to her plight began asking everyone they could to sign. The writer Dan Wakefield, who was reporting on the heroin problem in the community of East Harlem, was one of those asked to circulate it.

"I said of course I would help," he recalled.

I took the subway uptown to Maely's, and she introduced me to McKay and gave me the petitions. Then I set out on Saturday night to get signatures. I thought it would be easy. I figured people would be lining up to sign for one of the great singers of our time. I was wrong. That old McCarthyite fear of signing your name to anything was still alive in the land, even in New York. The attitude of many people I asked was summed up by a young man I encountered at a party at Ted the Horse's apartment who nervously refused on the grounds that "I'm not a signer."

But thousands of other people uptown signed it, along with many in the jazz community.

When the district attorney decided that Lady's condition was no longer "grave," an arraignment was scheduled at her bedside for June 22, but it was canceled because their chief prosecution witness, the nurse who had found the dope, was ill.

Another possible reason the arraignment was canceled was the pickets from the community who'd appeared outside of Lady's window, carrying protest signs with three words that expressed their deepest feelings:

LET LADY LIVE!

2.

There was one more experience that Ruby Rosano shared in common with Billie Holiday, yet another similarity that would later only deepen her emotional identification with her. At some point Ruby was informed by a doctor that she had developed ovarian cysts, which needed to be removed. Of course, Ruby proceeded to ignore the symptoms for the next two years. Eventually the pain became so bad that she went stumbling once again into the emergency room of St. Vincent's Hospital.

"The intern in the emergency room told me I needed immediate surgery. I was drunk, pilled up and having trouble standing. I told him I couldn't have the operation—my 'work' would suffer if my body was scarred. He reassured me that there would eventually only be a thin scar—a 'Hollywood incision,' he called it. I could still wear bikinis. But

I told him I couldn't stay, that I'd lose my apartment and possessions if I was gone too long. People were always breaking in and cleaning out my apartment when I was gone because they knew I was in jail, and I was worried that if I had the operation they would think I was in jail again, and I'd lose everything—and meanwhile here it was, I was going to lose my life, right?"

The young doctor got very angry at her and told her to go ahead and leave. "What's the loss of one more lousy dirty dope fiend to the world?" he said.

It stopped her right in her tracks. "I started to cry. I said, 'Wait a minute, I'm a human being!'"

"If you have any desire to live, the surgery has to be done immediately," he told her matter-of-factly, and just walked away. It was then that Ruby allowed herself to be led to the stretcher and taken away to surgery.

After the operation, her pill connection brought drugs to her in the ward, and she would just pull the curtains and get high. She just stayed stoned, wandering around the corridors at night all the time holding onto the IV stand. What happened next was unexpected. Before she left, the doctor told her she would never be able to have children.

"I wasn't prepared for how it was going to affect me. Okay, I was thirty-one years old and convinced I would make a terrible mother, and I knew I didn't want to raise a child alone, and I always thought I never wanted to bring a child into this stinking world anyway, but somehow there must have been some fantasy somewhere that one day a man would rescue me from this life of degradation and I'd settle down to that little white cottage with ivy around it and have kids and everything would turn out to be just hunky-dory. . . . Now that choice was gone. The last fantasy was over. I was completely outside the possibility of a normal family life and respectability. There was nothing left. It just shattered me."

After leaving the hospital, Ruby could think of nothing but heroin. She immediately went in search of a dealer she knew named Tony. As fate would have it, he was sitting on a very large quantity of dope. Ruby had finally found her junkie's fantasy: an unlimited supply of heroin.

"He lived in a hotel in the West 40s, and he was a nice guy. I was living with him, but it wasn't a romantic thing. He was strung out, too, and we were dope companions, and we lived in this strange world of using dope together that only junkie companions can truly understand, only we could use all the dope we wanted to. He used to keep his stash on the top of the door, where he had dug out the whole entire top, and he kept more in a dresser drawer next to a chair by the room's window, and he could always get more after that. I would never have to leave! I would just simply sit there, and cook up, and every time I came out of a nod I would just shoot up again. Oh, it was glorious, like being surrounded forever by this warm protective veil from life's realities—and by that time, believe me, there were plenty of life's realities I needed to be protected from—and worst of all was knowing that I could never have a child."

It went on and on like it would never end—one shot after another, the days turning to weeks, the weeks to months. "Then one day I realized, *You know what, Ruby, this motherfucker's gonna get* popped*!*—I just felt it in my gut—*and if he gets busted, there ain't no way in hell I'm ever gonna be able to support this habit.* I was shooting up about four hundred dollars a day, which was a lot of money in those days. Also, I was down to about ninety pounds. Who the hell needed to eat?"

One day she went out to get some air, and as she was returning she saw police cars parked outside the hotel. She watched from down the street as they dragged Tony out in handcuffs and threw him in the back of the car. Was it luck, or fate? Ruby had avoided arrest, but there she was, with the worst habit she'd ever had in her life. There she was facing the same questions all over again that seem to torment every junkie. What was she going to do? Where was she going to go? In her case the answer was nowhere. Ruby was now homeless, truly homeless, for the first time in her life. For a couple of weeks, she was able to sleep behind the stairs of her old building, on a piece of cardboard; then she had to start moving.

"Many times I had to choose between a place to sleep or a bag of dope. I'd sleep in the movie houses up on 42nd Street and wash up in a bar, or use someone's shower. All of life was boiled down to a matter of which floor could I sleep on and where I could get my next shot. Do you know it's possible to sleep on two chairs pushed together in someone's hotel room? You learn all kinds of things like that when you're homeless."

Less than two weeks later, Ruby was working in a cheap whore-house, getting paid ten dollars a person and giving the hotel clerk four dollars of it. To support her heroin habit, she would sleep with twenty-five men a night.

"As long as I live, I'll never be able to understand what manner of man was able to touch that pitiful blob of humanity."

Ruby Rosano had been reduced to nothing more than a pile of bones with a hank of long black hair hanging down to her waist. It was all over. She moved into the Lincolnview Hotel, a dingy welfare hotel on 69th Street and Broadway.

"I went there to die, really. My only goal was to be carried out of there in a plastic bag. I figured that would be a fitting end for a piece of shit like me."

Each night Ruby prayed for death. Each night she would scream, "If there is a fuckin' God, let me die! Let someone live who wants to, and take me, *you cocksucker!*"—and she would wait for the bolt of lightning, but it never came, and she would pass out, and in the morning when she had to wake to still another day of it, she would spit and curse God's name again. She felt the tempting magnetic pull of every open window. Then one day in an uncontrollable wave of despair she took a syringe and banged a shotful of air right into her mainline because she had heard it would kill you. She actually felt the bubble travel up her arm and head for her heart, but as messed up as she was at the time on pills and booze, the feeling was just too creepy, she couldn't stand it, and she started running insanely around the apartment like a chicken with its head cut off, hyperventilating, afraid her heart was going to burst at any second, and then she rushed out into the street, screeching about what she had done to anyone who passed by. Some-time later, after she calmed down, she was sitting there on a bench in the middle of Broadway, reckoning with the fact that she had just tried to kill herself and failed, when she saw a copy of the *New York Daily News* and learned that Billie Holiday was dying in Metropolitan Hospital.

"I just got on the subway. I had to go up there. . . . Something seemed to be pulling me."

It was when she turned the corner on East 99th Street that she saw the protesters carrying the signs—

LET LADY LIVE!

3.

The demonstration that Ruby Rosano encountered outside Billie Holiday's hospital window was more than ten years in the making.

Since the arrival of heroin in 1946–47, Harlem had found itself in the crosshairs, at a nexus where powerful forces of crime, policy, politics, race, and culture all intersected with the phenomena of drug use and addiction, with dire results. As the Mafia was building the global heroin trade into a multinational business that would exceed the gross national product of many nations, marketing their product in places like Harlem, the profile of the heroin addict had shifted dramatically, from white working-class males, frequently of ethnic background, to young black males of the inner cities, where it would remain for the next twenty-five years. Those who had argued for a more progressive approach to drug addiction had hoped that the establishment of the US Public Health Service Narcotics hospitals in 1935 might be the beginning of a breakthrough in the campaign to treat drug abuse without formally invoking criminal sanctions, but it was not to be.

Peddling drugs on the street quickly became a vocation in Harlem during the 1950s. The whole pathology of the heroin problem in Harlem began with youngsters who were never really bad boys. "Most were just kids and young adults like me who panicked once they got addicted and felt the nasty bite of horse, and got scared when they realized there was no place to go, nowhere to run," recalled Sonny Wright, who wore the Harlem heroin epidemic on his arms—forty years later, they were still criss-crossed with scars, like a road map of his addiction. As Wright portrayed it, the whole street trade in heroin really began with local kids from the neighborhoods motivated by the need for heroin and the spirit of entrepreneurship. For kids willing to apply the simple capitalist work ethic and the skill of simple mathematics to the business of investing twenty dollars in an eighth of an ounce of heroin, the street trade represented a perfect way for idle youth to make money, and there was always lots of idle youth in Harlem.

"It meant that kids like me could make a living without even having to leave their blocks. If I had twenty dollars, I could go into business for myself. I could buy an eighth and make up five or six sixteenths and sell them for ten dollars—and still have my shot. So that's what

I did, and then I could buy two eighths . . . and I could get high if I wanted to, and if I decided to use it all up, then that's what I'd do, and I wouldn't be threatened or hurt. That's what I did for a long while. We called it 'jugglin.'"

Jugglin' fed right into what would become one of the most intractable aspects of the drug problem in the African American community: the nexus of drugs, joblessness, and poverty. As the situation in Harlem worsened, Harry Anslinger always maintained that tougher trafficking penalties were the only solution that would work. Judges who were too lenient were the problem. Tougher laws were necessary, and he orchestrated them. The Boggs Act of 1951 compelled federal judges to give minimum jail sentences of two, five, or ten years, respectively, for first, second, and third offenses for possession; after the first offense, there was no parole, probation, or suspension. Legal devices that were granted to traitors or murderers were thus denied to drug addicts. When President Dwight D. Eisenhower signed the Narcotic Control Act of 1956 into law, penalties for heroin increased to ten, twenty, and forty years. Anyone over eighteen convicted of selling heroin to a minor could expect a minimum of ten years with a possible life sentence or even the death penalty upon recommendation of a jury; all discretion to suspend sentences or permit probation was eliminated. Thus, as heroin seized hold of Harlem and spread to other cities and more and more people found themselves desperately in need of help, policies were put into place that represented the most severe federal drug laws and penalties in American history.

"It was like a plague, and the plague usually afflicted the eldest child of every family, like the one of the firstborn with Pharoah's people in the Bible," recalled Claude Brown, author of *Manchild in the Promised Land*, the first book to document and portray the vast and shattering effects of heroin on the Harlem of his generation. "Sometimes it was even worse than the biblical plague. In Danny Rogers's family, it had everybody. There were four boys, and it had all of them. . . . It was as though drugs were a ghost, a big ghost, haunting the community."

People became afraid to go out in the streets. Multiple locks appeared on their doors, and pulling out any money on the street became a very dangerous thing to do. Fire escapes became desperate places of confrontation and violence as apartment dwellers encountered junkies trying to enter and sometimes sent them flying out of windows to their deaths. Worst of all was what was happening to families. Claude Brown remembered the fathers "picking up guns and saying, 'Now, look, if you fuck wit that rent money, I'm gon' kill you,' and they meant it. Cats were taking butcher knives and going at their fathers because they had to have money to get drugs."

The very context and connotation of dope had changed in only a few years. The use of heroin had gone from the neighborhood thing kids did to achieve "instant hipness" to something apocalyptic, something akin to a generational holocaust.

"The people in my parents' generation had known about heroin but it had never been a problem," Brown pointed out. "From 1950 on it wasn't considered dope anymore. It had an ominous connotation. If you had been born black and had come up in that southern black culture, when our parents talked about dope now it had an ominous ring like 'roots,' and I don't mean what Alex Haley wrote about. This roots was something else—what people did to you. It was like juju or voodoo. When people from the South talked about 'working roots' on you, it wrecked you for life. You came down with illnesses that doctors could not diagnose and there were no cures for. Well, the only thing worse than roots, was dope."

The ruthlessness and corruption of the police only increased commensurately with the levels of dope pouring into Harlem. Cops were shaking down dealers and junkies, being paid off by gangsters to look the other way or else to provide actual security for drug transactions, confiscating dope and reselling it on the streets, planting dope and setting people up for arrest, and using the testimonies of heroin-addicted informers and witnesses to make collars and convictions. The growing drug trade would make the Thirtieth Precinct in Harlem one of the most crooked in the United States, giving it the infamous name of "the Dirty Thirty." Consequently, as drugs spread to other black neighborhoods in New York and eventually to other communities in large cities during the late 1950s, there was an increasing tendency among African Americans to see a conspiratorial element of genocide in the whole paradigm of drugs. As African American communities grew more suspicious of all drug policies and their enforcement, these feelings of distrust and victimization were only compounded by the public treatment of drug addicts.

Only seven days before Billie Holiday's arrest, the office of Mayor Robert F. Wagner had announced a controversial new program to set up small detoxification units and allow addicts in city hospitals for the first time, in cooperation with medical schools, calling it a "milestone . . . endeavor to deal with the adult addict by means of modern, enlightened methods, recognizing that narcotics addiction presents a medical-psychiatric problem."

The proposed program may have been historic, but it was quite modest considering the magnitude of the problem, and Wagner had not gone down that progressive path of medicalization willingly. The new program was the result of years of intensive agitation by church-based neighborhood groups in Harlem like Reverend Norman Eddy's East Harlem Protestant Parish and Reverend Eugene Callender's Mid-Harlem Protestant Parish and several groups from other areas of the city that had organized themselves into the New York Neighborhoods Council on Narcotics Addiction (NYNCNA). These groups represented communities where for ten years people had witnessed a heroin epidemic raging in their communities, while all the city could think to do in response was to throw more and more people in jail.

Before 1951, the only city-supported treatment options were those located at the Women's House of Detention and Rikers Island Penitentiary for Men, neither of which accepted voluntary patients or young users. After a demonstration by a group of angry parents called the Bronx Committee for the Socio-Medical Treatment of Drug Addicts called on the city to establish a hospital, and after the state legislature passed measures calling for the civil commitment for at least ninety days for young drug addicts, Riverside Hospital was established on North Brother Island in 1951.

Riverside was a narcotics hospital for juveniles modeled after the US Public Health Service Narcotics Hospital in Lexington, Kentucky. It was small, detoxification lasted only five to seven days, the waiting list was endless, and the psychiatric staff was tiny. From the very beginning, the expectations for the hospital were ridiculously high—Governor Thomas Dewey and New York mayor Thomas Impellitteri had promised, incredibly, that the hospital would completely eradicate youthful narcotics addiction. The relapse rate was astronomical, but for the first time a community began to coalesce that included drug addicts, their families, doctors, psychiatrists, ministers, neighborhood activists, health-care workers, volunteers, social workers, social scientists, and criminal-justice experts. Over time, new debates and groundbreaking perspectives emerged out of this community about the nature and context of drug use and addiction, the psychology of recovery, and the role and ability of the state in treating and ending addiction. Nothing approaching a consensus emerged about what actually constituted rehabilitation—it meant different things to different groups—or about what treatments would best accomplish that goal, but as actual experience and information was lived and shared, all could agree on a few basic assumptions upon which to build.

The first and foremost theory was biomedical: that addiction was most usefully understood as a disease, and therefore was fundamentally a medical rather than a moral or criminal issue. This position held that addiction should fall exclusively under the authority of physicians, who should be allowed to treat addicts as they saw fit, up to and including the use of other narcotic substances, like methadone, on a maintenance basis.

The second belief was that treatment required not only psychiatric medicine but also basic counseling and attention to the fraying social and economic fabric of the community. Throughout the 1950s, the church-based neighborhood groups, moving back and forth between hospitals, homes, churches, schools, and workplaces, began to see the problems of drugs and addiction as inseparable from issues like jobs, housing, education, public health, and police integrity. The groups were supported in their views by a new breed of progressive drug sociologists, like Eva Rosenfeld, who urged the public to think of drug use in a social context and not simply as a moral weakness. The consensus approach called "socio-medical" redefined rehabilitation in terms of social reintegration, and this could only be accomplished by establishing a network of public and semipublic social services involving social work, legal aid, vocational assistance, psychological and group counseling, and medical treatment. As the East Harlem Protestant Parish expressed it, "The initial decision to use heroin may have been unwise, even immoral, but once an individual is an addict, his mind, body and soul are dependent upon the drug and he must have it unless he receives prolonged treatment which continues after his return to his home community and which involves multiple community resources."

The third basic supposition was that nothing would ever happen without forceful public advocacy. In May of 1956, after eight years of work in East Harlem, the East Harlem Protestant Parish declared that "we know that most of the problems dealt with here can only be solved effectively through political action." Over the years this grassroots political movement to change public drug policy in the city was shaped by the sensibilities of the growing civil rights movement as well as other strains of postwar urban liberalism, and as the problem worsened, the new politics of drug addiction and rehabilitation became ever more complex, tense, and volatile.

Since taking office in 1953, Mayor Robert F. Wagner had ignored the neighborhood organizations for as long as possible. As a conservative Democrat, these communities were not part of Wagner's natural political constituency and he was not at all receptive to their protests against the city's policies of criminalization and dramatic police action. Wagner dragged his heels even as the problem degenerated and the neighborhood movements grew and were supported by Ed Fancher and the *Village Voice,* and the issue started attracting the attention of people like Governor Nelson Rockefeller, Eleanor Roosevelt, judges like Morris Ploscowe and John Murtaugh, and newsmen like Mike Wallace. The neighborhood groups had been calling for a network of detoxification, residential therapy, and aftercare in the city's hospitals and jails since 1956, but Wagner saw them as an expensive option that would only empower his critics. Wagner's official position was that because there were so many factions and opinions, he wanted to be confident that "research" and a "cure" for addiction would be provided for in any program he supported. He did indicate a willingness, however, to at least study and consider the use of a pharmaceutical substitute for heroin like methadone in a program being developed at Rockefeller Institute by Dr. Marie Nyswander and Dr. Vincent Dole.

Things came to a head in 1958 when Wagner formed the Health Research Council (HRC) and the Mayor's Advisory Council on Narcotics

Addiction. No members of any of the religious organizations that came from the affected neighborhoods were included in any of these councils; and then, to make matters worse, Wagner announced the closing of Riverside Hospital. Because of its high rates of relapse, the Wagner administration determined that the hospital had failed to "cure" drug addiction—that is, to impose permanent drug abstinence, even though by this time a consensus had emerged within the Riverside community that relapse seemed to be a common part of the rehabilitation process.

In October of 1958, the NYNCNA sent a delegation that included Reverends Eddy and Callender to meet with William Peer, executive secretary to Mayor Wagner, but the results of the meeting were negligible because City Hall had already formulated its plans for 1959. When they realized that the mayor's plans did not provide for any of the kinds of psychiatric and social services that they had come to believe were essential for long-term rehabilitation, they escalated their campaign with prayer marches and submitted to the mayor's eight recommendations, which included the establishment of at least one medical clinic per borough for addicts and the provision of a certain number of beds at all city hospitals for those seeking detoxification. Then they marched on City Hall to deliver a letter that was signed by many of the city's leaders and alleged that people who been arrested and held at Rikers Island without proper detoxification had died of severe withdrawal symptoms. Wagner had no choice but to agree to meet with representatives of thirty-five churches, and with members of his own party on the City Council now vocally supporting medicalization—Earl Brown had threatened to open public hearings on the "health and social aspects of narcotics use"— Wagner finally relented. In June of 1959, only seven days before Billie Holiday was arrested on her hospital bed, he announced that addicts would be allowed to enter city hospitals for the first time.

But even this small measure was antithetical to the absolutist agenda of Harry Anslinger and the Federal Bureau of Narcotics, who believed, along with state officials, local members of the law enforcement community, a significant portion of the medical establishment, and conservative organizations, that drug addicts should be kept out of the hospitals at all costs because they would ruin them. Anslinger denounced the very concept of treatment for addicts because it would "elevate a most despicable trade to the status of an honorable business . . . and drug addicts would multiply unrestrained to the irrevocable impairment of the moral fibre and physical welfare of the American people." As they viewed it, Billie Holiday's arrest was an example of exactly the kind of thing that would happen if addicts were ever allowed as patients in the hospitals: they would smuggle drugs inside and corrupt the institution by their very presence. Those who vehemently opposed Wagner's program believed that society's laws should reflect its disapproval of the addict—and moreover, that society wasn't doing nearly enough to reflect that condemnation. The New York City police wanted a bill that would make it illegal for two addicts to congregate together anywhere in the city, for example. Police officials were presenting the bill as the most effective means of breaking up the uptown shooting galleries, but people like the Reverend Eugene Callender who had set up clinics in their churches to try and help addicts were worried that such a law might just as easily be used to control or break up the clinics and even criminalize the meetings of a group like the newly formed Narcotics Anonymous.

Callender himself was a passionate advocate for a humane policy of medicalization. His awareness of the issue began when he was the first African American minister in Rikers Island. As a true lover of jazz, Callender had been astonished to see so many of the artists he admired—J. J. Johnson, Walter Bishop, Ike Quebec—in jail. "Man," he thought, "I've got all of these guys on records at home, and here they are sitting in jail," and he wanted nothing more than to help them: "They were fantastic artists, but so many were tortured, exploited and broken by their demons, race-based oppression, and the mistreatment or misdiagnosis of their sickness."

Callender began to see that the way to help them was to "break through the negativity in their personalities and strengthen their self-esteem," and it was his time at Rikers and love of jazz that helped form "the blueprint for our clinic's success and for the transformation of attitudes toward the drug problem in New York City." As heroin seemed to take over Harlem, Callender saw his mission as serving "the drug-addicted, the homeless, and victims of the legal system." He turned the entire fifth floor of his church at the corner of Seventh

Avenue and 122nd Street into a detox clinic and started housing and legal clinics and began providing several other services.

Callender particularly loved and admired Billie Holiday, recognizing that she was "so gifted, but like so many other artists, she was haunted by some demon in her life that was only pacified by heroin." Even as her tragic image as a "drug-addicted woman with a fifth-grade education" grew, he saw her as royalty—"so unique that she cannot be completely defined by her color, gender, sparse education, or any other limits." When she was busted, Callender rushed to her bedside, and it was he who organized the protest with the signs from people in his parish and from the music scene: "Our protest for Billie was held to expedite her release so that she could be cared for with dignity."

To the protesters, the message of "Let Lady Live" was deeply personal and viscerally emotional. Many of them had drug addicts in their families and knew many others in their communities and had watched them suffer grievously. They had come to view the old policies as not simply repressive but barbaric. In their view, the timing of Lady's arrest, as well as the zealousness of the police and district attorney's office in prosecuting her, seemed unneccessary and particularly vindictive given the gravity of her condition—the epitome of a form of persecution. In a letter to the district attorney, Wilkes accused the police of treating Lady "as if she were a re-incarnation of Ma Barker (a gang leader of the 1930s), rather than one of the most gifted, brilliant and creative artists in the history of American music."

To the people carrying signs outside her window, it looked like Billie Holiday was literally being hounded to death by the police. As Callender and his committee declared in a press release, "The police have a function in this area. Let them halt the flow of narcotics into this country. Let then arrest the top echelon of importers and distributors of narcotics here. But unable or unwilling to do so they harass the ill and the defenseless, sabotage the Mayor's constructive and enlightened program and interfere with efforts by concerned community leaders."

With three police guards posted outside her door around the clock, the fate of Billie Holiday—Arrest Number 1660—was now embroiled in all of these issues, caught between Harry Anslinger's war on heroin and the new urban politics of rehabilitation.

4.

While the controversy erupted around her, Lady Day tried her best to carry on. According to Alice Vrbsky, her personal assistant, who was visiting her in the hospital, "She was bitter about the arrest, in the sense that it was the last thing she wanted at that point. They took everything away in the hospital, even the hope that she had." But at the same time, "she was still not in terrible spirits, even after she got arrested. She sort of reacted like, 'What do you expect?'"

Lady had her hair and her nails done; she broke the rules by asking for cigarettes and a beer and actually got permission for Dufty to go out and get her one, watching as the nurse poured it into a glass—"What kind of trained nurse are you, baby, if you can't pour a beer?"

The next day she tried and failed to get another one. What never left was her sardonic humor, her honesty, and her boldness. She was reading one of her own tabloid pre-obituaries titled "Billie Doomed" when she turned to one of the policewomen: "We're all doomed, baby, what the hell else is new?"

Another of those pre-obituaries, titled "Billie Holiday Is Dying of Dope Addiction and Alcoholism," reported, "Her voice is shot—cracked and eroded by the careless years of drug addiction, whiskey drinking and other malign influences." To which Lady said, "I've never had much of a voice to begin with, but I've got more today then I ever had"—and to prove it, she broke out into "Night and Day."

When she read another article about how whiskey and heroin had taken their toll and that she was on the verge of death, she commented that neither her mother or father had ever touched dope in their lives—"and neither lived to be as old as me. I've been on and off heroin for fifteen years. Who knows? Maybe heroin kept me alive."

When she read another report that quoted a psychiatrist she had never seen who pronounced her the self-destructive victim of a death urge, she laughed. "I'm not the suicide type. Never have been. Homicide, maybe, but not suicide!"

The comment about homicide may very well have been directed at her estranged husband, Louis McKay, who was hovering around her room like a carrion bird. Dufty would claim that Zaidans and McKay were trying to get him and Lady to sign over the rights to her book—"He couldn't wait for her to die." One day Dufty arrived to find Lady with her eyes closed and McKay at her bedside saying the Twenty-Third Psalm. He judiciously waited until McKay was gone before entering; then Lady opened her eyes and asked, "Is he gone? I've always been a religious bitch, but if that dirty motherfucker believes in God, I'm thinking it over."

Her health seemed stable—even improving—until doctors discovered a kidney infection even more serious than the original threat posed by the cirrhosis of the liver. Not surprisingly, different accounts of what really happened during the endgame have emerged. In the version formed by Dufty and advanced by biographer Donald Clarke, Joe Glaser brought in a doctor from Rockefeller Institute who recommended methadone, and it was administered for ten days, after which it was stopped because no hospital was allowed to legally maintain a patient on a narcotic for more than that amount of time. In this version Lady was addicted upon arrival at the hospital, was even putting on weight during the administration of the synthetic narcotic, and went downhill after it was stopped. In the counter version in which she was always clean, it was the stress of her arrest and pending arraignment that marked her turn for the worse. Indeed, some would even claim that her autopsy report showed no traces of narcotics whatsoever, although nobody who makes this assertion has ever stated that they've actually *read* the report.

Lady had signed a contract for a film based on her life and was making plans for a wardrobe conference. She was still talking about music and wanted to write a song called "Bless Your Bones" about FBN agent Jimmy Fletcher, who had so moved her by trying to visit her in the hospital, when her heart began to fail. She went into extremis for a period of about twenty-four hours. She was being bathed by nurses when they were astonished to discover a sum of cash on her person. It was money from an article that Dufty had written and that was published in *Confidential* as "I Needed Heroin to Live," given to her in cash so that it could be withheld from McKay. As Dufty relates what happened, "What she did, she wanted a piece of Scotch tape, because she rolled the bills tight, tight, tight, and she put a piece of Scotch tape around them to keep them from springing open, and it was up her vagina. Talk about a place to hide things. They didn't find it until an hour before she died."

And even the details of this story, now a part of Lady Day's legend, are wholly unreliable. Was the amount $1500? Or $750? Or $50? And was this tabloid lucre taped to her thigh or inserted in a more private location, as Dufty maintained? The only certainty is that some of Lady's last earthly thoughts were about this article and money. She was walking the tightrope between the law, her legend, and her addiction, to the very end.

After forty-seven days in the hospital, at around three o'clock in the morning on July 17, 1959, with "her face relaxed, in an incredible repose," it was all over for the Lady of the White Gardenias. Dufty, who was with her as she passed, along with a nurse, penned a touching obituary for the *New York Post*: "She was beautiful; no one who saw her exquisite brown head agaist the hospital white pillow would dare talk of her loveliness in bygone days."

He painted a portrait of a woman who was brave, regal, proud, and in the end triumphant—"For 15 years the government had paraded her through a whirligig of courts, jail, bail, as a horrible example of something called a drug addict; in the end she turned the tables on them."

But had she?

Billie Holiday died with seventy-five cents in her bank account. She also left us with over three hundred recorded songs that set the very standard for jazz singing—an invaluable treasure trove of work that deeply moved an entire generation of jazz lovers and changed American popular music forever—but you would never know it from the two-line obituary that ran in *Time*—

Died. Billie Holiday, 44, Negro blues singer, whose husky, melancholy voice reflected the tragedy of her own life; in Manhattan. Born of indigent teenagers, schooled in a Baltimore brothel, she stubbornly nursed her resentment, poured it out in songs that reached their height of popularity in the early '40s—Billie's Blues, The Man I Love, above all, Strange Fruit, a description of a Negro lynching in the South—succumbed to the dope addiction which dogged her to the end.

Of course, those who knew and loved her had a very different view, one much more in tune with the simple heartfelt eloquence of pianist Errol Garner's comment about her—

"She was like ice cream and cake."

5.

There was no white-light experience like Bill Wilson's in Towns Hospital for Ruby Rosano as she stood vigil outside the hospital, no great sense of peace and communion with a higher power like what had come over John Coltrane during his spiritual awakening. She was overcome with rage thinking about how Lady had been handcuffed and fingerprinted on her deathbed, but the anger gave way to the most unremitting kind of shame at the realization that Lady was up in that room fighting for her life as Ruby had tried to take her own life. It was a line from *Lady Sings the Blues* that came back to her at that moment: "If you beat the habit . . . no jail on earth can worry you too much." Was it even possible? She didn't know a single person who had, and that was when she started to panic, and what produced the terror was the sudden recognition that somehow there had to be more; this couldn't be all that there was to it. She couldn't die, and she knew that she couldn't die for the simple reason that she had never really lived.

This moment of clarity—the acknowledgment of the most basic human desire to live—was the closest thing to a spiritual awakening that Ruby would know. She had no idea how she was going to live, only that she would do anything possible. It was when Ruby began to fathom how much help she was going to need and that she had no idea where it would come from that she began to weep. She had no idea how long she stood there, sobbing convulsively. People in the street assumed she was crying for Lady, but she was really crying for all of the heroin addicts in the world.

In the end, nothing would do more to secure the implementation of the Wagner Program to allow addicts into the hospitals of the city than the death of Billie Holiday. If her deathbed arrest was intended to reflect society's "disapproval" of another addict, it also turned her into a martyr—one of the most dramatic and emotional symbols of its intolerance.

Ruby Rosano was among the second group of heroin addicts treated at Bernstein Hospital at 18th Street and Second Avenue, the first detoxification unit for adult drug addicts in the history of the city.

"That was quite an experience. In those days, the doctors believed whatever you told them. They were so ignorant that people said to me, 'When you go in, tell them that you were on any amount of drugs you want, because they will give you the equivalent in methadone.' So we all went in and lied, of course, and for the first week we were walking around stoned out of our skulls. We were medicated twice a day. We'd roll up our sleeves, get our injection, and stagger around the ward for hours, with legal highs the likes of which we would never know again. They were giving it to you intramuscularly. See, that was how we dope fiends educated the physicians. The detox was for thirty days, and they would keep you on intramuscular methadone for twenty-one days. On the twenty-second day, we all left—against all medical advice, of course. That's how they began to learn that addicts were as addicted to the needle as to the drug. Then they started realizing they had to give it to you orally. It was all new to everyone. They didn't understand addicts. They didn't realize that unless an addict like me was truly ready to stop, I would just find a way to keep getting high."

But something shifted, something fundamental changed in Ruby after that day outside Lady's hospital window and her first detox at Bernstein Hospital. She was now on a very different path. She would relapse and come back, relapse and come back again; it was a long hard road, but there came a day in 1962 when she was drug-free, and after that her life changed in ways she could never have imagined. Eventually Ruby became a resident expert in addiction counseling, joining the community that had emerged out of the now-closed Riverside Hospital. She found herself on the front lines of the struggle to deal with a whole new generation of addicts, immersed in the heat of the personalities, politics, and debates over the modalities of drug treatment as it developed to meet the challenge. All of it was new territory. She saw things she could scarcely have imagined in her days as a drug addict during the fifties. The "haircuts" of treatment communities like Daytop. Addicts with thirty-year-old habits. The spread of heroin to the middle-class suburbs. The institutionalization of methadone maintenance. The first application of acupuncture for heroin addiction. Debates over cross-addiction, disease models, trigger drugs, tough-love encounter groups, maturing out. Vietnam veteran heroin addicts suffering from post-traumatic stress disorder. The proliferation of the twelve-step fellowships.

As far as Ruby got from her last shot of dope or drink, she never forgot her days as a drunken, brawling, pill-popping, hope-to-die junkie whore. It was called "keeping it green" in the program. She would think about the little shooting gallery in the basement apartment on 116th Street back in the fifties. She would envision herself slouched against the wall with a needle in her arm as the nepenthe of dope coursed through her body, Charlie Parker with the saxophone in his mouth blowing his blues and Billie Holiday nodding with her in the back room. Ruby often thought about Lady and how Lady had died and she had lived, and wonder about why it had worked out that way. There were no easy answers, but of one thing she was certain. Above all else, addiction is a thief. It can rob those who suffer from it of family, friends, health, jobs, opportunities, resources, peace of mind, sometimes life itself. The elements and levels of the loss may vary, but nobody comes out unscathed. The part of Billie Holiday that was an addict was only one part, and certainly should never be the sole defining context through which we view her life, but it was her undoing. The recognition that she was a great artist—a musical genius—should never be superseded by the unfortunate personal consequences of her addiction, any more than her significance as a major figure in the story of addiction in America should be overlooked.

For Ruby Rosano, the elemental meaning of Billie Holiday was always very easy to articulate: "On any given day, there is never a doubt in my mind that she saved my life."

The End of the Beginning:
An Epilogue

1.

For the rest of the fifties and beyond, the journeys of musicians into and out of heroin continued to shape jazz, but never again to the degree they did in the period from 1947 to 1957. In 1959, Jackie McLean joined the cast of Jack Gelbar's groundbreaking play about heroin addiction at the Living Theatre, *The Connection*. McLean's brilliant performance as a heroin-addicted jazz musician in the production was completely authentic because every night there was virtually no transition as he stepped from street to stage. Every night he would wait for the dope man in the play exactly as he had waited for Shorty outside the Café Bohemia. He toured Europe with the play but eventually lost the appeal of his three-year-old narcotics conviction after his return and served time in prison.

McLean's life as an addict never changed until he met Dr. Marie Nyswander in the early 1960s. Dr. Nyswander had already worked with jazz musicians in her Musicians Clinic with the psychologist Charles Winick and was then developing the experimental program for addicts at Rockefeller Institute for Medical Research based on the use of methadone. McLean became a shining example of how a long-term addict could use the substance as a bridge back to a life of normalcy. Eventually he would work in the burgeoning methadone program as a counselor and wean himself from everything, but it would be twenty-five long years from the time of his first snort of heroin before he became completely drug-free.

Over time, McLean found himself increasingly discomfited by the portrayal of Charlie Parker and Billie Holiday and other jazz musicians of the time who were addicts as tragic figures. Similarly, critics like Stanley Crouch sought to reclaim these great artists by extolling their pure talent, elegance, and professionalism over the tabloid sensationalism that had defined them to the cultural mainstream. These concerns had only been compounded by myriad sensitivities about the whole relationship of jazz, race, and the cultural transmission of drugs in America. As Norman Mailer expressed it, "I felt that jazz and marijuana were one. I never thought of one without the other." Perhaps nothing romanticized this connection more than the Beat Generation. Over time, writers like Ishmael Reed would recognize in the Beats the same fascination for avant garde African American culture that white American and European artists had displayed for the primitive forms of other cultures since the turn of the century. "What was so interesting about Ginsberg and those guys was that they marketed this aesthetic to the American middle class," Reed commented. "There was a black connection to it but it was based on stereotypes: blacks as uninhibited, existential, living on the edge and all that. It was just another form of distortion, but you had to give them credit because at least they were reaching out for other cultural experiences, trying to understand and empathize, which was very rare in America, and they promoted more tolerant attitudes that impacted on the mainstream culture."

But even as writers and critics like Crouch and Reed and musicians like McLean might credit Kerouac and Ginsberg with opening the minds of young white Americans to an appreciation of jazz and African American culture, they also came to view depictions that largely focused on the addictions of artists like Bird and Billie Holiday as mere caricature. All have pointed out that the image of the tormented and tragic black junkie genius is a racial stereotype that can be as misleading, offensive, and one-dimensional as any other.

After becoming a professor of music at the University of Hartford in 1968, McLean and his wife, Dolly, opened the Artist's Collective at Albany Avenue and Woodland Street in 1970, in one of the worst parts of the city. On the day he first arrived to check out the run-down abandoned school building that they would renovate into the Collective, he couldn't help but see the name "Parker" on the door lock, and as he entered the dingy hallway, he felt the spirit of Bird there with him. The Collective was dedicated to preserving the art and culture of the African Diaspora; in place of litter, crime, crack, and broken bottles, it would offer music, theater, dance, and education. As Jackie McLean saw it, this was the true legacy of Charlie Parker. "It all comes from bebop," he said. "It's not just music, it's a movement."

2.

By the dawn of the sixties, there was more interest in drugs than ever before. As the writers of the Beat Generation were deeply influenced by the culture of jazz, so did they in turn spawn the counterculture of the 1960s and beyond. As the poet Gregory Corso remarked, "The hippies acted out what the Beats were writing about"—and the new counterculture embraced both the sacramental and recreational use of drugs as a central element.

Allen Ginsberg always saw the Beat Generation as a "decisive moment in American consciousness." As he fulfilled his destiny as an epic bard and became one of the most famous American poets of the twentieth century, he remained focused on drug use and how it could affect consciousness, creativity, and culture. He also remained a passionate advocate for changes in drug laws and policies. On a snowy December day in 1964, Ginsberg made good on his vow to challenge Harry Anslinger and the Marihuana Tax Act by appearing in Lower Manhattan with a small band of activists carrying signs that read "Pot Is Fun" and "Pot Is a Reality Kick." The group that Ginsberg formed with Ed Sanders was called LEMAR (for "Legalize Marijuana"), and it marked the beginning of the campaign to legalize marijuana in America. Fred McDarrah photographed Ginsberg wearing both signs. "A lot of people were paranoid," recollected Sanders, "but we felt it was a legitimate political position. . . . It quickly became a worldwide image—this bearded poet with a gleam in his eye, carrying these signs in the snow."

Ginsberg's *Howl* turned out to be only the first shot in a cultural war of values and attitudes about drugs and consciousness and sex and politics and art that would permeate and polarize American life for the next forty years. The peyote that had made its way into his life and the lives of others during the 1950s had initiated a small but growing number of people into an experience that burgeoned into an entire psychedelic movement. "This drug automatically seems to produce a mystic experience," Ginsberg wrote his father in May of 1959 after taking a new substance called lysergic acid diethylamide tartrate 25 at the Mental Research Institute in Palo Alto, embarking on a journey that would make him a cynosure of that movement. "Science is getting very hip."

Over the decades Allen Ginsberg watched his country change from a place where he was the only one smoking marijuana on the campus of Columbia in the 1940s to one where thirty million Americans were smoking it in the 1970s. "I was somewhat disappointed later on, when the counterculture developed the use of grass for party purposes rather than for study purposes," he reflected, making it clear that he never imagined the masses of stoner kids with their Doritos staring at television screens or getting wasted and going to the mall. "I always thought that was the wrong direction, that grass should be used for mindful attentiveness rather than for kicks—that's silly."

The uproar over the use of LSD and marijuana by the counterculture of the 1960s and the mass drug culture of the 1970s made the drugs of the Beat Generation seem like a quaint little donnybrook by comparison. Ginsberg witnessed the decriminalization of marijuana by ten states during the 1970s—the direct result of what he began on that snowy day in 1964—only to see it swept away by the coming of Ronald Reagan and his ever-escalating war on drugs during the 1980s. As Ginsberg sallied into the 1990s, he was convinced that "acid and rock and roll and blue jeans have helped to overturn the communist system, just like drugs during the Sixties liberated kids from the kind of narrow-minded mom-and-pop American chauvinism of the Vietnam War." And when it came to grass, he had this to say: "Everybody should try it at least once. Marijuana can be a very useful educational tool. It's as much a part of natural life as getting laid, having a homosexual experience, or going to Europe!"

Unfortunately, time would prove that a level of attrition was also a natural by-product of drug culture, and perhaps nobody would wrestle with the consequences and responsibility more honestly than Gary Snyder. In a 1959 essay called "Note on the Religious Tendencies," Snyder noted that "within the Beat Generation you find three things going on," identifying the first as "Vision and Illumination-seeking." "This is most easily done with systematic experimentation with narcotics. Marijuana is a daily stand-by and peyote is the real eye-opener. These are sometimes supplemented by dips into yoga technique, alcohol, and Subud." Snyder acknowledged that "a good deal of personal insight can be obtained by intelligent use of drugs," but warned that "being high all the time leads nowhere because it lacks intellect, will and compassion; and a personal drug kick is of no use to anyone else in the world." As Snyder later looked back at what happened in the 1960s from the vantage point of the late 1970s, he recognized that "in the 50s we really did have to protect, defend and nurture our freaks because they were valuable people. . . . Something else has happened in the meantime. . . . The Beats are responsible for plenty of freakouts. I don't know if it bothers anybody else but I take it into account. I mean I see it as my karma. . . . I've had people turn up at my door who are half insane, who told me that I had set them on their path. And I've had to deal with them, and it's not easy."

Neal Cassady, the very heartbeat of the Beat generation, was released from San Quentin on July 4, 1960, leaving prison without money or prospect of employment, heading to Palo Alto on the lookout for comely Stanford coeds. He greeted the new decade and added new dimensions to the ever-growing mythology of his life by seeking out Ken Kesey, the young author of a novel he had read in prison called *One Flew Over the Cuckoo's Nest,* which featured a rebel convict character named Randall P. McMurphy, whose wild and intractable life seemed as much an expression of Cassady's truth as Dean Moriarty. Trading one myth for another, he became the hammer-flipping, motor-mouthed Merry Prankster called Sir Speed Limit, who drove the legendary psychedelic bus Further on the 1964 cross-country odyssey that Tom Wolfe chronicled in *The Electric Kool-Aid Acid Test.* The man whom Kesey also called Fastestmanalive was found in February of 1968 naked and comatose along the railroad tracks between San Miguel de Allende and Celaya, Mexico, where he had dropped from pulque and a handful of Seconals consumed at a wedding bash.

"He often said to me that he really didn't want to be this hip hero; that being this hip hero was bugging him and causing him a lot of pain and suffering," observed the writer and poet Pierre Delattre, who was in San Miguel at the time of Cassady's death. "He didn't know how to get out of the role that everyone wanted him to play. It was noblesse oblige. In fact the last thing he said to me before the last time I saw him, he said, all I want to do is go back to working on the railroad. And that is what he actually ended up doing, is walking down the railroad tracks to his death."

Neal Cassady had lived and died by his myth, burning incandescently to his very last moments of consciousness, counting the railroad ties until he just wore out and dropped: "Sixty-four thousand nine hundred and twenty-eight," he said before dying in the hospital. It would be easy to see him as an example of the very kind of wreckage that Snyder was referring to, but his impact as a literary muse and a paragon of American freedom at a time when so many people were trying to break all kinds of barriers would turn him an enduring icon.

Cassady's spiritual brother on the road also never made it out of the 1960s.

Jack Kerouac never abandoned his love of jazz or his veneration for the African American culture that produced it, declaring in *Desolation Angels* that "the Negro people" would be "the salvation of America." The prolific body of work that he shaped as a result changed the very sound of American literature. "Someone handed me *Mexico City Blues* in St. Paul in 1959," Bob Dylan later told Allen Ginsberg, acknowledging that it was the first poetry he'd ever read that spoke his own American language. "It blew my mind."

By the beginning of the sixties, millions of young Americans had found awakenings in Kerouac's enraptured prose, uncovering what Joyce Johnson characterized as "that nagging secret itch they felt for a fuller, more meaningful, much freer life," which sent many of them "out in search of that elusive 'It' right in their own country." *The Dharma Bums* had all but predicted the hippies with its vision of "a great rucksack revolution." Kerouac could easily recognize the spiritual questing of these long-haired kids who claimed him as their cultural father, but as the decade progressed he had little use for them, especially as they demonstrated against the war in Vietnam.

Jack Kerouac accomplished what all great writers aspire to— "arriving at the voice that matched his vision," as Johnson puts it in her majestic biography, the aptly titled *The Voice Is All: The Lonely Victory of Jack Kerouac.* Kerouac's line from *On the Road* about the "mad ones" who " burn, burn, burn, like fabulous yellow roman candles exploding like spiders across the stars" became one of the most famous of twentieth-century American literature. In a single image he captured the ethos of the whole way of life personified by people like Charlie Parker and Billie Holiday, auguring an era of brilliant human supernovas and flameouts that followed, like Jimi Hendrix and Jim Morrison and Janis Joplin. It was also a prescient forecast of his own fate, as well as Cassady's. In 1952, Kerouac wrote that "at this time in my life I'm making myself sick to find the wild form that can grow with my wild heart" and he had done exactly that: found his wild form and in the process tragically made himself sick. At the end of his life he was drinking over a quart of Johnny Walker Red Label a day. He died puking blood into a toilet, the classic alcoholic's death of hemorrhaging esophageal varices, on October 19, 1969, in St. Petersburg, Florida. Make of it what you will—mere coincidence, fate, or karmic irony—but he died the same exact death as Lester Young, the man who had so changed his life by turning him on to marijuana in 1943.

The controversy of Prez's legacy of marijuana would never really go away. In 1988 a city council member in Lowell vehemently objected to the dedication of an eight-column granite memorial at Kerouac's gravesite. In the recriminatory atmosphere of the great "drug crisis" of that year, this particular Lowell city council member objected to the fact that Kerouac had been so involved in "substance abuse," a phrase that did not even enter the cultural vernacular for another thirty years after the publication of *On the Road.* One can hardly imagine such objections being raised to proposed memorials for, say, William Faulkner in Yoknapatawpha County, Mississippi, or Thomas Wolfe in Asheville, North Carolina, both of whom were notorious alcoholics, of course, but neither of whom ever smoked marijuana. Conservative columnist George Will also inveighed against the memorial, reproaching the "liberation from restraint" unleashed by the Beats, linking it to the AIDS and crack epidemics. It seemed that the "readily recognizable stigmata" of drug use and the culture war it unleashed followed Jack Kerouac past the grave, even as the park was established in his honor.

The dark legend of William Burroughs and his notorious novel, *Naked Lunch,* only grew after the American edition was published by

Grove Press on November 20, 1962, and detectives in Boston arrested Theodore Mavrikos, owner of a bookstore at 545 Washington Street, for selling an obscene book. Attorney Edward de Grazia took on the case and got the attorney general to agree that instead of proceeding with a trial against a single bookseller, the book itself would be put on trial. In the landmark obscenity case that followed, the book prevailed, and it has since been published in at least seventeen languages. No author was more embraced by America's underground avant-garde and counterculture, which acclaimed his novels as postmodernist masterpieces of deconstructionism and extolled Burroughs as a great visionary. The sixties generation viewed the novel exactly as Burroughs had intended—as "a frozen moment when everyone sees what is on the end of every fork." As Barry Miles notes, "If you wanted to be seen as cool in the early sixties, you had to have a copy of *Naked Lunch* casually displayed on your coffee table—preferably next to a big bowl of marijuana."

The influence of the novel extended far beyond literature, into popular culture. The notorious "Mugwumps," "heavy metal," and the dildo Burroughs called "Steely Dan" all found their way from the novel into the culture of pop music; Marianne Faithfull read the book and recognized that her destiny was to shoot heroin as she tried to live her life "by William Burroughs's rules." As Kerouac put his stamp on the fifties and Ginsberg marked the sixties as a major cultural and political figure, the seventies, eighties, and nineties became the period of Burroughs's greatest influence, when he was claimed as an inspiration by Patti Smith, Gus Van Sant, and the cyberpunks of the nineties.

At the same time, no author has been more damned by America's puritan moralists, who reviled the book as the violent and perverse rantings of a scabrous homosexual junkie. Of course, Burroughs didn't give a damn about any of it. In an age when drug addicts like him were supposed to self-destruct spectacularly on some public stage, or else apologize, perhaps William Burroughs's greatest sin was the fact of his survival, for not only did Burroughs survive, he lived and continued to write to a ripe old age, forever unredeemed, leaving as his legacy a book that begins with the following deposition: "I awoke from the Sickness at the age of forty-five, calm and sane, and in reasonably good health except for a weakened liver and the look of borrowed flesh common to all who survive the Sickness."

3.

By the the time *Naked Lunch* was published in America in 1962, cracks were already starting to appear in Harry J. Anslinger's reputation along with challenges to his policies. That year, the Supreme Court declared addiction to be a disease and not a crime, and judges, prosecutors, the Federal Bureau of Prisons, and the American Psychiatric Association became increasingly critical of the harsh mandatory penalities of Anslinger's regime. He was seventy years old—the mandatory retirement age for a federal employee—when he submitted his resignation in July of that year. It remains unclear whether Anslinger retired voluntarily or was pressured by the administration of John F. Kennedy to step down. Attorney Rufus King claimed that the Kennedys detested him; White House press secretary Pierre Salinger stated, "It was Mr. Anslinger's wish to retire."

For thirty-two years Anslinger had been an omnipresent and virtually omnipotent figure in the world of illicit drugs. Although his old bombastic newsreel style was becoming passé and would soon become the object of scorn, the shadow he cast was long and commanding, and continues to the present day. The moral panic and press sensationalism of his antimarijuana campaign, along with his penchant for playing fast and loose with the facts about drugs in America, established the template for all of the drug hysterias that followed. It was Anslinger who first institutionalized the entire ideology of drug prohibitionism that launched our drug war. The laws he orchestrated and championed, like the Boggs Act of 1951 and the Narcotic Control Act of 1956, became the precedents for the harsh sentencing guidelines in draconian pieces of legislation like the Rockefeller laws in New York and the Anti–Drug Abuse Act of 1986. Anslinger set the mold for the drug warriors of the eighties like William Bennett who became known for high moral dudgeon and an apocalyptic vision of how drugs would be the ruin of American civilization as they presided over the greatest escalation of the drug war in American history. Likewise, it was the racial component of Anslinger's wars on marijuana and heroin that marked the beginning of the institutionalization of racism in the drug war. It's hard to imagine that the crack statutes of the 1980s or the aggressive stop, frisk, and search practices in minority communities since, could have ever have been possible without Harry Anslinger. Therefore any real understanding of how and why America today finds itself with the largest prison population in the world with its gross racial disparities must begin with this single man—the nation's very first drug czar. Any true and fundamental drug reform will always run headlong into the foundational structures and views that Anslinger put in place.

Moreover, by overtly targeting African Americans, Mexicans, and jazz musicians in his crusade, Anslinger also created the very context for the culture war over drugs, and it is here that his legacy becomes truly scrambled by the ironies of history. As he spent his retirement years in Hollidaysburg, Pennsylvania, taking his daily three-block walk downtown to pick up his mail at the post office, stopping at Lusardi's Luncheonette for a cup of coffee and conversation with townspeople, Anslinger was increasingly befuddled and infuriated by the baby boom generation's romance with the evil weed and LSD. He railed against the drug revolution, blaming it on "permissive parents, college administrators, pusillanimous judiciary officials, do-gooder bleeding hearts and new-breed sociologists with their fluid notions of morality"—words that just as easily could have come out of the mouths of Drug Czar William Bennett or Attorney General Ed Meese in the 1980s.

As Anslinger surveyed the world of the 1960s from the quaintness and quietude of small-town Hollidaysburg, he saw drugs as "nothing less than an assault on the foundations of Western civilization." The spectacle of Haight-Ashbury was particularly mortifying to him—"The only persons who frighten me are the hippies"—as were the mounting voices for marijuana legalization: "To legalize marijuana would be to legalize slaughter on the highway."

Thanks to Anslinger, sale of marijuana to a minor in Georgia during the 1960s was punishable by life imprisonment, even if it was a first offense. In Alabama, a judge was required to sentence the possessor of one joint to not less than five years. Given the severity of these laws, it isn't hard to understand why the man who wanted to save America from drugs was utterly flummoxed that the campuses of America were chockablock with young Americans who were smoking pot and laughing at *Reefer Madness*—kids who had grown up hearing about how marijuana was an inevitable stepping-stone to heroin, smoked it, and when they realized that they were not turning into heroin addicts, only felt empowered to smoke more.

In 1968, one of Harry Anslinger's successors, John Finlator of the Bureau of Narcotic and Dangerous Drugs, reported hearing a certain chant becoming familiar on college campuses across America—

Anslinger, Anslinger
Creator of farces
Anslinger, Anslinger
Kiss our arses!

Acknowledgments

Much of the research and interviewing for this book was done in the early nineties, as I prepared my last book, *Can't Find My Way Home*, which contained a chapter on the bebop era and the Beat Generation called "Bop Apocalypse." I was so fascinated by that period and had done so much research and writing on it but had only been able to use a fraction of the material at the time. I'd always wanted to publish a book-length version of that chapter that went all the way back to the early twentieth century and the roots of jazz, fleshed out with a much more complete cast of characters. This, at long last, is that book.

The following people were kind enough to sit for interviews; in the decades since quite a few of them have passed on. I shall always be indebted to Michael Aldrich, the Rev. James Allen and Sonny Wright of the Addicts Rehabilitation Center of Harlem, Al Aronowitz, Peter Berg, Bernard Brightman, Claude Brown, Peter Coyote, Gregory Corso, Stanley Crouch, Diane di Prima, Gary Giddins, Dizzy Gillespie, Herbert Huncke, Joyce Johnson, Orrin Keepnews, Michael McClure, Lewis Merenstein, Dr. John P. Morgan, Edie Kerouac-Parker, David Rattray, John Rechy, Ishmael Reed, Larry Rivers, Paul Rothchild, Ed Sanders, Hubert Selby Jr., Terry Southern, Robert Stone, and Anne Waldman.

I owe a special debt of gratitude to poet Allen Ginsberg and the great saxophonist Jackie McLean. Both were extremely generous with their time and suggestions and went out of their way to bring this period to life for me. This book could not have been done without them.

As a baby boomer coming of age during the mid to late 1960s, I did not come to the pleasures of jazz until I was well into my twenties, during the 1970s. While students at some of my speaking engagements have expressed envy at my having seen such legendary artists as Jimi Hendrix perform, I have come to feel exactly that way about those lucky enough to have seen Bird at the Royal Roost, Miles at the Café Bohemia, or Monk at the Five Spot. But alas, I was not yet born, or a baby in diapers, or a mere toddler while such events were taking place. Jazz writers are a deeply passionate and opinionated lot. Many of them who have written so eloquently and insightfully over the years about the music and culture have served as my true guides and educators. I must therefore acknowledge the work of Donald Clarke, Stanley Crouch, Gary Giddins, Ira Gitler, Ted Gioia, Nat Hentoff, Dan Morgenstern, John Szwed, Sam Charters, Terry Teachout, Ralph J. Gleason, Martin Williams, Whitney Balliett, Eric Nisenson, Albert Murray, Robert O'Mealley, Lewis Porter, Farah Jasmine Griffin, Nate Chinen, and Ben Ratliff. Also, the jazz writing of Ralph Ellison, John Clellon Holmes, and Jack Kerouac.

Likewise, many of those who have written and spoken authoritatively about the Beat Generation have also been instrumental in my understanding of it. I am indebted to Ann Charters, Diane di Prima, Gregory Corso, Michael McClure, Gary Snyder, Lawrence Ferlinghetti, Joyce Johnson, John Tytell, Barry Miles, Ted Morgan, Bill Morgan, Carolyn Cassady, John Clellon Holmes, Michael Schumacher, Ed Sanders, Gerald Nicosia, and Dennis McNally.

There are a few excellent histories of marijuana, but I must single out Larry Sloman's *Reefer Madness*, as it was particularly indispensable for this project.

Thanks also to Steven Saporta for making many valuable suggestions, and special thanks to Jeff Levenson for opening so many doors when I began this journey. I'm also grateful to Mary Skafidas for her encouragement, and to Jeffrey Livingston for his time and insight.

The late Dr. John P. Morgan was both immensely knowledgeable about drugs and drug policy as well as a great aficionado of jazz—the perfect person to talk to about this subject. Also, thanks to the always invaluable Ethan Nadelmann of the Drug Policy Alliance.

My old friend Alison Rigney at the Everett Collection was tremendously helpful and generous with photographs, as was Peter Hale of the Allen Ginsberg Estate.

My longtime agent and friend, Russell Galen, never ceases to encourage my literary aspirations—I'm always grateful for his counsel, and for his efforts on my behalf.

Heartfelt thanks to Ben Schafer, my editor at Da Capo Press. When he acquired this book he said that he doubted I would ever find a more sympathetic editor for this book. How right he was.

And finally, a shout-out to my wife, Laura Last, and to my son, William. They are the lights of my life. Living with a writer is no easy task, especially in this day and age. My greatest sustenance is always their love, support, and understanding.

Bibliography

Acker, Caroline Jean. *Creating the American Junkie: Addiction Research in the Classic Era of Narcotic Control.* Baltimore, MD: Johns Hopkins University Press, 2006.

Albert, Richard N. *From Blues to Bop: A Collection of Jazz Fiction.* New York: Anchor Books, 1992.

Albertson, Chris. *Bessie.* New Haven, CT: Yale University Press, 2003.

Alexander, Bruce K. *The Globalization of Addiction: A Study in the Poverty of the Spirit.* New York: Oxford University Press, 2008.

Alexander, Michael. *Jazz Age Jews.* Princeton, NJ: Princeton University Press, 2001.

Alexander, Michelle. *The New Jim Crow.* New York: New Press, 2010.

Algren, Nelson. *The Man with the Golden Arm.* 1949. New York: Four Walls Eight Windows, 1990.

Amburn, Ellis. *Subterranean Kerouac: The Hidden Life of Jack Kerouac.* New York: St. Martin's, 1998.

Amram, David. *Vibrations: The Adventures and Musical Times of David Amram.* New York: Macmillan, 1968.

Anderson, Jervis. *This Was Harlem: A Cultural Portrait, 1900–1950.* New York: Farrar, Straus and Giroux, 1982.

Ansell, Derek. *Sugar Free Saxophone: The Life and Music of Jackie McLean.* London: Northway Books, 2012.

Ansen, Alan. *William Burroughs.* Sudbury, CT: Water Row, 1986.

Anslinger, Harry J. *The Murderers: The Shocking Story of the Narcotics Gang.* New York: Garden City Press, 1962.

———. *The Protectors: Our Battle Against the Crime Gangs.* New York: Farrar, Straus and Giroux, 1966.

Anslinger, Harry, and William F. Tomkins. *The Traffic in Narcotics.* New York: Funk and Wagnalls, 1953.

Armstrong, Louis. *Louis Armstrong in His Own Words.* Edited by Thomas Brothers. New York: Oxford University Press, 1999.

———. *Satchmo: My Life in New Orleans,* Boston: Da Capo Press, 1986.

Aronowitz, Al. *Bob Dylan and the Beatles.* Bloomington, IN: 1st Books Library, 2003.

Artaud, Antonin. *The Peyote Dance.* New York: Farrar, Straus, and Giroux, 1976.

Baker, Charles E., Jr. *Physicians' Desk Reference.* Oradell, NJ: Medical Economics, 1982.

Baker, Chet. *As Though I Had Wings.* New York: St. Martin's, 1997.

Balliett, Whitney. *American Musicians: 56 Portraits in Jazz.* New York: Oxford University Press, 1986.

Baraka, Amiri. *The Autobiography of Leroi Jones.* New York: Freundlich, 1984.

Basie, Count, with Albert Murray. *Good Morning Blues: The Autobiography of Count Basie.* New York: Da Capo Press, 2002.

Baudelaire, Charles. *The Poem of Hashish.* 1850. Trans. Sallie Sullivan. New York: Harper & Row, 1971.

The Beatles. *The Beatles Anthology.* San Francisco: Chronicle Books, 2000.

Beaulieu, Victor-Lévy. *Jack Kerouac: A Chicken Essay.* Translated by Sheila Fischman. Toronto: Coach House Press, 1979.

Bechet, Sidney. *Treat It Gentle: An Autobiography.* London: Cassett & Co., 1960.

Becker, Howard. *Outsiders: Studies in the Sociology of Deviance.* New York: Free Press, 1963.

Black, Jack. *You Can't Win.* 1926. Kukukuihaele, HI: Omnium, 1992.

Blackburn, Julia. *With Billie: A New Look at the Unforgettable Lady Day.* New York: Vintage, 2005.

Blank, A. R. *My Darling Killer: How Lucien Carr Introduced Jack Kerouac, Allen Ginsberg & William Burroughs, Killed David Kammerer, and Shaped the Beat Generation.* CreateSpace Independent Publishing Platform, 2013.

Blesh, Rudi. *They All Played Ragtime.* New York: Oak Publications, 1974.

———. *Shining Trumpets: A History of Jazz.* New York: Da Capo Press, 1980.

Bockris, Victor. *With William Burroughs: A Report from the Bunker.* New York: Seaver Books, 1981.

Bonnie, Richard J., and Charles H. Whitebread II. *The Marijuana Conviction: A History of Marijuana Prohibition in the United States.* Charlottesville, VA: University of Virginia Press, 1974.

Boon, Marcus. *The Road to Excess: A History of Writers on Drugs.* Boston: Harvard University Press, 2002.

Booth, Martin. *Cannabis: A History.* New York: St. Martin's, 2003.

Boujut, Louis. *Louis Armstrong.* New York: Rizzoli International, 1998.

Brecher, Edward M., and the Editors of Consumer Reports. *Licit and Illicit Drugs.* Boston: Little Brown, 1972.

Brothers, Thomas. *Louis Armstrong's New Orleans.* New York: W. W. Norton, 2006.

Brown, Claude. *Manchild in the Promised Land.* New York: Signet/New American Library, 1965.

Brown, Peter, and Steven Gaines. *The Love You Make.* New York: Signet Books, 1984.

Bruce, Lenny. *The Essential Lenny Bruce.* Edited by John Cohen. New York: Random House, 1967.

Büchmann-Møller, Frank. *You Just Fight for Your Life: The Story of Lester Young.* New York: Praeger, 1990.

Burns, Glen. *Great Poets Howl: A Study of Allen Ginsberg's Poetry, 1943–1955.* New York: Peter Lang, 1983.

Burns, Jim. *Radicals, Beats, and Beboppers.* n.p.: Penniless Press Publications, 2011.

Burroughs, William S. *The Adding Machine: Selected Essays.* New York: Seaver, 1986.

———. *The Burroughs File.* San Francisco: City Lights, 1984.

———. *Exterminator!* New York: Viking Press, 1973.

———. *Interzone.* New York: Viking Press, 1989.

———. *The Job.* New York: Grove Press, 1972.

———. *Junky.* New York: Ace Books, 1953.

———. *Junky: The Definitive Text of "Junk."* London: Penquin, 2003.

———. *The Letters of William S. Burroughs, 1945–1959.* Edited by Oliver Harris. New York: Viking Press, 1993.

————. *Letters to Allen Ginsberg.* New York: Full Court Press, 1982.

————. *My Education: A Book of Dreams.* New York: Viking/Penguin, 1998.

————. *Naked Lunch.* New York: Grove Press, 1962.

————. *Queer.* New York: Viking Press, 1985.

————. *Roosevelt After Inauguration.* San Francisco: City Lights, 1979.

Burroughs, William S., and Jack Kerouac. *And the Hippos Were Boiled in Their Tanks.* New York: Grove Press, 1999 (reprint edition).

Bushnell, Garvin. *Jazz from the Beginning.* New York: Da Capo Press: 1998.

Callender, Reverend Eugene S. *Nobody Is a Nobody: The Story of a Harlem Ministry Hard at Work to Change America.* New York: CreateSpace Independent Publishing Platform, 2012.

Calloway, Cab. *The New Cab Calloway's Hepster's Dictionary: The Language of Jive.* New York: C. Calloway, 1944.

Campbell, James. *This Is the Beat Generation.* London: Seeker & Warburg, 1999.

Campbell, Nancy J., J. P. Olsen, and Luke Walden. *The Narcotic Farm: The Rise and Fall of America's First Prison for Drug Addicts.* New York: Abrams, 2008.

Carr, Ian. *Miles Davis: A Biography.* New York: Morrow, 1982.

Carr, Roy, Brian Case, and Fred Deller. *The Hip: Hipsters, Jazz, and the Beat Generation.* London: Faber and Faber, 1986.

Cassady, Carolyn. *Heart Beat: My Life with Jack and Neal.* Berkeley, CA: Creative Arts Books, 1976.

————. *Off the Road: My Years with Cassady, Keoruac, and Ginsberg.* New York: Morrow, 1990.

Cassady, Neal. *Grace Beats Karma: Letters from Prison, 1958–1960.* New York: Blast Books, 1999.

————. *The First Third.* 1971. San Francisco: City Lights, 1981.

Caveney, Graham. *The "Priest" They Called Him: The Life and Legacy of William S. Burroughs.* London: Bloomsbury, 1998.

Chambers, Jack. *Milestones 1: The Music and Times of Miles Davis to 1960.* New York: Beech Tree Books, 1983.

————. *Milestones 2: The Music and Times of Miles Davis Since 1960.* New York: Beech Tree Books, 1983.

Charters, Ann. *Beats and Company.* New York: Doubleday, 1986.

————. *Beat Down to Your Soul.* New York: Penguin, 2001.

————. *A Bibliography of Work by Jack Kerouac.* New York: Phoenix Bookshop, 1967.

————. *Kerouac: A Biography.* San Francisco: Straight Arrow, 1973.

————, ed. *The Portable Beat Reader.* New York: Penguin, 1992.

————, ed. *The Portable Kerouac.* New York: Viking, 1995.

Charters, Ann, and Samuel Charters. *Brother Souls: John Clellon Holmes, Jack Kerouac and the Beat Generation.* Jackson, MS: University Press of Mississippi, 2010.

Charters, Samuel. *Jazz: A History of the New York Scene.* New York, Da Capo Press, 1996.

————. *A Trumpet Around the Corner: The Story of New Orleans Jazz.* Jackson, MS: University of Mississippi Press, 2008.

Chilton, John. *Billie's Blues.* New York: Quartet Books, 1975.

————. *The Song of the Hawk: The Life and Recordings of Coleman Hawkins.* Ann Arbor, MI: University of Michigan Press, 1990.

Clarke, Donald. *Wishing on the Moon: The Life and Times of Billie Holiday.* New York: Viking Press, 1994.

Cohen, Harvey G. *Duke Ellington's America.* Chicago: University of Illinois Press, 2010.

Cole, Bill. *John Coltrane.* New York: Schirmer, 1976.

———. *Miles Davis: The Early Years.* New York: Da Capo Press, 1994.

Collier, James Lincoln. *Benny Goodman and the Swing Era.* New York: Oxford University Press, 1989.

———. *Louis Armstrong: An American Genius.* New York: Oxford University Press, 1983.

Cook, Bruce. *The Beat Generation.* New York: Charles Scribner's Sons, 1971.

Corso, Gregory. *Elegiac Feelings American.* New York: New Directions, 1970.

———. *Gasoline.* San Francisco: City Lights, 1958.

Courtwright, David T. *Addicts Who Survived: An Oral History of Narcotic Use in America, 1923–1965.* Knoxville, TN: University of Tennessee Press, 1989.

———. *Dark Paradise: Opiate Addiction in America Before 1940.* Cambridge, MA: Harvard University Press, 1982.

———. *Forces of Habit: Drugs and the Making of the Modern World.* Cambridge, MA: Harvard University Press, 2001.

Crouch, Stanley. *Considering Genius: Writings on Jazz.* New York: Basic Civitas, 2007.

———. *Kansas City Lightning: The Rise and Times of Charlie Parker.* New York: HarperCollins Publishers, 2013.

Dahl, Linda. *Stormy Weather: The Music and Lives of a Century of Jazzwomen.* New York: Pantheon, 1984.

Daniels, Douglas Henry. *Lester Leaps In.* Boston: Beacon Press, 2002.

Darnowsky, M., B. Epstein, and R. Flacks, eds. *Cultural Politics and Social Movements.* Philadelphia: Temple University Press, 1995.

Davenport-Hines, Richard. *The Pursuit of Oblivion: A Global History of Narcotics.* New York: W. W. Norton, 2002.

Davis, Francis. *Bebop and Nothingness: Jazz and Pop at the End of the Century.* New York: Simon & Schuster, 1996.

Davis, Miles, with Quincy Troupe. *Miles: The Autobiography of Miles Davis.* New York: Touchstone Books, 1989.

de Grazia, Edward. *Girls Lean Back Everywhere: The Law of Obscenity and the Assault on Genius.* New York: Random House, 1992.

De Ropp, Robert S. *Drugs and the Mind.* New York: Grove Press, 1961.

DeVeaux, Scott. *The Birth of Bebop: A Social and Musical History.* Berkeley, CA: University of California Press, 1997.

DeVito, Chris, ed. *Coltrane on Coltrane: The John Coltrane Interviews.* Chicago: Chicago Review Press, 2010.

Dexter, Dave. *Jazz Cavalcade: The Inside Story of Jazz.* Whitefish, MN: Literary Licensing, 2011.

di Prima, Diane. *Memoirs of a Beatnik.* New York: Olympia Press, 1969.

———. *Recollections of My Life as a Woman.* New York: Penguin Books, 2001.

———. *Revolutionary Letters.* San Francisco: City Lights, 1971.

Driggs, Frank, and Chuck Haddix. *Kansas City Jazz: From Ragtime to Bebop—A History.* New York: Oxford University Press, 2005.

Du Bois, W. E. B. *The Souls of Black Folk.* Mineola, NY: Dover Publications, 1994.

Duke, Steven B., and Albert C. Gross. *America's Longest War.* New York: G. P. Putnam's Sons, 1993.

Duster, Troy. *The Legislation of Morality: Law, Drugs and Moral Judgment.* New York: Free Press, 1970.

Ebin, David. *The Drug Experience.* New York: Grove Press, 1961.

Elkholy, Sharin N., ed. *The Philosophy of the Beats.* Lexington, KY: University Press of Kentucky, 2012.

Ellington, Duke. *Music Is My Mistress.* Garden City, NY: Doubleday, 1973.

Ellison, Ralph. *The Invisible Man.* New York: Vintage, 1989.

———. *Living with Music: Ralph Ellison's Jazz Writings.* Edited by Robert O'Meally. New York: Alfred A. Knopf, 2002.

———. *Shadow and Act.* New York: Random House, 1965.

Epstein, Edward Jay. *Agency of Fear: Opiates and Political Power in America.* New York: Verso Books, 1990.

Escohotado, Antonio. *A Brief History of Drugs: From the Stone Age to the Stoned Age.* South Paris, ME: Park Street Press, 1993.

Feather, Leonard. *Encyclopedia of Jazz,* revised edition. New York: Bonanza, 1960.

———. *Encyclopedia of Jazz in the Sixties.* New York: Bonanza, 1966.

———. *From Satchmo to Miles.* London: Quartet, 1974.

Feather, Leonard, and Ira Gitler. *Encyclopedia of Jazz in the Seventies.* New York: Horizon, 1976.

Finlator, John. *The Drugged Nation.* New York: Simon & Schuster, 1973.

Fletcher, Tom. *100 Years of the Negro in Show Business.* New York: Da Capo Press, 1984.

Friedwald, Will. *Jazz Singing.* New York: Scribner, 1990.

Gahlinger, Paul. *Illegal Drugs: A Complete Guide to Their History, Chemistry, Use, and Abuse.* Yucca Valley, CA: Sagebrush Press, 2001.

García-Robles, Jorge. *At the End of the Road: Jack Kerouac in Mexico.* Minneapolis, MN: University of Minnesota Press, 2014.

———. *The Stray Bullet: William S. Burroughs in Mexico.* Minneapolis, MN: University of Minnesota Press, 2013.

Gelly, Dave. *Being Prez: The Life and Music of Lester Young.* New York: Oxford University Press, 2007.

George-Warren, Holly. *The Rolling Stone Book of the Beats: The Beat Generation and American Culture.* New York: Hyperion, 1999.

Gertz, Stephen. *Dope Menace: The Sensational World of Drug Paperbacks, 1900–1975.* Los Angeles: Feral House, 2008.

Giddins, Gary. *Celebrating Bird: The Triumph of Charlie Parker.* New York: Birch Tree Books, 1987.

———. *Rhythm-a-ning: Jazz Tradition and Innovation.* New York: Oxford University Press, 1981.

———. *Riding on a Blue Note: Jazz and American Pop.* New York: Da Capo Press, 2000.

———. *Satchmo: The Genius of Louis Armstrong.* New York: Doubleday, 1988.

———. *Visions of Jazz: The First Century.* New York: Oxford University Press, 1998.

Giddins, Gary, and Scott DeVeaux. *Jazz.* New York: W. W. Norton, 2009.

Gifford, Barry. *Kerouac's Town.* Berkeley, CA: Creative Arts Books, 1977.

Gifford, Barry, and Lawrence Lee. *Jack's Book.* New York: St. Martin's, 1978.

Gillespie, Dizzy, with Al Fraser. *To Be or Not to Bop.* New York: Doubleday, 1979.

Ginsberg, Allen. *Allen Verbatim: Lectures on Poetry, Politics, Consciousness by Allen Ginsberg.* Edited by Gordon Ball. New York: McGraw-Hill, 1975.

———. *Collected Poems, 1947–1980.* New York: Harper & Row, 1984.

———. *Howl and Other Poems.* San Francisco: City Lights, 1956.

———. *Howl: Original Draft Facsimile, Transcript and Variant Versions.* Edited by Barry Miles. New York: Harper & Row, 1986.

———. *Journals: Early Fifties, Early Sixties.* Edited by Gordon Ball. New York: Grove Press, 1977.

———. *Snapshot Poetics: Allen Ginsberg's Photographic Memoir of the Beat Era.* San Francisco: Chronicle Books, 1993.

Ginsberg, Allen, and William S. Burroughs. *The Yage Letters.* San Francisco: City Lights, 1956.

Ginsberg, Allen, and Neal Cassady. *As Ever: The Collected Correspondence.* Edited by Barry Gifford. Berkeley, CA: Creative Arts Books, 1997.

Gioia, Ted. *The Birth (and Death) of the Cool.* Golden, CO: Speck Press, 2009.

———. *The History of Jazz.* New York: Oxford University Press, 2011.

———. *The Imperfect Art: Reflections on Jazz and Modern Culture.* New York: Oxford University Press, 1988.

———. *West Coast Jazz.* Berkeley, CA: University of California Press, 1998.

Gitler, Ira. *Jazz Masters of the Forties.* New York: Macmillan, 1966.

———. *Swing to Bop: An Oral History of the Transition in Jazz in the 1940s.* New York: Oxford University Press, 1985.

Gleason, Ralph J. *Celebrating the Duke . . . and Other Heroes.* Boston: Little, Brown, 1975.

Goffman, Ken, and Dan Joy. *Counterculture Through the Ages: From Abraham to Acid House.* New York: Villard, 2004.

Gold, Herbert. *Bohemia.* New York: Simon & Schuster, 1993.

Goldberg, Joe. *Jazz Masters of the Fifties.* New York: Macmillan, 1956.

Gourse, Leslie. *Louis' Children: American Jazz Singers.* New York: William Morrow, 1984.

Grace, Nancy, and Ronna Johnson. *Girls Who Wore Black: Women Writing the Beat Generation.* Piscataway, NJ: Rutgers University Press, 2002.

Green, Michelle. *The Dream and the End of the World: Paul Bowles and the Literary Renegades in Tangier.* London: Bloomsbury, 1992.

Griffin, Farah Jasmine. *In Search of Billie Holiday: If You Can't Be Free, Be a Mystery.* New York: Random House, 2001.

Grinspoon, Lester, and James B. Bakalar. *Marijuana: The Forbidden Medicine.* New Haven, CT: Yale University Press, 1993.

———. *Drug Control in a Free Society.* New York: Cambridge University Press, 1984.

Hadlock, Richard. *Jazz Masters of the Twenties.* New York: Macmillan, 1965.

Halberstam, David. *The Fifties.* New York: Villard, 1993.

Hammond, John, with Irving Townsend. *John Hammond on Record: An Autobiography.* New York: Penguin Books, 1977.

Hari, Johann. *Chasing the Scream: The First and Last Days of the War on Drugs.* New York: Bloomsbury, 2015.

Harris, Oliver. *William Burroughs and the Secret of Fascination.* Carbondale, IL: Southern Illinois University Press, 2003.

Harris, Oliver, and Ian MacFadyen, eds. *Naked Lunch @ 50: Anniversary Essays.* Carbondale, IL: Southern Illinois University Press, 2009.

Hawes, Hampton, and Don Asher. *Raise Up Off Me.* New York: Coward, McCann and Geohegan, 1974.

Hayes, Kevin J. *Conversations with Jack Kerouac.* Oxford, MS: University Press of Mississippi, 2005.

Helmer, John. *Drugs and Minority Oppression.* New York: Seabury Press, 1975.

Hentoff, Nat. *At the Jazz Band Ball.* Berkeley, CA: University of California Press, 2010.

———. *Jazz Is.* New York: Random House, 1976.

———. *The Jazz Life.* New York: Da Capo Press, 1961.

Hentoff, Nat, with Nat Shapiro. *Hear Me Talkin' to Ya.* New York: Dover, 1955.

Herrer, Jack. *The Emperor Wears No Clothes.* Seattle, WA: Queen of Clubs Publishing, 1985.

High Times Encyclopedia of Recreational Drugs. New York: Stonehill Publishing, 1978.

Hill, Lee. *A Grand Guy: The Life and Art of Terry Southern.* New York: Harper, 2001.

Himmelstein, Jerome L. *The Strange Career of Marijuana: Politics and Ideology of Drug Control in America.* Westport, CT: Greenwood, 1983.

Hofstadter, Richard. *The Paranoid Style in American Politics.* 1964. New York: Vintage Books, 2008.

Holiday, Billie, with William Dufty. *Lady Sings the Blues. New York:* Doubleday Books, 1956.

Holladay, Hilary. *Herbert Huncke: The Times Square Hustler Who Inspired Jack Kerouac and the Beat Generation.* Tucson, AZ: Schaffner Press, 2015.

Holmes, John Clellon. *Go.* 1952. New York: Thunder's Mouth Press, 2002.

———. *The Horn.* New York: Random House, 1958.

———. *Nothing More to Declare.* New York: Dutton, 1967.

———. *Visitor: Jack Kerouac in Old Saybrook.* California, PA: Unspeakable Visions of the Individual, 1981.

Horowitz, Michael, and Cynthia Palmer, eds. *Shaman Woman, Mainline Lady: Women's Writings on the Drug Experience.* New York: Quill, 1982.

Hughes, Langston. *I Wonder As I Wander: An Autobiographical Journey.* 1956. New York: Hill and Wang, 1999.

———. "Motto." *Montage of a Dream Deferred.* New York: Henry Holt. 1951. 19.

Huncke, Herbert. *The Evening Sun Turned Crimson.* Cherry Valley, NY: Cherry Valley Editions, 1980.

———. *Guilty of Everything.* New York: Paragon House, 1990.

———. *Huncke's Journal.* New York: Poet's Press, 1965.

James, William. *The Varieties of Religious Experience.* 1902. New York: New American Library, 1958.

Jay, Mike. *Emperors of Dreams: Drugs in the Nineteenth Century.* London: Dedalus, 2000.

Johnson, Bruce. *Taking Care of Business: The Economics of Crime by Heroin Abusers.* Lexington, MA: Lexington Books, 1985.

Johnson, Joyce. *Minor Characters.* Boston: Houghton Mifflin, 1983.

———. *The Voice Is All: The Lonely Victory of Jack Kerouac.* New York: Penguin Books, 2012.

Jones, Hettie. *How I Became Hettie Jones.* New York: E. P. Dutton, 1990.

Jones, LeRoi. *Blues People: Negro Music in White America.* New York: Quill, 1963.

Jones, Max, and John Chilton. *Louis: The Louis Armstrong Story, 1900–1971.* Boston: Da Capo Press, 1971.

Jones, Papa Jo. *Rifftide: The Life and Opinions of Papa Jo Jones.* Edited by Paul Devlin. Minneapolis, MN: University of Minnesota Press, 2011.

Jonnes, Jill. *Hep-Cats, Narcs, and Pipe Dreams: A History of America's Romance With Illegal Drugs.* Baltimore, MD: Johns Hopkins University Press, 1999.

Kahn, Ashley. *The House That Trane Built: The Story of Impulse Records.* New York: W. W. Norton, 2006.

Kaplan, John. *Marijuana—A New Prohibition.* New York: World Publishing, 1970.

Kastin, David. *Nica's Dream: The Life and Legend of the Jazz Baroness.* New York: W. W. Norton, 2011.

Kelley, Robin D. G. *Thelonious Monk: The Life and Times of an American Original.* New York: Free Press, 2009.

Kerouac, Jack. *Big Sur*. New York: Farrar, Straus and Cudahy, 1962.

———. *Book of Dreams*. San Francisco: City Lights, 1961.

———. *Desolation Angels*. New York: Coward-McCann, 1965.

———. *The Dharma Bums*. New York: Viking Press, 1958.

———. *Dr. Sax*. New York: Grove Press, 1959.

———. *Jack Kerouac and Allen Ginsberg: The Letters*. Edited by Bill Morgan and David Stanford. New York: Penguin Books, 2011.

———. *Mexico City Blues*. New York: Grove Press, 1959.

———. *On the Road*. New York: Viking Press, 1957.

———. *On The Road: The Original Scroll*. Penguin Classics, 2008.

———. *Pull My Daisy*. New York: Grove Press, 1961.

———. *Selected Letters, 1940–1956*. Edited by Ann Charters. New York: Viking, 1995.

———. *Selected Letters, Vol 2, 1957–1969*. Edited by Ann Charters. New York: Penguin Books, 2000.

———. *The Subterraneans*. New York: Grove Press, 1958.

———. *The Town and the City*. New York: Harcourt, Brace, 1950.

———. *Vanity of DuLuoz*. New York: Penguin Books, 1994.

———. *Visions of Cody*. New York: McGraw-Hill, 1972.

———. *Windblown World: The Journals of Jack Kerouac, 1947–1954*. Edited by Douglas Brinkley. New York: Viking, 2004.

Kerouac, Jack, and Joyce Johnson. *Door Wide Open: A Beat Love Affair in Letters, 1957–1958*. New York: Viking, 2000.

Kerouac, Joan Haverty. *Nobody's Wife: The Smart Aleck and the King of the Beats*. Berkeley, CA: Creative Arts Book Company, 2001.

Kesey, Ken. *The Further Inquiry*. New York: Viking, 1990.

———. *One Flew Over the Cuckoo's Nest*. New York: Viking, 1962.

———. *Sometimes a Great Notion*. New York: Penguin USA, 1998.

King, Rufus. *The Drug Hang-Up: America's Fifty-Year Folly*. New York: W. W. Norton, 1972.

Knapp, Bettina L. *Antonin Artaud: Man of Vision*. New York: Discus Books/Avon, 1971.

Knight, Arthur, and Kit Knight, eds. *The Beat Angels*. California, PA: Unspeakable Visions of the Individual, 1984.

———. *The Beat Diary*. California, PA: Unspeakable Visions of the Individual, 1977.

———. *The Beat Journey*. California, PA: Unspeakable Visions of the Individual, 1978.

———. *The Beat Road*. California, PA: Unspeakable Visions of the Individual, 1984

———. *The Beat Vision: A Primary Sourcebook*. New York: Paragon House, 1987.

Knight, Brenda. *Women of the Beat Generation*. Berkeley, CA: Conari Press, 1995.

Korall, Burt. *Drummin' Men: The Heartbeat of Jazz, The Swing Years*. New York: Schirmer, 1990.

Kramer, Jane. *Allen Ginsberg in America*. New York: Random House, 1969.

Krim, Seymour. *The Beats*. Greenwich, CT: Fawcett, 1960.

———. *What's This Cat's Story?* New York: Paragon House, 1991.

Krist, Gary. *Empire of Sin: A Story of Sex, Jazz, Murder, and the Battle for Modern New Orleans*. New York: Crown Publishers, 2014.

Lee, Martin A. *Smoke Signals: A Social History of Marijuana—Medical, Recreational and Scientific*. New York: Scribner, 2012.

Lee, Martin A., and Bruce Shlain. *Acid Dreams: The CIA, LSD and the Sixties Rebellion*. New York: Grove Press, 1986.

Lees, Gene. *Waiting for Dizzy*. New York: Oxford University Press, 1991.

Leland, John. *Hip: The History.* New York: Harper Perennial, 2005.

———. *Why Kerouac Matters: The Lessons of "On the Road" (They're Not What You Think).* New York: Penguin, 2008.

Lewin, Lewis. *Phantastica, Narcotic and Stimulating Drugs.* New York: E. P. Dutton, 1931.

Lindesmith, Alfred R. *The Addict and the Law.* Bloomington, IN: Indiana University Press, 1965.

———. *Opiate Addiction.* Evanston, IL: Principia Press, 1947.

Lindner, Robert. *Must You Conform?.* New York: Grove Press, 1961.

Lingeman, Richard. R. *Drugs From A to Z.* New York: McGraw-Hill, 1969.

Lomax, Alan. *The Land Where the Blues Began.* New York: Pantheon, 1993.

Lomax, Alan. *Mister Jelly Roll.* New York: Pantheon, 1994.

Long, John. *Drugs and the "Beats": The Role of Drugs in the Lives and Writings of Kerouac, Burroughs and Ginsberg.* College Station, TX: Virtualbookworm.com, 2005.

Louria, Donald. *The Drug Scene.* New York: Bantam, 1970.

Lukas, J. Anthony. *Don't Shoot—We Are Your Children!* New York: Random House, 1971.

Lusane, Clarence. *Pipe Dream Blues: Racism and the War on Drugs.* Boston: South End Press, 1991.

MacAdams, Lewis. *Birth of the Cool: Beat, Bebop, and the American Avant-Garde.* New York: The Free Press, 2001.

Mailer, Norman. *The White Negro.* San Francisco: City Lights, 1958.

Malcolm X, with Alex Haley. *The Autobiography of Malcolm X.* New York: Grove Press, 1964.

Margolick, David. *Strange Fruit: Billie Holiday, Café Society, and an Early Cry For Civil Rights.* Edinburgh: Canongate Books, 2001.

Margolis, Jack S., and Richard Clorfene. *A Child's Garden of Grass: The Official Handbook of Marijuana.* New York: Pocket Books, 1970.

Marihuana: A Signal of Misunderstanding: The Official Report of the National Commission on Marihuana and Drug Abuse. Washington, DC: US Government Printing Office, 1972.

Masters, R. E. L., and Jean Houston. *The Varieties of Psychedelic Experience.* New York: Holt, Rinehart & Winston, 1966.

Mayor's Committee on Marijuana. *The Marijuana Problem in the City of New York.* New York: Jacques Cattell, 1944.

McClure, Michael. *Scratching the Beat Surface.* San Francisco: North Point Press, 1982.

———. *Selected Poems.* New York: New Directions, 1986.

McCoy, Alfred W. *The Politics of Heroin: CIA Complicity in the Global Drug Trade.* Chicago: Lawrence Hill Books, 1991.

McDarrah, Fred, ed. *Kerouac & Friends: A Beat Generation Album.* New York: William Morrow, 1985.

McDarrah, Fred, and Gloria McDarrah. *Beat Generation: Glory Days in Greenwich Village.* New York: Schirmer, 1996.

McKenna, Terence. *The Archaic Revival: Speculations on Psychedelic Mushrooms, the Amazon, Virtual Reality, UFOs, Evolution, Shamanism, the Rebirth of the Goddess, and the End of History.* San Francisco: Harper San Francisco, 1991.

———. *Food of the Gods: The Search for the Original Tree of Knowledge: A Radical History of Plants, Drugs, and Human Evolution.* New York: Bantam Books, 1992.

McNally, Dennis. *Desolate Angel: Jack Kerouac, the Beat Generation and America.* New York: McGraw-Hill, 1980.

———. *On Highway 61: Music, Race, and the Evolution of Cultural Freedom.* Berkeley, CA: Counterpoint, 2014.

McWilliams, John C. *The Protectors: Harry J. Anslinger and the Federal Bureau of Narcotics, 1930–1962*. Newark, DE: University of Delaware Press, 1990.

Meltzer, David, ed. *The San Francisco Poets*. New York: Ballantine Books, 1971.

Mezzrow, Mezz, and Bernard Wolfe. *Really the Blues*. New York: Random House, 1946.

Mikuriya, Tod H. ed. *Marijuana: Medical Papers, 1839–1972*. Oakland, CA: MediComp Press, 1973.

Miles, Barry. *The Beat Hotel. Ginsberg, Burroughs and Corso in Paris*. New York: Grove, 2000.

———. *Call Me Burroughs: A Life*. New York: Hachette, 2013.

———. *Ginsberg*. New York: Simon & Schuster, 1989.

———. *Jack Kerouac, King of the Beats: A Portrait*. New York: Henry Holt, 1998.

———. *William Burroughs, El Hombre Invisible: A Portrait*. New York: Hyperion, 1993.

Mingus, Charles. *Beneath the Underdog: His World as Composed by Mingus*. New York: Knopf, 1971.

Morgan, Bill. *The Beats Abroad: A Global Guide to the Beat Generation*. San Francisco: City Lights, 2016.

———. *Beat Atlas: A State-by-State Guide to the Beat Generation in America*. San Francisco: City Lights, 2011.

———. *The Beat Generation in New York: A Walking Tour of Jack Kerouac's City*. San Francisco: City Lights, 1997.

———. *The Beat Generation in San Francisco*. San Francisco: City Lights, 2003.

———. *I Celebrate Myself: The Somewhat Private Life of Allen Ginsberg*. New York: Viking, 2006.

———. *The Typewriter Is Holy: The Complete Uncensored History of the Beat Generation*. New York: Free Press, 2010.

Morgan, Bill, and Nancy J. Peters, eds. *"Howl" on Trial: The Battle for Free Expression*. San Francisco: City Lights, 2006.

Morgan, Bill, and Bob Rosenthal, eds. *Best Minds: A Tribute to Allen Ginsberg*. New York: Lospecchio Press, 1986.

Morgan, Ted. *Literary Outlaw: The Life and Times of William S. Burroughs*. New York: Henry Holt, 1988.

Morgenstern, Dan. *Jazz People*. New York: Abrams, 1976.

———. *Living with Jazz*. New York: Pantheon, 2004.

Moscow, Alvin. *Merchants of Heroin*. New York: Dial Press, 1968.

Mottram, Eric. *Allen Ginsberg in the Sixties*. Seattle, WA: Unicorn Bookshop, 1972.

———. *William Burroughs: The Algebra of Need*. Buffalo, NY: Intrepid Press, 1971.

Mulligan, Gerry. *The Complete Birth of the Cool* by Miles Davis, Capitol M-11026, 1971. Liner notes.

Murray, Albert. *Stompin' the Blues*. New York: McGraw-Hill, 1976.

Musto, David. *The American Disease: Origins of Narcotic Control*. New Haven, CT: Yale University Press, 1973.

———, ed. *Drugs in America: A Documentary History*. New York: New York University Press, 2002.

———, ed. *A Hundred Years of Heroin*. Westport, CT: Greenwood, 2002.

Newark, Tim. *Boardwalk Gangster: The Real Lucky Luciano*. New York: St. Martin's, 2010.

Newsday Editors. *The Heroin Trail*. New York: Signet Books, 1973.

Nicholson, Stuart. *Billie Holiday*. London: Victor Gollancz, 1995.

Nicosia, Gerald. *Memory Babe: A Critical Biography of Jack Kerouac*. New York: Grove Press, 1983.

Nicosia, Gerald, and Anne Marie Santos. *One and Only: The Untold Story of "On the Road."* Berkeley, CA: Viva, 2011.

Nisenson, Eric. *Ascension: John Coltrane and His Quest.* New York: St. Martin's, 1993.

———. *'Round About Midnight: A Portrait of Miles Davis.* New York: Da Capo Press, 1996.

Norman, Philip. *Shout.* New York: Warner Books, 1982.

Nyswander, Marie. *The Drug Addict as Patient.* New York: Grune and Stratton, 1956.

O'Day, Anita, with George Eels. *High Times, Hard Times.* New York: G. P. Putnam's Sons, 1981.

Odier, Daniel. *The Job: Interviews with William Burroughs.* New York: Grove Press, 1970.

O'Meally, Robert. *Lady Day: The Many Faces of Billie Holiday.* New York: Arcade Publishing, 1993.

———, ed. *The Jazz Cadence of American Culture.* New York: Columbia University Press, 1998.

Orlovsky, Peter. *Peter Orlovsky: A Life in Words: Intimate Chronicles of a Beat Writer.* New York: Routledge, 2014.

Owens, Thomas. *Bebop: The Music and Its Players.* New York: Oxford University Press, 1995.

Palmer, Cynthia, and Michael Horowitz, eds. *Sisters of the Extreme: Women Writing on the Drug Experience.* Rochester, VT: Park Street, 2000.

Pass It On: The Story of Bill Wilson and How the A.A. Message Reached the World. New York: A.A. World Services, Inc., 1984.

Pearson, Nathan W. *Goin' to Kansas City.* Champaign, IL: University of Illinois Press, 1995.

Pepper, Art, and Laurie Pepper. *Straight Life: The Story of Art Pepper.* New York: Schirmer, 1979.

Perreti, Burton W. *The Creation of Jazz Music, Race and Culture in Urban America.* Champaign, IL: University of Illinois Press, 1994.

Pettinger, Peterr. *Bill Evans: How My Heart Sings.* New Haven, CT: Yale University Press, 1998.

Piazza, Tom. *The Guide to Classic Recorded Jazz.* Iowa City, IA: University of Iowa Press, 1995.

———, ed. *Setting the Tempo: Fifty Years of Great Jazz Liner Notes.* New York: Anchor, 1996.

Pinfold, Mike. *Louis Armstrong.* New York: Universe, 1987.

Plummer, William. *The Holy Goof.* Englewood Cliffs, NJ: Prentice-Hall, 1981.

Podhoretz, Norman. *Making It.* New York: Random House, 1967.

Polsky, Ned. *Hustlers, Beats and Others.* New York: Anchor, 1969.

Porter, Lewis. *John Coltrane: His Life and Music.* Ann Arbor, MI: University of Michigan Press, 1998.

———, ed. *A Lester Young Reader.* Washington, DC: Smithsonian Institution Press, 1991.

———. *Lester Young.* Ann Arbor, MI: University of Michigan Press, 2005.

Ratliff, Ben. *Coltrane: The Story of a Sound.* New York: Farrar, Straus and Giroux, 2007.

Rattray, David. *How I Became One of the Invisible.* Cambridge, MA: The MIT Press, 1992.

———. *Opening the Eyelid.* Brooklyn, NY: Diwan, 1990.

Rechy, John. *City of Night.* New York: Grove Press, 1963.

Reed, Jeremy. *Saint Billie.* London: Enitharmon Press, 2001.

Reisner, Robert. *Bird: The Legend of Charlie Parker.* New York: Citadel Press, 1962.

Rimbaud, Arthur. *Rimbaud: Complete Work, Selected Letters: A Bilingual Edition.* Translated by Wallace Fowlie. Chicago: University of Chicago Press, 2005.

Rivers, Larry, with Arnold Weinstein. *What Did I Do? The Unauthorized Autobiography.* New York: Harper Collins, 1992.

Rosenthal, David. *Hard Bop: Jazz and Black Music, 1955–1965*. New York: Oxford University Press, 1992.

Rudgley, Richard. *Essential Substances: A Cultural History of Intoxicants in Society*. New York: Kodansha International, 1995.

Russell, Ross. *Bird Lives!: The High Life and Hard Times of Charlie (Yardbird) Parker*. New York: Charterhouse, 1973.

———. *Jazz Style in Kansas City and the Southwest*. New York: Da Capo Press, 1973.

Sanders, Ed. *Tales of Beatnik Glory*. New York: Stonehill Press, 1975.

Sante, Luc. *Low Life: Lures and Snares of Old New York*. New York: Farrar, Straus and Giroux, 1991.

Schoener, Alan, ed. *Harlem on My Mind: Cultural Capital of Black America, 1900–1968*. New York: W. W. Norton, 1995.

Schuller, Gunther. *Early Jazz*. New York: Oxford University Press, 1968.

———. *The Swing Era: The Development of Jazz, 1930–1945*. New York: Oxford University Press, 1989.

Schumacher, Michael. *Dharma Lion: A Critical Biography of Allen Ginsberg*. New York: St. Martin's, 1992.

Seaver, Richard, Terry Southern, and Alexander Trocchi, eds. *Writers in Revolt: An Anthology*. New York: Frederick Fell, 1963.

Shapiro, Harry. *Waiting for the Man: The Story of Drugs and Popular Music*. New York: William Morrow, 1990.

Shaw, Arnold. *The Street That Never Slept*. New York: Coward, McCann and Geohegan, 1971.

Shelton, Robert. *No Direction Home: The Life and Music of Bob Dylan*. New York: William Morrow, 1986.

Simon, George T. *The Big Bands*. New York: Macmillan, 1967.

Sloman, Larry. *Reefer Madness: The History of Marijuana in America*. New York: Bobbs-Merrill, 1979.

Smith, Willie "the Lion." *Music On My Mind*. New York: Da Capo Press, 1978.

Snyder, Gary. *Back on the Fire: Essays*. Berkeley, CA: Counterpoint, 2007.

———. *Myths & Texts*. New York: Totem Press/Corinth Books, 1960.

———. *The Real Work: Interviews and Talks, 1964–1979*. New York: New Directions, 1980.

Solomon, David, ed. *The Marihuana Papers*. New York: Bobbs-Merrill, 1966.

Southern, Eileen. *The Music of Black Americans: A History*. New York: W. W. Norton, 1997.

Southern, Terry. *Flash and Filigree*. 1958. New York: Grove Press, 1996.

———. *The Magic Christian*. 1959. New York: Grove Press, 1996.

———. *Red-Dirt Marijuana and Other Tastes*. New York: New American Library, 1967.

———. *Texas Summer*. Arcade, 1992.

Southern, Terry, and Mason Hoffenberg. *Candy*. 1958. New York: Grove Press, 1996.

Spellman, A. B. *Black Music: Four Lives*. New York: Schocken, 1970. Published in 1966 as *Four Lives in the Bebop Business*.

Starks, Michael. *Cocaine Fiends and Reefer Madness: An Illustrated History of Drugs in the Movies*. London: Cornwall Books, 1982.

Stearns, Marshall W. *The Story of Jazz*. New York: Oxford University Press, 1956.

Sterling, Claire. *Octopus: How the Long Reach of the Sicilian Mafia Controls the Global Narcotics Trade*. New York: Touchstone Books, 1991.

Straussbaugh, Josh, and Donald Blaise, eds. *The Drug User: Documents, 1946–1960*. New York: Blast Books, 1990.

Sukenick, Ronald. *Down and In: Life in the Underground*. New York: Collier Books, 1987.

Szwed, John. *Billie Holiday: The Musician and the Myth*. New York: Viking, 2015.

———. *Crossovers: Essays on Race, Music, and American Culture*. Philadelphia, PA: University of Pennsylvania Press, 2006.

———. *Jazz 101: A Complete Guide to Learning and Loving Jazz*. New York: Hachette Books, 2000.

———. *So What: The Life of Miles Davis*. New York: Simon & Schuster, 2002.

Teachout, Terry. *Pops: The Wonderful World of Louis Armstrong*. New York: Houghton Mifflin Harcourt, 2009.

Thomas, J. C. *Chasin' the Trane*. New York: Doubleday, 1974.

Thompson, Robert Farris. *Aesthetic of the Cool: Afro-Atlantic Art and Music*. Periscope, 2011.

———. *Flash of the Spirit: African and Afro-American Art and Philosophy*. New York: Random House, 1984.

Torgoff, Martin. *Can't Find My Way Home: America in the Great Stoned Age, 1945–2000*. New York: Simon & Schuster, 2004.

Travis, Trysh. *The Language of the Heart: A Cultural History of the Recovery Movement from Alcoholics Anonymous to Oprah Winfrey*. Chapel Hill, NC: University of North Carolina Press, 2009.

Trebach, Arnold. S. *The Great Drug War*. New York: Macmillan, 1987.

———. *The Heroin Solution*. New Haven, CT: Yale University Press, 1982.

Trebach, Arnold, and Kevin B. Zeese. *Drug Prohibition and the Conscience of Nations*. Washington, DC: Drug Policy Foundation, 1990.

Trocchi, Alexander. *Cain's Book*. New York: Grove Press, 1960.

Turner, Steve. *Jack Kerouac: Angel Headed Hipster*. New York: Viking, 1996.

Tytell, John. *Beat and Other Occasions of Literary Mayhem*. Nashville, TN: Vanderbilt University Press, 2014.

———. *The Beat Interviews*. Temple, PA: Beatdom Books, 2014.

———. *The Living Theatre: Art, Exile, and Outrage*. New York: Grove Press, 1995.

———. *Naked Angels: The Lives and Literature of the Beat Generation*. New York: McGraw-Hill, 1976.

Tytell, John, and Mellon Tytell. *Paradise Outlaws: Remembering the Beats*. New York: William Morrow, 1999.

Ullmann, Michael. *Jazz Lives*. Washington, DC: New Republic Books, 1980.

Vail, Ken. *Bird's Diary: The Life of Charlie Parker, 1945–1955*. London: Castle Communications, 1996.

———. *Lady Day's Diary: The Life of Billie Holiday, 1937–1959*. London: Castle Communications, 1996.

Valentine, Douglas. *The Strength of the Wolf: The Secret History of America's War on Drugs*. London: Verso, 2004.

Von Eschen, Penny M. *Satchmo Blows Up the World: Jazz Ambassadors Play the Cold War*. Cambridge, MA: Harvard University Press, 2004.

Wakefield, Dan. *New York in the Fifties*. New York: Houghton Mifflin/Seymour Lawrence, 1992.

Waldman, Anne, ed. *The Beat Book*. Boston: Shambala, 1996.

Walker, Rebecca, ed. *Black Cool: One Thousand Streams of Blackness*. Berkeley, CA: Soft Skull Press, 2012.

Walton, Stuart. *Out of It: A Cultural History of Intoxication*. New York: Harmony, 2001.

Ward, Geoffrey C. *Jazz: A History of America's Music*. New York: Alfred A. Knopf, 2000.

Watson, Steven. *The Birth of the Beat Generation: Visionaries, Rebels, and Hipsters, 1944–1960.* New York: Pantheon, 1995.

Weinreich, Regina. *Kerouac's Spontaneous Poetics: A Study of the Fiction.* New York: Thunder's Mouth, 1987.

White, John. *Billie Holiday: Her Life and Times.* New York: Universe Books, 1987.

White, William. *Slaying the Dragon: The History of Addiction Treatment and Recovery in America.* Bloomington, IN: Chestnut Health Systems, 1998.

Williams, Martin. *Jazz Masters of New Orleans.* New York: Macmillan, 1967.

———. *The Jazz Tradition.* New York: Oxford University Press, 1983.

Woideck, Carl. *The Charlie Parker Companion.* New York: Schirmer, 1998.

———. *Charlie Parker: His Life and Music.* Ann Arbor, MI: University of Michigan Press, 1998.

Wolfe, Leonard, ed. *Voices of the Love Generation.* Boston: Little, Brown, 1968.

Woodward, Vann C. *The Strange Career of Jim Crow.* New York: Oxford University Press, 1974.

Articles and Essays

Adams, J. Donald. "Speaking of Books." *New York Times,* May 18, 1958.

Anslinger, Harry J. "Marihuana: Assassin of Youth." *American Magazine* 124, no. 1 (July 1937).

Aronowitz, Al. "The Beat Generation" (series). *New York Post,* March 1959.

Becker, Howard S. "Becoming a Marihuana User." *American Journal of Sociology* 59, no. 3 (1953): 235–242.

———. "Marihuana: A Sociological Overview." In *The Marihuana Papers,* edited by David Solomon. New York: Bobbs-Merrill, 1966.

Bierowski, Ted. "The Art of Fiction: Jack Kerouac." In *Conversations with Jack Kerouac,* edited by Kevin J. Hayes. Jackson, MS: Mississippi University Press, 2008.

"Books: The Ganser Syndrome." *Time,* September 16, 1957.

Burroughs, William. Foreword to *Guilty of Everything,* by Herbert Huncke. New York: Paragon House, 1990.

Caen, Herb. "Pocketful of Notes." *San Francisco Chronicle,* April 2, 1958.

Cassady, Neal. "The First Third" [the Joan Anderson letter]. *Notes from Underground,* 1964. http://sensitiveskinmagazine.com/joan-anderson-letter-neal-cassady/.

Charters, Ann. Introduction to *On the Road,* by Jack Kerouac, xxi–xxv. New York: Penguin, 1976.

Cunnell, Howard. "Fast This Time: Jack Kerouac and the Writing of 'On the Road.'" In *On the Road: The Original Scroll,* by Jack Kerouac. New York: Viking, 2007.

Dufty, William. "Billie Holiday Dies After Relapse: First Lady of the Blues Was 44." *New York Post,* July 17. 1959.

Ferlinghetti, Lawrence. Introduction to *"Howl" on Trial: The Battle for Free Expression,* edited by Bill Morgan, and Nancy J. Peters. San Francisco: City Lights, 2006.

Ginsberg, Allen. "A Version of the Apocalypse." In *The Beat Vision,* edited by Arthur Knight and Kit Knight. New York: Paragon House, 1987.

———. "The Great Marijuana Hoax." In Dr. Lester Grinspoon's Marijuana Uses, November 13, 1965. October 19, 2008. www.marijuana-uses.com/essays.

———. Introduction to *The Evening Sun Turned Crimson,* by Herbert Huncke. Cherry Valley, NY: Cherry Valley Editions, 1980.

——. Introduction to *Visions of Cody*, by Jack Kerouac. New York: McGraw-Hill, 1972.

Green, Martin. "The Loneliest Writer in America." *Literary Review* 32 (1988): 123–128.

Grennard, Elliot. "Sparrow's Last Jump." *Harper's Magazine*, May 1947.

Harris, Oliver. Introduction to *The Letters of William S. Burroughs, 1945–1959*, edited by Oliver Harris. New York: Viking Press, 1993.

Hart, Carl L. "How the Myth of the 'Negro Cocaine Fiend' Helped Shape American Drug Policy." *The Nation*, February 17, 2014.

Hawksley, Rupert. "Marianne Faithful: Heroin Saved My Life." *The Telegraph*, December 2, 2014.

Holiday, Billie. "I'm Cured for Good Now." *Ebony*, July 1949.

Holmes, John Clellon. "The Name of the Game." In *Passionate Opinions: The Cultural Essays of John Clellon Holmes*. Fayetteville, AR: University of Arkansas Press, 1988.

——. "This Is the Beat Generation." *New York Times Magazine*, November 16, 1952.

Jones, James. Introduction to *Jazz People*, by Dan Morgenstern. New York: Abrams, 1976.

Kerouac, Jack. "Are Writers Made or Born?" In *The Portable Jack Kerouac*, edited by Ann Charters. New York: Penguin, 1996.

——. "Belief and Technique for Modern Prose." In *The Portable Jack Kerouac*, edited by Ann Charters. New York: Penquin, 1996.

——. "Essentials of Spontaneous Prose." In *The Portable Jack Kerouac*, edited by Ann Charters. New York: Penguin, 1996.

——. "Jazz of the Beat Generation." In *From Blues to Bop: A Collection of Jazz Fiction*, edited by Richard N. Albert. New York: Anchor Books, 1992.

Mabley, Jack. "Filthy Writing on the Midway." *Chicago Daily News*, October 25, 1958.

McKenzie, James. "Moving the World a Millionth of an Inch: Gary Snyder." In *The Beat Vision: A Primary Sourcebook*, edited by Arthur and Kit Knight, 16. New York: Paragon House, 1987.

Millstein, Gilbert. Review of *On the Road*, by Jack Kerouac. *New York Times*, September 5, 1957.

Morgenstern, Dan. "Lester Leaps In." *Jazz Journal*, August 1958.

Mortensen, Erik. "High Off the Page: Representing the Drug Experience in the Work of Jack Kerouac and Allen Ginsberg." *Janus Head* 7, no. 1 (2004): 54–72.

"Pierre Delattre Remembers Neal Cassady." In *The Beat Vision: A Primary Sourcebook*, edited by Arthur and Kit Knight, 60. New York: Paragon House, 1987.

Plimpton, George. Introduction to *Red-Dirt Marijuana and Other Tastes*, by Terry Southern, xiv–xv. New York: New American Library, 1967.

Podhoretz, Norman. "The Know-Nothing Bohemians." *The Partisan Review*, Spring 1958, 305–319.

——. "Where Is the Beat Generation Going?." *Esquire*, December 1958.

Roberts, Samuel. "Rehabilitation as Boundary Object: Medicalization, Local Activism, and Narcotics Addiction Policy in New York City, 1951–1961." *Social History of Alcohol and Drugs* 26, no. 2 (Summer 2012): 147–166.

Sewell, Rhonda B. "Biographer Remembers Billie Holiday's Greatness." *The Blade*, April 1, 2001.

Snyder, Gary. "Note on the Religious Tendencies." *Liberation* 4 (June 1959): 11.

Wallace, Mike. "Mike Wallace Asks Jack Kerouac: What Is the Beat Generation?" *New York Post*, January 21, 1958.

Wilentz, Sean. "Bob Dylan, the Beat Generation, and Allen Ginsberg's America." *The New Yorker*, August 13, 2010.

Will, George. "Daddy, Who Was Jack Kerouac?" *Newsweek*, July 1988.

Williams, Edward Huntington. "Negro Cocaine 'Fiends' Are a New Southern Menace." *New York Times*, February 8, 1914.

Wilson, John M. "Defending Kerouac." *Los Angeles Times*, September 18, 1988.

Yankah, Ekow N. "When Addiction Has a White Face." *New York Times*, February 9, 2016.

Archives and Libraries

Federal Bureau of Narcotics Archives, Virginia

Harry Anslinger Archives at Penn State University, Pennsylvania

Schaffer Library of Drug Policy, www.druglibrary.org, Hearings on H.R. 6385 (April 27, 28, 29, 30 and May 4, 1937), Hearing on H.R. 6906 (July 12, 1937), Marihuana Conference (December 5, 1938). Correspondence about the legal status of hemp, 1930–1938.

Filmography

Bach, Jean, dir. *A Great Day in Harlem*. 1995. Stamford, CT: SABC Home Video.

Burns, Ken, dir. *Jazz*. 2001. PBS/WNET.

Clarke, Shirley, dir. *The Connection. 1961*. New York: Living Theatre Production. Mystic Fire Video, New York, 1998. VHS.

Palmer, Robert, dir. *The World According to John Coltrane*. 1990. Tony Byron/Multiprises. New York: BMG Video, 1991.

Smeaton, Bob. "Four (August '64 to August '65)." *The Beatles Anthology*. Aired November 22, 1995. DVD. Hollywood, CA: Capitol, 2003.

Notes

Author's Note

xi   "*smoking marijuana for breakfast*": Beatles, *Beatles Anthology*, 167.

xi   "*herbal jazz cigarettes*": *Beatles Anthology* video series.

xii   75 percent of Americans believe the repeal of marijuana prohibition is now inevitable: 2014 Pew poll cited in "Weed Nation," *Newsweek* Special Edition, 2015, 89.

xiii   "*These are people and they have a purpose in life*": Yankah, "When Addiction Has a White Face."

xiii   the vast wreckage of disproportionately black mass incarceration: Alexander, *The New Jim Crow*, 2–12, 180–182, 174–175.

xiii   rates twenty to fifty times greater than whites: Human Rights Watch. *Punishments and Prejudice: Racial Disparities in the War on Drugs*, HRW Reports vol. 12, no. 2 (New York, 2000).

xiv   "*the eclipse of the generations-long failed war on drugs*": Yankah, "When Addiction Has a White Face."

Chapter 1: Red-Dirt Marijuana

1   "*What's the matter with this cow?*": Terry Southern, interview with the author, 1992.

2   "*We went back to the barn*": Southern, interview.

3   *Murder Weed Found Up and Down Coast*: Lee, *Smoke Signals*, 50.

3   "*hot bed of marihuana fiends*": Sloman, *Reefer Madness*, 30.

3   "*After that incident*": Southern, interview.

4   "*I guess I surprised him*": Ibid.

4   "*part of the city called Nigger Town*": Ibid.

5   "*lean-to shacks, beside which great black-charred iron wash pots*": Southern, *Texas Summer*, 17.

6   "*I tried to make it even wilder*": Southern, interview.

6   *Not for nothing did the Beatles place Southern*: Plimpton, introduction to *Red-Dirt Marijuana*, xiv–xv.

7   "*How come it's against the law*": Southern, *Red-Dirt Marijuana*, 12.

7   "*By the time I wrote that story*": Southern, interview.

8   "*It's hard to believe*": Ibid.

Chapter 2: Stompin' at the Savoy

9   *Bernie Brightman was sixteen:* All details of this chapter were related to the author by Bernard Brightman in a 1992 interview. Also very useful was the chapter on Brightman in Sloman, *Reefer Madness*, 90–100.

Chapter 3: The Paranoid Spokesman

14   *"this traffic in marihuana is increasing":* Statement of H. J. Anslinger, Commissioner of Narcotics, Bureau of Narcotics, Department of the Treasury, Hearings on Marihuana Tax Act, April 27, 1937, available online Schaffer Library of Drug Policy, www.druglibrary.org.

15   *"the moral equivalent of war":* George Bush, "Address to the Nation on National Drug Control Policy" (speech, September 5, 1989), available online at The American Presidency Project, http://www.presidency.ucsb.edu.

15   an incident that happened in 1904: McWilliams, *The Protectors*, 27; Jonnes, *Hep-Cats, Narcs and Pipe Dreams*, 91.

16   *"I never forgot those screams":* Anslinger, *The Murderers*, 8.

16   *"When he grew into a man":* Hari, *Chasing the Scream*, 8.

17   *"ginger-colored nigger":* Sloman, *Reefer Madness*, 46.

17   *"It would seem to me that a man in such a responsible position":* Quoted in Ibid., 46.

17   *"His fame spread throughout the world":* Quoted in Jonnes, *Hep-Cats, Narcs and Pipe Dreams*, 154.

18   *"The Police Department here in New Orleans":* Quoted in Sloman, *Reefer Madness*, 43.

18   *"bureaucratic overkill":* Musto, *The American Disease*, 225.

19   *"ten either explicitly acknowledged the help of the Bureau":* Becker, "Marihuana: A Sociological Overview," 62.

19   *"An entire family was murdered":* Anslinger, "Marihuana: Assassin of Youth."

21   *"style of mind, not always right wing":* Hofstadter, *The Paranoid Style in American Politics*, 3.

21   *"overheated, oversuspicious, overaggressive":* Ibid., 4.

21   *"the desire of Yankee Americans to maintain an ethnically and religiously homogeneous society":* Ibid., 19.

21   *"all-out crusade":* Ibid., 29.

21   *"always a conflict between absolute good and absolute evil":* Ibid., 31–32.

21   *"The sexual freedom often attributed to him":* Ibid., 34.

22   *"The Marihuana Menace":* A. E. Fossier, "The Marihuana Menace," quoted in Sloman, *Reefer Madness*, 41–42.

23   *"Projection of blame on foreign nations":* Musto, *The American Disease*, 248.

23   a *"boundary-dissolving"* experience and a *"deconditioning"* agent: McKenna, *The Archaic Revival*, 82.

24   *"Colored students at the Univ. of Minn":* Quoted in McWilliams, *The Protectors*, 53.

24   *"a primary stimulus to the impulsive life":* Dr. Walter Bromberg's 1933 paper to the American Psychiatric Association, as summed up by Bromberg during hearings on marijuana held by FBN at Internal Revenue Building, US Department of Treasury, December 5, 1938, available online at Shaffner Library of Drug Policy, www.druglibrary.org.

24   *"releases inhibitions and restraints imposed by society":* Ibid.

Chapter 4: Two Hits of That Stuff, and Jack, You'd Be Mellow

25   *"I think I spent every Saturday night there"*: Bernard Brightman, interview with the author, 1992.

26   *"That's where all the hip guys went"*: Ibid.

26   *"Here's how a viper spent the evening"*: Ibid.

27   *"There must have been dozens"*: Ibid.

27   *"Kaiser was this big black stud"*: Ibid.

27   *"Mae was a black chick from Carolina"*: Ibid.

Chapter 5: The White Mayor of Harlem

30   *"When it came to hearing Louis"*: Mezzrow, *Really the Blues*, 212.

31   *"As soon as we got some of that Mexican bush"*: Ibid., 214.

31   *"Hey, there, Poppa Mezz"*: Ibid., 216; the "translation" of the conversation is from the appendix of that text, 354.

32   *"Overnight I was the most popular man in Harlem"*: Ibid., 215.

33   *"You know who they were"*: Ibid., 226.

34   *"Every Friday night"*: Ibid., 236.

35   *"I don't mean to boast"*: Ibid., 210.

36   *"a sawed-off runt of a jockey"*: Ibid., 71.

36   *"Say tff, tff, only breathe in when you say it"*: Ibid., 72.

36   *"The first thing I noticed"*: Ibid., 72–73.

37   *"stripped of its dirty gray shrouds"*: Ibid., 73.

37   *"All your pores open like funnels"*: Ibid.

37   *"Them first kicks are a killer, Jim"*: Ibid.

Chapter 6: Pops

38   *"one of the very few areas in American life"*: Hentoff, *The Jazz Life*, 21.

38   Marijuana appeared on the streets of New Orleans for the first time around 1910: Jonnes, *Hep-Cats, Narcs and Pipe Dreams*, 122.

39   *"the most beautiful Creole prostitutes"*: Hentoff with Shapiro, *Hear Me Talkin' to Ya*, 8.

39   *"standing in their doorways nightly"*: Ibid., 8.

39   *"The streets were crowded with men"*: Ibid., 6.

40   *"all of the cocaine, morphine, heroin"*: Ibid., 12.

40   *closed down Storyville in 1917*: Ibid., 64.

41   Fate Marable's steam calliope: Ibid., 75–76.

41   *"the opiate that inflames the mind"*: Shapiro, *Waiting for the Man*, 45.

41   *"I can say from my own knowledge"*: Shapiro, *Waiting for the Man*, 47.

42   *"We did call ourselves vipers"*: Jones and Chilton, *Louis*, 132.

42   a daily laxative: Jones and Chilton, *Louis*, 134–135; Teachout, *Pops*, 154.

42   *"I was never born to be a Square"*: Teachout, *Pops*, 155.

43   stand on their chairs and shout: Hentoff with Shapiro, *Hear Me Talkin' to Ya*, 85.

43   a big mirror ball: Ibid., 99–100.

43   *"born poor, died rich"*: Ibid., 371.

44   *"Anytime you make generalizations"*: Stanley Crouch, interview with the author, 1992.

44   *"For the early jazz artists, marijuana was a revelation"*: Lee, *Smoke Signals*, 46.

44–45   *"I felt as if I had stared into the sun's eye"*: Gioia, *The History of Jazz*, 62.

45   *"he tried to make a picture"*: Hentoff with Shapiro, *Hear Me Talkin' to Ya*, 46.

45   *"a mirror which magnifies"*: Baudelaire, *The Poem of Hashish: Hashish will be, indeed, for the impressions and familiar thoughts of the man, a mirror which magnifies, yet no more than a mirror.*

45   *"Budd Johnson once told me"*: Crouch, interview.

46   *"Buddy got to drinking too much"*: Hentoff with Shapiro, *Hear Me Talkin' to Ya*, 39.

46   *"Now, when it comes to summing it up"*: Jones and Chilton, *Louis*, 134.

46   On November 14, 1930, Louis Armstrong became the first celebrity marijuana bust in American history: Teachout, *Pops*, 157.

47   *"packed and jammed with all sorts of my fans"*: Jones and Chilton, *Louis*, 133.

47   *"His protestations were considered hilarious in jazz circles"*: Giddins, *Satchmo*, 95–96.

48   *"gage is more of a medicine than a dope"*: Jones and Chilton, *Louis*, 138.

48   *"But the price got a little too high"*: Ibid.

Chapter 7: The Misdo Gets Meanor and Meanor (Jailhousely Speaking)

50   The congressional and Senate hearings: Transcripts available online, Shaffner Library of Drug Policy, www.druglibrary.org.

53   *"This nation's laws were born in imperialism"*: Michael Aldridge, interview with the author, 1992.

53   uniquely murderous "Negro cocaine fiends": Williams, "Negro Cocaine 'Fiends' Are a New Southern Menace"; Hart, "How the Myth of the 'Negro Cocaine Fiend' Helped Shape American Policy."

54   *"under its influence men become beasts"*: McWilliams, *The Protectors*, 78.

54   *"jail offenders, then throw away the key"*: Ibid.

54   *"Marijuana has become our greatest problem"*: Lee, *Smoke Signals*, 55.

55   the *"Marijuana and Musicians"* file: Ibid., 134–142.

55   *"Music hath charms"*: Quoted in ibid., 135.

55   forced to promote the growing of *Cannabis indica*: Lee, *Smoke Signals*, 58.

56   *"one vast City of Night stretching from Times Square to Hollywood Boulevard"*: John Rechy, interview with author, 1992. *City of Night* is also the title of Rechy's 1963 novel.

Chapter 8: The Great Tenor Solo in the Shoeshine Jukebox

57   She liked to smoke between shows in a taxicab: Chilton, *Billie's Blues*, 66.

58   What the audience saw for a brief and shocking instant: Ibid., 66–67.

58   *"the right place for the wrong people"*: Clarke, *Wishing on the Moon*, 156.

58   *"a nightclub to take the stuffing out of stuffed shirts"*: Margolick, *Strange Fruit*, 40.

58   *"Fuck 'em"*: Clarke, *Wishing on the Moon*, 161.

58   *"That was one time a black person said, 'Kiss my ass'"*: Ibid.

58–59   pick up her tips off the tabletops with the labia of her vagina: Hentoff, *Jazz Is*, 53.

59   Tuskegee Institute estimations of lynchings in US: Margolick, *Strange Fruit*, 14.
60   *"When I sing it, it affects me so much I get sick"*: Ibid., 62.
60   *"Don't you sing that song again!"*: Ibid., 89.
60   *"the first significant protest in words and music, the first unmuted cry against racism"*:
      Ibid, 17.
60   *"Surely a song that forced a nation to confront its darkest impulses"*: Ibid., 21–22.
60   *"I've made a lot of enemies"*: Quoted in Blackburn, *With Billie*, 111.
60   It was this song that first brought Billie Holiday to the attention of the FBI: Ibid.
61   *"Jim's got the best panatela"*: Holiday with Dufty, *Lady Sings the Blues*, 45.
62   *"She was just something I stole at fifteen"*: Hentoff, *Jazz Is*, 52.
62   *"being without proper care and guardianship"*: Clarke, *Wishing on the Moon*, 18.
62   *"I screamed and banged on the door"*: Holiday with Dufty, *Lady Sings the Blues*, 18.
62   *"The documentary evidence"*: Clarke, *Wishing on the Moon*, 34.
63   *"like a damn cripple"*: Hentoff, *Jazz Is*, 55.
63   *"Eleanora sings if we ask"*: Clarke, *Wishing on the Moon*, 55.
63   *"sung and boozed and smoked them real skinny reefers"*: Ibid., 35.
63   *"The fellas that was crazy for her"*: Ibid.
64   *"somebody's damn maid"*: Holiday with Dufty, *Lady Sings the Blues*, 119.
64   *"like a gypsy fiddler in a Budapest café"*: Chilton, *Billie's Blues*, 14.
64   *"crying in their beer"*: Holiday with Dufty, *Lady Sings the Blues*, 34.
65   *"The first girl singer I'd come across"*: Hentoff, *Jazz Is*, 53.
66   being struck by his heavy-lidded light green eyes: Related by Holiday in con-
      versation with Ruby Rosano, circa 1953, included in unpublished manuscript
      given to this author.
66   *"When some reefer started going around"*: Chilton, *Billie's Blues*, 42.
70   he was a confirmed daily user of marijuana: Blackburn, *With Billie*, 125; Porter,
      Lester Young, 18; Büchmann-Møller, *You Just Fight for Your Life*, 122.
71   *"He didn't like nothing harsh"*: Gitler, *Swing to Bop*, 40.
72   When one of the top ARC executives walked in: Chilton, *Billie's Blues*, 42.
72   one of the great recording sessions in the history of American popular music:
      Gelly, *Being Prez*, 49.
73   *"you listen to him and can almost hear the words"*: Porter, *Lester Young*, 17.
73   *"like two of the same voices"*: Ibid.
74   Theirs would be a great musical romance: Porter, *Lester Young*, 17–18;
      Clarke, *Wishing on the Moon*, 122–126; Blackburn, *With Billie*, 121–122; Büch-
      mann-Møller, *You Just Fight for Your Life*, 70–71; Gioia, *The History of Jazz*, 165;
      Szwed, *Billie Holiday*, 123–124; Gelly, *Being Prez*, 47.
74–75 *"the dominant cultural stereotypes of black women were Mammy and the Tragic Mulatto"*:
      Griffin, *In Search of Billie Holiday*, 28.
75   *"welcoming gathering places"*: Szwed, *Billie Holiday*, 134.
75   *"everybody would get buck naked"*: Clarke, *Wishing on the Moon*, 78.
75   *"Lester's flow of obscenity was magnificent"*: Porter, *Lester Young*, 2.
76   *"he epitomized everything that I could aspire to"*: Bernard Brightman, interview with
      the author, 1992.
76   *"Lester Young was blowing"*: Ibid.
76   Prez invented nicknames and jive: Gioia, *The Birth (and Death) of the Cool*, 74;
      MacAdams, *Birth of the Cool*, 19; Gelly, *Being Prez*, 55–56; Büchmann-Møller, *You
      Just Fight for Your Life*, 85, 95, 104; Porter, *Lester Young*, 2, 17; Blackburn, *With
      Billie*, 122.

77 the first person ever to use the expression "cool": MacAdams, *Birth of the Cool,* 19; Gioia, *The Birth (and Death) of the Cool,* 77; Jackie McLean, interview with the author, 1992.

77 Prez's aesthetic: Giddins and DeVeaux, *Jazz,* 252; Gioia, *The Birth (and Death) of the Cool,* 73; Porter, *Lester Young,* 104; Crouch, *Kansas City Lightning,* 155–160.

77 *"The vision of jazz that entered the mainstream of American life"*: Gioia, *The Birth (and Death) of the Cool,* 73.

77 the way Prez dressed: Blackburn, *With Billie,* 124; Gioia, *The Birth (and Death) of the Cool,* 73; MacAdams, *Birth of the Cool,* 19; Büchmann-Møller, *You Just Fight for Your Life,* 104; Gelly, *Being Prez,* 94.

77 his droll and extraordinarily singular being: Blackburn, *With Billie,* 122–123; Gioia, *The Birth (and Death) of the Cool,* 73; MacAdams, *Birth of the Cool,* 19; Büchmann-Møller, *You Just Fight for Your Life,* 95, 111.

78 *itutu,* or "mystic coolness": Thompson, *Flash of the Spirit;* Thompson, *Aesthetic of the Cool: Afro-Atlantic Art and Music* (2011).

78 *"the ultimate revenge of the powerless"*: MacAdams, *Birth of the Cool,* 20.

78 *"I play it cool"*: Hughes, "Motto."

79 the dark glasses that Prez wore onstage at the Savoy: Brightman, interview.

79 *"Lester Young turned Jack on to marijuana"*: Edie Kerouac-Parker, interview with the author, 1992.

79 it was there that his fragile paradise was burst: Blackburn, *With Billie,* 127–129; Porter, *Lester Young,* 23–25; Büchmann-Møller, *You Just Fight for Your Life,* 119–120.

79–80 *"this young guy came out one night"*: Büchmann-Møller, *You Just Fight for Your Life,* 117.

80 a *"Constitutional Psychopathic State"*: Gelly, *Being Prez,* 100.

80 *"to be confined at hard labor"*: Büchmann-Møller, *You Just Fight for Your Life,* 126.

81 *"a nightmare, man"*: Ibid., 128.

81 *"The army just took all his spirit"*: Ibid., 129.

81 *"Man, what a fine hat"*: Clarke, *Wishing on the Moon,* 125–126.

81 *"that gloomy saintly goof in whom the history of jazz is wrapped"*: Kerouac, "Jazz of the Beat Generation," 167.

82 *"a roar of subterranean excitement that is like the vibration of the entire land"*: Kerouac, "Jazz of the Beat Generation," 168.

Chapter 9: You Mean There's Something Like This in This World?

84 a truant from Lincoln High: Giddins, *Celebrating Bird,* 28.

85 *"Charlie decided to jump during Jones's jam session"*: Giddins, *Celebrating Bird,* 40.

85 *"I'll fix those cats"*: Reisner, *Bird,* 186.

87 *"Bird's mind was of such a keenness"*: Reisner, *Bird,* 58.

87 *"When Bird was sixteen he looked thirty-eight"*: Ibid., 68.

87 a local drummer named Little Phil: Ibid., 67.

87 *"some character in Kansas City"*: Ibid., 172.

88 *"when he went north and got permission from the Chicago mob"*: Crouch, *Kansas City Lightning,* 213.

88 a *"darkskinned, nicely proportioned and vivacious"* woman named Little Mama: Ibid., 213–214.

88   heroin was already very likely in Kansas City by the summer of 1937: Court-wright, *Dark Paradise*, 108.

88   cheaper, stronger, and faster-acting than morphine: Ibid.

88   *"in every part of the United States except the Pacific Coast"*: Ibid., 108.

88   the ratio of heroin use to morphine use was 7.7 to 1: Ibid., 110.

88   reading Sir Arthur Conan Doyle's Sherlock Holmes mysteries: Crouch, *Kansas City Lightning*, 214.

88   Gary Giddins mentions the death of his close friend: Giddins, *Celebrating Bird*, 40.

89   *"Getting high the first time at fifteen"*: Reisner, *Bird*, 124.

89   *"got her first look at a needle"*: Giddins, *Celebrating Bird*, 46.

89   *"Charlie, I'd rather see you dead than use that stuff"*: Ibid.

90   *"from eleven to fifteen hours a day"*: Crouch, *Kansas City Lightning*, 88.

90   *"In the summer of 1937"*: Reisner, *Bird*, 186.

91   *"He got into his music all the sounds around him"*: Ibid.

91   *"Charlie might bring disorder to your border"*: Crouch, *Kansas City Lightning*, 246.

91   *"Rebecca, you are a good person"*: Ibid., 254–255.

92   And yet, as he jumped a train heading north to Chicago, he was clean: Ibid., 256.

92   *"to unlock the genie that was hidden somewhere in his soul"*: Ibid., 333.

92   The nickname he would shortly acquire: Giddins, *Celebrating Bird*, 58.

93   *"We were standing around when a guy comes up"*: Reisner, *Bird*, 84.

Chapter 10: Once Known, Never Forgotten

94   *"I've always wanted to be an opium addict"*: Herbert Huncke, interview with the author, 1992.

94   *"Here once the kindly dope fiend lived"*: Nicosia, *Memory Babe*, 162.

94   *"I'm sort of a legend"*: Huncke, interview.

95   *"As far as I know the ethos of what's charmingly Hip"*: Ginsberg, introduction to *The Evening Sun Turned Crimson*, 8.

95   *"On the evening of this story as I walked from the interior of the house out to the porch"*: Huncke, *The Evening Sun Turned Crimson*, 13.

96   *"I was a little late for the hard-core old junkies of New York"*: Huncke, interview.

97   *"Oh, it's quite a story"*: Ibid.

97   *"a small, dark, Arabic-looking man with an oval face"*: Kerouac, *The Town and the City*, 364.

97   *"the greatest storyteller I know"*: Kerouac, *Selected Letters*, 127.

97   *"Everything I did was wrong"*: Huncke, *The Evening Sun Turned Crimson*, 15.

98   *"Man, I started to use drugs back in the thirties"*: Huncke, interview.

98   *"You look like a pretty wise kid"*: Huncke, *Guilty of Everything*, 25.

98   *"unable to move"*: Ibid., 26.

98   *"smugglers and Chinese junks"*: Ibid.

98   *"with hennaed hair a fire engine red, and gigantic deep blue eyes"*: Ibid., 29.

99   *"At that time in my life I could scarcely have imagined that such a person could really exist"*: Allen Ginsberg, interview with the author, 1992.

99   *"At an early age Huncke was cut off"*: Burroughs, foreword to *Guilty of Everything*, vii.

99   *"petty cheats, phony braggarts"*: Algren, *The Man with the Golden Arm*, 143.

99   *"It's still my favorite thing to do"*: Huncke, interview.
99   *"If you were a drug addict"*: Ibid.
100 *"I was a natural for it"*: Huncke, *Guilty of Everything*, 43–44.
100 *"At the time the streets of New York"*: Huncke, *The Evening Sun Turned Crimson*, 41–42.
101 *"In those days the so-called drug addicts"*: Huncke, interview.
101 *"in some stool pot in hell"*: Ibid.
101 *"Six big black guys"*: Huncke, *Guilty of Everything*, 47.
102 *"the guard passing with the flashlight"*: Huncke, interview.
102 *"Later on I went to the US Public Hospital"*: Ibid.
102 *"After all that pain and discomfort"*: Ibid.
102 *"There are innumerable ways to woo"*: Huncke read this story to me as he was in the process of writing it. I am not aware that it has ever been published.
103 *"Once known, never forgotten"*: Ibid.
103 *"and everything is going to the beat"*: Kerouac, *Desolation Angels*, 123.
103 *"Yes, it's good"*: Huncke, interview.
104 *"It's funny now"*: Ibid.

Chapter 11: The Shot Heard 'Round the World

105 William Burroughs was standing stiffly at the door: Herbert Huncke, interview with the author, 1992; Huncke, *Guilty of Everything*, 68–71; Huncke, *The Evening Sun Turned Crimson*, 109–111; Burroughs, *Junky*, 5–7; Morgan, *Literary Outlaw*, 120–122.
106 *"small and very thin, his neck loose in the collar of his shirt"*: Burroughs, *Junky*, 5.
107 *"an open sore where I can slip a needle right into my vein"*: Burroughs, *Naked Lunch*, 59.
107 Barry Miles avows that none of this ever happened: Miles, *Call Me Burroughs*, 123–124.
108 *"If God made anything better he kept it to himself"*: Burroughs, *Naked Lunch*, 210.
108 *"Junk wins by default"*: Burroughs, *Junky*, xv.
108 The facts of his life: Burroughs's early years in Morgan, *Literary Outlaw*, 14–96; Miles, *William Burroughs*, 21–35; Miles, *Call Me Burroughs*, 7–92.
109 *"The general consensus among his analysts"*: Miles, *Call Me Burroughs*, 24.
109 *"Hey, looky, someone just did it"*: Miles, *William Burroughs*, 22.
109 *"a walking corpse"*: Morgan, *Literary Outlaw*, 32.
109 *"People laughed and said: 'You mean the biography of a wolf"*: Miles, *William Burroughs*, 21.
109 *"He claimed he just wanted to see how it worked"*: Morgan, *Literary Outlaw*, 48.
110 *"Got any bugs, lady?"*: Miles, *William Burroughs*, 33.
110 *"I had never met a girl quite like Joan"*: Huncke, *Guilty of Everything*, 73.
111 *"My storytelling ability"*: Huncke, interview.

Chapter 12: You're Buzzing, Baby

112 Benzedrine entered the life of Jack Kerouac: This chapter is based on interviews with Herbert Huncke, Allen Ginsberg, and Edie Kerouac-Parker; Huncke, *Guilty of Everything*, 72–73; Burroughs, *Junky*, 14–15; Miles, *Call Me Burroughs*,

126–127; and Miles, *Ginsberg*, 64–65; but mostly it's based on Kerouac's own recollections, as tape-recorded while smoking marijuana with Neal Cassady and rendered in *Visions of Cody*, 192–196.

112 *"What do you think happens when we die?: Visions of Cody*, 195, *On the Road*, 144.

112 *"we might pick up a little junk"*: Visions of Cody, 192.

112 *"a typical clean-cut American"*: Huncke, *Guilty of Everything*, 72.

112 *"At that time Jack would smoke a little pot"*: Ibid.

113 *"I have a boy friend I the navy"*: Ibid, 193.

113 *"Do you pick up, jazz baby?"*: Ibid, 193.

113 *"Are we in St. Petersburg?"* Ibid, 195.

113 *"Nothing, ba-by"*: Ibid, 195.

114 *"You're buzzing, baby"*: Ibid, 195

114 *"fucked her solid"*: Ibid, 196

Chapter 13: And the Hippos Were Boiled in Their Tanks

116 *"the New Vision"*: Schumacher, *Dharma Lion*, 33–34.

117 *"this romantic seaman who wrote poem books"*: Nicosia, *Memory Babe*, 115.

117 *"Ginsberg was going through a stage"*: Huncke, *Guilty of Everything*, 73.

117 *"my soul and his were akin"*: Schumacher, *Dharma Lion*, 36.

118 *"nothing was secure, not even his own name"*: Nicosia, *Memory Babe*, 21.

118 *"inscrutable because ordinary-looking"*: Morgan, *Literary Outlaw*, 91.

119 *"the war, the second front (which occurred just before this time), the poetry, the soft city evenings"*: Kerouac, *Vanity of Duluoz*, 16.

120 Ginsberg would look back on the episode: Allen Ginsberg, interview with the author, 1992.

120 *"Jack, you know I love you"*: Schumacher, *Dharma Lion*, 49.

120 Kerouac felt that it was a demonstration of the truth of the New Vision: Ginsberg, interview.

120 *"a great seeker of cities and souls"*: Morgan, *Literary Outlaw*, 133.

121 *"Burroughs was primarily a master of gnostic curiosities"*: Schumacher, *Dharma Lion*, 41.

121 *"Edify yer mind, my boy"*: Morgan, *Literary Outlaw*, 91.

121 *"a year of low, evil decadence"*: Kerouac, *Vanity of Duluoz*, 269.

122 *"It was aesthetic, more of a curiosity"*: Ginsberg, interview.

122 *"There was really no place to even go to get any reliable information on drugs"*: Ibid.

123 *"When they had a narcotics bust"*: Sloman, *Reefer Madness*, 173.

123 *"I didn't know what it was"*: Ibid., 172–173.

123 *"an eager, intense, sharply intelligent boy"*: Kerouac, *The Town and the City*, 365.

123 *"and so I had the honor of bringing the first box of grass back"*: Ginsberg, interview.

124 *"this great mound of snowlike ice cream but absolutely sweet and pure and clean and bright"*: Sloman, *Reefer Madness*, 174; Ginsberg, interview.

125 *"I would later come to understand it in Buddhist terms"*: Sloman, *Reefer Madness*, 175.

125 *"only the beginning of the exploration of the senses"*: Ibid.

125 *"fear and trembling"*: Ibid.

125–126 *"this giant official government propaganda machine"*: Ginsberg, interview.

126 *"what it had to offer"*: Ibid.

126 They would station themselves underneath the great Pokerino sign: Nicosia, *Memory Babe*, 157–58; Ginsberg, interview.

126   "*All the characters that were asked to leave Bickfords*": Ginsberg, "A Version of the Apocalypse," 190.

127   "*enamel particles*": Ibid., 186.

127   "*What have you got to say tonight, old phantom?*": Nicosia, *Memory Babe*, 158.

127   "*From the beginning I was leery of amphetamines*": Ginsberg, interview.

128   "*little white hairs that appear out of the eyes and nose and mouth*": Ginsberg, "A Version of the Apocalypse," 186.

128   "*Kerouac and I ran downstairs*": Ginsberg, interview.

128   "*Benny has made me see a lot*": Kerouac, *Selected Letters*, 100.

129   "*Night after night we'd go to the clubs*": Edie Kerouac-Parker, interview with the author, 1992.

Chapter 14: Parker's Mood

130   "*Do you know what that muthafucka is doing?*": Gillespie with Fraser, *To Be or Not to Bop*, 235.

131   "*I lit my fire*": Reisner, *Bird*, 21.

132   "*Everybody at one time or another smoked marijuana*": Gillespie with Fraser, *To Be or Not to Bop*, 283–284.

132   "*like putting whipped cream on Jell-O*": Ibid., 231.

132   "*the architect of the new sound*": Giddins, *Celebrating Bird*, 68.

132   "*We were pretty close philosophically*": Gillespie with Fraser, *To Be or Not to Bop*, 235.

134   "*Bird couldn't find nobody with no shit*": Gitler, *Swing to Bop*, 172.

134   "*He couldn't get started on anything*": Reisner, *Bird*, 98.

134   "*a handful of Benzedrine tablets*": Ibid., 174.

134   causing his limbs and muscles to jerk: Nat Hentoff quotes Leonard Feather about this in *Jazz Is*, 186.

134   "*He founders in shallow waters*": Giddins, *Celebrating Bird*, 93.

135   "*Yeah, Sparrow's last recording would sure make a collector's item*": Grennard, "Sparrow's Last Jump."

135   "*I got this cat goin' around in circles*": Gitler, *Swing to Bop*, 175.

135   "*'Gimme eight doubles'*": Ibid., 175–176.

136   "*Those of us who were affected the strongest*": Chambers, *Milestones 1*, 139.

136   "*Oh, the* pathos—how does one even speak *of it?*": Herbert Huncke, interview with the author, 1992.

137   "*in short, hard bursts of breath*": Davis with Troup, *Miles*, 102.

Chapter 15: A Ghost in Daylight on a Crowded Street

138   "*Bill acted as the shill*": Herbert Huncke, interview with the author, 1992.

138   "*A ghost in daylight on a crowded street*": Burroughs, *Junky*, 29.

138   "*mooches, fags, four-flushers*": Ibid., 47.

139   "*Things began to change*": Edie Kerouac-Parker, interview with the author, 1992.

139   "*As a habit takes hold*": Burroughs, *Junky*, 22.

139   "*Almost worse than the sickness is the depression*": Ibid., 28.

140   "*You should write a book with that title one day, Bill*": Miles, *Burroughs*, 44.

141   "*I can feel the heat closing in*": Burroughs, *Naked Lunch*, 3.

142   "*Young man, I am going to inflict a terrible punishment on you*": Morgan, *Literary Outlaw*, 129.

142   "*More than anything else, the use of drugs that year*": Allen Ginsberg, interview with the author, 1992.

142   "*it was only the beginning*": Ibid.

142   "*When I watched Burroughs get his habit*": Ibid.

143   "*When I looked at Huncke*": Ibid.

143   "*The biggest impact was the realization of the enhancement of sensibility and consciousness*": Sloman, *Reefer Madness*, 79.

143   "*in addition to deriding the dangerous aspects and being a glorification of marihuana smoking*": Shapiro, *Waiting for the Man*, 59.

143   it was through *Really the Blues* that Ginsberg and Burroughs first learned about the La Guardia Committee Report: Ginsberg, interview.

144   "*shipped over the King's County Hospital, where they were used as guinea pigs*": Mezzrow, *Really the Blues*, 317.

144   "*does not lead to addiction in the medical sense of the word*": Mayor's Committee on Marijuana, *The Marijuana Problem in the City of New York*, online at Schaffer Library of Drug Policy, www.druglibrary.org.

144   "*From then on, I realized that marijuana was going to be an enormous political catalyst*": Sloman, *Reefer Madness*, 180.

145   "*If one law was full of shit and error, then what of all those other laws?*": Gisnberg, interview.

145   "*with his baby son in one hand and a hypo in another, a marvelous sight*": Kerouac, *The Town and the City*, 372.

145   "*one of the strangest and most curiously exalted youngsters*": Ibid., 365.

145   "*You'll see the great tycoons of industry suddenly falling apart*": Ibid., 371.

Chapter 16: Ain't Nobody's Business If I Do

146   "*dignified bearing and her wonderful poise*": Vail, *Lady Day's Diary*, 86.

146   "*She was so elegant*": Blackburn, *With Billie*, 93.

147   "*And he could be a big help to me*": Ibid.

147   "*I spent the rest of the war on 52nd Street*": Ibid., 116.

147   "*it was a real drag to go to Hollywood and end up as a make-believe maid*": Ibid, 119.

148   "*Lady Day had an awful lot to forget*": Blackburn, *With Billie*, 203.

148   "*We should not be shocked*": Szwed, *Billie Holiday*, 107.

149   "*This woman was only feelings*": Clarke, *Wishing on the Moon*, 202–203.

150   "*Now he gave her an ultimatum*": Ibid., 249.

150   Billie Holiday had already been watched for years by the Federal Bureau of Narcotics: Ibid., 252; Blackburn, *With Billie*, 209.

150   "*She flaunted her way of living*": Blackburn, *With Billie*, 219.

150   "*Joe Glaser wants a colored agent*": Ibid, 210.

150   When Lady let them in: Ibid., 212–213.

151   "*She sealed our friendship*": Ibid., 213.

151   "*She was the type that would make anyone sympathetic*": Ibid.

151   staying at the Hotel Attucks when it all came down: Clarke, *Wishing on the Moon*, 256–261; Blackburn, *With Billie*, 215–216; Holiday with Dufty, *Lady Sings the Blues*, 123–126.

152   *United States v. Billie Holiday*: Clarke, *Wishing on the Moon*, 161; Holiday with Dufty, *Lady Sings the Blues*, 127–131; Chilton, *Billie's Blues*, 115–116; Anslinger, *The Protectors*, 150–157; Griffin, *In Search of Billie Holiday*, 41–43.

152   *"It was all over in a matter of minutes"*: Holiday with Dufty, *Lady Sings the Blues*, 131.

152   *"I felt like the fool of all time"*: Ibid., 132.

152   *"They don't cut you down slow"*: Ibid., 133.

153   she appears to have done her time well: Blackburn, *With Billie*, 183–184; Clarke, *Wishing on the Moon*, 161–162; Chilton, *Billie's Blues*, 116–118; Holiday with Dufty, *Lady Sings the Blues*, 133–137, Vail, *Lady Day's Diary*, 102–103.

153   One couple in Switzerland: Holiday with Dufty, *Lady Sings the Blues*, 137.

153   *"Lady, how could you?"*: Clarke, *Wishing on the Moon*, 263.

154   On the night of Saturday, March 27: Clarke, *Wishing on the Moon*, 279–280; Blackburn, *With Billie*, 185–186; Holiday with Dufty, *Lady Sings the Blues*, 143–148; Griffin, *In Search of Billie Holiday*, 48–49; Chilton, *Billie's Blues*, 120–121; Szwed, *Billie Holiday*, 106.

154   *"one of the most thunderous ovations""*: Vail, *Lady Day's Diary*, 104.

154   *"She was nervous and perspiring freely"*: Ibid., 105.

154   *"the biggest thing that ever happened to me"*: Holiday with Dufty, *Lady Sings the Blues*, 119.

154   *"here to watch me fall on my ass"*: Blackburn, *With Billie*, 185.

155   *"I came out expecting to to be allowed to go to work"*: Holiday, "I'm Cured for Good Now."

155   *"a new image, that of the tragic, ever-suffering black woman singer"*: Griffin, *In Search of Billie Holiday*, 31.

155   *"There are images and myths that seem to swallow up individuals"*: Ibid., 28.

Chapter 17: The Sacralization of the Mundane

157   *"How did we get here, angels?"*: Allen Ginsberg, interview with the author, 1992.

157   *"This life is our last chance to be honest"*: Ibid.

157   *"a young Gene Autry"*: Kerouac, *On the Road*, 2.

158   *"rush down the street together, digging everything in the early way they had"*: Kerouac, *On the Road*, 8.

158   the *"whole mad swirl"* of everything that is going to happen: Ibid., 8.

158   he grew up with his father: Plummer, *The Holy Goof*, 11–14.

159   *"the great experiencer and Midwest driver and talker"*: Ginsberg, introduction to *Visions of Cody*, ix.

159   *"simply an awareness that time"*: Cassady, *The First Third*, 112–113.

160   *"a young jailkid hung-up on the wonderful possibilities of becoming a real intellectual"*: Kerouac, *On the Road*, 6.

160   *"a kind of holy lightning"*: Ibid., 7.

160   *"Yes! That's Right! Wow! Man!"*: Ibid.

161   "Man, wow, there's so many things to do": Ibid.

161   *"except you've got to stick to it with the energy of a benny addict"*: Ibid., 6.

161   to *"sacralize the mundane"*: Nicosia, *Memory Babe*, 133.

161   to elitch: Ibid., 322.

162   By 1948, Ginsberg was seeing a Reichian therapist in New York: Schumacher, *Dharma Lion*, 90.

162   *"Bird was the supreme hipster"*: Reisner, *Bird*, 13.

162   *"amoral, anarchistic, gentle, and over-civilized"*: Reisner, *Bird*, 25.

163 *"the way the young hipsters of Times Square walked down the street"*: Holmes, "The Name of the Game," 54.

164 *"changing, becoming sweeter, no more wars, sweet presidents"*: Nicosia, *Memory Babe*, 253.

164 *"dingy backstairs 'pads,' Times Square cafeterias"*: Holmes, *Go*, 36.

164 *"the year of consciousness that runs through everything"*: Schumacher, *Dharma Lion*, 94–97.

164 *"the impression of the entire universe as filled with poetry and light"*: Miles, *Ginsberg*, 100.

165 *"I've seen God!"*: Ibid., 101.

165 a *"giant octopus serpent-monster consciousness"*: Schumacher, *Dharma Lion*, 98.

165 *"I thought for many years"*: Miles, *Ginsberg*, 103–104.

165 One freezing morning in February of 1949: Schumacher, *Dharma Lion*, 106–108, 110–113.

Chapter 18: That Was Our Badge

167 During the day, you could see them all hanging around: Jackie McLean, interview with the author, 1992; Davis with Troupe, *Miles*, 129–130, 145.

167 *"Clean as a motherfucker"*: McLean, interview.

168 *"getting famous at exactly the same time "*: Davis with Troupe, *Miles*, 127.

168 *"If it hadn't been for the women who supported me"*: Ibid., 163.

168 *"higher than a motherfucker"*: Ibid., 145.

169 McLean was in the audience at Smalls Paradise: Jackie McLean, interview with the author, 1992.

169 One night Bird came out, smiled at him: Ibid.

169 *"I would go to a party"*: Ibid.

169 *"and then, finally, one day I was gone"*: Ibid.

170 Dope for Coltrane was an unfathomable thing: Thomas, *Chasin' the Trane*, 63, 66–67.

170 walking the bar with his saxophone in Philly clubs: Thomas, *Chasin' the Trane*, 55–56.

170 changing his reed, adjusting his mouthpiece: Ibid., 47.

171 They would get high at Bishop's: McLean, interview.

171 *"There were a lot of tasters"*: Orrin Keepnews, interview with the author, 1992.

173 *"It would take a very unique individual"*: Ibid.

173 *"That first night he was so scared and high"*: Davis with Troupe, *Miles*, 144.

173 *"Bud Powell and those guys"*: McLean, interview.

174 *"It consisted of the front line of Miles and Sonny Rollins"*: Ibid.

174 *"You consolidate all your loans into one payment"*: Szwed, *So What*, 88.

174 *"heroin narrowed the emotional and visual fields"*: Ibid., 88.

175 *"in spite (or because?)"* of the use of the drug, *"a great music was made"*: Gitler, *Swing to Bop*, 282.

175 *"That's what you were playing—your lifestyle"*: Ibid.

175 *"the tempos for one thing"*: Ibid, 283.

175 *"Hostility, pettiness"*: Ibid.

176 *"For the first time critics and commentators on jazz"*: Jones, *Blues People*, 189.

176 *"Narcotics users, especially those addicted to heroin"*: Ibid., 201–202.

177   *hep cat,* as derived from the Molof *hipicat:* Gillespie with Fraser, *To Be or Not to Bop,* 297.

177   *"I just knew that Parker did it":* Larry Rivers, interview with the author, 1992.

177   *"If they don't own us":* Mingus, *Beneath the Underdog,* 188.

178   *"King Spook don't even own fifty percent of himself!":* Ibid., 189.

178   *"Oh, it's a hard wrinkle, Mingus":* Ibid., 190.

178   *"bugged by the fact that, being a Negro, he could go just so far and no farther":* Reisner, *Bird,* 126.

178   *"Once he finished a set to great acclaim":* Ibid.

179   *"the first jazz musician I have ever met":* Hentoff, *Jazz Is,* 194.

179   *"Wait until everybody gets rich off your style":* Ibid.

179   *"a young Buddhist monk pouring oil on himself":* Gillespie with Fraser, *To Be or Not to Bop,* 398.

179   *"the first time the black ego was expressed in America with assurance":* McLean, interview.

180   *"they didn't like all them black men being with them rich, fine, white women:"* Davis with Troupe, *Miles,* 71.

180   *"Are you kidding? To the point of death":* McLean, interview.

181   *"There were people who used to say":* Keepnews, interview.

181   *"That's right, and you didn't have to be a musician to be in that club, either":* McLean, interview.

181   *"That was our badge":* Gitler, *Swing to Bop,* 282.

Chapter 19: Blues for a Junkie Whore

183   Ruby Rosano's first arrest: "Ruby Rosano" is the pseudonym of someone I encountered in a twelve-step recovery fellowship in the early 1990s, whose anonymity I guaranteed as a condition of her participation in this book. Even though she has passed away, I've decided to honor that agreement out of respect for her family. All of the writing about her—details, scenes, quotes—are based directly on interview transcripts, notes, and personal writings she furnished to this author.

Chapter 20: Wild Form, Man, Wild Form . . .

197   *"a tremendous clap of thunder":* Reisner, *Bird,* 133–135.

198   BIRD LIVES: Sukenick, *Down and In,* 86.

198   *"It was the worst feeling in the world":* Dizzy Gillespie, interview with the author, 1992.

198   *"For all the adulation heaped upon him by fans":* Reisner, *Bird,* 135.

198   *"In attempting to escape the role, at once sub- and super-human":* Ellison, *Shadow and Act,* 227.

199   *"For us, who had replaced religion":* di Prima, *Recollections of My Life as a Woman,* 369.

200   *"a huge Dostoyevskean novel":* Kerouac, *Selected Letters,* 371.

201   *"wrapped in wild observation of everything":* Ibid., 231.

201   *"What is my own voice?":* Ibid.

201   *"here I was, nude, no clothes, and all exits blocked"*: Cassady, "The First Third" [the Joan Anderson letter].

202   *"You gather together all the best styles"*: Kerouac, *Selected Letters*, 242.

202   the *"Colossus risen to destroy Denver"*: Schumacher, *Dharma Lion*, 133.

202   *"proceed into the actual truth"*: Kerouac, *Selected Letters*, 246.

202   *"I want to fish as deep as possible into my own subconscious"*: Nicosia, *Memory Babe*, 324.

202   *"from moment to moment, incomprehensible, ungraspable yet terribly clear"*: Ibid., 279.

202   *"Now, eyeball kicks are among the world's greatest"*: Cassady, *The First Third*, 196.

202   *"as one looks into a picture"*: Ibid., 196.

202   *"You must and will go on at all costs including comfort & health & kicks"*: Kerouac, *Selected Letters*, 242.

203   *"What was it like, Jack?"*: Haverty Kerouac, *Nobody's Wife*, 202.

203   The book that Kerouac produced: Nicosia, *Memory Babe*, 343; Kerouac, *Selected Letters*, 315; Charters, introduction to *On the Road*, xviii–xxvi; Charters, *Kerouac*, 124–128; Tytell, *Naked Angels*, 67–68; Johnson, *The Voice Is All*, 392–404.

204   *"Benny tea, anything I KNOW none as good as coffee"*: Kerouac, *Selected Letters*, 318.

204   *"lifestyle as music"*: Gitler, *Swing to Bop*, 282.

204   *"the dawn of jazz America"*: Kerouac, *On the Road*, 204.

204   *"you know everything and all is decided forever"*: Ibid, 129.

205   *"rolled it out on the floor and it looks like the road"*: Kerouac, *Selected Letters*, 316.

205   *"I've telled all the road now"*: Ibid., 315.

205   *"write all my books in twenty days"*: Ibid., 317.

205   *"He was in a funny state"*: Johnson, *The Voice Is All*, 399.

205   a *"crass idiot"*: Nicosia, *Memory Babe*, 349.

205   *"the loneliest writer in America"*: Green, "The Loneliest Writer in America."

206   *"I'm afraid I need Miss Green to write"*: Kerouac, *Selected Letters*, 400.

206   *"Why don't you just sketch in the streets like a painter but with words?"*: Ibid, 356.

206   *"a big multi-dimensional conscious and subconscious character ionvocation of Neal"*: Ibid., 356.

206   *"everything activates in front of you in myriad profusion"*: Ibid.

207   *"He'd blast, get high, and he'd write all night"*; Gifford and Lee, *Jack's Book*, 77.

208   *"They drink to 'come down' or 'get high', not to illustrate anything"*: Holmes, "This Is the Beat Generation."

208   *"Like Proust be an old teahead of time"*: Charters, *The Portable Beat Reader*, 59.

208   *"I realize how right you are"*: Schumacher, *Dharma Lion*, 204.

208   *"He said Anything is good because it is everything"*: Ginsberg, *Howl: Original Draft Facsimile*, 149–150.

209   *"a perfect place to write, think, blast"*: Kerouac, *Selected Letters*, 383.

210   *Charley Parker forgive me*: Kerouac, *Mexico City Blues*, 241st Chorus, 243.

210   *"a jazz poet blowing a long blues"*: Kerouac, Note to *Mexico City Blues*.

210   "PREDICT EARTHQUAKES": Kerouac, *Selected Letters*, 514.

211   a *"spontaneous bop prosody and original classic literature"*: Johnson, *The Voice Is All*.

Chapter 21: Trust the Germans to Concoct Some Really Evil Shit

212   *"the best junk kick I ever had"*: Burroughs, *The Letters of William S. Burroughs*, 199.

213   *"an end-of-the-world feeling"*: Ibid., 215.

213   *"the orgasm of a hanged man when the neck snaps"*: Burroughs, *Junky*, 94.

213   *"the first intelligent modern confession on drugs"*: Kerouac's unpublished blurb for *Junky* in Morgan, *Literary Outlaw*, 209–210.

214   *"a paranoid obsession, like anti-Semitism under the Nazis"*: Burroughs, *Junky*, 42.

214   *"police-state legislation penalizing a state of being"*: Ibid., 142.

215   *"I guess it's time for our William Tell act"*: Burroughs recounts the story in Howard Brooker's 1980 documentary, *Burroughs: Movie*, which is quoted in Miles, *Call Me Burroughs*, 207.

215   *"You know I can't stand the sight of blood"*: Miles, *Call Me Burroughs*, 208; Morgan, *Literary Outlaw*, 193–196; Miles, *El Hombre Invisible*, 53.

215   *"Why I did it, I don't know"*: Quoted in Morgan, *Literary Outlaw*, 194.

215   *"a mad genius in littered rooms"* : Kerouac, letter to Ginsberg, quoted in Miles, *Call Me Burroughs*, 220.

216   *"Burroughs is gone at last"*: Kerouac, *Selected Letters*, 389.

216   *"afraid. . . . Not exactly to discover unconscious intent"*: Burroughs, *The Letters of William S. Burroughs*, 263.

217   *"I am forced to the appalling conclusion"*: Burroughs, introduction to *Queer* (New York: Viking Press, 1985), quoted in Miles, *Call Me Burroughs*, 3.

217   *"desert of beautiful boys"*: Burroughs, *The Letters of William S. Burroughs*, 204.

218   *"Trying to write novel"*: Ibid., 201.

218   *"When the druggist sells me my daily box"*: Ibid., 215.

219   *"I have an open sore where I can slip a needle right into a vein"*: Ibid.; Burroughs, *Naked Lunch*, 59.

219   *"Kiki has confiscated all my clothes"*: Burroughs, *The Letters of William S. Burroughs*, 224.

220   *"Once I get off junk, anything is possible"*: Ibid., 283.

220   *"The critical point of withdrawal"*: Burroughs, *Naked Lunch*, 49.

221   *"strangled with routines"*: Burroughs, *Letters*, 245.

221   *"The incredibly obscene, thinly disguised references"*: Ibid., 259.

221   a *"vast, Kafkian conspiracy to prevent me from ever getting off junk"*: Ibid., 307.

221   *"I just experienced indescribable, nightmare flash"*: Ibid., 309.

222   *"kissed the vein, calling it my 'sweet little needle sucker'"*: Ibid., 312.

222   *"The days glide by strung on a syringe"*: Burroughs, *Naked Lunch*, 56.

Chapter 22: Holy the Bop Apocalypse!

224   *"It is hard, in our present era of self-righteousness"*: di Prima, *Recollections of My Life as a Woman*, 202.

224   *"There was a mystery about drugs"*: McClure, *Scratching the Beat Surface*, 5.

225   *Howl* began with a single line: Schumacher, *Dharma Lion*, 200–204.

225   *starving, mystical, naked*: First draft of the poem published in *The Annotated Howl*, 12.

225   *"not with the idea of writing a formal poem"*: Ginsberg, preface to *Howl: The Original Draft Facsimile*, xii.

225   *"It was a line that could never have been written"*: Allen Ginsberg, interview with the author, 1992.

225   *"One of the accused"*: *New York Times*, April 23, 1949.

226 "*a lament for the lamb in America*": Miles, *Ginsberg*, 191.

226 "*a tragic custard-pie comedy of wild phrasing*": Ibid., 188.

226 "*They are hip without being slick*": Kerouac, *The Subterraneans*, 1.

227 "*three distinct musical movements*": Schumacher, *Dharma Lion*, 207.

228 As they went out into the San Francisco night after having eaten the peyote buttons: Schumacher, *Dharma Lion*, 206; Miles, *Ginsberg*, 192; Ginsberg, interview.

228 "*two phantom ghosts with empty eyes*": Miles, *Ginsberg*, 192.

228 "*the fulfillment of all my desires since I was nine.*" Schumacher, *Dharma Lion*, 193.

228 "*Moloch! Molock!*": *Annotated Howl*, 58–59.

228 The conduit directly responsible for bringing this visionary substance into Ginsberg's life: Ginsberg, interview.

229 Artaud had traveled to northern Mexico: Artaud, *Peyote Dance*, 78.

229 "*The legend of peyote*": Ginsberg, interview.

229 "*metallic imaginary aftertaste & feeling of stomach sickness*": Ginsberg, *Journals*, 7.

229 "*The sky is a solid light blue*": Ibid., 8.

229 "*The great mystery is that of being*": Ibid.

229 "*A bird just shat on me!*": Ibid., 9.

229 "*Peyote is not God—but is a powerful force*": Ibid., 12.

229 the next time Ginsberg took it, in October of 1954: Schumacher, *Dharma Lion*, 205–206; Ginsberg, interview.

230 "*This is deep-gong religious*": Journal entry quoted in Schumacher, *Dharma Lion*, 206.

230 "*What I had heard about peyote*": Ginsberg, interview.

231 "*The world that we tremblingly stepped out into*": McClure, *Scratching the Beat Surface*, 12.

232 in an "*aura of jazz, William Blake, Swedenborg, and the Visionary Surrealists*": Michael McClure, interview with the author, 1992.

232 a bebopper from Kansas City named Don: Ibid.

232 "*The first time I got high*": Ibid.

232 "*Six poets at the Six Gallery*": Schumacher, *Dharma Lion*, 214.

232 "*pieces of orange crates*": McClure, *Scratching the Beat Surface*, 13.

233 "*It was a mad night*": Kerouac, *The Dharma Bums*, 13–14; Schumacher, *Dharma Lion*, 215.

233 "*out-of-this-world genteel-looking Renaissance Italian*": Kerouac, *The Dharma Bums*, 11.

233 "*delicate pale handsome*": Ibid., 11.

233 "*a hundred and eighty pounds of poet meat*": Ibid., 12.

233 a "*truly illuminated intelligence*": Ibid., 32.

233 "*in Oriental scholarship, Pound, taking peyote and seeing visions*": Ibid., 32.

234 "*deep and resonant and somehow brave*": Ibid., 14.

234 "*howl with joy, it was so pure*": Ibid.

234 "*a world full of rucksack wanderers*": Ibid., 97.

234 "*hornrimmed intellectual hepcat with wild black hair*": Ibid., 11.

235 "*Allen began in a small and intensely lucid voice*": McClure, *Scratching the Beat Surface*, 13.

235 "*In all our memories no one had been so outspoken*": Ibid.

235 "*I knew the world had been waiting for this poem*": Ferlinghetti, introduction to "*Howl*" *on Trial*, xii.

235 "*Ginsberg, this poem will make you famous in San Francisco*": Miles, *Ginsberg*, 196.

237   *"I may have conjured the pleasure of a 'teahead joyride'"* : Ginsberg, interview.

237   *"carefully figgering where to place these bombs"*: Schumacher, *Dharma Lion*, 238.

Chapter 23: 'Round Midnight

238   Every night after the gig with the Miles Davis Quintet: Details of this entire portrait of John Coltrane and Elvin Jones using drugs together furnished to the author by the poet David Rattray, as told to him by Elvin Jones when the two of them were heroin addicts and would shoot up together in the bathroom of Elvin's apartment at 424 East 11th Street (which Elvin called his "office"), circa 1961–1962.

241   *"32-bar song form, improvising on a simple line the way an Indian musician would do with a raga"*: Thomas, *Chasin' the Trane*, 77.

241   *"You can't use that boy"*: Szwed, *So What*, 121.

241   *"Can't you play twenty-seven choruses instead of twenty-eight?"*: Szwed, *So What*, 122.

242   *"He didn't even have to put the horn to his lips"*: Lewis Merenstein, interview with the author, 1992.

243   *"a dry, unplaned tone that sets Davis off like a rough mounting for a fine stone"*: Davis with Troupe, *Miles*, 196.

243   *"honey mixed with liquid fire"*: Chambers, *Milestones 1*, 135.

243   after the great Sonny Rollins bottomed out on heroin: Davis with Troupe, *Miles*, 94; Jackie McLean, interview with the author, 1992.

244   the long and arduous journeys of scores of musicians who had been caught in the vise of addiction for years: Davis with Troupe, *Miles*, 209–211; Chambers, *Milestones 1*, 249; Szwed, *So What*, 125–126; McLean, interview.

245   John Coltrane was another story: Details of Coltrane's troubles with drugs and drink in Davis with Troupe, *Miles*, 207–209; Porter, *John Coltrane*, 104–105; Nisenson, *Ascension*, 39–40, Thomas, *Chasin' the Trane*, 80–82; McLean, interview.

246   *"One night I got so mad I slapped him"*: Davis with Troupe, *Miles*, 207.

246   *"We were getting high together"*: McLean, interview.

247   What happened to Miles: Details of Miles kicking his habit in Davis with Troupe, *Miles*, 169–170; Chambers, *Milestones 1*, 176–179; Szwed, *So What*, 107–108.

249   *"one of the quintessential heroes of the jazz life"*: Hentoff, *Jazz Is*, 135.

249   What happened to John Coltrane: Details of Coltrane kicking his habit in Nisenson, *Ascension*, 39–40; Porter, *John Coltrane*, 106–107; Davis with Troupe, *Miles*, 216; Thomas, *Chasin' the Trane*, 82–84; McLean, interview.

249   a channel of God: Coltrane's spiritual awakening in Nisenson, *Ascension*, 40–42.

250   *"If there be a God"*: Pass It On, 121.

250   *"the sway of alcohol over mankind"*: James, *The Varieties of Religious Experience*, 387.

251   *"the equivalent on a low level of the spiritual thirst"*: Pass It On, 384.

251   *"I heard the Supreme One playing music through John Coltrane's mind"*: Thomas, *Chasin' the Trane*, 217.

252   *"The etiology of liver cancer is still basically unknown"*: Nisenson, *Ascension*, 217.

252   Sometimes for Jackie McLean the endless waiting was worse than getting sick: McLean, interview.

253   He was particularly haunted by the last time he saw Bird alive: Ibid.

254   *"Hey, Jackie, how you doin', you got yourself together?"* Details of this scene with Miles Davis, ibid.

Chapter 24: Why Are All These Young Boys Being Hanged in Limestone Caves, Bill?

256 Dr. Dent believed that drug addiction was a metabolic illness: On Dr. Dent and his treatment, Miles, *William Burroughs: El Hombre Invisible*, 76; Morgan, *Literary Outlaw*, 257–258.

256 *"stumbling with fatigue"*: Burroughs, *Letters of William S. Burroughs*, 317.

257 *"sexy as an eighteen-year-old and healthy as a rat"*: Ibid., 320.

257 *"a period of change more drastic than adolescence or early childhood"*: Ibid., 329.

257 *"a straight continuation of Interzone"*: Ibid., 327.

258 *"Fuck your nabor. He may like it"*: Burroughs, *Naked Lunch*, 333.

259 *"random insect doom"*: Ibid., 187.

260 *"I will send along about 100 pages of Interzone"*: Burroughs, *Letters of William S. Burroughs*, 346.

260 *"hitting the majoun pretty heavy of late"*: Ibid., 353.

260 *"almost automatic writing"*: Ibid., 355.

260 *"several novels all interlocking and taking place simultaneously in a majoun dream"*: Ibid., 367.

260 *"great long baloneys"*: Miles, *Burroughs*.

261 *"Why are all these young boys being hanged in limestone caves, Bill?"* Morgan, *Literary Outlaw*, 263.

261 *"Gilt and red plush"*: Burroughs, *Naked Lunch*, 67–68.

261 *"Belch . . . They'll hear this fart on Jupiter"*: Ibid., 141.

261 *"precise, clinically observed and unemotionally rendered details"*: Tytell, *Naked Angels*, 118.

262 *"huntsmen strut about with imbecile narcissism"*: Burroughs, *Naked Lunch*, 113.

262 *"a future possibility far more dismal and terrifying"*: Tytell, *Naked Angels*.

262 *"strange circuits revealing the future"*: Ibid., 121.

263 *"Me and Peter Orlovsky"*: Allen Ginsberg, interview with the author, 1992.

263 *"that was when Burroughs began changing it around"*: Ibid.

263 *"drug-induced sensitivity to the place's strange collage of histories"*: Harris, introduction to the *Letters of William S. Burroughs*, xxxiv.

264 *"Nurse: Adrenalin, doctor?"*: Burroughs, *Naked Lunch*, 55.

Chapter 25: The Empirical Soul of Jazz

265 *"We must not put into America's homes"*: Szwed, *Billie Holiday*, 63.

267 *"I've had my troubles with the habit for fifteen years"*: Holiday with Dufty, *Lady Sings the Blues*, 189.

267 *"I knew when I started to work on this book"*: Ibid.

268 *"a lot to answer for"*: Blackburn, *With Billie*, 201.

268 *"Well, let me tell you"*: Holiday with Dufty, *Lady Sings the Blues*, 182.

268 *"On a recent Sunday"*: Ibid., 183.

269 *"I can't help it, I just told what happened to me"*: Szwed, *Billie Holiday*, 23.

269 *"Readers who had seen Lady in concert"*: Griffin, *In Search of Billie Holiday*, 50.

269 *"The only way I can answer that question, Mike"*: Clarke, *Wishing on the Moon*, 445.

270 Herridge delivered the message that if Billie Holiday was not allowed to appear: Szwed, *Billie Holiday*, 63.

270   *"Billie Holiday is one of a handful of really great jazz singers"*: "Fine and Mellow," CBS Studios, 1957, available on www.YouTube.com.

270   *"There's two kinds of blues"*: Ibid.

271   *"She was just a little bitty woman"*: Blackburm, *With Billie*, 326.

271   *"a little light housekeeping"*: Ibid., 327.

271   *"He blew the sparest, purest blues chorus I have ever heard"*: Hentoff, *Jazz Is*, 50.

272   *"the empirical soul of jazz"*: Ibid.

272   As soon as Ruby Rosano heard that Billie Holiday had published her autobiography: "Ruby Rosano" is a pseudonym. Her story is continued here from Chapter 19.

275   *"Who can tell what detours are ahead?"*: Holiday with Dufty, *Lady Sings the Blues*, 192.

Chapter 26: Peyote Solidities of Halls

277   *"This fellow was vaguely related to somebody from Texas"*: Peter Berg, interview with the author, 1992.

277   He was the son of an alcoholic: Ibid.

277   a strange world of Cuban émigrés and redneck kids who looked like the young Montgomery Clift: Wolfe, *Voices of the Love Generation*, 252–253.

278   *"To really set the scene here"*: Berg, interview.

279   *"We knew so little about it"*: Ibid.

279   *"It came out in a straight line"*: Ibid.

279   *"I heard and saw unbelievable things"*: Ibid.

280   *"The policeman said, 'Boy, what in the world you been drinkin'?'"*: Ibid.

280   *"How did it change me?"*: Ibid.

281   *"We were not taking peyote to get high"*: Michael McClure, interview with the author, 1992.

281   *"They were five beautiful buds"*: Ibid.

281   *"It was a profound and moving experience"*: Ibid.

282   *"It seemed greater than exploring Siberia"*: Ibid.

282   *"All things beam inner light and color"*: McClure, *Meat Science Essays*, 43.

282   *"extreme fright and demon-seeing"*: Ibid., 42.

283   *"It backfired on me"*: McClure, interview.

283   an *"arrogant and supercilious young man"*: Ibid.

283   *"one of THE most handsome men I've ever seen"*: Kerouac, *Big Sur*, 105.

283   *"I didn't feel like I was floating in timelessness"*: Ibid.

283   *"fear, horror and self-blockading"*: McClure, "Peyote," 47.

283   *"To walk a hundred yards in freedom"*: Ibid., 48.

Chapter 27: A Readily Recognizable Stigmata

284   *"an authentic work of art"*: Millstein, review of *On The Road*.

285   *"he was enraged"*: Wakefield, *New York in the Fifties*, 163.

285   Kerouac was soon appearing on John Wingate's *Nightbeat*: Kerouac described this experience in a letter to Neal Cassady in the fall of 1957, reprinted in Knight and Knight, eds., *The Beat Vision*, 120.

287   *"Ask him if we can get any tea"*: Kerouac, *On the Road*, 281.

287 "*Somewhere along the way I knew there'd be girls*": Ibid., 11.
287 "*by sheer wild insight and sudden revelatory genius*": Ibid., 285.
287 "*flared in the golden mysterious afternoon*": Ibid., 287.
287 "*like a long, spectral Arabian dream*": Ibid., 189.
288 "*a conspiracy to overthrow civilization*": Podhoretz, "Where Is the Beat Generation Going?"
288 Kerouac's "*love for Negroes and other dark-skinned people*": Podhoretz, "The Know-Nothing Bohemians."
288 "*Nothing gave the Beat scene the image of cool more than the media rap*": Ed Sanders, interview with the author, 1992.
289 "*far out*": Caen, "Pocketful of Notes."
289 "beatniks" were one of the "greatest threats" facing America: Sloman, *Reefer Madness*, 181. Allen Ginsberg recalled Hoover's speech as having been given in Salt Lake in 1961 and reported in the *New York Daily News*.
290 "*If the medium is the message*": Ibid.
290 "*Suddenly he would go to all these literary parties*": Joyce Glassman, interview with the author, 1992.
290 "*What is the Beat Generation?*": Wallace, "Mike Wallace Asks Jack Kerouac: What Is the Beat Generation?"
291 "*Well, how do you like fame?*" Allen Ginsberg, interview with the author, 1992.
291 "*drugs, drunkenness, and aimless wandering*": Adams, J. Donald. "Speaking of Books."
292 "*What's goin' on, Allen?*": Schumacher, *Dharma Lion*, 314.
292 "*Just like in New York or Frisco or anywhere*": Kerouac, *Desolation Angels*, 258.
293 "*Holy Goof . . . He was beat—the root, the soul of beatific*": Kerouac, *On the Road*, 194–195.
293 "*Excitement and movement mean everything*": "Books: The Ganser Syndrome."
293 "*the tremendous energy of a new kind of American saint*": Kerouac, *On the Road*.
293 "*He became a kind of Johnny Appleseed of grass*": Ginsberg, interview.
294 "*I was at a party at Ferguson's*": Cassady, *Off the Road*, 296–297.
295 "*two stony monsters*": Ibid., 298.
295 "*Suddenly I was afraid*": Ibid.
295 "*they wanted me to tell them everybody I knew who smoked marijuana*": Ibid,. 305.
296 "*the controversial Allen Ginsberg*": Plummer, *The Holy Goof*, 106.
296 "*I stepped right in between them and stopped the fight!*": Cassady, *Off the Road*, 305.
297 "*treated with respect bordering on the friendly*": Ibid., 312.
297 "*In that case I must assume*": Ibid., 312.
297 "*But your Honor, we haven't any proof!*": Ibid., 313.
298 "*In my disillusionment*": Ibid.
298 "*an unparalleled opportunity to attain greater grace*": Plummer, *The Holy Goof*, 107.
298 "*shining with earthly fire*": Ibid., 111.

Chapter 28: Goodbye Pork Pie Hat

299 The whole way home from Paris: Gelly, *Being Prez*, 140; Frank Büchmann-Møller, *You Just Fight for Your Life*, 218–219.
299 "*They're picking the bones while the body is still warm*": Büchmann-Møller, *You Just Fight for Your Life*, 204.

300   "*The downbeat is soft, the tempo medium*": Morgenstern, "Lester Leaps In."

300   " '*The Pres' still wore his celebrated pork pie hats*": Jones, introduction to *Jazz People*, 16.

300   "*somebody you wouldn't believe, too, a great person*": François Postif interview quoted in Büchmann-Møller, *You Just Fight for Your Life*, 217.

300   "*You just fight for your life*": Ibid., 218.

301   "*Well, I never want to lose that feeling*": Ibid., 109.

301   "*definitely schizophrenic*": Ibid., 203–204.

302   "*the greatness of America in a single Negro musician*": Kerouac, "Jazz of the Beat Generation," 167.

302   "*So much of my roots, my definition of hipness*": Paul Rothchild, interview with the author, 1992.

302   "*The black musicians seem to be the ones who suffer the most*": Büchmann-Møller, *You Just Fight for Your Life*, 220.

303   "*a beautiful fuckin' love story*": Clarke, *Wishing on the Moon*, 423–424.

304   "*It was so sad*": Blackburn, *With Billie*, 273.

304   after 1957 Lady's use of heroin was largely "*incidental*": Nicholson, *Billie Holiday*, 212.

304   "*a hip little dude*": Clarke, *Wishing on the Moon*, 430.

305   "*Faults? Well, of course, she drank too much*": Blackburn, *With Billie*, 203.

305   "*She looked totally wasted*": Chilton, *Billie's Blues*, 186.

305   "*She who had always been the center of attention*": Chilton, *Billie's Blues*, 181–182.

305   "*Ask him to take away that damn mustard*": Clarke, *Wishing on the Moon*, 453.

306   "*It takes a very bad woman to be a good godmother*": Ibid., 454.

306   "*cried for days and days*": Blackburn, *With Billie*, 305.

306   "*cuts through like a painful knife*": Clarke, *Wishing on the Moon*, 430.

306   "*She had a lightness to her voice I hadn't heard in years*": Ibid., 431.

306   "*and there was this little old Negro lady*": Ibid., 432.

307   "*You seen a ghost or something?*" Ibid.

Chapter 29: It's All a Part of Their Poetic— No, Their Metaphysical—Education

308   "*like some cat explaining to a former friend*": Burroughs, *The Letters of William S. Burroughs*, 392.

309   a "*crucifixion*": Schumacher, *Dharma Lions*, 285.

309   "*To me, Neal's arrest was the most graphic proof*": Allen Ginsberg, interview with the author, 1992.

309   "*I knew that the fundamental issues of drug use in America*": Ibid.

309   "*one of the foulest collections of printed filth I've seen publically circulated*": Mabley, "Filthy Writing on the Midway."

310   "*In the end I knew you couldn't have it both ways*": Ginsberg, interview.

310   "*I began the files*": Ibid.

310   "*the original culture warrior for cannabis*": Lee, *Smoke Signals*, 73.

310   "*We were going to discuss the modern sensibility*": Ginsberg, interview.

311   "*What outraged me the most*": Ibid.

311   "*I wrote a long, long letter to Anslinger*": Ibid.

311   "*When I got my Freedom of Information Act*": Ibid.

312   *"That was a stereotype"*: Sloman, *Reefer Madness*, 181; Ginsberg, interview.

314   *"I'd been commissioned to write a serious, no-holds-barred report"*: Wakefield, *New York in the Fifties*, 177.

314   *"You've got to see Allen"*: Ibid.

314   *"Almost everyone has experimented with it"*: Ibid.

314   *"a cutting-edge issue"*: Ginsberg, interview.

Chapter 30: Let Lady Live

315   she was completely clean when she entered the hospital: Blackburn, *With Billie*, 307.

316   *"There were no withdrawal symptoms"*: Clarke, *Wishing on the Moon*, 435.

316   *"You watch, baby, they're going to arrest me in this damn bed"*: Ibid., 436–437.

316   *"Mind your own damn business"*: Ibid., 437.

316   *"six feet away from the bottom of her bed"*: Ibid.

317   they would deal with that by simply removing her from the critical list: Ibid.

317   *"Far from attempting to deprive the petitioner of any constitutional or statutory rights"*: Blackburn, *With Billie*, 297.

317   *"I said of course I would help"*: Wakefield, *New York in the Fifties*, 316.

318   *"The intern in the emergency room told me I needed immediate surgery"*: "Ruby Rosano" is a pseudonym. Her story is continued from Chapter 25.

322   more than ten years in the making: For the history of medicalization movement and New York Neighborhoods Council on Narcotics Addiction (NYNCA), see: Roberts, "Rehabilitation as Boundary Object"; Wakefield, *New York in the Fifties*, 93–107; Callender, *Nobody Is a Nobody*, 73–77, 79–95; Brecher, *Licit and Illicit Drugs*, 72–78.

322   *"Most were just kids and young adults like me who panicked once they got addicted"*: Sonny Wright, interview with the author, 1992.

322   *"It meant that kids like me could make a living without even having to leave their blocks"*: Ibid.

323   Anslinger always maintained that tougher trafficking penalties: McWilliams, *The Protectors*, 108–120; Jonnes, *Hep-Cats, Narcs and Pipe Dreams*, 160–163, Musto, *The American Disease*, 230–232.

323   *"It was like a plague"*: Brown, *Manchild in the Promised Land*, 170.

324   *"picking up guns"*: Ibid., 171.

324   *"instant hipness"*: Brown, interview.

324   *"The people in my parents' generation had known about heroin"*: Ibid.

325   a *"milestone . . . endeavor to deal with the adult addict by means of modern, enlightened methods"*: Roberts, "Rehabilitation as Boundary Object," 162.

326   *"The initial decision to use heroin may have been unwise"*: Roberts, "Rehabilitation as Boundary Object," 156.

327   *"we know that most of the problems dealt with here can only be solved effectively through political action"*: Ibid., 157.

328   *"health and social aspects of narcotics use"*: Ibid, 161.

329   *"elevate a most despicable trade to the status of an honorable business"*: Anslinger, *The Traffic in Narcotics*, 186.

329   *"I've got all these guys on records at home"*: Callender, *Nobody Is a Nobody*, 80.

329   *"break through the negativity of their personalities"*: Ibid.

330   *"so unique that she cannot be completely defined by her color"*: Ibid., 84.

330   *"Our protest for Billie"*: Ibid., 85.

330   *"as if she were a re-incarnation of Ma Barker"*: Chilton, *Billie's Blues*, 195.

330   *"The police have a function in this area"*: Clarke, *Wishing on the Moon*, 440.

331   *"She was bitter about the arrest"*: Blackburn, *With Billie*, 320.

331   *"What kind of trained nurse are you, baby"*: Clarke, *Wishing on the Moon*, 443.

331   *"We're all doomed, baby"*: Szwed, *Billie Holiday*, 51.

331   *"I've never had much of a voice to begin with"*: Ibid.

331   *"and neither lived to be as old as me"*: Ibid.

331   *"I'm not the suicide type"*: Ibid.

331   *"He couldn't wait for her to die"*: Clarke, *Wishing on the Moon*, 441.

332   *"Is he gone?"*: Szwed, *Billie Holiday*, 51–52.

332   some would even claim that her autopsy report showed no traces of narcotics whatsoever: Griffin, *In Search of Billie Holiday*, 27.

332   *"she rolled the bills tight, tight, tight"*: Clarke, *Wishing on the Moon*, 444.

333   *"her face relaxed, in an incredible repose"*: Ibid.

333   *"She was beautiful"*: Dufty, "Billie Holiday Dies After Relapse."

333   *"Died. Billie Holiday, 44, Negro blues singer.* Obituary in *Time* magazine, July 27, 1959.

334   *"She was like ice cream and cake"*: Sewell, "Biographer Remembers Billie Holiday's Greatness."

334   *"If you beat the habit"*: Holiday with Dufty, *Lady Sings the Blues*, 191.

The End of the Beginning: An Epilogue

338   *"I felt that jazz and marijuana were one"*: Wakefield, *New York in the Fifties*, 310–311.

338   *"What was so interesting about Ginsberg and those guys"*: Ishmael Reed, interview with the author, 1992.

339   *"It all comes from bebop"*: Jackie McLean, interview with the author, 1992.

339   *"The hippies acted out what the Beats were writing about"*: Torgoff, *Can't Find My Way Home*, 207.

339   *"decisive moment in American consciousness"*: Allan Ginsberg, interview with the author, 1992.

339   *"A lot of people were paranoid"*: Ed Sanders, interview with the author, 1992.

340   *"This drug automatically seems to produce a mystic experience"*: Miles, *Ginsberg*, 260.

340   *"I was somewhat disappointed later on"*: Sloman, *Reefer Madness*, 178.

340   *"acid and rock and roll and blue jeans have helped to overturn the communist system"*: Torgoff, *Can't Find My Way Home*, 461. Ginsberg made these comments to this author at the Twenty-Fifth Anniversary Woodstock Festival of 1994.

340   *"Everybody should try it at least once"*: Ibid., 460.

340   *"within the Beat Generation you find three things going on"*: Snyder, "Note on the Religious Tendencies."

341   *"in the 50s we really did have to protect, defend and nurture our freaks"*: McKenzie, "Moving the World a Millionth of an Inch: Gary Snyder."

341   *"He often said to me that he really didn't want to be this hip hero"*: "Pierre Delattre Remembers Neal Cassady," 60.

342   *"the salvation of America"*: Kerouac, *Desolation Angels*, 123.

342   "*Someone handed me* Mexico City Blues *in St. Paul in 1959*": Wilentz, "Bob Dylan, the Beat Generation, and Allen Ginsberg's America."

342   "*that nagging secret itch*": Johnson, *The Voice Is All*, xvii.

342   "*arriving at the voice that matched his vision*": Ibid.

342   "*great rucksack revolution*": Kerouac, *The Dharma Bums*, 97.

342   he had little use for these long-haired kids: Nicosia, *Memory Babe*, 687.

343   "*liberation from restraint*": Will, "Daddy, Who Was Jack Kerouac?."

344   "*a frozen moment when everyone sees what is on the end of every fork*": Burroughs, *Naked Lunch*, ix.

344   "*If you wanted to be seen as cool in the early sixties*": Miles, *William Burroughs: El Hombre Invisible*, 84.

344   Marianne Faithfull read the book and recognized that her destiny was to shoot heroin: Hawksley, "Marianne Faithfull: Heroin Saved My Life."

344   "*I awoke from the Sickness at the age of forty-five*": Burroughs, *Naked Lunch*, ix.

345   "*It was Mr. Anslinger's wish to retire*": McWiliams, *The Protectors*, 180.

346   "*permissive parents, college administrators*": McWiliams, *The Protectors*, 186.

346   "*The only persons who frighten me are the hippies*": Ibid.

346   "*To legalize marijuana*": Ibid.

347   *Anslinger, Anslinger / Creator of Farces*: Quoted in Finlator, *The Drugged Nation*, 187.

Permissions Acknowledgments

Index